CRASH

OF THE

TITANS

CRASH
OF THE
TITANS

GREED, HUBRIS, THE FALL OF
MERRILL LYNCH,
AND THE NEAR-COLLAPSE OF
BANK OF AMERICA

GREG FARRELL

CROWN
BUSINESS
NEW YORK

CROWN BUSINESS is a trademark and CROWN and the Rising Sun colophon are
registered trademarks of Random House, Inc.

Crown Business books are available at special discounts for bulk purchases for
sales promotions or corporate use. Special editions, including personalized covers,
excerpts of existing books, or books with corporate logos, can be created in large
quantities for special needs. For more information, contact Premium Sales at
(212) 572-2232 or e-mail specialmarkets@randomhouse.com.

Library of Congress Cataloging-in-Publication Data is available upon request.

ISBN 978-0-307-71786-3

Printed in the United States of America

2 4 6 8 10 9 7 5 3 1

First Edition

In memory of my father,

DAVID J. FARRELL,

a righteous man

CONTENTS

PROLOGUE

THE WONDER OF IT ALL

STAN O'NEAL, CHIEF EXECUTIVE officer of Merrill Lynch, a Wall Street firm on the verge of disaster, had only himself to blame. He calculated the damage that had been wrought. He reviewed the mistakes he had committed, the strategic blunders, the errors in judgment, and disregard for risk, all of which was exacerbated by faulty execution. Of course it wasn't entirely his fault, since he relied on the advice of the one person who should have known better—his caddy.

The final tally for O'Neal's round of golf was 88, one stroke better than the day before, but well off the 80 he had shot just a week earlier at Waccabuc, near his home in a remote corner of Westchester County, north of New York City. It was near twilight on a Sunday in late September 2007, and as mediocre as his round of golf at the Country Club of Purchase had been, at least it was a better experience than the meeting he'd had in the city that day, where he had flirted with the unthinkable.

. . .

JUST A FEW HOURS earlier, O'Neal found himself squirming in the backseat of his Audi A8 as his driver navigated the Sunday afternoon traffic of Manhattan, crawling inexorably, block by block, red light by red light, toward his destination, the Time Warner Center on the southwest corner of Central Park.

As always, when the Merrill Lynch chief executive was hatching a plan of any magnitude—from the firing of top executives to the outright sale of Merrill Lynch, which was the reason for his meeting this day—he relied on the counsel and advice of the only person he absolutely, unconditionally trusted: himself.

Throughout his career, that trust had been well-placed. The story of O'Neal's rise to the pinnacle of Wall Street was by now legendary. The fifty-seven-year-old African-American, born in Roanoke, Alabama, and raised in the dirt-poor town of Wedowee, Alabama, the grandson of a man born into slavery in the 1860s, had shattered every glass ceiling and stormed through, over, or around every obstacle placed in his way to become chief executive of Merrill Lynch at the end of 2002.

Over the next five years, he transformed the business. The backbone of Merrill Lynch had always been its nationwide network of financial advisors—the 16,000 men and women spread across the U.S. who managed not only the investments of the wealthiest people in Philadelphia, Chicago, San Francisco, Los Angeles, and other large cities, but the slender portfolios of the hardworking citizens in second-tier towns like Cincinnati, Wichita, Lansing, Spokane.

Most Wall Street banks and brokerage firms catered to huge institutional investors—pension funds with billions of dollars in assets—and plutocrats sitting atop massive fortunes. It was the genius of Charlie Merrill, the founder of Merrill Lynch, to look beyond the super-wealthy and build an investment advisory business at the grassroots level, by courting "the modest sums of the thrifty," as he wrote early in his career.

Starting in the 1940s, when most Americans still had searing memories of the stock market crash of 1929 and the Great Depression that followed, Merrill pursued his vision. Over the course of several decades Merrill Lynch became a powerhouse through its incomparable network of brokers across the U.S., connecting Wall Street to Main Street. In the second half of the twentieth century, most large companies that sold stock to the public wanted to use Merrill Lynch as their sales force to reach investors not just in the big cities, but in the midsized burgs of flyover country. A TV commercial in the 1970s, showing a stampede of longhorns, declared that Merrill Lynch was "bullish on America," and from that point forward, the symbol of the bull became synonymous with Merrill Lynch. The firm's retail brokers became known as Merrill's thundering herd.

Across the United States, in every town where they set up shop, members of Merrill's thundering herd were among the most prominent citizens, stalwarts of the local Rotary clubs, people who could be counted on to raise money for charitable causes. They were the pillars of their communities.

By 2000, the world of capital markets had changed. In order to keep growing, Merrill Lynch had built up its own investment bank so it could originate the stock offerings that were then distributed and sold through its network. It had also constructed a world-class sales and trading operation allowing the firm not only to buy and sell stocks directly for its clients but also to traffic in the lucrative world of fixed-income derivative products, a market in which Merrill Lynch could bet large sums of money to generate easy revenues.

In 2001, Stan O'Neal beat out his competitors for the top job at Merrill Lynch in part because he convinced the board of directors he could whip the firm's disparate businesses—weighed down by a low-growth network of financial advisors—into a more profitable, full-service investment bank.

From 2002 through 2006 he delivered on that promise, de-emphasizing the company's roots as a retail brokerage network and building up Merrill's sales and trading operations, which generated billions of dollars in profits each year. Through the first two quarters of 2007, Merrill Lynch continued its streak of record breaking profits, establishing itself as a Wall Street colossus that rivaled Goldman Sachs, the ultimate Wall Street money machine.

The date was Sunday, September 30, 2007. O'Neal was about to meet with Ken Lewis, chief executive of Bank of America, who was prepared, as a precondition of the meeting, to offer $90 a share to buy Merrill Lynch outright. The stock price had closed at $71.28 the previous Friday. Merrill Lynch had more than 853 million shares outstanding, so at $90 per share, Lewis was prepared to pay almost $77 billion for the company. Based on its own share price, Bank of America had a market capitalization of $223 billion, about three times the size of what Lewis was willing to put on the table for Merrill.

O'Neal had kept the meeting secret from the firm's directors and everyone else at Merrill Lynch except for his general counsel, Rosemary Berkery, and treasurer, Eric Heaton, from whom he needed specific information for his discussion. He swore both executives to keep the matter to themselves.

The Merrill Lynch CEO was sitting on another secret as well, one which the world outside of Merrill's board and senior management did not know about. There was a hole in Merrill Lynch's balance sheet that would wipe out most of the bank's profits for the quarter and threatened to destroy the institution completely.

After more than five years of easy credit in the banking system— the equivalent of pleasant weather and favorable breezes on the high seas of global finance—a shift had taken place over the summer. The great real estate bubble that had helped fuel growth in the financial sector for much of the decade had burst in early 2007. Companies that originated subprime mortgages were in trouble, if not in bankruptcy, based on an alarming spike in foreclosures. Banks that had gladly provided overnight funding to each other on easy terms suddenly pulled back automatic lines of credit.

Ken Lewis knew all that. What he did not know was that Merrill Lynch, which had more than doubled its balance sheet to $1 trillion in assets over the previous two years, had been mortally wounded by the wipeout of the subprime mortgage market. O'Neal only tuned in to the problem in late July, after the implosion of two hedge funds run by a competing firm, Bear Stearns. The funds had been gigantic, multi-billion-dollar bets on collateralized debt obligations—CDOs, for short—which were securities constructed from subprime mortgages. Following the collapse of the Bear Stearns funds, other Wall Street firms, including Merrill Lynch, scoured their own balance sheets for any signs of exposure to the subprime market.

Then on August 9, 2007, a French bank, BNP Paribas, announced it would suspend the valuation of three subprime mortgage–based investment funds because liquidity in the market had disappeared. The fact that all trading in the market for these funds had stopped meant there was no longer a market.

The BNP announcement caused the normal flow of overnight interbank funding to seize up on the Continent, spurring the European Central Bank to put 95 billion euros into the market as an emergency measure.

For the first time in nine years, when Long Term Capital Management imploded in 1998 and threatened to take down several investment banks, including Merrill Lynch, O'Neal felt fear in the pit of his stomach. Back then, he was Merrill's chief financial officer and the firm's exposure to Long Term Capital, a hedge fund that bet the wrong way on interest rates, threatened Merrill's access to overnight funding.

O'Neal had to return from vacation in the summer of 1998, and for the next three months he spent every day and night worrying about how and whether Merrill Lynch would be funded. A consortium of banks, including Merrill, eventually worked together to unwind Long Term Capital's positions, but the possibility that Merrill Lynch might get shut out of the market for overnight loans frightened O'Neal and caused him physical pain. Because of that experience, O'Neal shifted Merrill Lynch away from its reliance on overnight funding and toward longer-term debt.

The overnight-funding failure in Europe was surely a harbinger of things to come. There was no way, O'Neal vowed to himself, that he was going to let this CDO problem inflict the same kind of emotional anguish and physical discomfort on him that he had suffered in 1998.

O'Neal summoned Ahmass Fakahany, the co-president of the firm, and told him to assemble a team and deal with the CDO positions in August. When he returned from vacation after Labor Day, O'Neal said, he wanted Merrill's books to be clean. It didn't matter if Fakahany hedged the positions or bought insurance from a third party. The only thing that mattered was for the exposure to be removed.

And with that, O'Neal was off on his 2007 summer holiday on Martha's Vineyard. He threw himself into his favorite sport—golf—playing almost every day, often by himself. O'Neal checked in with the office regularly, but playing golf relieved the tension he felt building up from the firm's precarious exposure. On Labor Day, O'Neal came back to learn that the CDO positions were still on the books. Fakahany couldn't find any buyers or people willing to insure the complex positions.

O'Neal had two options: He could immerse himself in Merrill's business once again, taking control of the situation as he had in 1998 and again after the terrorist attacks of September 11, 2001, when Merrill's business was threatened and he became the firm's hands-on leader. Or he could sound out some potential merger partners, large banks that would be able to absorb Merrill's losses. It wouldn't hurt to test the market and find out what Merrill Lynch was worth, he told himself.

O'Neal placed a call to Ed Herlihy of Wachtell Lipton, the lawyer who advised Ken Lewis and Bank of America on all of its major acquisitions. O'Neal and Herlihy crossed paths regularly, either at business events in Manhattan or on the golf course. Whenever they met, Herlihy always left O'Neal with the impression that if the situation ever arose in which Merrill Lynch wanted to find a strategic partner, BofA would be interested.

"Ed, I've thought many times about a combination between Bank of America and Merrill Lynch," said O'Neal. "I think you have, too."

"Yes, we have," Herlihy replied. "Ken has always been interested in Merrill Lynch."

"This would be a very difficult deal for people to accept because of heritage and history and the culture and brand of Merrill and the perception that Merrill Lynch would be absorbed by Bank of America," said O'Neal. "In order to even engage in discussions, if it warranted it, there would have to be a very compelling reason."

Herlihy asked what "compelling" meant.

"I think north of $90 a share," O'Neal said. "If there were an interest on your end, I might be willing to listen."

Over the next several weeks, even as he traveled to Tokyo, then London and Germany, O'Neal had an ongoing dialogue with Herlihy about the meeting. Herlihy pressed O'Neal for details that he could pass on to Ken Lewis in Charlotte. Throughout, O'Neal's posture was clear: This would *not* be a negotiation to sell Merrill Lynch, it was simply an exploratory meeting to help O'Neal determine if it made sense to sell the firm. An expert in the bluffs and feints that accompany most discussions about mergers and acquisitions, Herlihy assured O'Neal that he and Lewis understood the ground rules.

As the date of the meeting got closer, O'Neal warned Herlihy that Merrill would be announcing a significant write-down on some of its assets in October. He also said he wasn't sure $90 a share was an adequate price. Herlihy said he would pass along that information.

KENNETH DOYLE LEWIS, a guarded and taciturn fifty-nine-year-old southerner, became uncharacteristically excited after hearing from Ed Herlihy, the New York lawyer who brokered Bank of America's biggest acquisitions. Merrill Lynch was willing to sell!

During his six years as chief executive, Lewis had cemented his reputation as a good operating executive, a man who knew how to run the country's largest commercial and depository bank. But as the fourth CEO of the Charlotte-based bank (it had been known as North Carolina National Bank, and then NationsBank, before the 1998 merger with San Francisco–based Bank of America), Lewis had yet to leave an imprint worthy of his predecessors. Through a series of mergers, Addison Reese had created the bank in the 1960s, Tom Storrs had expanded into Florida, before interstate banking was widely allowed, and Hugh McColl used the interstate platform to buy banks across the U.S. during his two decades at the helm, establishing himself as a legend in the business.

In his six years, Lewis had cleaned up some of the operational mess created by McColl's quest for empire. Then in 2004 he did an acquisition of his own, buying Boston's Fleet Financial for $47 billion. In 2007, he was at it again, buying Chicago-based LaSalle Bank for $21 billion, but those deals improved Bank of America's growth only at the margins.

Lewis had been an important member of McColl's team, but he would never be compared favorably with his predecessor. No one would ever use the word "legendary" in the same sentence as "Lewis," unless the name "McColl" was squeezed somewhere in between.

And now here it was, out of the blue, an opportunity for Lewis to pull off something even the great Hugh McColl couldn't achieve. In the 1990s McColl saw how the combination of Merrill Lynch's thundering herd of financial advisors could be grafted on to BofA's nationwide base of "mass affluent" customers to create a superpower in the industry, a demonstrable advantage for the Charlotte bank against its nearest competitors.

The timing wasn't perfect, since Lewis was about to pay out $21 billion in cash for LaSalle, and had just invested $2 billion in Countrywide Financial, the huge mortgage originator that was hobbled by the real estate downturn. But the acquisition of Merrill Lynch was something Lewis could not pass up. He put Greg Curl, his head of strategy, in charge of drawing up plans that could be presented to the BofA board of directors.

Curl's team laid out, in a series of charts, how the combination of businesses would turbocharge the bank's earnings. Merrill's capital market businesses were much larger than BofA's, so Lewis could cut costs by folding the division Bank of America Securities into Merrill. Across all of their combined businesses, Curl calculated that BofA could save $6 billion in costs by firing tens of thousands of employees.

To highlight the magnitude of the deal to BofA's directors, and capture the special nature of the opportunity that lay before them, Lewis affixed the following title to the board presentation: "Merrill Lynch: The Wonder of It All."

AS HIS DRIVER FINALLY pulled up to the Time Warner Corporate Center, where Bank of America owned a corporate apartment, the squirming O'Neal felt some relief. The drive from his home in Westchester County had been more than an hour and he was desperate to visit a bathroom.

After ushering the Merrill CEO into the BofA apartment on the sixty-fourth floor, which had a view to the northeast, looking out over Central Park, Lewis introduced O'Neal to Greg Curl, the Charlotte bank's head of strategic planning. O'Neal said hello in his usual calm, businesslike fashion, then excused himself and went directly to the toilet.

Curl and Lewis, who thought O'Neal had zipped across town from his Manhattan apartment, exchanged glances as the moments ticked by and O'Neal remained secreted in the washroom. Finally, the Merrill Lynch CEO emerged, as coolly as if nothing had happened, and sat down with the two men.

For the next fifteen minutes or so, Curl walked through the presentation he had crafted for his own board of directors, showing how the combination of businesses would be sorted out. O'Neal sat quietly, listening to Curl, before finally breaking his silence. "As you know, Merrill Lynch is an incredibly valuable franchise. While this meeting was predicated on a price of at least $90 a share, I think it needs to be more like $100 a share."

Lewis said he heard that might be the case, and took out a smaller book, a ledger crammed with numbers. He moved away so O'Neal could not see what was in the book, and said that $100 a share might be possible, but only if an additional $2 billion in cost cuts could be achieved.

At this point, Curl left the room so Lewis and O'Neal could negotiate alone.

"What do you want?" Lewis asked O'Neal. "You need to think about what you want to make this happen."

What did Stan O'Neal *want*? That was easy. He wanted the one thing Lewis could never give him. He wanted a *mulligan,* a do-over. He wanted to take his golf ball out of the water hazard on the eighteenth hole, bring it back to the tee, and hit a nice, easy, low-risk shot into the middle of the fairway. He had screwed everything up. All O'Neal wanted was for someone to turn the clock back and give him another chance.

CHAPTER 1

THE YOUNG TURK

"MY NAME'S TOM SPINELLI," said the man at the microphone. "Good morning, Mr. O'Neal, members of the board, executive committee, and fellow shareholders. I would like to apologize in advance if my voice appears to be too loud. The reason is because I have subjective tinnitus; it's a hearing disorder."

Spinelli was in the auditorium of Merrill Lynch's sprawling corporate center outside Princeton, New Jersey, on the occasion of the company's annual meeting on April 27, 2007. Merrill Lynch's chief executive, Stan O'Neal, had just reviewed the ninety-three-year-old firm's record-breaking results in 2006 for his audience. The company he had led since 2002 posted $7.3 billion in profits for the previous year, dwarfing the 2005 earnings of $5 billion, which were also a record. O'Neal could now bask in the glow of his success and soak up the praise bestowed by Spinelli and other investors.

"I would like to emphasize that I've been an employee, client, and shareholder for over thirty-five years," Spinelli continued. "I do know that during your tenure here at Merrill Lynch I have discovered a wealth of new products and services unlike anything I've ever seen in the past. As a client it has enabled me to take full advantage of so many excellent investment opportunities in the marketplace. I am now in a position to provide a much more secure financial future for members of my family and myself.

"This is a comment and a personal observation. I neither have the inclination or frame of mind to put you in an awkward position. However it should be stated that thanks to your knowledge, skills, superb leadership, and the expertise of designated members of the executive committee, Merrill is now back and in excellent competitive form."

Annual shareholder meetings, supposedly the great democratizing force of corporate America, are curious affairs, with CEOs re-elected almost by acclamation by the votes of institutional investors representing huge blocs of votes. The few individual shareholders who do attend often fall into one of two categories: activists agitating for change and well-meaning individuals entranced by the prospect of getting themselves in front of a microphone before a captive audience.

"As you know, the 2008 presidential election is starting to heat up again," Spinelli went on. "I'm convinced that the Democrats will win back the White House in the aforementioned election. Under our new presidential administration I am confident that you will be called upon [by] our president-elect to serve as his, as an elite member of his or her new cabinet.

"It would be similar to what late President Ronald Reagan did for former chairman and CEO of Merrill Lynch, Don Regan, in 1980, who quietly slipped away in 2003. If you accept to do for our country what you have done for Merrill Lynch, I would no longer just be a content American, I would be a proud American. Thank you and have a nice day."

O'Neal smiled at this bouquet of gushing praise. "Just the opposite of being too loud," the CEO said facetiously, pretending not to hear. "If you would say that again . . . I'm not sure I caught all of it." The audience broke up in laughter.

"Thank you very much for your comments," O'Neal continued. "And I have no intention of going anywhere, I'm afraid, because this is where I want to be. Thank you."

The annual meeting ended, and O'Neal exulted in his achievements. He had, single-handedly it seemed, rescued Merrill Lynch from irrelevance and established himself as one of the most successful CEOs on Wall Street and in corporate America.

Leaving the conference center, O'Neal would join his directors for a board meeting at the Nassau Inn, in Princeton, just a short drive away.

EARLY IN 2007, PROBLEMS emerged in the U.S. real estate market— the great engine of growth across the country over the previous decade. Home prices had stopped appreciating in high growth markets such as California, Nevada, Arizona, and Florida, and as a result, mortgage companies reported an alarming increase in foreclosures. The mortgage companies with the weakest credit standards, such as New Century, failed, while Countrywide, the largest mortgage originator in the country, had fallen on hard times.

While the problems of the real estate market in other parts of the country seemed distant from Wall Street, investment banks such as Merrill Lynch had derived more and more of their revenues from underwriting mortgage-backed securities—bonds which had been created by packaging large groups of mortgages together. For that reason, O'Neal thought it prudent to present his board with an overview of the market for mortgage-related products. Osman Semerci, a rising star at Merrill Lynch, would make this presentation and walk the board of directors through Merrill Lynch's fixed-income exposures.

Just nine months earlier, O'Neal had encouraged the selection of Semerci, a thirty-eight-year-old native of Turkey, to be head of Merrill Lynch's fixed-income, commodities, and currencies business, an area known on Wall Street as "FICC." The term "fixed income" had grown more important on Wall Street over the previous decade because of the proliferation of products that, like bonds, provided a steady stream of payments to the owner. When he was stationed in Tokyo and then in London, Semerci had established himself as a master in the art of selling fixed-income products to other banks and investors.

Nestled comfortably in a dining room at the Nassau Inn, the directors listened closely as Semerci outlined the successes he had engineered in less than one full year on the job: record revenues in FICC for 2006, followed by record revenues in the first quarter of 2007. In addition to the board, several other Merrill Lynch executives sat in on the presentation, including Ahmass Fakahany, the head of treasury and risk management; Jeff Edwards, the chief financial officer; Rosemary Berkery, the general counsel; and Laurence Tosi, chief operating officer of the global markets and investment banking division of Merrill Lynch.

From a competitive standpoint, Semerci explained, Merrill Lynch was trouncing its competition in year-over-year improvement in his department, with a 36 percent increase in FICC revenues for the first quarter of 2007 over the previous year's first quarter. By contrast, Morgan Stanley showed a 31 percent improvement, while mighty Goldman Sachs—the perennial leader in almost every Wall Street category—had improved by only 20 percent.

It was now clear why O'Neal had touted Semerci to the board as potential CEO material. Poised and elegant, Semerci demonstrated to the board how he had figured out the formula for maximizing the company's revenues in an overheated real estate market without exposing Merrill Lynch to any of the downside of the real estate crash. Of the company's $9.2 billion in FICC revenues for 2006, Semerci explained, only 6 percent—or some $550 million—came from U.S. mortgages. Another 15 percent, or $1.4 billion, came from securitization and foreign mortgages. Merrill's total exposure to the subprime market amounted to less than 2 percent of its revenues.

Semerci then handed the presentation over to Michael Blum, a subordinate who managed global structured finance and investments. If there was any danger on Merrill's balance sheet from mortgage-related bets, it would be in Blum's department, which securitized large pools of mortgages and then sold them to other banks and investors. In the previous two years, Merrill Lynch had generated $700 million in revenues from packaging mortgages into CDOs, large concentrations of similar-type mortgages that could either turn into bars of gold for the acquirer or radioactive bricks that disintegrated in value.

When the real estate market was strong, CDOs were enormously popular, since they promised investors a steady stream of payments at a higher percentage rate than most corporate bonds would pay. For several years, the manufacturing of CDOs was akin to the smelting of gold bars. Merrill Lynch and other banks received fees for forging the CDOs, and were able to sell the products with ease.

As the real estate market overheated in 2005 and 2006, the quality of the mortgages being used to manufacture CDOs deteriorated. Wall Street banks started making CDOs from subprime loans to people who normally wouldn't qualify for a home loan or who put little or no down payment on a house. In these conditions, CDOs forged from questionable ingredients might turn into bars of gold, if the economy remained strong and the home buyers behind the mortgages kept making their payments, but these latter vintage CDOs were no longer a sure bet. Just the opposite: In the spring of 2007, many of the CDOs circulating in the marketplace were already showing signs of turning into bricks of radioactive waste. It was one thing to make and market these products, but Merrill Lynch's board and management did not want to own the CDOs.

Blum was unsparing in his description of the shift that had taken place in the markets. The quality of mortgages had dropped dramatically and posed dangers to any bank, such as Merrill Lynch, that participated. He walked the directors through his efforts to limit Merrill Lynch's exposure to CDOs. He showed how his department had reduced a $17.7 billion subprime mortgage exposure the previous September to $3.5 billion as of the date of his presentation.

At the end of his talk, the directors seemed satisfied with Merrill's position in the declining mortgage markets. One member of the board, Virgis Colbert, asked a follow-up question.

"Is that all the subprime you have?" he asked Blum.

Blum turned to his boss, Semerci, who was responsible for all FICC investments, not just deals struck in the global structured finance department.

"That's it," said Semerci.

. . .

IT WAS KNOWN AMONG some of the traders on the seventh floor as the "Voldemort book" because, like the villain of the Harry Potter stories, the mere mention of it was discouraged. Few people outside Semerci's tight circle were told about the portfolio of super senior CDOs held within the department. But after the blow-up of two Bear Stearns hedge funds in June 2007, Stan O'Neal requested a board presentation about Merrill's CDOs, and details about what was in the "Voldemort book" began to trickle out.

In early July, John Breit returned from a conference in France when he heard from some of his people that they had been contacted by Dale Lattanzio, Semerci's second in command. Breit, a physicist by training, had been a risk manager for Merrill's fixed-income group until a year earlier. The people in his group, who had studied mathematics in great depth, were known as "quants" because of their expertise in complex quantitative calculations. Lattanzio had shown the quants some paperwork for exotic CDO products comprised of subprime mortgages known as "CDO-squareds" to make sure their valuation was correct.

Breit was puzzled. There was a group in place in the FICC department that could have handled this request from Lattanzio easily. It seemed suspicious that Lattanzio would want to go outside the usual channels for an opinion on a product of this sort. In presenting the package of CDO-squareds, Lattanzio eventually told Breit that it was a small position, $6 billion maximum, and that he just wanted to make sure his method of evaluating the amount of losses on that $6 billion position was right. But Breit told him that his valuation was way off. Lattanzio, a forceful man with the build of a football player, backed down, urging the former risk manager not to worry, because the investment was just a small part of a much bigger position. Struck by the irregular nature of Lattanzio's request, and the revelation that there was a much larger trove of CDO products where this one position had come from, Breit brought the matter to Greg Fleming's attention. Fleming, Merrill Lynch's co-president, encouraged Breit to keep digging into the FICC positions and see if there were other problems with Semerci's books.

· · ·

TWO WEEKS LATER, on July 17, 2007, Merrill posted second-quarter earnings of $2.1 billion, on revenues of $8.7 billion. But the widely reported news of losses at the Bear Stearns hedge funds—billions of dollars—raised widespread concern on Wall Street that the mortgage meltdown might affect other banks. On July 22, Merrill's board of directors met at the St. Regis Hotel on East 55th Street in Manhattan, just off Fifth Avenue, and one of the topics on the agenda was how Merrill Lynch would be affected by recent events in the markets.

During a meeting of the board's finance committee, Tosi, the chief operating officer of Merrill's global markets and investment banking division, made a presentation about the spin-off of Barry Wittlin, one of Merrill's top bond traders, into Wittlin Capital Group, a hedge fund in which Merrill would retain a stake. After finishing his presentation, Tosi decided to stay for the balance of the meeting, and plopped himself down in a seat near Stan O'Neal to hear the update of subprime exposures in FICC from Semerci and Lattanzio.

Lattanzio had relocated to New York after Semerci was promoted the year before. He and his boss talked about the CDO market in the U.S. for all banks and presented a chart that showed Merrill Lynch as the leader in CDO production for the first half of 2007, with $34.2 billion in volume. The nearest competitor was Citigroup, which had done $30.1 billion in CDOs for the first six months of 2007, and then eight other banks, rounding out the top ten. Goldman Sachs didn't even make the list, having apparently dropped out of the business of manufacturing CDOs. On a separate slide, Lattanzio revealed something that would have shocked some of his own traders: The firm had accumulated $31 billion in CDOs on its balance sheet.

But Merrill Lynch was managing its CDO business prudently, Lattanzio said, describing several hedges, or counter-bets, the firm had made to protect itself from the continuing decline of the real estate market. As Semerci looked on approvingly, Lattanzio said that if the market continued the negative trend that had taken hold in the second quarter, Merrill Lynch would only lose $73 million on its mortgage exposures, a tiny sum for a bank with earnings of more than $7 billion the year before.

Sitting at the far end of the table, Tosi grew alarmed. As chief operating officer of global markets and investment banking, he felt he should know what the FICC unit's positions were. Three months earlier, Semerci had told the entire board that Merrill's mortgage exposures were minimal—less than 2 percent of the firm's revenues. But now he and Lattanzio were saying that Merrill Lynch had manufactured a total of $34 billion in CDOs in the first half of 2007 alone, of which $31 billion remained on Merrill's balance sheet, at a time when no savvy investor was putting money into those products. Tosi began scribbling notes furiously to Jeff Edwards, Merrill's chief financial officer, who was sitting beside him. The back and forth messaging seemed to distract O'Neal.

After Semerci and Lattanzio finished, O'Neal thanked them, and the FICC executives stepped out into the hallway. Tosi was furious and went up to Semerci and started challenging him about the mass of CDO positions, of which he'd been completely unaware, sticking his finger in his colleague's chest. Lattanzio, much larger than either, came over to separate the men physically.

"I'm not talking to you anymore!" Semerci shouted at Tosi, before storming off.

Tosi, a graduate of Georgetown Law School who had been hired from General Electric a decade earlier, was a rising star at Merrill. He had been made a managing director before he was even thirty, caught the eye of Fakahany, and risen to one of the top jobs in Merrill's capital markets group by the age of thirty-eight. Up until this moment, he had been a booster of Semerci's, just as his boss Fakahany had been. But now he sensed that something was wrong. Semerci had told the board in April that Merrill had almost no exposure to the subprime mortgage market, but Lattanzio had just said Merrill was holding $31 billion worth of CDOs. Almost every respectable player in the market, starting with Goldman Sachs, had *reduced* its CDO positions during the first half of the year, and yet Merrill Lynch was loading up its balance sheet with these products for the past six months. Why would anyone want to corner the market on radioactive waste?

Not long after the board meeting, Tosi went to Fakahany, with whom he had a close relationship.

"We've got a real problem here," he said.

Fakahany urged Tosi not to get overexcited about the situation, but encouraged him to take a closer look at the positions in the FICC books.

In subsequent days, Tosi tried to find out more information about what Semerci and Lattanzio had done in the CDO market, but his requests for information from the seventh floor, where Semerci ruled the FICC operations, were met with limited assistance. When Tosi did find someone who could talk to him about investment positions that had been established, it was only with trepidation that the person cooperated. Semerci made it clear to everyone in the department that all financial information channeled upstairs had to go through him first.

Tosi connected with John Breit, who was on his own mission to determine the value of the CDO positions in the seventh floor's "Voldemort book." By mid-August, the two men were on complementary tracks: Tosi was trying to figure out, from the top down, what had been going on in the FICC unit over the past year under Semerci. Breit and his team of quants were building a case from the ground up, looking at all the mortgage positions salted away on Merrill's balance sheet and calculating the losses being generated by those positions, losses which Semerci seemed to be understating by a wide margin.

A FEW DAYS AFTER the July board meeting, O'Neal went out to dinner with the two co-presidents of Merrill Lynch—Fakahany and Fleming—and a member of his board of directors, John Finnegan. The foursome went to San Pietro, an expensive Italian restaurant on East 54th Street favored by Wall Street's heavy hitters.

Also at the restaurant that evening was James "Jimmy" Cayne, CEO of Bear Stearns, who had spent the past month grappling with the meltdown of his two subprime-mortgage-oriented hedge funds, an implosion that cost his firm $200 million and damaged its relationship with the institutions that invested in the funds, such as Bank of America.

Cayne stopped by the table to exchange a few words with O'Neal.

"This is a watershed day," said Cayne, referring to the collapse of his firm's hedge funds and the ramifications of that failure. "This is a game-changing event."

O'Neal disagreed. "I don't think this will contaminate the rest of the market. It will stay contained in the mortgage area."

Cayne shook his head and said the damage would extend far beyond that, and walked away.

THE ANNOUNCEMENT BY THE French bank BNP Paribas on August 9 that it was suspending valuation of its mortgage-backed investment funds was an admission of massive losses on its balance sheet that damaged the bank's capital levels. It caused the normal flow of overnight interbank funding to seize up on the Continent, spurring the European Central Bank to put 95 billion euros into the system as an emergency measure.

When he saw the news about the European bank's extraordinary decision to throw that much money into the marketplace in order to keep it liquid, O'Neal began to worry that Jimmy Cayne was right. If subprime problems were affecting interbank loans in Europe, they could affect Merrill Lynch as well. O'Neal asked Fakahany, who oversaw the company's finance and risk operations, to gather more information about Merrill's exposure to the subprime market.

O'NEAL WASN'T THE ONLY Wall Street executive to link the Bear Stearns hedge fund blowup with the European Central Bank's emergency funding program.

Dick Fuld, CEO of Lehman Brothers, which had emerged as a powerful force on Wall Street over the previous decade through its aggressive investments in real estate, called O'Neal to see how he was doing.

"I've had near death experiences, Stan, and this isn't one of them!" said Fuld.

After the call, O'Neal turned to several executives sitting in his office and said, "Dick just doesn't get it."

IN LATE AUGUST, TOSI came back from a ten-day trip with his wife to Spain. It was supposed to be a vacation, but every day, Tosi found himself obsessing about what had happened in Semerci's FICC business, poring over financial statements he brought with him and calling Merrill Lynch employees who worked on the seventh floor to pump them for more information.

The first and most obvious issue concerned the $31 billion in CDOs. The size of the position itself was enormous, capable of bankrupting the firm. Under normal risk controls, Merrill Lynch traders would not be able to amass a $1 billion position in a liquid, reliable stock like General Electric. When bankers in Merrill's private equity division wanted to invest $475 million in a joint buyout of Hertz in 2005, the approval process had taken months and required the backing of the board of directors. Somehow Merrill's FICC department had amassed the largest single CDO position in the history of Wall Street. Somewhere in the hull of the good ship Merrill Lynch was an enormous concentration of toxic assets that could take the entire enterprise down. Tosi had to find a way to identify it so it could be off-loaded or neutralized before the whole thing blew up.

Then there was a problem with the hedges that supposedly protected Semerci's CDO positions. At the board meeting in July, Semerci's right-hand man, Lattanzio, said that he and his boss had bought almost $290 million in insurance to protect against CDO losses, among other hedging activities. This was little comfort to Tosi. Yes, Merrill Lynch did have a $290 million insurance policy on risky subprime investments, but Michael Blum had taken out that insurance policy to protect the investments within his small division of FICC, the global structured finance division. Semerci was attempting to take that hedge out of Blum's department and move it over to his side of the ledger, which to Tosi appeared to be a violation of basic accounting standards.

Tosi brought the issue of the shifting hedges to Fakahany's attention, but his boss told him not to worry about it. Tosi insisted that hedges purchased by Michael Blum in his unit be attached to trading positions that Blum himself had purchased and pushed the matter up to O'Neal. At first, the CEO didn't see what all the fuss over the hedges was about, but eventually he relented as well, and Tosi got his way.

In late August, O'Neal left for a two-week vacation on Martha's Vineyard. He was aware that concerns had been raised about how much exposure Merrill Lynch had, so he instructed Fakahany to get a grip on the CDO problem and give him daily updates on what was happening.

Semerci, meanwhile, became angry and defensive about the incessant requests by outsiders—Breit and Tosi—for information from the seventh floor. At one point, when Breit was relaxing on a beach, Semerci called him up and berated him, telling Breit that FICC's books were "none of your fucking business." Semerci reminded everyone in his department that any requests for information from outside the department be forwarded to him.

Semerci still had the support of Fakahany, who was growing tired of Tosi's conspiracy theories about what was happening in FICC. Every time the thirty-eight-year-old came up to his office to discuss the situation, or give him an update, Fakahany would wave him off, addressing him by his nickname: "Please, LT, not one more time!"

Tosi would not relent. He knew enough people on the seventh floor that he could keep gathering information, just not at the pace he'd like. Tosi conferred regularly with Eric Heaton, the treasurer, and Greg Fleming, both of whom agreed with him that something was seriously wrong in the FICC department. Fleming agreed to work on O'Neal, to try to convince him that Semerci was "ahead of his skis" in grappling with the complexities of Merrill's massive CDO position. Tosi, who had a better relationship with Fakahany than Fleming, would keep trying to persuade Fakahany to look more closely at the FICC books.

But taking on Semerci posed challenges for the men, even for Fleming, who was higher up in the organizational chart. Fleming had opposed Semerci's promotion to the job a year earlier, in July 2006. He viewed Semerci as a ruthlessly political executive who only wanted to advance himself in the organization.

Semerci cut an interesting figure at Merrill Lynch. His father had been a major general in the Turkish army, but Semerci's colleagues had somehow come to believe that the old man was a high-ranking official in the Turkish intelligence service. The whiff of a connection to an extrajudicial organization and his father's presumably influential connections lent Semerci an air of mystery and power.

Then there was his background. Semerci had taken an unusual career path at Merrill Lynch, starting off as a retail broker before securing himself a position as an institutional salesman, where the dollar level and complexity of the products being sold required a much higher level of sophistication.

As for the mystery surrounding his start in finance, it was only enhanced by the story Semerci used to tell about his hardscrabble beginnings in Istanbul. One of his first jobs, Semerci told subordinates, was selling hand-crafted oriental carpets to foreign tourists. But the direct sale of these carpets was difficult, so Semerci established himself as a tour guide in Istanbul, where he would lead groups of foreign vacationers through the labyrinthine warrens of the old city, before bringing them to the carpet shop which he represented. Once inside, the tourists were made to feel as though they were being afforded intimate access by their guide to one of Istanbul's best-kept secrets, a feeling which enhanced their desire to buy.

A meticulously neat man, Semerci exuded an old-world European charm and proved himself to be a terrific salesman when he was posted to London, then subsequently to Tokyo. As a manager, he walked around the trading floor with a notebook, and would ostentatiously write something down in it when someone disagreed with him over a trade or another matter, implying that the incident would be remembered.

In 2003, Dow Kim, a forty-year-old Korean, had been put in charge of all sales and trading operations. But by 2006, the fixed-income division was generating so much revenue every quarter (much of which came from Semerci, who was based in London), that Stan O'Neal felt the unit should have a full-time manager for the position. Kim had come under increasing pressure from O'Neal to boost Merrill's FICC revenues up to the levels of Goldman Sachs, the industry leader in the category. Kim's first choice for the job was an internal candidate, Jeff Kronthal, one of the top fixed-income people on Wall Street, who had a deep understanding of risk. But neither O'Neal nor Fakahany was enamored of the fifty-one-year-old Kronthal, who had recently become cautious about trades involving the real estate market.

Instead, top management let Dow Kim know that Semerci would be a good choice for the position. Fakahany was a big booster of Semerci, having overseen his progress in Tokyo and London, and he saw that Semerci had the potential to become a top executive at Merrill Lynch. O'Neal liked Semerci as well. During meetings of the firm's top global sales force in New York, O'Neal would always attend the large dinner for the team, and more often than not, Semerci seemed to find a way to be seated at O'Neal's table. (When O'Neal took a summer holiday to Turkey in 2005, Semerci put the CEO in touch with a tour guide who squired the O'Neal family around Istanbul for the day.)

Kim didn't think Semerci was the right person for the job, in part because of the star salesman's lack of risk experience, and also because Kim didn't want to lose his top performer in the London office. Unable to promote the insider he wanted, Kim looked outside the firm, and began negotiations with Jack DiMaio, who had recently spun his hedge fund out of Credit Suisse. Running a fixed-income department is a lot like running a hedge fund. Managers of FICC departments at Wall Street banks aren't allowed to bet as much of their firm's money on trades as they could if they were running their own fund, but other than those limits, the skill sets are similar. Good hedge fund operators know how to measure and manage risk.

Negotiations with DiMaio over the acquisition of his hedge fund and his installment as head of FICC were nearly finalized in July 2006. Merrill Lynch acquired part of DiMaio's hedge fund, and Alberto Cribiore, the director in charge of Merrill's compensation committee at the time, approved the pay package to be awarded to DiMaio. Greg Fleming met with DiMaio and supported the idea.

But when Semerci found out that a big opportunity for advancement had opened up and that he wasn't going to get the promotion, he discussed the matter with Fakahany. If he didn't get the top FICC job, Semerci said, he might as well leave and take some of his top people with him, a move that would hurt the financial performance of the unit. On the other hand, if he were running the FICC department, the business would grow much more quickly than it was under the watch of the older, risk-averse guys currently in place, referring to Kronthal and one of his partners, Harry Lengsfield. With him in charge, there was no reason why Merrill's FICC department couldn't generate the kind of profits coming out of Goldman Sachs or Lehman Brothers.

Faced with the prospect of losing a rising star in their organization, someone who had great potential at Merrill Lynch, Fakahany and O'Neal agreed that Semerci should get the job. Fakahany informed Dow Kim that Jack DiMaio wasn't the right guy for the position and that if he insisted on hiring DiMaio, he would lose Semerci, his top producer in London, and Semerci's immediate team.

Dow Kim did the math: His bosses didn't want him to promote Kronthal, and didn't support his effort to hire Jack DiMaio. Further, if he hired DiMaio, his revenues would take an immediate hit from the departure of Semerci and his team in London.

In late July 2006, Osman Semerci was promoted from his position as a top salesman for Merrill Lynch in London and Europe to head of fixed income, commodities, and currencies at the firm, one of the most complex jobs on Wall Street.

To some extent, the sales and trading desks of every Wall Street bank functioned like in-house casinos, where the banks wagered their own funds in the marketplace. The best firms, such as Goldman Sachs, put strict limits and controls on each trader and kept up-to-the-minute tabs on the bank's firm-wide exposure at all times. Goldman vested its internal monitors with the full authority of top management to stop any trade, unwind any position, and shut down any trader who trespassed his limit.

By pushing Semerci for the FICC job, O'Neal and Fakahany were taking a salesman with the instincts of a riverboat gambler and making him general manager of the casino. Semerci's compensation—north of $15 million including bonus and restricted stock—was tied directly to how much business he could gin up.

Fleming was irate over the selection of Semerci and, for the first time since he had been named head of investment banking, capital markets, and private equity in 2003, he confronted the CEO directly.

"You can't do this," Fleming told O'Neal over the phone. "You know how Semerci operates. It would be the wrong move."

"You don't get it," O'Neal snapped back. "And I don't appreciate your advice on this."

"But, Stan, you know what Semerci is like. This would be completely dysfunctional."

"What you don't seem to understand, Greg, is that sometimes, dysfunction is a good thing. Some of the most successful people on Wall Street operate that way," he added, referring to Anshu Jain as an example. Jain, a hard-charging trader, had left Merrill years earlier for Deutsche Bank, where he was regarded as a star.

Fleming couldn't believe what he was hearing from the CEO of Merrill Lynch, that dysfunction was somehow a salutary quality in a manager. "You know what, Stan, there's too big a gap between us on this," he continued. "At the end of this conversation, we are not going to be in agreement."

"That's right," snarled O'Neal, who insisted that his decision was final and terminated the discussion.

As for Fleming, he knew at that moment that his career at Merrill Lynch had been derailed. In keeping with the dysfunctional management style he espoused, O'Neal shut Fleming off for several weeks, not responding to any calls or e-mails. About a month later, after Semerci had moved into his new job, O'Neal summoned Fleming to his summer home on Martha's Vineyard for the ritual round of golf, a favor that the CEO dispensed as a way of affirming the value of an underling. During the visit, O'Neal said he still needed Fleming and urged his young executive to stay on board.

In a decision that he would eventually rank as the worst of his career,

Fleming agreed to stay, becoming to all outward appearances a lackey in the court of Stan O'Neal.

SEMERCI WAS PROMOTED TO the FICC job in late July 2006. As a condition of his move, he insisted that the existing management team of the FICC department, which included Kronthal and Lengsfield, be fired. The ouster of two highly regarded fixtures of the trading floor—on the same day that several board members were taking a tour of the trading desks—made for unusual theater.

When Semerci arrived a few days later and was introduced to everyone by Dow Kim as the new FICC leader, fixed-income traders gathered on the seventh floor to take the measure of the new boss. Semerci made a few introductory remarks, talking about what he had been doing in Europe, then addressed the topic at hand: "I think the U.S. is very important," he said. "I don't know much about U.S. fixed income, but I'm excited to learn." Most of the veteran traders, who had relied on the decades of expertise that Kronthal and his crew had brought to the game, listened in disbelief. Afterward, Dow Kim went around the room asking individual traders what they thought of the new guy, hoping for an enthusiastic response. Instead, most of the veterans shrugged their shoulders, wondering what to make of the cipher who had just been put in charge of the department.

Within a month, Semerci fired a group of experienced fixed-income traders and replaced them with his own hand-picked collection of salespeople. There would be no time for settling into the job. Semerci had promised Fakahany that he could drive revenue growth, and he had his own aggressive timetable. "I've got six months to make this work or I'm out of here," he told members of his team.

A year later, in the midst of the U.S. real estate meltdown, an expanding group of Semerci's own colleagues were trying to figure out what he'd done in the fixed-income unit. The market for CDOs had disappeared, meaning that Merrill couldn't sell any of the billions of dollars in risky assets sitting on its books without dropping their prices so dramatically as to set off a wave of panic about the firm's overall health.

. . .

BY NOW, ONE OF Tosi's complaints about Semerci had gained traction with upper management. Starting right after the July board meeting, the Georgetown grad had insisted that there was no way the third-quarter losses from the CDOs would be the minuscule sum of $73 million that Lattanzio had predicted. Tosi said the losses from July alone would be $1.4 billion. In a meeting with Fakahany, Semerci acknowledged as much, admitting that his unit might have sustained as much as $800 million in losses for the month of July. Fakahany had become annoyed with Tosi's incessant updates about what was wrong with Semerci's books, but Semerci's own admission that losses would be much worse than what Lattanzio had told the board put the co-president on alert. Fakahany began paying much closer attention to what was going on in the FICC department than he had over the previous year.

Part of being a good salesman is to be able to address the concerns and fears of the buyer. Semerci was a master of the art, and between the July board presentation, when O'Neal first felt that Merrill's CDO problems might be worse than advertised, and September, Semerci worked on the CEO incessantly, visiting his office when he was in New York and constantly updating him.

From the other side, Fleming was receiving regular updates about what Tosi was learning regarding the financial positions in the fixed-income unit. But in one-on-one sessions with O'Neal, Semerci defended himself, pointing out that Fleming had always disliked him and had opposed his promotion to head of FICC in the first place. Besides, most of Merrill's CDO problems were positions he inherited from Jeff Kronthal a year earlier, Semerci insisted.

With these deft pivots, Semerci neutralized Fleming's influence with O'Neal. By September, the advice of Fleming—the co-president of Merrill Lynch—was being ignored by the chief executive, who discounted any criticism of Semerci as being driven by a political agenda. It had taken only thirteen months, but now O'Neal himself was being held captive by the very same "dysfunctional" management style he had lectured Fleming on at the time of Semerci's promotion.

Tosi's incessant pestering of Fakahany, however, was having an effect. Every time Tosi found something unusual in the FICC books, he brought it to his boss's attention.

On Tuesday, September 4, O'Neal returned from his vacation and met Fakahany over a cup of coffee to get a status report on the CDO issue. Fakahany informed him that not only did it seem impossible to sell the CDO positions at anything close to their carrying value, but he was starting to lose confidence in Semerci's abilities as the head of FICC.

This was grim news. Not only had both men believed Semerci was the right guy for the job, but they had presented him to the board of directors as one of the future stars of Merrill Lynch. O'Neal told Fakahany to have an in-house lawyer, Pete Kelly, do a review of what had happened in the FICC department. Then he told Fakahany, who was his primary interface with the board, to prepare the directors for what might eventually come down the road: Semerci's ouster and the announcement of sizable write-downs of Merrill's CDO positions.

Fakahany kept his loss of confidence in Semerci a closely held secret. But on September 12 the situation began to change. The executive committee of the global markets and investment banking unit held a conference call at 10:30 a.m., on the thirty-second floor of Merrill Lynch headquarters in New York. The participants included Rohit D'Souza, the head of equities, Nate Thorne, who managed Merrill's private equity investments, Tosi, Semerci, and Andrea Orcel, the head of international investment banking. Semerci and Orcel dialed in from London and D'Souza called from an airport. Tosi and D'Souza had discussed their concerns about Semerci prior to the meeting and both men agreed to take a firm line on Merrill's exposures during the call.

Shortly after the conference call began, Tosi went on the offensive, pointing out that losses in the fixed-income unit now appeared to be at least $2.1 billion. When confronted with this fact, Semerci became defensive, insisting that the losses came from positions he inherited a year earlier. "These are all legacy positions; we've been through this before, LT. It's Kronthal," he said.

D'Souza then asked where Semerci was marking his CDO positions, given that the general market was pricing some of those assets at about

80 cents per dollar. "Are you sure you have your CDOs marked correctly, Osman? We are seeing market prices that are different."

Semerci declared that Merrill's CDO positions were marked appropriately and that the firm would hardly lose any money on them. "I inherited all this risk," he explained. "I swam upstream. We're not going to lose money on this. I've got short positions in place."

D'Souza said he'd heard from traders at Morgan Stanley that they felt Merrill's CDO prices were way above market.

Now Semerci began to stutter. "Those aren't priced properly," he said of Morgan Stanley's CDO positions.

"What's the size of our balance sheet?" asked Thorne, the private equity manager.

"We've got about $40 billion in CDO exposures," Tosi said.

"No, no, that's not true!" Semerci insisted. "It's all hedged."

"The only hedges I can see here are from Michael Blum's positions," said Tosi, "not the CDOs."

Semerci, even more agitated, insisted that everything was under control. The call ended abruptly, without any consensus on where the firm was or what it should be doing about its exposures.

Immediately after the meeting, Semerci spent an hour composing an e-mail to Fakahany, complaining that Tosi and D'Souza were ganging up on him. To defend himself, Semerci set forth his accomplishments over the past year, explaining in minute detail how he had taken the mess left by Jeff Kronthal and transformed everything into better shape. Once Fakahany received and read Semerci's e-mail, he forwarded all of it to Tosi—except for the part where the Turk complained about people ganging up on him.

"LT—fyi this note excerpt is the view on this subject," Fakahany wrote above Semerci's long letter. "I think Osman does show that the CDOs were built from Feb onwards but goes through the thought process and lays it out. A lot fits with your thinking. Let's talk end game strategy tonight. Thanks. AF."

Tosi then read the contents of Semerci's original e-mail to Fakahany, an eleven-point rebuttal of the facts that had been raised at the 10:30 meeting that morning concerning Merrill's CDO positions and whose fault they were. The sheer brazenness of Semerci's assertions staggered him for some minutes, and then Tosi realized what had just been bestowed upon him: a detailed series of excuses and arguments that could be tested against the facts.

Tosi called Pete Kelly and asked him up to his office on the thirty-fourth floor. Kelly—who was forbidden from discussing the assignment he'd been given by Fakahany to review Semerci's work—read the e-mail, and the two men reviewed some of Semerci's claims. Kelly suggested that Tosi dig in and analyze the e-mail, and see if the facts supported Semerci's assertions.

For two months, Semerci had avoided doling out any more responses than necessary to his examiners and the only information he did pass along was in such granular form as to be almost meaningless without context. Here, finally, in an e-mail, was a broad position statement, an explanation of everything Semerci had done in the past year, and Tosi, who had begun his career as a Justice Department lawyer, shut himself in his office and attacked it point by point.

Tosi spent most of the next forty-eight hours tracking down every scintilla of information concerning the claims that Semerci had made, squeezing his sources on the seventh floor for details of every transaction involving CDOs that Semerci had referenced. Semerci was in London, so Tosi and several subordinates—Frank D'Alessio, Rob Abdel-Malek, and Alan Seklar—could extract information directly from the finance team at FICC without triggering any kind of scene or shouting match with the Turk, given his temper. Even though Semerci was an ocean away, the FICC finance people were scared for their jobs when Tosi approached them. Nevertheless, they cooperated with the probe, and turned over specific information about the department's balance sheet and sales records, details that had been treated like a state secret by Semerci.

Tosi and his crew worked on and off through the night and straight through the next day, comparing notes, sharing what they had found on the seventh floor and reconstructing what had gone on in the FICC department over the previous twelve months. Pete Kelly occasionally popped in to see what was going on and beheld a scene that looked like a Wall Street version of a college dorm room, minus the beer and pizza: four guys scattered in different corners of the room, each buried in paper. Tosi kept at it through Thursday night, composing his response, decamping to his apartment in the nearby Tribeca neighborhood only briefly to take a jog and a shower to keep himself going, then returning to finish his work on the morning of Friday, September 14.

By midday, after more than forty-eight hours of continuous work, Tosi alerted Heaton and Kelly to what he had found, and sent an e-mail to Fleming. Semerci had been blaming everything on Kronthal, but Tosi had determined the opposite to be the case: "It was all his risk, he could have sold everything and got out, but he increased the risk," he wrote to Fleming in an e-mail.

Then Tosi took his own work—a heavily annotated version of Semerci's e-mail—and walked it down to Fakahany's office on the thirty-second floor. Fakahany was surprised and amused at Tosi's appearance. Shuffling into a conference room adjoining the co-president's office, Tosi—the clean-cut Boy Scout from New Hampshire—seemed bedraggled. He was unshaven, tired-looking, and wearing rumpled clothes. He sat down across from Fakahany as if he'd finally found a place to rest following an all-night bender.

"You're not going to believe what's in here," Tosi began, and the amused look left Fakahany's face. "Not only is it all Semerci's risk, but he could have sold out a long time ago. He took down his hedges, increased his risk, and we now have eight times the exposure we had under Kronthal. This is all Semerci."

The manufacturing of CDOs is a two-step process. First, an investment bank has to open a "warehouse" for mortgages. The warehouse isn't a physical location, but a commitment to fund loans offered by mortgage origination companies to home buyers. Once the "warehouse" has enough mortgages in its pool, the investment bank turns around and securitizes this pool of funds into financial products that resemble bonds. These mortgage-backed bonds then produce a regular stream of payments over many years, the same way corporate bonds or U.S. Treasury bonds do. Because mortgages could be broken down into various categories, such as prime and subprime, the CDOs that were constructed from them contained prime assets (rated AAA) and subprime assets. Until 2006, investors lapped up these products because they paid higher rates of interest than corporate bonds and government bonds.

Semerci claimed in his e-mail that the only thing he did starting in November 2006 through June 2007 was to convert warehouse funds assembled by his predecessor, Jeff Kronthal, into CDOs so that the riskiest portions of these loans—the subprime parts—could be sold off, thus protecting Merrill Lynch. Semerci had even attached a chart showing that the total amount of CDOs and warehouse funds in November was about $32 billion, an amount that didn't change substantially through the following June, when the total of the two ledgers reached $35.7 billion.

Tosi ripped the chart apart, starting with Semerci's timing. The new head of FICC took over in late July 2006 and by November he'd already added $9 billion of unhedged risk. Semerci had been able to sell the CDOs that were on the books when he took over, which he did, but then he went out and opened twenty-one new warehouses in late 2006 and 2007. This was a period when every other investment bank, including Bear Stearns—the most aggressive of the Wall Street firms—had scaled back its involvement in the manufacture of CDOs.

Semerci's eagerness to collect the upfront fees that came with securitizing mortgages—fees which made his performance look good in the short term—blinded him to what was going on in the market. Other banks had stopped creating warehouses because the quality of the mortgages being originated in the U.S. had deteriorated to their worst level in modern history. Merrill Lynch had doubled down, buying First Franklin, an originator of subprime mortgages. The fact that Merrill kept the lights on at its warehousing facility meant it was scraping the bottom of the barrel, accepting the lowest quality mortgages being written at the moment when the real estate bubble was bursting.

Month after month in the winter of 2006 and 2007, Semerci and Lattanzio kept creating one CDO after another from the dregs of the mortgage business. The largest chunks of these CDOs still carried triple-A ratings, at least in name, because the credit rating agencies hadn't bothered to recalibrate their antiquated ratings models. But almost no one was willing to buy the triple-A portion of these bonds from Merrill because the rest of the marketplace knew what the credit rating agencies and Semerci didn't know: that the entire world of mortgages had turned into radioactive waste.

All told, in his year as head of fixed income, commodities, and currencies, Osman Semerci inherited some $5 billion in CDOs from his predecessor, Jeff Kronthal, created $70 billion in new CDOs, and sold approximately $40 billion of the stuff, leaving Merrill Lynch saddled with a total of almost $35 billion of the most toxic assets in the marketplace on its balance sheet, more than enough to wipe out the company.

Fakahany sat stunned as he reviewed the totality of the damage his protégé had done in the FICC department. Merrill Lynch had just violated the cardinal rule of every financial institution on Wall Street, which holds that no one business unit should ever be given enough leeway to sink the entire firm.

Fakahany, who along with O'Neal, had pushed for Semerci's promotion the year before, slumped over beside the conference table with tears in his eyes and held his head in his hands.

Tosi stared at his boss despondently. "I love this firm," he said. "I would never do anything to hurt it, but I can't work in an environment like this. We have 60,000 families that depend on us to manage this place responsibly. I can't believe this happened."

Visibly shaken, Fakahany echoed the sentiment. "For everything I've done for this firm . . ." said the co-president, who had been responsible for risk management, his voice trailing off. "I guess I took my eye off the ball." Fakahany assured Tosi that he'd bring the matter to O'Neal's attention, and Tosi left, reporting his conversation with Fakahany in vivid detail to Heaton and subsequently to Fleming.

FAKAHANY EVENTUALLY RELAYED THE gist of Tosi's findings to O'Neal. The CEO now realized that all those meetings he had held with Semerci over the past two months, in which the Turkish salesman had explained what he had done to "clean up" after Kronthal, had only obscured, not clarified his understanding of what was going on at the firm. As for Semerci's firing, it was no longer a matter of whether, but simply when.

At one meeting in his office to discuss the CDOs, O'Neal asked for a copy of the briefing Semerci had prepared for the board in April. As he flipped through it, page by page, O'Neal's face contorted in disgust. Every page, it seemed, featured one sunny portrait of the unit's health after another. Finally, O'Neal picked up the entire briefing book and hurled it against a wall.

"There's not one fucking mention of CDOs in this entire presentation," he barked.

Tosi's annotated e-mail was given a special designation, "attorney-client privilege," to protect it from the prying eyes of plaintiffs' lawyers who were sure to bring class action lawsuits in the wake of Merrill's upcoming losses.

Fakahany reconnected with Pete Kelly to see how the FICC review was going. Kelly, who was working with Ed Moriarty III, a risk executive, had spent nearly a week gathering information about the CDOs from the seventh floor, in some cases piggybacking on Tosi's work. Within a few days, he'd be ready to interview some of the key figures in FICC, including Semerci and Lattanzio, to figure out the process by which the FICC group had built up Merrill's CDO positions. Kelly was to summarize his findings in time for the next board meeting, which would be in mid-October. O'Neal and Fakahany had, in effect, put Semerci and Lattanzio into Kelly's custody, and then provided the lawyer with a horse, a rope, and directions to the nearest tree. Kelly knew what to do from there.

Fakahany dubbed the postmortem "Project Horizon." Kelly and Moriarty scheduled eight interviews with FICC executives between September 21 and 26. One of the interviews was with John Breit, who was continuing to do his own independent review of Merrill's subprime mortgage exposures, but Tosi and his investigative work were not included in the probe.

EVEN WHILE HE WAS handling these issues, O'Neal kept in touch with Herlihy, the deal lawyer who represented Bank of America, to review the protocol surrounding his September 30 meeting with BofA's chief executive, Ken Lewis.

O'Neal was also exploring other options. On a trip to Tokyo that month, he had met with the top executives of two large commercial banks, Mizuho and the Bank of Tokyo Mitsubishi. Both banks had expressed interest in some form of strategic partnership with Merrill in the past, and Merrill's retail brokerage unit was already working closely with Mitsubishi.

As an alternative plan, O'Neal flew to London for a secret meeting with Anshu Jain, the former Merrill Lynch trader who was now a top executive at Deutsche Bank. O'Neal's offer to Jain was blunt: If he agreed to return to Merrill Lynch, O'Neal would put him in charge of cleaning up the mess in FICC and designate him as the next CEO of the firm. After discussing the matter for several hours, the men agreed to revisit the topic in a few weeks.

As his September 30 meeting with Ken Lewis of Bank of America approached, O'Neal was already developing a sense of how much Merrill Lynch was worth in the eyes of potential partners. When he finally met with Lewis at the Time Warner Corporate Center, he was determined to play hard to get, to see how much value he could possibly extract if he wanted to sell Merrill Lynch to the Charlotte bank.

As he sat with Lewis and Greg Curl in BofA's corporate apartment, listening to Curl's outline of how Merrill Lynch would fit into BofA's corporate structure, he betrayed little interest in the charts and diagrams shown to him.

"I just don't see how we could make this work," O'Neal said. "I don't see any synergies."

That statement caught Lewis by surprise. There were legitimate reasons to oppose a merger between Merrill Lynch and Bank of America, but lack of synergies was not among them. A deal between the two organizations would graft Merrill's thundering herd of retail brokers on to BofA's "mass affluent" customer base across the U.S. The potential for growth in the category seemed unlimited and would allow Merrill's sales force, already the industry leader, to put even more distance between itself and its competitors.

After Curl left the room, Lewis asked O'Neal what he wanted in order to make the deal happen.

"I want to be president," O'Neal said. "My team will not accept this unless I have an ironclad deal to become your successor."

Lewis balked at the notion. "It makes more sense for you to head up the capital markets business," he said.

"That's too narrow a scope," replied O'Neal.

"I can't promise that you'd be my successor but I can guarantee that you'd get a fair shot."

The two men went back and forth for a time over the issue of O'Neal's position in a combined organization before the conversation came to an end.

"My board's really behind this," Lewis said.

"I think I've heard everything you had to say," O'Neal replied. "It's an interesting proposal. And I appreciate the time." O'Neal said he'd bring the matter up with his board and get back to Lewis, but he didn't demonostrate any enthusiasm for the proposal. And with that, he was gone. On the drive back to Westchester, O'Neal called a friend to see if he was free for a quick round of golf. Sure, came the reply. O'Neal instructed his driver to bring him to the Country Club of Purchase where he and his friend, an investment banker, would squeeze in eighteen holes before the early autumn darkness set in.

After O'Neal's exit, Lewis tried to make sense of what had happened. Despite all the foreplay between O'Neal and Herlihy in the weeks leading up to the meeting, it was clear to Lewis that O'Neal had no real interest in doing the deal. It was also clear to him that the Merrill CEO was like most Wall Street bankers Lewis had encountered: All he cared about was himself.

FROM 2002 THROUGH EARLY 2007, Stan O'Neal was one of the best paid executives on Wall Street. His base salary of $500,000 per year grew to $700,000 in 2004. Over that five-year period, he received $53.2 million in cash bonuses, $98.9 million in restricted stock, and another $5 million worth of stock options. On top of that, he received $2.2 million worth of perks, primarily to pay for a car and driver, and his personal use of Merrill's corporate jet. Other Wall Street CEOs and O'Neal's top lieutenants, including Fleming, also had access to a car and driver, but in an unusual arrangement, O'Neal's wife, Nancy Garvey, got her own car and driver, paid for by the company.

Despite accumulating just over $163 million by 2007, O'Neal spent time and energy trying to figure out ways to save a few thousand dollars of personal expenses. In the fall of 2005, after deciding to spend Christmas on safari at Malu Malu game park in South Africa with his family, he ordered his subordinates to drum up business meetings for him in Johannesburg. Martin Wise, who worked for O'Neal, reached out to Brian Henderson, a banker with an extensive history in Africa and the Middle East. Henderson explained to Wise that it would be impossible for O'Neal to meet with anyone of real stature in Johannesburg at that time of year, because in the Southern Hemisphere, Christmas coincides with summer vacation for schoolchildren. Everyone goes away and the city and government are virtually shut down. Wise wouldn't hear any of it and reiterated O'Neal's request that meetings be arranged for him, even if they were with lower level executives or government officials. There was one other thing, Wise said: O'Neal needed at least one meeting in Cape Town on December 31 to justify a stopover with the corporate jet. Henderson leaned on the managing directors in Merrill's Johannesburg office to come up with a few meetings for the boss. He was thus able to put together a business itinerary for O'Neal, and even arranged for the first African-American CEO on Wall Street to visit with Nelson Mandela, the legendary apartheid opponent who had helped bring a peaceful end to white rule in South Africa.

By generating a work-related premise for the African safari vacation, O'Neal was able to fuse the family adventure with a legitimate business trip, underwritten in part by Merrill Lynch shareholders.

CHAPTER 2

A QUESTION OF CHARACTER

"**WHAT DO YOU THINK** of Alberto Cribiore?" Stan O'Neal asked his mentor at Merrill Lynch, Barry Friedberg.

"What do you mean? What's the context?" replied Friedberg.

It was early 1998 and O'Neal, who was the newly installed chief financial officer of Merrill Lynch, had just returned from a weekend skiing in Jackson Hole with Cribiore, who ran his own private equity firm, Brera Capital. Ever since Friedberg had recruited him to Merrill from the finance department of General Motors in January 1987, O'Neal had relied on the veteran investment banker for the occasional piece of career advice.

"Alberto has offered me a partnership at his firm," said O'Neal.

Friedberg didn't understand what O'Neal was thinking. It was as though a young, highly touted backup quarterback for the Dallas Cowboys—someone being groomed for great things on a big stage—had just received an offer to join the Arena Football League or the Canadian Football League, and wanted to know if it would be a good idea to accept.

Private equity firms bought companies that were in trouble,

reorganized them for growth, loaded them down with debt—which generated losses and tax benefits—then brought the companies public, generating huge payouts. The men who ran the biggest private equity firms—Kohlberg Kravis & Roberts (KKR) and the Blackstone Group—made hundreds of millions of dollars for themselves through these deals.

After being the top deal guy in the 1980s for Steve Ross, the CEO of Time Warner, Cribiore moved to a large private equity firm, Clayton, Dubilier & Rice. It was there that he met O'Neal, pitching the young Merrill Lynch executive on deals. Cribiore wanted to run Clayton, Dubilier himself, but after an attempt to maneuver himself into the executive suite misfired, he left. Based on his track record in the industry, he raised $650 million to start his own fund, Brera.

"Are you really interested in the private equity business, or is there something wrong here at Merrill?" Friedberg asked O'Neal.

O'Neal said he wasn't interested in being a chief financial officer. He wanted a job where he could be doing deals. On top of that, he added, "I'm finding it increasingly difficult to work with Herb," referring to Herb Allison, the Merrill Lynch president, who had championed O'Neal's career and installed him as CFO.

"I understand," said Friedberg, who knew that Allison's micromanaging style had rubbed some executives the wrong way. "But don't be in such a hurry. If you really want to be in private equity, you should aspire to one of the top-tier firms, like KK&R, not a second-tier operation. Be patient. Things could change here as well."

O'Neal thanked Friedberg for the advice and left. It wasn't the first time the investment banker had done a favor for the young man in a hurry. After recruiting him from GM, Friedberg had gotten O'Neal's career launched in Merrill's junk bond department. In 1990, when the junk-bond business shrank following the collapse of Drexel Burnham Lambert, O'Neal suddenly quit Merrill Lynch and accepted a similar job at Bankers Trust. Like every Wall Street firm, Merrill Lynch was under pressure to diversify its workforce, so Friedberg did something he never would have if O'Neal had been white: Four days after O'Neal left,

Friedberg called him and recruited him back to Merrill Lynch, by offering him a bigger job with better pay.

O'NEAL NEVER LEFT MERRILL for Brera, but the two men maintained a close relationship. In 2002, when O'Neal became CEO of Merrill Lynch, Cribiore sent him an expensive case of French white wine, Baron d'L. Months later O'Neal replaced a departing board member, Robert Luciano, with Cribiore, whose private equity firm was by that time struggling.

For several years on the Merrill Lynch board, Cribiore proved himself to be a loyal supporter of O'Neal. He was put in charge of a powerful subgroup, the management development and compensation committee, where he modeled Merrill Lynch's bonus schemes on those of competitors such as Goldman Sachs.

But as Brera's fortunes got worse and worse, Cribiore became erratic. He lost his temper at Merrill employees who worked with him in conjunction with board activities. When Merrill staffers brought their complaints about Cribiore's temperamental behavior to the CEO, O'Neal would dismiss his antics, explaining that "Alberto is exhaustive and exhausting." Cribiore alienated Merrill's lead director, the noted academic and author Jill Ker Conway, pestering her on a wide range of issues. Finally, Cribiore approached O'Neal, asking permission to discuss job opportunities at Merrill with some of the firm's business leaders. O'Neal quietly removed Cribiore from his perch at the top of the compensation committee, but otherwise avoided addressing the conflict of interest that had sprung up concerning one of his own directors. Instead, the two men maintained their friendly relationship and O'Neal continued to drop by Cribiore's office on a regular basis for coffee and a discussion about mergers and acquisitions, their favorite subject.

By September 2007, as O'Neal was grappling with the problems looming on Merrill's balance sheet, it appeared as though Cribiore was going to land a job at Citigroup, where an old friend from his Time Warner days, Richard Parsons, served on the board of directors. O'Neal passed the word quietly to several other board members that Cribiore was about to leave.

Despite his impending departure, O'Neal liked to use Cribiore as a sounding board for ideas. The day after his discussion with Lewis, O'Neal dropped by Brera Capital for his regular cup of coffee.

Throughout September, Fakahany had been keeping the board members apprised of the worsening developments on Merrill's balance sheet, and how Semerci had gotten in over his head and would be asked to leave the firm. Because of these communications, Cribiore, who had become the lead director after the retirement of Jill Ker Conway, was already aware that the firm had serious problems. O'Neal now discussed his plight.

"I'm not sure I have a solution for this," he said.

Cribiore was almost nonchalant in his response. "Take the largest write-off you can, and then go raise more capital," he said in his thickly accented baritone.

"But that's the problem, Alberto," said O'Neal. "I don't know what that number looks like."

Neither man brought up the inconvenient fact that, since 2004, Merrill Lynch had bought back $21 billion of its own stock, frittering away a massive war chest of cash. The buybacks pumped up the company's share price and turbo-charged the annual bonuses paid out to the firm's top executives.

Because it was unclear how deep the problem was, O'Neal continued, he thought it might be a good time to consider some kind of strategic partnership with a bigger bank.

Was O'Neal thinking of selling Merrill Lynch? Cribiore asked.

"A deal might be possible," O'Neal said. "Bank of America has expressed an interest, and made a very attractive offer."

Cribiore brushed away the notion that Merrill Lynch should be sold. Cribiore loved New York, Wall Street, and the world of high finance. He thought it ridiculous to sell Merrill Lynch to a bunch of hillbilly commercial bankers in North Carolina.

O'Neal decided to drop the matter for the time being. After all, there was no rush, and Cribiore would be leaving the board in the near future anyway, at which point the CEO would have an easier time convincing his board to sell, if it ever came to that. O'Neal left Cribiore's office at Brera. He was alone. There was no one at Merrill Lynch in whom he could confide. There used to be two people he trusted at Merrill Lynch, Tom Patrick and Arshad Zakaria, and they had helped him become CEO. And then in 2003 O'Neal found out he couldn't trust them, so he fired them. And he would never let anyone get that close again.

In addition to the help he got from Patrick and Zakaria, one of the biggest reasons for O'Neal's rise to the top of Merrill Lynch was his decisiveness. In 2000 and 2001, when O'Neal was competing for the top job, he demonstrated an ability to act quickly that his other rivals for the top job lacked. The Merrill Lynch board viewed O'Neal's decisiveness as a positive attribute, but few people, other than O'Neal's closest associates, grasped the secret of his quick-mindedness.

Stan O'Neal, as a creature of Wall Street, viewed most challenges and decisions through the prism of how they would impact his career and his paycheck. The ability to cast every problem in the context of how it would affect him had always clarified issues for O'Neal and simplified his choices. But now, on October 1, 2007, he found himself in a situation where the options were bad, worse, and worst. It was not yet clear that most other Wall Street banks would find themselves in similar predicaments in the months to come, so O'Neal felt alone in having presided over a screwup of monumental proportions.

IN MID-SEPTEMBER, AFTER REVEALING the truth about Semerci to Fakahany, Tosi was on to the next challenge, which was figuring out a way for Merrill Lynch to extricate itself from its disastrous situation. Merrill was faced with an exposure of $35 billion to $40 billion incurred on Semerci's watch. To put that number in context, Merrill Lynch's earnings for the year 2006 were just over $7 billion, and the sum total of its shareholders' equity at the end of that year was $39 billion.

The company would need to raise cash, quickly, so Tosi mentioned the possibility that Merrill could sell its 20 percent stake in Bloomberg L.P., the powerhouse financial information company founded by Michael

Bloomberg, who had become mayor of New York City in 2001. Tosi also floated the idea of creating a "bad bank," a separate entity to be funded by Merrill Lynch that would house all of the firm's toxic assets, thus removing them from the parent company's books.

AFTER HIS BRIEF DISCUSSION with Cribiore about his meeting with Ken Lewis, O'Neal had to deal with a more urgent matter. The losses for Merrill's third quarter, which had just ended, were so steep that the firm would have to give its investors a warning. Merrill's auditor, Deloitte & Touche, recommended that the bank not wait until its regularly scheduled earnings announcement on October 24. Instead, O'Neal had his finance team prepare for an early earnings warning at the end of that week, on Friday, October 5. Based on their calculations, Merrill's finance staff determined by Thursday, October 4, that declining asset prices would call for a $4.5 billion markdown of its CDO positions, and a $463 million write-down of its private equity investments.

Ever since Tosi had exposed Semerci in mid-September, the plan had been to fire the head of fixed income and his deputy, Lattanzio, after third-quarter earnings were announced on October 24, by which time Pete Kelly's postmortem report would have been completed.

But on the evening of Tuesday, October 2, Fakahany realized that when investors learned of the sudden, precipitous losses at the end of that week, there would be questions about who was responsible. It dawned on him that Friday's pre-announcement would lead to a demand for scalps, and if Merrill Lynch hadn't done anything by then, investors would assume that the firm was covering for someone, or hiding worse things. Around 9:00 p.m. that evening, Fakahany called O'Neal and received approval to speed up the termination process.

As luck would have it, Semerci, who traveled frequently between London and New York on his British passport, was already scheduled to visit Fakahany's office at 8:00 a.m. on Wednesday. Fakahany didn't want to give his former protégé any prior notice about his upcoming execution. Instead, he alerted Merrill's human resources staff to the fact that two senior executives would be fired Wednesday morning and both would need to be escorted out of the building.

On the morning of Wednesday, October 3, Semerci took the elevator up to the thiry-second floor for his appointment with Fakahany. The co-president told the HR people that once Semerci was there, that Dale Lattanzio should also be summoned to his office, immediately.

Semerci entered the conference room adjoining Fakahany's office—the same room where Tosi had exposed his actions to Fakahany a few weeks earlier—and sat down, across from his boss, with all the confidence and brio he had displayed throughout his career at Merrill. Starting in London in the early 1990s, then in Tokyo, where he emerged as a top salesman, and then back in London, where he eventually assumed responsibility for fixed-income sales across Europe, the Middle East, and Africa, Semerci had successfully advanced his career through a series of all-or-nothing bets. He was decisive, because he viewed every action as a choice between an outcome that would propel him forward, or one that would impede him.

As soon as his boss started talking, Semerci realized that the game was over. "We've decided to go in a different direction," Fakahany said euphemistically, as though the accumulation of $35 billion in toxic assets on the balance sheet had, until recently, been part of some larger strategy at Merrill Lynch.

Semerci's eyes watered slightly, but he remained otherwise composed. The fact that Kelly had interviewed him a week earlier was enough to alert him that he had lost the unconditional support he once enjoyed on the thirty-second floor. Lattanzio by now was sitting in a waiting room outside of Fakahany's office. It was clear to Semerci's deputy—whom Fakahany had begun referring to as "Sancho Panza"—that he too was about to be fired and as he sat, he lamented, "I knew I never should have left London."

One by one, two top HR executives—Peter Stingi and Joe Casey—escorted Semerci and Lattanzaio from the thirty-second floor down to the lobby, where cars were waiting to take them home. Semerci remained upbeat, like a seasoned Las Vegas gambler who understands that the luckiest player is always one roll of the dice away from crapping out. Lattanzio was crestfallen, his brilliant career in finance in shambles.

Semerci consoled his subordinate, turned to Stingi and said, "We don't need the other car." Turning back to Lattanzio, he said, "Dale, let's go have some coffee." Then the two men left the building.

At Semerci's request, Joe Casey returned to his seventh floor office to retrieve a few items left behind. One of these items was a large nondescript envelope stashed in a drawer of Semerci's desk. Casey opened it to examine its contents. Inside was approximately $15,000 in cash, in sequentially numbered hundred-dollar bills.

Semerci, who also kept his Turkish passport in New York, promptly checked out of the Four Seasons Hotel, where Merrill Lynch had been paying for his suite, and returned to London on the first flight he could catch. Thus ended the Wall Street career of one of the most remarkable characters ever to pass through the doors of Merrill Lynch, a young rug merchant who parlayed the sales skills he had honed in the alleys of Istanbul into one of the most sensitive and complicated posts in global finance, a position just a few steps down from the corner office of the best-known investment bank in the world. After he was fired, Semerci phoned Bob McCann, a friend at Merrill Lynch who was in charge of the firm's thundering herd. "It was a wild ride," Semerci said.

After several weeks of negotiations between his lawyers and attorneys for Merrill Lynch, Semerci secured the stock that had been awarded to him the previous February as a bonus for his phenomenal success in 2006, a sum slightly larger than the $15 million awarded to Lattanzio that year. Six months later, in April 2008, Semerci was hired by Duet, a London-based hedge fund group, to oversee $1.7 billion spread across thirteen funds.

CHAPTER 3

BEAT THE WACHOVIA

IN THE GENTLEMANLY WORLD of post–World War II banking, Addison Reese was an anomaly. Where the vast majority of U.S. bankers in the late 1940s and 1950s were content to sit on their franchises and let them grow organically, along with the surging postwar economy, Reese was an intense competitor.

Reese had been recruited south to Charlotte, then a sleepy backwater, in 1951 from his native Baltimore to become second in command at the American Trust Company. Torrence Hemby, the bank's president, had been looking for a leader who could help his bank grow, and found his own executive team lacking. In Reese, the forty-two-year-old head of the Nicodemus National Bank in Hagerstown, Maryland, Hemby saw someone who could make a difference.

After several years as Hemby's understudy, Reese became president in 1954, and from that point forward, his vision was to grow. In 1957, he merged his bank with Commercial National to form the American Commercial Bank. Two years later, Reese reached an agreement to merge with First National Bank in Raleigh, giving him access to business in the state capital. One year after that, in 1960, he combined with Security National, which had offices in Greensboro, and rechristened the enterprise North Carolina National Bank, or NCNB.

At this point, with offices across a wide swath of North Carolina, Reese sought to unify his fractious group of bankers around one goal: to beat Wachovia, the dominant force in North Carolina banking since the Great Depression. Wachovia, which was based in Winston-Salem, had the best corporate clients in the state, and the best contacts with local government. Until Reese decided to take on Wachovia, its primacy in the Tar Heel State was unchallenged, and most of the state's other banks were content to pursue smaller pieces of business rather than attack the unassailable industry leader.

Many of the bankers in Reese's organization were older men who had witnessed the damage wrought by the Great Depression. In that grim period of the 1930s, thousands of banks across the country had failed. This vivid memory left these older executives conservative by nature and less fit to lead an organization that wanted to grow aggressively. Throughout the late 1950s and 1960s, Reese devoted an enormous amount of his energy to recruiting hard-charging young bankers who bought in to his vision, and training them for future leadership roles. One of these recruits was a young ex-Marine from South Carolina whose father had been in the banking business, Hugh McColl. Reese also needed a strong number two, someone who shared his vision but who had the gravitas to continue the fight against Wachovia. He found the perfect candidate in 1960 in the person of Thomas Storrs, manager of the Federal Reserve's branch operations in Charlotte. Upon joining NCNB, Storrs was put in charge of the bank's offices in Greensboro.

By 1974, when Storrs succeeded Reese as CEO, North Carolina National Bank had caught up to Wachovia in terms of assets. Over the remainder of the decade, Storrs would continue the battle against his in-state rival, while looking for ways to expand beyond North Carolina. At the same time, he had to manage his own bank carefully through a period of economic turmoil and deteriorating loans.

Storrs was a proponent of international banking, and even before he became CEO, NCNB started opening offices in global financial centers such as London and Hong Kong. But it was a small investment that Addison Reese had made in 1972, when he bought the Trust Company of Florida, which ended up giving Storrs the platform he would need to expand into the Sunshine State. In 1981, Storrs used NCNB's preexisting ownership of the small Trust Company to navigate around Florida laws against out-of-state banks invading their turf to acquire the First National Bank of Lake City, a small concern with $21 million in deposits.

The sudden arrival of a major out-of-state commercial bank in Florida, executed with military precision during a period when the Florida legislature was out of session, became a template for future growth at NCNB and demonstrated the importance of speed to the top managers in Charlotte. It was McColl, who had risen to become Storrs's top lieutenant, who announced NCNB's arrival in Florida in the warlike terms he would employ through the remainder of his career. "We have stolen a march on the world into one of the fastest-growing banking markets," he declared after the Lake City acquisition went through.

Two years later, McColl succeeded Storrs and continued NCNB's expansion into Florida. Many top bankers in the market, who enjoyed a comfortable life owing to the state's booming growth, welcomed the arrival of an aggressive out-of-state competitor who was willing to pay top dollar to acquire their operations. The employees of these acquired banks, however, often suffered in the changeover, as NCNB tried to figure out how to run this ever increasing assortment of banks and unify the system. When he encountered severe problems in 1985, McColl dispatched one of his top managers, Ken Lewis, to Tampa to straighten out NCNB's far-flung operations.

Ken Lewis was born in Meridian, Mississippi, because, he liked to say, "that's where you go to get born when you live in Morgan Grove." His father was an Army sergeant and his mother was a registered nurse. Lewis was recruited by NCNB after graduation from Georgia State in 1969. He fit the personality mold sought by the Charlotte bank perfectly: He was from the Deep South, had a strong head for figures, and, best of all, had a chip on his shoulder toward anyone who had had an easier time of it in life. His starting salary was $8,000.

Lewis's father, Vernon, had grown up dirt poor and dropped out of school before getting to the eighth grade. He worked in a lumber yard and then joined the Army, where, owing to his lack of education, he never rose above the rank of sergeant. Lewis's mother, Alice Byrdine Franklin, had grown up in different circumstances, the daughter of an affluent doctor. She had ambitions of becoming a doctor herself. But life changed for Byrdine in medical school when her father, then eighty years old, married his thirty-year-old nurse, and the young wife inherited all the old man's money. Byrdine dropped out of med school and became a registered nurse. Although she married beneath her station, and her Army sergeant husband abandoned her after Ken was born in 1947, she never lost her ambitious spirit, and channeled her energies into her hardworking son.

Lewis established himself as a solid credit analyst in his first years on the job. McColl recognized the young man's talent, put him in charge of lending to corporate customers in the western United States, and in the late 1970s, he sent Lewis to New York to grow NCNB's fledgling international lending operations, a business that allowed local banks to extend credit to U.S.-based multinationals. By day, Lewis assembled a team to call on large corporations from Philadelphia to Boston and by night, he took courses in international finance at New York University. During some business meetings, he kept a textbook on his lap so he could crib the meaning of some of the arcane terminology used in international lending. His only failure occurred when he tried to get a mortgage from Manufacturers Hanover and was turned down because his salary, $30,000 a year, was too low. The banker at Manny Hanny actually called down to Charlotte to tell Lewis's superiors that they weren't paying the young man enough money to live in the New York market. Lewis eventually did get a loan from a small New Jersey bank and bought his first piece of property, a house at 143 Colonial Road in Summit, New Jersey.

McColl brought Lewis back to Charlotte in 1980 and put him in charge of NCNB's U.S. division, and three years after that added responsibilities for middle market lending to Lewis's portfolio. By 1985, when the Charlotte bank had acquired so many Florida banks that the businesses were unfocused and veering off in different directions, McColl summoned Lewis to his office and told him about the situation.

"I need you to go down there and make some money," the CEO said. The next day, McColl went looking for Lewis around the office to give him some more direction about what needed to be done in Florida, but couldn't find his young deputy. Lewis had already left and started work in Tampa. Over the next three years, Lewis organized NCNB's Florida banks. He suffered the jeers and insults flung at him by the market leader, Barnett Bank, which asked Floridians if they wanted to do business with a local bank or with an outfit that kept running "troop trains" full of young bankers from Charlotte to the Sunshine State. Despite the home-grown resistance, NCNB's Florida banking operations became profitable under Lewis, and McColl took note.

For McColl, Florida was only the beginning. Short in stature at five-foot-seven, but gifted with an enormous competitive drive and strong leadership skills, McColl envisioned building a bank that would challenge the money-center institutions of New York and California. Early in his career, Reese had fired his imagination by getting McColl to focus his competitive drive on Wachovia. Then Storrs had unleashed him on Florida. But McColl wanted more, and he sought out ways to beat the New York banks at their own game. In 1989, McColl pulled off one of the signal achievements in the history of U.S. banking when he convinced the Federal Deposit Insurance Corporation to award NCNB control of First Republic, the largest bank in Texas and the biggest victim of the Lone Star State's boom and bust economy that decade. First Republic had crashed following the collapse of energy prices in Texas, which, when they were soaring, had fueled a binge of speculative real estate loans throughout the state.

First Republic's problems had driven it into the arms of the FDIC, which in 1988 began looking for a big bank willing to buy the floundering Dallas-based operation and its bad loans. Initially, only two large banks—Citibank in New York and Wells Fargo in San Francisco—expressed interest. But McColl approached FDIC chairman L. William

Seidman with a novel idea: NCNB would make a down payment on First Republic and run it on behalf of the government, buying it outright within several years. Unlike the two money-center banks, NCNB had another angle in its favor: Its lawyers had figured out that it would be perfectly legal for the Charlotte bank to take the losses generated by First Republic's bad loans and apply them toward its own tax liabilities going forward. NCNB applied for and received an IRS ruling to that effect. The tax benefit ended up improving the quality of the bid that the Charlotte bank made to the FDIC. Seidman delayed and delayed on making a decision, but McColl was persistent and eventually received the regulator's blessing to take over the largest bank in Texas in July 1989.

NCNB's triumph in the battle for First Republic was a stunning coup which vaulted the Charlotte bank from its status as an aggressive but distinctly regional player into a bank with national stature. McColl had bet—correctly it turned out—that the Texas economy would bounce back, and when it did NCNB reaped the benefits of owning the biggest bank in the state. Once again, McColl dispatched his top manager, Lewis, from Tampa to Dallas to run the business, under the guidance of Buddy Kemp, a more seasoned leader who served as chairman.

The trash talk Lewis had endured in Florida was nothing compared to what awaited him in Dallas. The downside of McColl's deal with the FDIC was that it required the Charlotte bank to settle all delinquent loans on the government's terms, which forced NCNB to collect on First Republic's best customers, many of whom were prominent business leaders in Dallas. The uncompromising approach that NCNB had to take in these matters generated deep antipathy within the Lone Star State. Lewis and Kemp were blackballed from Dallas's best country clubs—where membership was a requisite for the state's top bankers—and never welcomed into the upper reaches of the city's business circles. Lewis avoided explaining to his young daughter why her friend's father, a commercial real estate developer, had a license plate on his car that consisted of six letters: FU NCNB. When Lewis tried to join the Young Presidents Organization in Dallas, he was sponsored by Roger Staubach, the beloved

ex-quarterback of the Dallas Cowboys. It didn't matter. The city's love
for Staubach, a star player who had led its team to Super Bowl victories,
was outweighed by its leaders' visceral hatred of Lewis and his Charlotte
colleagues. After two years of such vehement rejection—at a time when
the bank's retail business in the Lone Star State was booming—Lewis
came close to snapping. He and his wife, Donna, were having dinner one
evening at a fashionable restaurant when Lewis overheard a remark from
a neighboring table about NCNB. "That's it," he said, standing up and
preparing to approach the offender when his wife grabbed his arm and
told him to sit down, that the overheard remark was a compliment, not
an insult.

In 1992, after the acquisition of C&S/Sovran in Atlanta, McColl
renamed his sprawling enterprise NationsBank, befitting its multistate
status, and put Lewis in charge of operations in Georgia. The new environment was far more hospitable, and Lewis was finally able to enjoy life
as a beloved civic leader, and help out the city of Atlanta by becoming a
sponsor of the 1996 Olympic Games. But McColl was never satisfied,
and continued his career-long crusade against the big banks of the northeast, the "northern money" that in his mind had frustrated the ambitions of downtrodden southerners since the Civil War. It all came back to
the textile mills, the biggest businesses in the region, which, when they
needed to borrow a large amount of money, went directly to New York
rather than to a local bank.

McColl delighted in tweaking his opponents, posing for magazine
cover stories and boasting about how he was going to overrun weaker
banks across the country. But he never received the respect he felt he
deserved from the New York establishment. In 1993, he offered to buy
Warburg Pincus, a New York–based investment fund. Lionel Pincus,
the well-bred founder and chairman of the organization, was practically
quivering with disgust when he brought the idea before a roomful of
managing directors and hollered, "Do you want to work for a bunch of
hillbillies?" The answer was a resounding "no," the same answer McColl
always got when it came to his quest for respect from New York.

Up to the time of the First Republic acquisition, Buddy Kemp had established himself as the lead candidate to be McColl's successor, but shortly after that deal, he was diagnosed with a brain tumor and spent most of the following year battling cancer. He succumbed in November 1990. Of his two top deputies, McColl had once described Kemp as the better leader and Lewis as the better manager. But over the course of the 1990s, Lewis worked on his leadership skills—aided by a human resources executive who was paired up with him in Georgia, Steele Alphin—and by the end of the decade Lewis had established himself as McColl's clear number two.

In 1998, McColl pulled off the deal of his career, a merger with San Francisco–based Bank of America. McColl convinced BofA's management that the combined bank should be based in Charlotte, but he conceded one important point: The name "Bank of America" was stronger in the marketplace and would therefore replace the name of his own beloved creation, NationsBank. The union created the largest bank in the country by deposits, and the first bank with a coast-to-coast network of retail operations. The deal also established Charlotte as a major money center in its own right, independent of New York. Thus, in the span of less than four decades, a hard-charging group of aggressive bankers, unified by Addison Reese against a common enemy, Wachovia, managed to build the largest bank in the nation.

In the annals of corporate history, there are few stories that can rival this transformation or the effect it had on the city of Charlotte. Paced by NationsBank, another Charlotte lender, First Union, also grew rapidly through the 1980s and '90s, culminating with its merger with the mighty Wachovia in 2001. (The combined bank kept the Wachovia name.) Between the growth of the two organizations, Charlotte became a boomtown and a financial destination in its own right. By the turn of the century, the natural order of the banking system in the U.S., which had been centered around New York since the nineteenth century, had been upended, and Charlotte was the default destination of any corporation that needed a line of credit. An apocryphal story that gained traction in the Carolinas involved a New York banker appealing to a large corporate client who has just turned him down: "But you don't have to go to North Charlotte to get money, sir. We've got money here!"

HUGH McCOLL FINALLY STEPPED down from the top job in 2001, after an eighteen-year run that established him as a legend in the world of banking. Ken Lewis became CEO of Bank of America, and told investors that his mission was clear: He would focus on unifying all the banks that were now flying under the BofA flag, rationalize their operations, and make the place run smoothly and more efficiently. For a few years he was good to his word, until he got bit by the acquisition bug and bought Fleet Financial Group of Boston for $47 billion in 2004.

Lewis had another mission as well, and that was to preserve the aggressive, can-do culture that he grew up with at NCNB. That culture could not thrive in a vacuum. It required an enemy, a target against which NCNB could compete. In his early days on the job, Lewis used to walk up the hill to NCNB's offices on Tryon Street and look at the big Wachovia billboard that had been strategically placed near his bank's headquarters. That was enough to get his blood going and focus him on the task at hand.

After Lewis relocated to Florida in 1985, a local reporter asked him to describe the culture of the North Carolina bank, which was now competing against Barnett, the biggest bank in Florida. Lewis said NCNB was a special place where people worked closely together and created an atmosphere of "winning with friends." It was, he added, a "cult."

The word "cult" has a negative connotation when applied to religious groups, but in the corporate world, many successful organizations—from Apple to Nike to Starbucks to Goldman Sachs—inspire a cultlike devotion among their employees. In these companies, workers display a dedication to their jobs that transcends the normal contours of the employer-employee relationship. This devotion, in turn, becomes a competitive advantage in the marketplace.

For most of McColl's tenure, the bank's cultlike devotion to the competitive ethos of NCNB flowed naturally from the top of the organization. After every acquisition, McColl let it be known among employees of the vanquished that there was a seat for them on the NationsBank train, but they had to want to get on, because the train was leaving the station. In this way, the Charlotte bank was able to inculcate its values into a large chunk of the workforce of every bank it acquired.

The Bank of America deal was different. It doubled the organization in size—to 180,000 employees—and McColl's aphorism about people needing to get on the train before it left the station no longer applied. McColl needed almost everyone to stay on board in order to keep the place running. The culture of the Charlotte bank finally became a hostage of its own appetite for growth.

As for Bank of America's legacy employees, some of them looked to A. P. Giannini—the Italian immigrant who founded BofA a century earlier—as a source of inspiration. Many other legacy BofA employees had no sense of their corporate culture whatsoever. They were just people who worked at a bank and collected their paychecks.

After Lewis became CEO, he named Steele Alphin, who had become a close friend, to be his head of personnel and gave him far-reaching authority at the bank. Over time, Alphin built up his department into an empire more powerful than any HR department at any other Fortune 500 company. At most companies, HR is a support function that helps executives achieve their business goals by assisting in the process of hiring the right people for the right jobs.

The power of the HR department of Bank of America went much further. Alphin believed that his HR people should help the bank grow its revenues and develop future leaders. To that end, every senior executive at the bank—people responsible for business units that produced revenue—had a "shadow" assigned to him or her by the HR department. This shadow followed the executive everywhere, sitting in on business meetings, taking notes, and reporting back to Alphin on what the executive had said to subordinates. This relentless monitoring of an executive's performance and every utterance on the job was done under the guise of helping Alphin develop future leaders for the firm, but it also made him the most powerful executive on Lewis's management team, because he knew the weaknesses and mistakes of every senior executive at the bank.

Outside of dealing with his own direct reports, Lewis did not wander around the various floors of the BofA tower, checking in on people two levels below to see what their concerns were. Instead, he relied on Alphin to supply him with intelligence as to which up-and-coming executives deserved promotion and which executives weren't with the program.

Alphin's team often weighed in about business matters, recommending that an executive pursue one course of action over another. Early on in Lewis's tenure, many of the bankers to whom these shadows had been assigned pushed back, rejecting the business advice from the HR person. But over time, these bankers learned from hard experience that it didn't pay to cross Steele Alphin.

Unlike a factory or other manufacturing facility, where production jobs are interchangeable, banking is a people business. On the ground level in each Bank of America office across the country are the tellers and store managers who deal with regular customers, local residents who have checking accounts, auto loans, and mortgages. Further up the food chain are the people responsible for making loans to small and medium-sized businesses in a particular region. At the higher levels are the people who make large loans to corporate clients. And then there's the investment bank, which helps corporate clients raise even larger sums of money through the issuance of bonds or the sale of stock. All of these activities are directed by a management team that reports to the CEO in Charlotte.

The most important decisions for the bank's senior executives often involved personnel: Picking the right person for the right job could determine whether a manager achieved a revenue target for the year. An executive's power over his subordinates also rested on the perception that he or she could promote or get rid of a particular employee. But under Alphin, even the staffing decisions at various business units were determined by HR, which further undermined the business leader's power within the organization. It didn't matter if the business leader wanted to hire someone for a particular job. Alphin's department controlled compensation, so if HR didn't sign off on a new hire, it didn't happen. Likewise, at bonus time, a department leader's ability to reward his best performers was constricted by what HR determined should be an appropriate amount. Thus, at BofA, the most important tools a manager had for motivating his troops—the ability to promote and reward—had been stripped away and were controlled by a team of HR people who answered to Alphin alone.

In this way, members of Alphin's department exerted enormous control over the executives they monitored. By 2004, the year in which BofA acquired Fleet, many business executives at the Charlotte bank acted like puppets, and the HR people were no longer their shadows, but the puppeteers.

THE ORIGINS OF THIS unusual system of management flowered in the late spring of 2000, when McColl was a year away from retirement. Even though Lewis would not ascend to the corner office for another year, McColl made it clear that the job was his, and that he should go ahead and assemble his own management team. But the future CEO of Bank of America found himself in a quandary: Several of his contemporaries—members of McColl's management team—still held important jobs in the organization. Lewis wasn't sure if their loyalties would translate to him, or whether they would fit into his own management team.

Adelaide "Alex" Sink, the most powerful woman in the corporate hierarchy, ran the bank's Florida operations, reporting to Joel Smith, the Charlotte-based executive in charge of BofA's East Coast banking system. Both had been loyal members of McColl's team who had proven themselves in the lean years and contributed to NCNB's transformation into the largest bank in the U.S. Under McColl, the bank had grown haphazardly, and his solution had been a decentralized system which allowed the regional heads of the banking system to act according to their best judgment. Lewis wanted to strip out that layer of oversight and centralize control in Charlotte. He didn't want his directives to be filtered through a layer of management and therefore didn't picture Sink, Smith, and others being integral players on his own team going forward. If Lewis kept them on, he'd be holding back the next layer of executives that he wanted to groom to run the bank.

Alphin, who could read Lewis's body language better than anyone at the bank, recognized the anguish Lewis was going through in trying to make a hard decision involving McColl's loyalists. This would be the future CEO's first significant personnel decision, one that would define the way Lewis ran the organization for years to come. Alphin—who had spent much of the previous decade helping Lewis develop the leadership skills needed for the top job—advised his boss that action was better than inaction, and that the longer he put off a difficult decision, the worse he would appear as a leader. But Lewis still struggled as he tried to figure out a way to build his own team without disenfranchising the core of McColl's group.

Finally, in early June, Alphin visited Lewis at his home in the affluent section of Charlotte where almost all of the bank's top executives lived. As the two men sat in the sunroom of Lewis's house, Alphin, a student of military history, explained that one of the core attributes of leadership was decisiveness, and that if Lewis kept putting off a difficult decision, then he wasn't doing his job. A leader, Alphin said, was supposed to lead, and not spend an inordinate amount of time thinking things over. Lewis's job, Alphin summed up, was to be a leader, to set an example for everyone who worked beneath him, and if Lewis kept spending all his time puzzling over a difficult decision, then he wasn't doing a very good job of leading, was he?

At that moment, the scales fell from Lewis's eyes. "You're right," he told Alphin. "I'm not doing my job. I cannot procrastinate."

Within days, an internal memo at the bank went out announcing that, as part of a reorganization, there would no longer be geographical units for the East Coast, Midwest, and West Coast, and that Alex Sink, at age fifty-two, had decided to retire. Taking her place as head of BofA's important Florida operations would be Catherine Bessant, thirty-nine.

ONE OF LEWIS'S BIGGEST challenges after taking over from McColl was the need for Bank of America to establish a strong presence on Wall Street. Unless BofA had its own investment bank, it risked losing some of its largest clients' capital markets business to rivals such as Citigroup, which could offer commercial loans, and raise capital through bond offerings or stock sales. A few years earlier, BofA had acquired Montgomery

Securities in San Francisco, but McColl clashed immediately with Thomas Weisel, the central figure at Montgomery. Weisel stormed off soon after the acquisition, taking many of his top people with him.

McColl replaced Weisel with Carter McClelland, a well-respected investment banker from Deutsche Bank. Eventually, BofA moved the Montgomery unit to New York and rechristened it Bank of America Securities, and McClelland built up his team in New York. Lewis never liked the idea of having an investment bank, but instead considered it a necessary evil in order to have a deluxe service to offer BofA's largest clients. Everything about the investment bank rubbed him the wrong way, from the outrageous pay packages doled out to everyone, which dwarfed the compensation for comparable work in Charlotte, to the fact that it was in New York. Lewis shared McColl's general dislike for the elitism of New York, and no segment of the financial world was more elite than the investment banking business. Lewis had spent his life building an institution that was far more important than any of the individuals who worked at that institution. But the investment bankers were prima donnas who thought the world revolved around them and viewed themselves as luminaries who outshone their companies.

By 2005, Lewis was wary of the size and scope of what McClelland was building in New York, and McClelland, who had struggled with his German overlords when building up Deutsche Bank's U.S. presence, now realized how much easier it had been to deal with German bankers in Frankfurt than Prussian-style bankers in Charlotte.

In order to be good citizen in the community, Ken Lewis agreed to lend his name to a fundraiser, in his own honor, at the Museum of Natural History in New York. McClelland took the lead on raising money, along with Louis Bernard of Morgan Stanley. A few weeks before the May 2005 event, only $1.3 million out of the museum's $2 million goal had been raised. McClelland and Bernard went into overdrive and drummed up as many corporate sponsors as they could find in the final weeks, reaching the $3 million mark and turning the fundraiser into a huge success. On May 5, Lewis attended the dinner in his honor and gave a speech in tribute to the museum as a cause worthy of supporting.

Lewis and his wife sat at the head table, along with McClelland and his wife.

Since Lewis was an unknown quantity in New York, and avoided unnecessary business trips to the city, McClelland had become the public face of Bank of America. On this evening, a stream of guests came up to the head table to congratulate McClelland and thank him for the wonderful fundraising job he'd pulled off. As McClelland was beaming, soaking up the praise that he knew would reflect well on the bank, Lewis turned to him and said, "You'd think they were honoring you here tonight."

A week later, Steele Alphin called up McClelland to inform him that the bank was removing one of his titles, head of the bank's New York City operations. Less than two months later, McClelland was pushed out altogether.

Following McClelland's departure, Lewis appointed Gene Taylor, a longtime friend, as head of the investment bank in New York. Unlike McClelland, Taylor did not have any significant experience in investment banking, but he was a good relationship banker, and would help sell the Bank of America Securities story to capital markets clients. Lewis paired Taylor with Al de Molina, a strong finance executive who knew the ins and outs of sales and trading, and who was willing to play Mr. Inside to Taylor's Mr. Outside.

The partnership only lasted a few months before Lewis fired his chief financial officer, Mark Oken, and replaced him with de Molina, leaving Taylor exposed in the investment banking job. The Cuban-born de Molina, who was respected in the financial community, rubbed Alphin the wrong way from the start by referring to his HR shadow as a member of the "Gestapo" or "Stasi." De Molina refused to read the talking points handed to him by HR for his meetings and goaded Alphin into doing something about it. But de Molina had a fiery temper, and after a blowup with Alphin, he lost support among his colleagues on the management committee. In December 2006, just as the credit crunch was about to begin, he quit.

During 2007, Taylor continued to excel as Mr. Outside at BofA's investment bank in New York, but without any Mr. Inside managing the firm's risk, or monitoring its trading positions, BofA Securities made some bad bets, including buying into a pair of Bear Stearns hedge funds constructed around CDOs.

On Thursday, October 18, just a few weeks after Ken Lewis met with Stan O'Neal to talk about the possible purchase of Merrill Lynch, Bank of America announced a 31 percent decline in its third-quarter earnings, largely due to $3.7 billion in write-downs of assets acquired by its investment banking operations in New York. During a conference call to discuss the disappointing earnings, an analyst asked Lewis if he was still interested in bolstering BofA's relatively small capital markets business. "I never say never," Lewis replied, "but I've had all the fun I can stand in investment banking at the moment."

A week later, on October 24, Lewis fired Taylor, a thirty-eight-year veteran of the Charlotte bank, and replaced him with Brian Moynihan, a forty-eight-year-old executive who had been with Fleet Financial when it was acquired by BofA in 2004.

The announcement surprised BofA's top management ranks in Charlotte, because Taylor had a long history with Lewis, going back to the late 1960s when they both launched their careers at the old NCNB. Not only were the men close friends, but each of them had had a failed first marriage, and wound up with their administrative assistants at the bank as second wives. Taylor had been best man when Lewis married his former secretary, Donna Chesser, in 1980, and Lewis had served as best man when Taylor married his secretary. Even closer friends than their husbands, Donna Lewis and Kathy Taylor were both shocked by the news.

Taylor blamed Alphin for the firing and barged into the HR chief's office in Charlotte to complain. The two men went at it verbally for some time, with Taylor shouting that Alphin was an idiot who didn't understand the banking business, and Alphin shouting back at Taylor that there was no room in the organization for someone who could lose $3.7 billion. The two men caused such a commotion that Alphin's assistant got up and closed the door to the office.

To his colleagues in New York, Taylor expressed gratitude for their hard work. But he did find one part of his firing a complete puzzle: the appointment of Moynihan to replace him.

"I can't believe Ken put someone in who knows even less about investment banking than I do," Taylor said of his successor.

Hugh McColl, who stepped down as CEO of Bank of America in 2001, still kept an office in the sixty-story Cesar Pelli–designed headquarters he constructed in the heart of Charlotte. In keeping with the strict code of loyalty that was part of the culture of the old NCNB, he never criticized Lewis to outsiders. But among friends he questioned the wisdom of letting a banker of Taylor's caliber go, especially for errors in judgment that occurred outside his area of expertise.

CHAPTER 4

BETRAYAL

EVERY CEO HAS HIS own management style, which tends to evolve from his personality. At Merrill Lynch, O'Neal's style grew out of his self-confidence. Not only had he proven himself to be smarter than his rivals for the top job earlier in the decade, O'Neal was more ruthless. After becoming CEO in 2002, he systematically eliminated any executive who had enough experience to challenge him, or marginalized him in such a way that the executive left. Few people who reported to him in his early years as CEO were surprised to learn that O'Neal's favorite TV show was *The Sopranos*.

O'Neal even rebuffed Barry Friedberg, the man who recruited him from GM, re-recruited him from Bankers Trust, and counseled him not to leave Merrill for Brera Capital in 1999. Friedberg called O'Neal late in 2001, after he was named president of the firm and heir apparent to David Komansky, the CEO. Friedberg, by this time the honorary head of investment banking, advised against some of the changes O'Neal was planning to make in that division. "Barry, I don't need your advice,"

O'Neal said. "I need you to do your job, and that means calling on clients."

By getting rid of all of the grown-ups at Merrill Lynch, even those who had helped him to the corner office, O'Neal could populate the management team with a younger, more diverse·group of people—such as Fakahany, Kim, and Fleming—none of whom had the experience or stature to challenge his wisdom.

And when one of those executives ultimately did rise up to challenge him—as when Fleming argued against Semerci's promotion—O'Neal simply tuned him out.

O'Neal's imperial style worked superbly in good times. Merrill's four-year run of healthy profits from 2003 to 2007 only served to reinforce the notion that the CEO was the all-knowing master and commander of Merrill Lynch.

But the sudden announcement of a $4.5 billion write-down on its assets in the first week of October punctured the myth of O'Neal's infallibility. On the morning of Friday, October 5, the firm's top finance people and O'Neal huddled to go over the final language that would be part of the earnings warning sent out just after 9 a.m. The finance group, headed by CFO Jeff Edwards, had come up with the $4.5 billion number for the write-down on the firm's CDO portfolio. Once the language was in place, the group dispersed, in the belief that the work was done.

But after a subsequent discussion involving Gary Carlin, who headed Merrill's internal controls, Edwards and the investor relations people decided to err on the side of caution and tell investors that the CDO write-downs related to an "incremental" impact in the quarter. At 9:06 a.m., the announcement went out on the wires. Sometime around 9:07 a.m., O'Neal called Eric Heaton, the treasurer, and screamed at him, demanding to know who had inserted the word "incremental" in the release. Normally a man of calm and businesslike demeanor, O'Neal laced his tirade with derivatives of the word "fuck," which seemed out of character. Then the CEO turned his fury on Edwards, unleashing another fusillade of f-bombs on the CFO, whom he blamed for adding the word "incremental." The earnings warning was supposed to let investors know that Merrill Lynch was on top of its problems, O'Neal hollered. Using a qualifier like "incremental" suggested that the firm didn't even know how bad its problems were.

In the days following the announcement, he was no longer the same old Stan, the intimidating but decisive leader who had righted a listing ship after the terrorist attacks of September 11, 2001. Subordinates who used to fear his displeasure now looked on as their cold-eyed, confident CEO moved around his offices tentatively, as if he'd been temporarily stunned in the boxing ring by a punch to the head. O'Neal was still standing, but his bell had been rung.

DAYS AFTER MERRILL LYNCH'S earnings warning, O'Neal's executive assistant called down to John Breit, the former risk executive who had been conducting his own probe into Merrill's subprime mortgage exposures, and arranged a meeting with the CEO. Before and during his postmortem investigation, Pete Kelly had listened as Breit spelled out the extent of the losses on Merrill's books, losses that were more severe than what the bank had told investors about on October 5. Kelly brought the matter up to Fleming, who passed along the information to O'Neal.

Breit went to O'Neal's office—the first time he'd spoken to the CEO since 2005—and walked him through his valuations for CDO exposures. Instead of a $4.5 billion decline, which had been announced October 5, the loss would be almost double that number, Breit explained. The dodgiest securites, known as CDO-squareds, were toast, Breit declared. As for the "mezzanine" portions of the CDOs, which consisted of a lot of subprime mortgages, they had probably lost half their value, just using back-of-the-envelope calculations. But the biggest position, some $30 billion in "super senior" CDOs, hadn't been valued properly, Breit explained. Even with Semerci gone, the FICC department kept insisting that there were hedges in place and countervailing short positions that insured the firm against losses, so the $30 billion exposure would retain most of its value. Not so, said Breit. If the mortgage market continued trending downwards, and all indications suggested it would, the insurance companies hedging those positions would be swamped with claims and unable to deliver, and the other short positions would be of little help. The $30 billion position would be decimated.

O'Neal looked like he was about to vomit. Just days earlier, he had told the world that there was a $4.5 billion hole, and now it emerged that Merrill's losses would be a multiple of that amount. When the firm announced its third quarter earnings two weeks later, it would have to disclose a number almost twice as large, accompanied by a warning that things could get worse.

The next few days were an emotional roller coaster for O'Neal as his mood shifted between paralysis—born of his realization that the problems were too big for him to fix—and a manic concern over Merrill's future.

O'Neal reached out to Cribiore, his "deal guy" on the board, and asked him if Warren Buffett, the billionaire stock picker, might be interested in making a strategic investment in the firm. O'Neal and Cribiore talked about how an infusion of capital from one of the world's most respected investors would allay any concerns about Merrill's health. Cribiore called Buffett in Omaha, Nebraska, and got the chairman of Berkshire Hathaway to agree to give O'Neal a call.

ON A SUNNY OCTOBER afternoon during this period, Tosi came to O'Neal's office on the thirty-second floor to review some questions about his "bad bank" idea. The CEO's office was modern in its décor, with smooth, white Formica walls and a large, kidney-shaped desk at the center, around which O'Neal would confer with his subordinates. Throughout were tasteful objects of African art, part of O'Neal's own collection. Tosi—whose metabolism was so fast that he didn't even need to drink coffee in the mornings—was always wound a little tighter than usual when he visited O'Neal, because the CEO was a tough taskmaster and if you weren't completely prepared with facts and figures, he would cut you to pieces, no matter who else was in the room.

But entering the office on this afternoon, Tosi no longer beheld the fierce master of Merrill Lynch. The room, which had a southwesterly exposure, was bathed in the afternoon sunlight, but Tosi noticed that none of the electric lights were on. There was O'Neal slouched back in his chair, looking disheveled, unshaven, wearing a gray cardigan, his hands at his temples to prop up his slumping head. Tosi had never seen the CEO like this, and it was unnerving.

"That fucking Semerci," O'Neal muttered. "I should have known I could never trust him." He then started talking about the Long Term Capital Management crisis almost a decade earlier, when he was CFO and Merrill Lynch nearly ran out of money. "Those fixed-income guys got me in 1998, and I swore I'd never let them do it to me again."

When Tosi left the office, he looked at Marian Brooks, O'Neal's longtime secretary. There were tears in her eyes.

A few hours later, after the sun had set, Greg Fleming came to O'Neal's office, hoping to find the CEO. He was sure his boss would be there, but there was no sign of him, and the lights were off. And then when he entered the corner office, Fleming saw O'Neal sitting at his desk, alone, in the dark.

"Stan," said Fleming, turning on the lights. "What is this, a metaphor? Come on, let's go. We've got work to do."

DAYS LATER, ON OCTOBER 18, O'Neal did something highly unusual: He asked Fleming for help. Even as Fleming had ascended the management ladder under O'Neal's rule, becoming president of investment banking in 2003, then co-president of the entire firm in 2007, he was never part of O'Neal's inner circle. That circle, such as it was, consisted of O'Neal and Fleming's co-president, Ahmass Fakahany.

Fakahany, who managed the inner workings of the firm, had worked closely with O'Neal for nearly a decade, and was among the first to articulate the political strategy by which O'Neal would vault himself into the CEO's job. After O'Neal took over, Fakahany accumulated more power at the firm, but his most important role was to serve as O'Neal's eyes and ears at Merrill Lynch.

But the blowup in the fixed-income department, engineered by Osman Semerci, the man identified by Fakahany as a future leader at Merrill Lynch, had damaged the credibility of O'Neal's closest confidant. An aggravating circumstance was that Merrill's risk-management systems, which had failed miserably in overseeing Semerci, also reported to Fakahany.

O'Neal asked Fleming if he still had a good relationship with Ken Thompson, chief executive of Wachovia Bank in Charlotte.

"Yes," said Fleming.

For more than a decade, like its crosstown competitor, BofA, Wachovia had been a serial acquirer of other banks. Merrill Lynch was Wachovia's primary advisor. In most of those deals, Fleming had been Merrill's lead banker, working with Thompson and other Wachovia executives to bring complicated transactions to fruition. Thompson had taken a liking to Fleming.

"I want you to ask Ken if he'd be interested in a strategic combination between our companies," O'Neal said. A few weeks earlier, when O'Neal met with BofA's Ken Lewis, Merrill's problems seemed manageable and so O'Neal didn't see any pressing need to move forward in that direction. Besides, Cribiore disdained the idea. But now that the blinders had been removed and O'Neal had developed an understanding of the magnitude of the problems facing Merrill, biding his time was no longer an option. He had to make a move, and quickly.

Fleming said he'd get on it. He had been in the doghouse with O'Neal for more than a year, ever since the argument over Semerci's promotion. Now O'Neal was asking him for help and he was eager to deliver.

Over the next two days, Fleming spoke with Thompson and the chief financial officer of Wachovia, Tom Wurtz. He explained Merrill's situation, which was not yet desperate, but distressed. Thompson was keenly interested, and said he'd bring the matter to the attention of his board. After all, the chance to acquire Merrill Lynch, one of the premier brands in financial services around the globe, was a once-in-a-lifetime opportunity, Thompson said.

IF MERRILL LYNCH WAS sold to Bank of America, the Charlotte colossus would crush the place and take full ownership, firing thousands of people and eviscerating the organization, O'Neal believed. That was Ken Lewis's style: He paid top dollar, then took full control. Wachovia,

O'Neal figured, would be different. There would be a "softer landing" for Merrill Lynch. The price would not be as high, but Ken Thompson might allow Merrill to retain some autonomy. A deal with Wachovia would resemble a merger more than an acquisition.

With a special board meeting a few days away, O'Neal started shopping for support among directors. Once again he approached his old friend Cribiore, in the hopes of enlisting his support for the idea of a Wachovia deal. But rather than hear O'Neal out, Cribiore dug in to his earlier position: Merrill Lynch should not be sold, especially to a bank in Charlotte. O'Neal should simply declare a big write-down of its CDO position, then go raise fresh capital.

ON FRIDAY, OCTOBER 19, Armando Codina, a Cuban-born real estate developer and member of Merrill Lynch's board, showed up at Harvard Business School to discuss a case study built around one of his deals. While he was explaining to the students the decisions he made with the proposed development, one of the school's administrative assistants came up to him in mid-lecture and handed him a note. Stan O'Neal needed to speak with him urgently, the message said.

Codina was well aware that Merrill was facing red ink. Fakahany had paid him a visit in Florida in late September to brief him on the CDO issue and warn him that Semerci was going to be fired. Then there was the $4.5 billion earnings warning, issued two weeks earlier. A Merrill Lynch board meeting was scheduled to begin the next day in New York, so he didn't understand why O'Neal would need to reach him with such urgency.

After class, on the drive back to a second home he kept in Litchfield County in northwestern Connecticut, Codina returned O'Neal's call.

"Armando," said O'Neal. "You're the first board member I wanted to talk to about this. I've had a conversation to sell the company to Wachovia. I hope you are okay with that."

Codina was dumbfounded. After several seconds, he spluttered something about how inappropriate it was for O'Neal to go off shopping the company on his own, without informing the board.

"You can't just tell me you're doing this because it's your judgment,"

Codina said. "That's not your role. That's a decision for the directors." Codina said he would discuss the topic further at Sunday's board meeting and hung up.

AT MERRILL LYNCH HEADQUARTERS in the World Financial Center in lower Manhattan, Fakahany and Jeff Edwards, the chief financial officer, spent Saturday with a team of people from finance and treasury putting together a major presentation for Sunday evening's board meeting, laying out the scope of the investment bank's exposure to subprime mortgages and CDOs.

Everyone involved in the presentation was surprised when Cribiore showed up. The director, who had never attended such a prep session before, didn't explain why he was there. After forty-five minutes, during which he thumbed through a briefing book and asked a few questions, Cribiore left. Neither Fakahany, the co-president of Merrill, nor anyone else involved in the presentation had any idea what was going on.

ON SUNDAY, OCTOBER 21, O'Neal called Fleming at home to see if there was any update on the state of the Wachovia talks. It dawned on Fleming that O'Neal was doing some last-minute cramming for a discussion with the directors later that day.

"Where are you on the dialogue with the board on this?" Fleming asked. O'Neal said he planned on telling the directors about Wachovia later that day.

"You're making a big mistake, Stan," Fleming said. "You've got to warm them up for this. You've got to lay the groundwork."

"Who are you talking to on my board?" demanded O'Neal, suspicion in his voice.

"I'm not talking to anybody," said Fleming. "What I'm telling you is good advice. I've done this a hundred times."

The younger man, who'd been treated like an annoyance by O'Neal for the past year, regained his footing as he warmed to his subject. "The board is going to want process," Fleming said. "You have to explain to them where we are, what our financial situation is. Then you go through our strategic options, whether it makes sense to stay independent or sell. And if we sell, then who is the right partner? It's then that you start to talk about Wachovia. It's a three- or four-step process."

THE MERRILL LYNCH board of directors meeting convened at the St. Regis Hotel in Midtown Manhattan that afternoon. Fakahany had worked many such meetings and developed a personal relationship with most of the directors. He could tell, right from the outset, that something was wrong at this one, and it went far beyond the CDO losses.

Prior to a presentation he was about to make to the board's four-member finance committee, he was approached by Charles Rossotti, the committee chair, and Ann Reese, a member of the panel.

"Can we talk about Stan?" Reese asked him. Reese and Rossotti assured Fakahany that he was doing a good job and that they had confidence in him. Fakahany wasn't aware that anyone thought he was doing a bad job.

Then, as he and Edwards led the presentation to the finance committee, Fakahany noticed something else: Armando Codina, who was not a member of the finance committee, had decided to sit in. From his posture and demeanor, it was clear that Codina was tightly wound.

The directors had taken over the east wing of the second floor, directly above the hotel's famous King Cole bar. The afternoon committee meetings were held in the smaller meeting rooms, the Rambouillet and Matignon. When the meetings broke up, the directors socialized in a hallway for a few minutes of small talk before helping themselves to a buffet-style dinner and repairing to the Fontainebleau Room for the evening's discussion. The board's ten outside directors were present, but instead of the usual camaraderie that bubbled up in similar meetings, Fleming, Fakahany, and Rosemary Berkery, the general counsel, all noticed an unusual level of tension in the air.

The Fontainebleau Room, with its deep red carpet and walls, along with baroque, gold-painted chairs, suggested a strange mixture of Louis XIV France and de Medici Italy. Fleming squirmed throughout the meal and Fakahany was bewildered by the bad chemistry that prevailed.

Finally, after everyone was settled, Fakahany and Jeff Edwards, the chief financial officer, walked the board through Merrill's balance sheet exposures and what the worsening economic environment meant for the firm. After that, Pete Kelly got up and delivered his report on Merrill's buildup of more than $30 billion in CDOs, and how it had happened under Semerci's watch. After he spoke, Ed Moriarty got up to talk about the CDOs. Not long after, O'Neal cut off the presentation abruptly.

"Okay, you guys have the general idea," O'Neal said to the board, bringing his subordinates' presentation to an abrupt end. Chris Hayward, Eric Heaton, Kelly, and Moriarty realized they had been given a cue to leave, and awkwardly departed.

O'Neal now made his case to the directors. The problems on Merrill's balance sheet could get far worse, and there was no way to quantify the potential losses at the moment, he said. He had lived through the Long Term Capital Management crisis in 1998, and once liquidity dries up, Merrill Lynch could get into deep trouble in almost no time. Given this situation, it was only prudent for the firm to look at potential partners, O'Neal explained. That's why he had reached out to Wachovia.

"Stan, this is a great franchise, an iconic brand," said Cribiore. "It's as famous as Coca-Cola. We don't want to be sitting with a bank in Charlotte." Neither Cribiore nor O'Neal mentioned the merger discussion with Bank of America CEO Ken Lewis from three weeks earlier.

"I don't like to make decisions with my back against the wall," declared Codina. "What has taken place with Wachovia?"

"It was just a phone call, just a feeler," O'Neal said, before indicating that it was Fleming who was the primary contact with the Charlotte bank.

Codina turned to Fleming and demanded to know what had transpired.

"It was just a casual call," Fleming replied. "Nothing's really happened."

"Do you think I was born on a banana boat?" Codina said with a snarl. "Do you take me for a fool? Tell me what has happened."

"It was only three conversations," said Fleming, flustered by the attack. "I made that phone call at the request of the CEO, who works for you. Talk to him if you've got a problem. What would you like me to do when I get a request from my chief executive officer, ignore him?"

O'Neal sat mute, a few feet away, as Fleming defended himself. It was but the latest example of why the CEO inspired so little loyalty in the company.

Finally, it was John Finnegan's turn to speak. Finnegan, who had worked alongside O'Neal earlier in his career at GM, was the chief executive of Chubb Insurance, the only director with a job comparable to O'Neal's. As such, he felt the board should show a certain amount of deference to O'Neal's judgment.

"Stan's the CEO," said Finnegan. "If he's saying that he thinks this is the best course of action, maybe we should listen." It was too late. There was already too much antagonism in the room for the other directors to be swayed.

Later that evening, the outside directors voted to retain their own legal counsel, Robert Joffe of Cravath, Swaine & Moore. To anyone familiar with the world of corporate governance, a board's decision to retain its own attorney, separate from the company's general counsel, is a sign of trouble. It would be akin to a wife, following a disagreement with her husband, hiring a lawyer to represent her interests. Even if the word "divorce" is never uttered, the act of hiring an independent lawyer represents an irreparable breach of trust in the relationship.

THE NEXT DAY, the board reconvened at Merrill Lynch headquarters downtown. During various meetings, board members were accompanied by Joffe, a top ranked securities lawyer who had represented boards of directors in numerous corporate battles over the previous two decades.

O'Neal met with his board first thing in the morning. One concern shared by various directors was the "change in control" clause in O'Neal's contract, which triggered a special payment of some $250 million in the event of a sale of Merrill Lynch. The clause, a standard feature in most CEO contracts, is designed to protect a top executive if his board opts for a sale of the company. In reality, the clause could act as an incentive for CEOs to give up in the face of adversity and sell their firms instead of fighting to fix problems.

When Codina raised the issue, O'Neal assured him that his desire to sell Merrill Lynch did not stem from the financial incentive in the change-in-control clause, and agreed to amend his contract to delete that language. O'Neal's decision mollified the board on that point, but did not convince the directors of the justness of his views.

Throughout the day, other Merrill Lynch executives went up to the boardroom on the thirty-third floor to be interrogated by the directors in the presence of their outside counsel while O'Neal sat and fumed in his office on the thirty-second floor. Each time someone returned, O'Neal would pepper the individual with questions about what the board was asking.

Finally, around 2:00 p.m., O'Neal returned to the boardroom. He ascended the stairs from the executive floor up to the "chairmen's gallery" on thirty-three, where portraits of his nine predecessors hung on the walls. Then he entered the boardroom. Joffe, the outside counsel, was sitting in his seat—the power seat—in the middle of one side of a long table. As Joffe stood up to excuse himself, Codina invited O'Neal to return to his usual spot at the table.

"No, I can see that it's been taken by someone else," said O'Neal as he plopped himself down in the chair closest to the door.

The previous evening, he had used scare tactics with the board, trying to paint the worst portrait imaginable of Merrill's financial condition in order to compel them to follow. By now the board, which had been taken over by Cribiore, had become satisfied that Merrill Lynch's position was not so dire. Cribiore announced that he'd conducted his own investigation and concluded that Merrill Lynch could work its way through the problem with the right leadership. What's more, Cribiore had swung Ann Reese and Codina around to his view.

"How do you know we won't be back here in February and the Federal Reserve has lowered rates and the value of the assets will come back?" Cribiore asked.

"Maybe that's true," said O'Neal, "but I don't care to run a business where I have to depend on outside events for things to work out."

Codina and Reese insisted that Merrill's problems could be solved. O'Neal, who no longer saw eye to eye with either one, despite having appointed them to the board, got fed up with his decisions being questioned.

"Well, if you're not going to listen to me, maybe I'm not the right person to lead this company," he said in an insolent tone.

That was it, as far as Codina was concerned. O'Neal's arrogance appalled him.

ON WEDNESDAY, OCTOBER 24, Merrill Lynch announced its third-quarter earnings, which were even worse than what investors had been warned about earlier in the month. At the insistence of Edwards, the chief financial officer, the firm re-evaluated its CDO positions and determined that they should be written down by $7.9 billion, wiping out all the revenues generated by other parts of the company and resulting in a quarterly loss of $2.3 billion.

O'Neal himself sat in on the conference call with analysts after the numbers were announced, something he hadn't done in a long time, a sign of the severity of the situation. He was forced to admit in public what was now widely known.

"We got it wrong by being overexposed to subprime mortgages," he said. "No one, no one is more disappointed than I am by that result."

Merrill's share price, which had managed to stay above $70 per share until a week earlier, continued its decline, closing at $63.22 on the date earnings were announced.

At 4:00 p.m. that day, O'Neal came out for a "town hall" meeting in Merrill's third floor, oversized conference room. Instead of speaking from a podium, he sat on a bar stool placed at the front of the room, and showed his employees a side he'd never shared before.

"Let me start by saying a couple of things," O'Neal began. "There are a lot of great things that go along with this job. One of them is not so great and that is being a public figure. One of the things that happens with public figures is that they are caricatured and they're characterized in various ways that people choose to do that. It's not necessarily who they are.

"That's neither here nor there except that some of the characterizations of me [are] as someone who doesn't really care, who's not emotionally involved or connected. And the first thing I want to tell you is I'm deeply, deeply connected to this firm. This place has given me extraordinary opportunity over the time that I've been associated with it. I've learned more, developed more, made more friends and connections across this firm than at any other place in my professional life.

"I care about the people. I came here because I had choices but I thought the people here were the kind of people I wanted to be affiliated with. That's never, never not been the case. And it's still true today.

"So the worst part of the results that we reported today is the fact that I'm deeply disappointed—not so much for anything other than the people of this firm. Deeply disappointed. Because I think, despite the fact that there were circumstances that touched every, virtually every aspect of the financial market, we could have done a better job and this could have had a lesser impact."

ON THURSDAY, OCTOBER 25, Stan O'Neal was in a no-man's-land. He had alienated several board members with his surly, take-it-or-leave-it attitude earlier in the week, but had staggered through the earnings announcement with a brave face, and confessed his most personal feelings about the firm to his employees afterward, generating some sympathy.

He wasn't sure if his board still wanted him, or if he wanted to stay on and fight through the big turnaround challenge that lay ahead.

Sensing O'Neal's isolation, Larry Fink, chief executive of BlackRock, the huge asset management group that was 49 percent owned by Merrill Lynch, invited him out to dinner that evening.

Starting with the disclosure of a big write-down on its CDO assets in early October, the entire month, it seemed, had been consumed with one admission after another of Merrill's disastrous foray into subprime-based businesses. In contrast to those horrible investments, O'Neal's decision to sell Merrill's own asset management business to BlackRock in February 2006 was now looking better than ever.

Merrill Lynch was in several businesses: investment banking, capital markets sales and trading—the private client business that was centered around the thundering herd—and asset management. BlackRock specialized in asset management only, investing hundreds of billions of dollars in global markets on behalf of large, sophisticated investors. In this way, BlackRock was different from Fidelity and other companies that managed the mutual funds of individuals and families. Merrill's own asset management business was constrained by its relationship to the parent company: Financial advisors were reluctant to push their clients into Merrill Lynch mutual funds because of the appearance that they were favoring captive products that benefited Merrill instead of selecting the best available investment for the client.

By spinning off its own asset management business to BlackRock, Merrill Lynch unlocked the value in its own unit, propelled BlackRock beyond the $1 trillion mark in terms of assets, and wound up with a 49.8 percent stake in Fink's company, which was growing at a much faster rate than Merrill's own asset management unit. Fink put O'Neal and Fleming, who was instrumental in setting up the deal, on BlackRock's board of directors. When Merrill announced its third-quarter losses, one of the few bright points in its earnings discussion involved the value of its stake in BlackRock, which had risen from $10 billion in 2006, when the deal was struck, to $13 billion by October 2007.

O'Neal was grateful for the dinner invitation and met with Fink at Sistina, a high-end Italian eatery on the Upper East Side of Manhattan, favored by the Wall Street elite. Midway through the meal, O'Neal received a call from Fleming.

"Stan, look at your BlackBerry," said Fleming.

O'Neal checked his messages and saw one from a reporter at *The New York Times,* who said the paper was planning to run a story the next day describing his overtures to Wachovia. Did Merrill Lynch have any comment?

"I've got to go," said O'Neal to Fink as he stood up and walked out of the restaurant.

O'Neal spoke to his head of public relations, Jason Wright, but both men knew there was nothing they could do to kill the story, especially since it was accurate. O'Neal wondered who would have leaked the news, since the disclosure of the Wachovia overture was certain to damage him irreparably. It could have been Fleming, Cribiore, or even Fink, each of whom stood to gain from his ouster. Or it could have been Bob McCann, the ambitious head of Merrill's private client business, who had run afoul of O'Neal in the past.

That evening O'Neal called Armando Codina, who made it clear that the revelation of the talks with Wachovia had undermined O'Neal's position.

Later, O'Neal doubled back to Fleming, calling him at home to tell his deputy that it was over for him as CEO.

THE NEXT DAY, CODINA, who headed up the corporate governance committee at Merrill, held a conference call with his fellow directors to discuss O'Neal's future at the firm.

Ever since the previous Monday, when O'Neal had challenged the directors—telling them that if they didn't support his initiative to sell to Wachovia, he wasn't sure if he wanted to remain CEO of Merrill Lynch—Codina and Cribiore had lost confidence in him. When the *New York Times* story about the Wachovia initiative appeared on Friday, several other directors began to harbor similar feelings.

But O'Neal, who had remained aloof from the board all week, suddenly launched a campaign to save his job. He called several directors, including his old friend Finnegan, telling them how much the job meant to him and that he was willing to work with the board on their terms if only he could stay.

O'Neal also reached out to Jill Ker Conway, who had stepped down from the board just a few months earlier after more than a quarter century as a Merrill Lynch director, stretching back to the Don Regan era. Conway had supported O'Neal unilaterally throughout his five-year tenure as CEO, even during the annual ritual in which O'Neal argued passionately before the board about how he deserved more than what they were paying him. Like O'Neal's bosses at Merrill before he became CEO, other directors would be taken aback by O'Neal's histrionics over the issue of his pay, but O'Neal and Conway connected on a deeper level. After raising his voice with Conway over the amount he should be paid, a final decision would be reached—often to O'Neal's satisfaction—and the two would be good friends again immediately afterward. Conway understood that the passion O'Neal displayed on the subject of his pay wasn't personal; it was strictly business.

Now her old friend was in an hour of need, and when O'Neal told her that there was a board conference call that evening, Friday, to discuss his future at the firm, she swung into action. Conway called about half of the directors, including Codina, Judith Mayhew Jonas, and Carol Christ, president of Smith College—the same position Conway had held when Don Regan tapped her for the Merrill Lynch board in the 1970s.

To each, Conway made the same argument: in almost thirty years on Merrill's board, she had seen executives come and go at Merrill Lynch and other Wall Street firms. In her experience, there was absolutely no one on Wall Street and especially not at Merrill who was up to the challenge of leading the firm out of the troubles in which it had become mired. When he was put in charge of the firm's thundering herd in 2000, O'Neal made tough decisions about downsizing its bloated cost structure. After the 9/11 terrorist attacks in 2001, O'Neal cut the firm's payroll by more than 20,000 jobs, right-sizing Merrill Lynch for the leaner days of 2002. At a time when Merrill Lynch needed strong leadership, there was no one out there who could match O'Neal.

Codina could not be swayed by her arguments, but Christ and Jonas reiterated Conway's case time and again during the multi-hour conference call. Virgis Colbert also remained staunchly loyal to O'Neal.

But the problems facing Merrill Lynch didn't favor the CEO. Once the board determined that the firm did not have to be sold to Wachovia—a point on which O'Neal relented during his pleas to keep his job—then it would have to raise billions of dollars in fresh capital to make up for the losses.

Codina and Cribiore pointed out that despite his vaunted executive skills, O'Neal's credibility in the marketplace was now gone. No one would invest billions of dollars in Merrill Lynch while he was still running the place. One by one throughout the long, arduous call, most of the directors came to agree with Codina and Cribiore and recommended a change in leadership at Merrill Lynch. Finally, in a show of unanimity, Christ, Jonas, and Colbert joined Codina and voted to remove Stan O'Neal. In just six months, O'Neal had gone from being arguably the most successful CEO in the ninety-three-year history of Merrill Lynch to the first one ever pushed out by a hostile board vote.

DURING ITS YEARS AS a private partnership and subsequently for two decades after Merrill Lynch became a public company, top leadership at the institution had usually been decided in a collaborative manner. The men in the most senior positions at the firm jockeyed for the top job in discreet, oblique fashion, knowing that any overt statement about their ambition would probably disqualify them from the corner office.

The most successful CEO of Merrill Lynch in the modern era, Don Regan—who would become Treasury secretary and then White House chief of staff under President Ronald Reagan—ascended to the top job by force of his effectiveness as a senior executive, prevailing over a powerful rival. Regan proved to be a fiery leader of Merrill Lynch in the 1970s, railing against the club of Wall Street firms that fattened their bottom lines at the expense of the average investor.

Bill Schreyer, a member of the thundering herd who moved up the management chain under Regan, took the top job after Regan's successor, Roger Birk, stepped down for health reasons. Schreyer steered the firm through the "Black Monday" crash of 1987 and a mortgage-related loss of $387 million. When the time came for Schreyer's retirement, the torch was passed to Dan Tully, who had served as Schreyer's right-hand man. Tully codified the five principles of Merrill Lynch, principles on which Charlie Merrill had built the modern Merrill Lynch in the 1940s. The principles, which Tully insisted be displayed in Merrill Lynch offices around the world, were: client focus, respect for the individual, teamwork, responsible citizenship, and integrity.

But Tully faced a problem during his stint as CEO. At a time when the financial markets were growing more complex, success in the financial advisory business was no longer the single most important factor in determining who could lead Merrill Lynch into the twenty-first century. Tully's top candidate as successor, Dave Komansky, had risen in the organization primarily through his successful career in the private client business. Komansky wasn't as strong in Merrill's two other business units, capital markets and investment banking. Tully's solution was to team Komansky up with Herb Allison, a hard-driving, numbers-oriented operational manager who would wear the green eyeshade and help the expansive Komansky run a tight ship.

Komansky took over as chief executive of Merrill Lynch in December 1996. For more than two years, the pairing of him and Allison seemed to work. But by 1999, Komansky and other members of Merrill's board of directors grew concerned about whether Allison would be the right man to step up to the top job when Komansky retired.

Allison, a Navy veteran who believed in the importance of a strong management structure, had succeeded at Merrill Lynch despite his unrelenting criticism of the firm's "affiliative" culture. Under Schreyer and Tully, a back-channel system flourished at Merrill. Through this system, mediocre people who enjoyed some personal tie to the top were able to build careers, despite the limits of their talent. Allison waged numerous battles against the nepotism of the system and the special treatment doled out to people who had friends on the thirty-second floor or in the boardroom. Tully, who saw real potential in Allison, used to ask the younger man why he was so stubborn about management issues. "Do you want to be right, or do you want to be president?" he'd say. Allison displayed no interest in playing the go-along, get-along game at Merrill, even when he did become president. By the middle of 1999, he had lost the support of Komansky above him and his top reports beneath him. Over the summer, Komansky informed Allison that he had to leave Merrill Lynch.

The sudden departure of Komansky's number two created a horse race for the job between two Merrill lifers—Jeffrey Peek and Tom Davis—and Stan O'Neal, who was chief financial officer. In 2000, each of the men was given a new position, with the clear understanding that whoever performed best would most likely become Komansky's successor. O'Neal was put in charge of Merrill's private client business, Peek was named head of asset management, and Tom Davis became head of investment banking.

The three candidates came not from Merrill's bread-and-butter business, but from its capital market operations. Instead of working quietly to build their candidacies, open warfare broke out for the top job.

O'Neal fought the battle of succession on two fronts. At the business level, he improved the performance numbers at Merrill's private client unit, cutting expenses and forcing smaller clients to deal with a call center rather than an actual financial advisor. But he wasn't content to let merit alone determine his success. He formed a small group within the firm, headed by CFO Tom Patrick and supported by Fakahany, to advance his candidacy for the top job in any way possible. Patrick had been with the company for more than two decades, since Merrill's acquisition of the investment bank White Weld in 1978. He and Jeff Peek had crossed swords in the past and Patrick was determined that the next chief CEO of Merrill Lynch be someone he favored, as opposed to a political competitor.

Paul Critchlow, Merrill Lynch's chief spokesman, came by O'Neal's office one day late in 1999 for a brief chat.

"What are you doing for me, Paul?" O'Neal asked the PR man.

"I'm not sure I understand," said Critchlow.

"What are you doing to help me become the next chief executive of Merrill Lynch?"

Critchlow said he wasn't taking sides in the horse race to succeed Komansky. He knew O'Neal would be a strong candidate, and he looked forward to supporting whoever eventually emerged as Komansky's successor.

O'Neal advised him to look at the situation from a different point of view, that professionally, Critchlow would be much better off supporting his candidacy.

"Life is a series of choices, Paul. It's time for you to make a choice," O'Neal said.

"I'll think about it," Critchlow said as he prepared to leave.

"Okay," replied O'Neal. "But don't think about it too long."

This was new territory for Critchlow. The Nebraska native and former political columnist for the *Philadelphia Inquirer* left journalism in 1978 to become campaign manager for Dick Thornburgh in his successful bid to become governor of Pennsylvania. Critchlow joined Merrill Lynch in 1985, where he worked for Bill Schreyer and Schreyer's successors, Tully and Komansky. Critchlow had always viewed his job as serving Merrill Lynch, as opposed to any one individual within Merrill Lynch. But that changed following his conversation with O'Neal. He did the math and realized he'd be better off siding with a winner than waiting to see how things played out. From that point on, Critchlow became part of the group headed by Tom Patrick that worked relentlessly to make sure O'Neal succeeded in his quest to become CEO.

In response to criticism from Peek's camp that a "cabal" of insiders was working to put O'Neal in the top job, the group started referring to itself as "the cabal." Schreyer himself became a vocal advocate for O'Neal and the group won allies on Merrill Lynch's board of directors, including Bob Luciano, the chief executive of Schering-Plough and a longtime friend of Schreyer's. Another board member, Jill Ker Conway, who had grown up on a farm in New South Wales, Australia, and risen to become president of Smith College, was completely taken with O'Neal and his inspiring story, how he had risen from humble roots in Alabama, attended Harvard Business School, and emerged as one of the top African-American executives on Wall Street.

Boosted by strong support from Merrill's board and from Schreyer, who relentlessly pushed his candidacy among the directors, O'Neal won the campaign to be president of Merrill Lynch and heir apparent to Komansky in July 2001. He immediately started acting on his own to bring the firm's costs in line with the shift to leaner times. After the terrorist attacks of September 11, which occurred adjacent to Merrill Lynch headquarters in lower Manhattan, Komansky was devastated. Three employees died in the attacks and O'Neal essentially took full control of the firm's day-to-day operations.

O'Neal fired some 22,000 people in the next year, cutting Merrill's workforce from 72,000 to 50,000. He also cleared out the executive suite of holdovers from the Tully era. Impressed with his decisiveness during a turbulent time and his relentless focus on costs, the board voted in 2002 to finalize the transfer of power, naming O'Neal chief executive.

The era of Mother Merrill, which O'Neal viewed as a "good old boy" system that protected underachievers and resisted change, was about to end. Like Herb Allison before him, O'Neal thought that the paternalistic culture spawned by his predecessors, who took care of their own—even if it meant carrying employees who were second-rate—was no way to run an investment bank in the twenty-first century. As an African-American who had to fight his way to one of the pinnacles of corporate America, O'Neal had little tolerance for the clubby atmosphere fostered by his predecessors.

O'Neal set out to eradicate the Mother Merrill culture. He moved aggressively to chop down deadwood in the organization and pare back its bloated cost structure. Most Merrill employees understood that the firm had overexpanded under Komansky, and would have to trim down in order to stay competitive. But O'Neal's slash-and-burn approach didn't win many friends. Instead of gently coaxing Merrill Lynch into the twenty-first century, O'Neal remorselessly hacked away at the existing structure. Thousands of employees were fired unceremoniously as O'Neal wiped out any internal rivals and assembled his own geographically and ethnically diverse team that was untainted by the Mother Merrill culture. His vision for Merrill Lynch was less focused on Charlie Merrill's initiative to bring Wall Street to Main Street. Instead, O'Neal wanted Merrill Lynch to be a lean and mean profit-oriented bank, along the lines of Goldman Sachs.

The "cabal" to install O'Neal as boss had succeeded. Tom Patrick and Arshad Zakaria, a brilliant young financial engineer, expected to reap the benefits of their efforts on the new CEO's behalf, but Zakaria overplayed his hand. In 2003, he pushed O'Neal to give him the title of president, but O'Neal refused, and fired him instead. Patrick tried to rescue his protégé, arguing at a board meeting that Zakaria had made a mistake, and urging the directors to prevail on O'Neal to reverse the decision.

Patrick misjudged his own importance. The board wanted nothing to do with the mini-drama and rallied behind O'Neal. Having ascended to the corner office in part through political maneuvering, there was no way O'Neal was going to allow himself to become a victim of similar intrigue. In the summer of 2003, he fired Patrick, the lone executive capable of standing up to him in meetings.

Over the next several years, the financial markets rebounded globally, helping Merrill Lynch increase its revenues. O'Neal reshaped his board of directors, ending the practice of having several Merrill insiders serve alongside the CEO. Instead, he replaced departing board members with a new group, including Cribiore; Finnegan; Charles Rossotti, the former IRS commissioner who had joined the Carlyle Group; and Ann Reese, who had worked with Cribiore at buyout firm Clayton, Dubilier in the 1990s.

O'Neal appointed Fakahany chief financial officer. Fakahany, an Egyptian-born executive who came to Merrill Lynch from Exxon, lacked the deep financial experience of Patrick, but he possessed the one key quality that O'Neal now valued above all others: absolute loyalty.

Zakaria's ouster paved the way for the promotion of the next layer of executives, Dow Kim and Greg Fleming, who became executive vice presidents of Merrill Lynch, and co-presidents of the firm's global capital markets and investment banking operations. Kim, who was Semerci's boss when the FICC chief built up the CDO positions, quit in the spring of 2007. After his departure, O'Neal named Fleming and Fakahany co-presidents of the firm.

NOW THAT HE WAS being pushed out the door, the shock from his sudden and precipitous fall from power overwhelmed O'Neal to the point where he failed to appreciate the irony of the situation. Starting in 1999, when he began competing for the top job in earnest, all the way through 2007, O'Neal had done whatever was necessary to advance his own career and defend himself from being outmaneuvered in the same way he had supplanted Komansky. Little did he suspect that the individual who would eventually supplant him wasn't an ambitious young Merrill Lynch executive like Fleming, but Cribiore, the pillar around which he'd built his own board of directors.

Up until this moment, O'Neal had never judged people on the basis of their character, only on what they could do for him. He had no use for Tully and his five principles, or the concept of Mother Merrill and loyalty. But after reaping the whirlwind he had sown by elevating Semerci and Cribiore to stratospheric levels in his organization, O'Neal learned that subprime mortgages were only part of his undoing.

ON SUNDAY, OCTOBER 28, Cribiore—who had secured himself a car and driver as part of his new role—arrived at Fleming's home in northern Westchester County.

O'Neal was leaving, he told Fleming. The details of his departure were still being worked out, but O'Neal was gone and he, Cribiore, would become non-executive chairman of Merrill Lynch. Cribiore wanted Fleming to take over day-to-day responsibility for running Merrill Lynch, while he, Cribiore, led the board's search for the next CEO.

"It won't be you," Cribiore told him point-blank.

"I understand," Fleming replied. He knew he was too young and had too little experience to be chosen to head up what would have to be the biggest turnaround in the history of Wall Street.

"We're going to bring someone in from the outside. Will that be a problem for you?"

"I'll stay if I can work with the guy," Fleming said.

He left Cribiore with one final thought on the search for O'Neal's successor. It was clear the board had no appetite for a merger, so the new CEO, whoever it was, would have to raise capital, quickly, to offset the losses that were metastasizing on the bank's balance sheet.

"You need to do this search fast and you need a big name," he told the Italian-born banker.

"I could not agree with you more," Cribiore said. Because of the thickness of his accent, Fleming couldn't tell if he was being earnest or patronizing.

CHAPTER 5

THE LISTING SHIP

"THERE'S A NEW NAME at Merrill Lynch today. It's Greg Fleming," blared the radio announcer at one of New York's all-news radio stations. It was 4:55 in the morning and the announcement startled the one listener who should have been least surprised—Greg Fleming—as he stood in the shower getting ready for his first day in the top job at Merrill Lynch.

Sitting in the backseat of his car, as his driver sped down an empty Westchester highway in the predawn darkness, ferrying him from his home toward Merrill Lynch headquarters in lower Manhattan, Fleming reflected on how appropriate it was that even in his departure, O'Neal had poisoned the one thing that he, Fleming, had worked for and aspired to during his fifteen-year career at the Wall Street bank.

Ever since he left the world of management consulting to join Merrill Lynch in 1992, Fleming's ambition to get the top job at the preeminent brokerage firm had been the driving force behind his career ascent.

Merrill Lynch had been dominated by its network of financial advisors, brokers who managed the assets of the wealthiest Americans in every big city and small town across the country. From the ranks of those brokers came the CEOs and other top executives.

By the 1990s, the power base from which CEOs and other top executives emerged was changing. Merrill Lynch had now established itself as a powerhouse investment bank and trading firm. Merrill's unrivaled ability to market and distribute all kinds of securities to individual investors and large institutional buyers gave it a strategic advantage over investment banks such as Goldman Sachs and Morgan Stanley, and protected it during the down cycles that periodically swept through Wall Street.

When Fleming joined Merrill's investment banking division in the 1990s, it was a business segment on the rise within the company. Most investment bankers have an MBA degree, which equips them to dissect the financial components of the deals they execute. Fleming, with his law degree, stuck out at first, but his excitable personality and strong relationship skills propelled him forward in his chosen profession.

After nearly a decade, Fleming emerged as the top "FIG" banker at Merrill—a reference to the "financial institutions group" within the investment banking division. In 2003, O'Neal tapped Fleming, then just forty, to be head of Merrill's investment banking division.

For the bright-eyed, optimistic young banker—who played up his modest roots as the son of two teachers from the hamlet of Hopewell Junction, New York—the promotion affirmed everything he believed about Merrill Lynch as an institution where the sky was the limit. That O'Neal had risen from the banking division to become CEO only reinforced Fleming's aspiration to the top job.

Over the next three years, Fleming rose to the challenge afforded him by O'Neal, driving growth in the investment banking business and improving Merrill Lynch's standing in the mergers-and-acquisition tables. But even while he thrived in his position, the truth behind his promotion gradually dawned on him: One by one, O'Neal had purged the company of any senior executive who could challenge him and replaced those executives with an entirely new crop of younger people, like Fleming, who didn't dare challenge the CEO's authority or judgment.

As long as he obeyed O'Neal, Fleming stayed in the CEO's good graces. But in February 2006, Fleming came to a fork in the road. He was in the middle of negotiating Merrill Lynch's investment in Black-Rock with Larry Fink, CEO of the asset management giant. Fleming and Fink had a strong relationship dating back to BlackRock's initial public offering in 1999, a transaction that Fleming managed.

O'Neal agreed with the strategy of swapping Merrill's undervalued asset management arm in exchange for the 49 percent stake in BlackRock, but he and Fink disagreed on how much stock should be exchanged as part of the transaction. The entire deal would be worth almost $10 billion, but the CEOs got hung up on whether Merrill Lynch would receive 68 million BlackRock shares for its asset management business, or 65 million shares, a difference worth several hundred million dollars. O'Neal, who could be stubborn when he didn't get his way, refused to budge.

Fleming and Eric Heaton, head of strategic planning at Merrill Lynch, held a conference call with O'Neal, trying to convince him to split the difference with Fink.

"You're handling it wrong," declared O'Neal through his speaker-phone, before abruptly hanging up.

Fleming followed up with an e-mail that evening, but received no response from O'Neal. The next morning, after a breakfast with Komansky, the former CEO who was on BlackRock's board, Fleming placed a call to O'Neal but the CEO's assistant, Marian Brooks, politely brushed him off, informing him that O'Neal couldn't speak to him.

"He has to see me!" Fleming pleaded, but Brooks said she couldn't help him.

Frustrated, Fleming called Heaton and told him to meet him on the thirty-second floor, where they would confront O'Neal face-to-face.

"Greg, you can't do that," said Heaton.

"Meet me up there. And if anyone asks you why you're up there, tell them I told you to come up."

Fleming arrived on the thirty-second floor, with Heaton, and barged into O'Neal's office. "You need to talk to me," he said petulantly.

O'Neal, who rarely lost his composure, even when cutting someone down to size, said, "All right. Sit down."

"Here's the way we could solve this," said Fleming, as he made his pitch. For all his issues about authority and subservience, O'Neal was a supremely rational executive. After hearing Fleming out, he agreed to proceed with the deal. In mid-February, the Merrill Lynch–BlackRock transaction was announced. It was hailed immediately by investors and the media as a winning combination and led to glowing articles in *The New York Times* and *The Wall Street Journal* that highlighted Fleming's role in the affair.

From that day forward, until O'Neal reached out to him to help on the Wachovia discussions some nineteen months later, Fleming's relationship with his boss was never the same. In April 2006, during one of their regular dinners at Nicola's, an Italian eatery on the Upper East Side of Manhattan, Fleming argued against the CEO's decision to move a small subgroup from his banking division to Dow Kim's trading division. O'Neal wouldn't listen and Fleming persisted until the CEO got fed up.

"I'm done with these meals," O'Neal told his subordinate. Fleming's job was not to question, but to listen and obey. "This is too painful for me. I'm not having any more dinners with you," the CEO said. A few months later, O'Neal ignored Fleming's warnings and pushed Dow Kim to install Semerci as head of FICC.

Now it was October 31, 2007—Halloween, appropriately enough—and Fleming finally had the job he had aspired to for the past fifteen years. Or rather, he had the *responsibilities* of the job—on a temporary basis—without the title, and under the worst conditions imaginable. O'Neal's implosion had left Merrill Lynch as a listing ship with a gaping hole in its side and no captain on the bridge in the worst storm that anyone on Wall Street had ever seen.

To make matters worse, O'Neal's exit package, consisting of $161 million in stock and options built up over the years, had become a scandal in the media. Outraged investors demanded to know how a man responsible for so much damage at Merrill Lynch could possibly walk away with such a windfall.

Fleming couldn't do anything about it. His job was to stand on that bridge until a new CEO was hired. And to keep the ship from sinking in the meantime.

JUST TWO DAYS INTO his temporary job, the listing ship hit another iceberg. As Fleming sat in the backseat of the car driving him to the office, he opened up that morning's edition of *The Wall Street Journal* and was stunned by the lead story, splattered across page one.

Merrill Lynch had been hiding losses from its subprime mortgage– related assets by engaging in tricky, *and possibly unlawful,* accounting transactions with hedge funds that year, the *Journal* reported. The article described one deal supposedly struck between Merrill Lynch and a hedge fund, by which the hedge fund would acquire commercial paper backed by mortgages that were eroding in value, with a guarantee that Merrill would repurchase the commercial paper a year later for a higher price. The article based its statement on the word of "a person close to the situa- tion." To Fleming, trained as a lawyer, it seemed like thin sourcing for an accusation of such magnitude.

Such a transaction would be a sham, not a true sale, designed to remove losses from Merrill's books in the near term. Alarmingly, the sup- posed transaction smelled just like the dubious deals that Merrill had helped Enron engineer a few years earlier. The Enron transactions, involv- ing a series of electricity barges moored off the cost of Nigeria, resulted in criminal charges against several Merrill executives. Confronted with evidence that Merrill Lynch had helped Enron park some of its assets for a few months in return for a $17 million fee, O'Neal cut off Dan Bayly, the Merrill banker implicated in the deal. The firm refused to give Bayly's attorney access to Enron-related documents that would have helped his defense. When Bayly was convicted and jailed for not providing "honest services" to his employer, longtime Merrill colleagues were outraged that O'Neal had abandoned one of them. Former CEO Dan Tully organized a defense fund to help Bayly pay for his lawyers. The conviction was eventually overturned, but not before Bayly had served time in prison and consumed his personal savings through lawyers' fees.

If the *Journal*'s allegations were true, the consequences would be horrific, possibly fatal to the firm. Top executives would almost certainly face civil fraud charges brought by the SEC, and criminal charges might also ensue. On top of the October announcement of Merrill's ballooning losses and Stan O'Neal's abrupt firing, the *Wall Street Journal* story now accused the firm of accounting trickery.

Even at 5:00 a.m. in the predawn darkness, Fleming knew that this would be the worst day in his professional career.

The story took him by complete surprise. No one in Merrill's PR department had given him any kind of warning. He sent off an e-mail to Rosemary Berkery, the firm's general counsel. She pinged him back immediately. They had to get on this first thing, she agreed.

Fleming felt as though he'd been physically slammed, punched in the gut. He couldn't tell which was worse: the publication of the story, splattered across page one of the influential business newspaper, or his own ignorance of whether the allegations being trumpeted by the *Journal* were even true.

He called Pete Kelly, the deal lawyer, waking him up. "Get in the shower and come to my office as fast as you can," he said.

Fleming called several other people he knew and trusted at the firm, with the same message: Report to my office as soon as you can get in. In addition to Kelly, he called Heaton, who was now Merrill's treasurer; Andrew Berry, another lawyer who worked on complicated deals and trades; Lisa Carnoy, who ran Merrill's equity capital markets business; and Carnoy's boss, Rohit D'Souza, who ran all equities trading operations.

Fleming also reached out to two senior investment bankers: Andrea Orcel, the top investment banker for Europe and the Middle East, who worked out of London; and Paul Wetzel, Merrill's top banker in Japan, who had been in New York since the board meeting two weeks earlier. He told them both to get ready for a long stretch in New York.

He also called two members of Merrill's PR team: Sara Furber of investor relations, who was already fielding calls from Merrill's biggest shareholders, and Michael O'Looney, who had done media relations for the New York Police Department during and after the September 11 attacks.

Most of the group, led by Kelly, made it to Fleming's office by 7:30, and Fleming outlined the problem posed by the *Wall Street Journal* story. The central allegation in the article was that Merrill had engaged in a sham transaction in the past few months that helped it hide billions of dollars in losses. Neither the editors at the *Journal,* nor the reporter who wrote the story, would tell Merrill's PR people who was involved in the transaction, only that the paper was sure it had taken place.

Fleming said Kelly and the rest of the team would have to dig up every individual transaction over the past few months that fit the *Journal*'s description, review every document associated with the deal, and find out if anything resembling the shady accounting reported in the *Journal* had actually taken place.

"You are going to nail this," Fleming told Kelly. "Unless they give us the name of the hedge fund, we can't say they're wrong until we've nailed it."

AFTER THE MEETING, FLEMING began to deal with the blowback generated by the article. Board members, top executives, and even Merrill's former CEOs were calling, trying to find out what was going on.

The heads of several business units urged Fleming to issue an immediate and unequivocal denial of the charges printed in the *Journal.* Of all the voices clamoring for attention that hectic morning, insisting that he issue a denial, one voice made sense to him. It was that of a board member, John Finnegan, CEO of Chubb Insurance. Finnegan cautioned Fleming against making any sweeping, categorical denials until he had all the facts.

Fleming got the message. "We can't deny it until we've confirmed that it's absolutely not true," he said to his top deputies when they pressed him for a strong reaction.

He told Sara Furber of investor relations that when investors called, she should inform them that Merrill Lynch is a highly ethical company that attempts to do the right thing for clients in thousands of situations, day in and day out.

In response to the story, Merrill Lynch issued a statement saying it was not aware of any transactions along the lines described by the *Journal,* designed to hide losses, taking place. "We have no reasons to believe that any such inappropriate transactions occurred," the firm said.

When the markets opened at 9:30 a.m., Merrill's stock price was at $54 per share, down $4 from where it was at the end of the previous day's trading. It began sinking further. Thousands of employees, many of whom had their retirement savings tied up in Merrill stock, grew worried. Members of Merrill's thundering herd of financial advisors across the country had to fend off questions from their clients about whether Merrill Lynch knew how to manage its own money.

Some of the advisors called in, demanding to know what the hell was going on, and some of Merrill's biggest clients, world-class corporations that had been with the firm for years, also wanted answers.

Then there were Merrill's former CEOs—Bill Schreyer, Dan Tully, and Dave Komansky—men who were respected throughout the firm. At his office on the thirty-second floor, Fleming's secretary told him that Schreyer was on line one and Tully was holding on line two. She couldn't take a message from each and tell them, "Greg's busy, but he'll call you back shortly." Fleming picked up, one after the other.

"What the fuck is going on!?" shrieked Komansky.

"Greg, you've got to get a grip on this," Schreyer urged. "Do you understand the degree of screwup that this is?"

Fleming said he already had a team on it.

The turmoil that one newspaper story had churned up at Merrill made it feel to Fleming as though the building itself was shaking. Merrill's share price continued to move down throughout the morning and into the afternoon. The decline was agonizing and, it seemed, inexorable.

A falling share price at an investment bank isn't just a measure of personal wealth for employees and a metric to use when senior executives wanted to figure out when they could retire. When a bank hits hard times, there are no factories to sell or hard inventory that can be used as collateral toward a loan. The assets of an investment bank are its loans, its funding commitments, and the securities it holds. The share price represents the excess reservoir of capital that a bank can draw on as a cushion against losses. At the worst possible time in Merrill Lynch's history, when it was holding more than $30 billion of toxic assets on its balance sheet—enough to wipe the firm out—a plummeting stock price was shrinking the firm's capital base. It was yet another hole in the ship's hull.

Fleming knew he had to do something to reassure Merrill's 60,000 employees. He called a "town hall" meeting for 4:00 p.m., after the trading day closed. It would be held in the bank's conference room on the third floor, but would be telecast to every Merrill office around the world.

Several executives cautioned against a live appearance, warning Fleming that such a move would be risky, and that he'd be better off recording a statement and making it available internally to all employees, the better to avoid a live question-and-answer session that could devolve into an unscripted, rage-infused free-for-all.

Just two weeks earlier, in response to the original shock of a multibillion-dollar write-down of assets, O'Neal had recorded a question-and-answer session with O'Looney, who had been a TV news reporter earlier in his career. The goal had been to subject O'Neal to what appeared to be rigorous questioning about Merrill's problems, but the fact that it was the company's own spokesman doing the questioning blunted the effectiveness of the message.

Given the uncertainty surrounding Merrill's losses, and its lack of leadership at the top, Fleming insisted on a live "town hall" format. "I'm doing it," he said. "These employees deserve to have somebody say, we're on top of it, go back to work, and we're a great company."

At 4:00 p.m., the markets closed for the week, with Merrill's share price at $52 per share, more than 10 percent lower than where it had been the day before, and 31 percent below where it had been a month earlier, when it was trading at $76 a share.

With his stomach churning, Fleming went to the front of the large, low-ceilinged room, which resembled a church basement, and looked out at several hundred employees, all jammed into seats and standing against the rear wall. In the front row sat members of the top management team—Jeff Edwards, Bob McCann, who ran the thundering herd end of the business, and Cribiore.

Fleming wanted to tell everyone that he had nothing to do with the CDOs that had wiped out the firm's earnings the previous month. He would have loved to tell everyone that the buildup of toxic assets on Merrill's balance sheet was orchestrated by Semerci, the former head of sales and trading. He wanted to deny categorically the allegations printed in *The Wall Street Journal* that day.

But he couldn't do any of that. He was the interim leader of the firm and he now represented the management of the entire company. Until a new CEO was named, he was the leader. Fleming had grown angry with O'Neal over the past few months, as the magnitude of Merrill's problems began to manifest itself. He was even angrier now at the disaster O'Neal had bequeathed to him.

"I wanted to speak to you directly today because this is clearly a challenging time for our firm," Fleming began. "And I didn't want to talk to you on Monday and I did not want to talk to you late next week, I wanted to talk to you today before everybody went home."

And with that introduction, Fleming reminded the employees that the company's underlying business remained sound. He said the story in the morning's paper was "nonspecific" and "relied on unidentified sources." He pointed to Cribiore and assured everyone that the search for a new CEO was proceeding "with speed and careful deliberation."

"This is not the first time that our firm has faced challenges," Fleming continued. "The crash of 1987, the credit crisis of 1998, the bursting of the technology bubble in 2000, and the terror attacks of 9/11. In many ways we can better navigate this challenge because it does not call for an overhaul of our strategy or a resizing of our business.

"We have accomplished a great deal in the past five years. Following the bursting of the tech bubble and 9/11, we pulled together as a firm and embarked on a new strategy to create a truly global, diversified financial services company. We did that. You did that. . . . We have a great firm with a well deserved, proud tradition. All of you, and the people who came before you, and there's many of them in a company almost a hundred years old, have built Merrill Lynch into one of the finest companies in the world. Together—together—we will continue that tradition."

Then Fleming welcomed employees' questions, which flooded in through the phone lines as well as on the floor.

"Bill" from New York: "Now that you are in charge of risk, can you assure us that there is a new approach to managing risk? Is there a new management team in place, and can we be comfortable that this debacle and gambling attitude will not take place in the future?"

Fleming assured the questioner that Merrill Lynch was already beefing up its risk-management capabilities under Ed Moriarty III.

An employee approached the microphone in the large conference room: "Are the recent events an indication of another problem like maybe a dysfunctional board and should we consider the separation of the chairmanship and the CEO roles?"

Fleming artfully avoided a direct answer, saying that the board was doing everything in its power to pick the next leader.

"Tom," a financial advisor from Fort Lee, New Jersey, called in: "Yeah, Greg, I have a couple of statements before my questions. First, with regard to your comment about the various events that the firm has survived in the past years, the crash of '87, Long Term Capital of '98, the terrorist attack, the tech bubble, and so on and so forth, the difference between those and this one is that this event was organically grown and obviously that gives me a great sense of concern. Either people at the top hid what was going on or didn't know what was going on, neither of which is very comforting. So there are two questions that I have on the piggyback of those statements.

"One is, besides O'Neal, who is ultimately responsible for allowing such a heavy bet to be taken by the institutional side of the firm? And if it means going right up to the board members and those responsible individuals, everybody should be let go who could be tied to allowing this event to happen. That's number one.

"Number two, there is a report of this additional possible $10 billion that we may have to write down. And, you know, being that back in July we were told that the firm had its arms around the risk-management side of the firm and two months later we're faced with unbelievable write-downs and two weeks later additional write-downs after that, there's a lack of confidence I guess that follows here with regard, you know, to responses from *you*. So at a minimum, if *you* could comment with regard to those two items, I'd appreciate it."

Finally, someone asked the question Fleming knew was coming, but dreaded hearing. Fleming was just another one of O'Neal's stooges, wasn't he? The golden boy from investment banking who had buckled under and accepted Semerci's promotion, and then received a $13 million cash bonus from O'Neal. Why should anyone believe a word he said? Fleming knew he should have stood up to O'Neal after Semerci was promoted. He should have threatened to quit. But he didn't have the wisdom or the guts and he would never forgive himself for that.

"Tom" was angry that someone in fixed income had been allowed by top management to put the entire organization in jeopardy. There was rage throughout the wealth management side of the business over that.

"Okay, Tom," Fleming began. "I can't tell you, given what I've done with my career, how painful it is to hear you talk about a lack of confidence. But such is where we are, at least in your eyes. I would say a couple of things here. Stan O'Neal is not the only executive to have lost his job as a result of this. Other people who were responsible for this business and these activities are also no longer with the firm.

"The other thing that I would say, Tom, is that mistakes were clearly made here. And I mentioned this in Chicago yesterday. I talk about Jim Collins, [who] has written several books on very effective management. And one of the ones that I have read that I think is particularly good talks about 'the bus' and getting the wrong people *off* the bus and making sure the right people are *on* the bus.

"Well, the reality is, in these businesses, we had some of the wrong people on the bus and they made some very bad decisions. And as a result of that, we're all here.

"It isn't entirely, Tom, organically grown. We had too much exposure to the subprime mortgage market. Nobody would argue that otherwise now. But this has come to the fore because of a very challenging and volatile credit market, without which a lot of the things that have come out here may not have otherwise come out. And that's what I want to say on that."

Bob McCann, who ran the wealth management business, got up, took the microphone and said he and Fleming realized that a lot of members of the thundering herd were angry about recent events.

"I understand it," McCann said. "We're both trying to respond to it. All of us in executive management are in a constructive way. I want to draw the line at one thing though, when people talk about the 'other side of the firm.'

"We are *one* company. And that's who and what we are. Our business model has been proven over many years, having a world-class wealth management organization, a world class global markets and investment banking profile, and our great profile right now in investment management. That is the strength of Merrill Lynch. It's easy on a day like today and at the end of a long week, at the end of a long month, to feel that emotion. We're going to continue to respond to you in the ways that we know how and the ways that we think are thoughtful."

Then McCann offered some insights on how the news media worked.

"I would like to tell you that today is going to be the last negative story that you read about Merrill Lynch or it's going to be the last story that you read that's fueled by innuendo, by speculation and rumor," he said. "That isn't how the world works though.

"Unfortunately there are likely to be many of these or several of these in the next [few] weeks. I think it's very important, as hard as it is, and I can only imagine how hard it was today, if you're a financial advisor or an institutional salesperson, to defend our company. But we find [out] the most about ourselves in times like this when we stand tall and stand together. It isn't 'the other side of the firm,' it's our firm. It's very important that we all work hard to separate what is fact from what is fiction from what is innuendo and what is rumor."

"Thanks, Bob. Very well said," Fleming responded.

The questions kept coming, and Fleming kept answering. The five thousand phone lines set up for outside callers were completely jammed, setting off dark speculation that management wanted to sandbag things so aggrieved employees couldn't call in.

By 5:30, the town hall meeting had ended. It was a gut-wrenching experience. Fleming reconnected with Pete Kelly for an update on the search for the crooked transaction reported in the *Journal*. On the drive back to Westchester, slumped in the back of his car, he watched the e-mails pour in, some 2,300 from all over the world, and tried to field or return as many phone calls as possible. Finally he arrived at his home, having survived the horrible day.

THE NEXT MORNING, SATURDAY, Fleming checked in with Kelly to find out what was going on with the hedge fund transaction task force. There would be no days off for that effort: They needed to get to the bottom of the issue as soon as possible. Fleming continued returning Friday's calls and answering e-mails well into Sunday, when Orcel arrived in New York.

He told Orcel and Wetzel to buy lots of shirts and underwear, because they were going to be camped out in New York for some time. Fleming described the firm's capital position, which had been dented by the losses reported in October. Obviously, Merrill Lynch would need to raise new capital, and the men brainstormed to come up with potential investors.

Wetzel knew that Temasek, the sovereign wealth fund of Singapore, was always looking for big investment opportunities in U.S. finance. He also knew that Mizuho, a Japanese bank, would be a good candidate to invest in Merrill Lynch. Orcel thought some of the sovereign wealth funds of the Middle East would be interested, along with some major European banks.

The men began seeding the ground with the potential investors, letting them know that the arrival of the next chief executive at Merrill Lynch would create a terrific opportunity for a select group of large players to buy in to the firm at a relatively low price. Other Merrill Lynch executives put out similar feelers to global fund managers, planting the idea that they might like to buy in to a major U.S. investment bank at a time when its stock was trading well below its normal levels.

This capital-raising SWAT team also began reviewing other ideas for generating capital. The most obvious one was to sell the firm's 20 percent stake in Bloomberg, the firm started by Michael Bloomberg, the mayor of New York City. Since the company was privately held, it was impossible to determine how much Merrill's 20 percent stake was worth, but industry experts believed Bloomberg L.P., the financial information company, to be worth anywhere from $25 billion to $35 billion, meaning that Merrill's stake was worth somewhere between $5 billion and $7 billion.

A pair of Merrill Lynch veterans, Victor Nesi and Todd Kaplan, made contact with Marty Geller, an accountant who served as an outside CFO of Bloomberg L.P., to review some of the contractual obligations regarding any divestiture by Merrill.

IN ORDER TO GET a better understanding of the complicated hedge fund trades that led to the *Wall Street Journal* story, Pete Kelly contacted Jeff Kronthal, the fixed-income trader who had been fired a year earlier to make room for Semerci in the FICC department. Fleming wanted Kronthal around to provide advice on the CDOs and what they were doing to Merrill's balance sheet. He offered him a six-month consulting gig designed to help the firm unwind its positions.

Fleming kept after his hedge fund task force, meeting with them every weekday at 7:00 a.m. and again at 5:00 p.m. In the week after the *Wall Street Journal* story, Kelly reported that the group had made some progress, breaking down scores of deals that involved CDOs, but finding no instance where Merrill had promised to buy something back, at a higher price, in a subsequent quarter.

Fleming also kept in close touch with Finnegan, the board member who had counseled him against saying anything rash in response to the *Wall Street Journal* story. As head of a large financial services firm, Finnegan was familiar with the issues and challenges Fleming was facing, and the older man's advice turned out to be helpful during this raucous period of uncertainty.

By November 9, a week after the story ran, and after seven full days of digging through every CDO transaction with hedge funds, Kelly reported to Fleming what they both wanted to hear: It didn't happen. Of the hundreds of deals that the firm had struck with hedge funds since the summer, there was not one transaction where Merrill Lynch would be on the hook to buy back a package of CDOs at a guaranteed profit for the hedge fund. They could now go back to *The Wall Street Journal* and demand a retraction, and if the *Journal* refused, they felt they had a strong case in court. But in all likelihood, things would never escalate to that level.

TO FLEMING'S ANNOYANCE, Alberto Cribiore—the non-executive chairman of Merrill Lynch—was spending a lot of time roaming about the company's offices at Four World Financial Center. Fleming pestered him repeatedly about the CEO search, asking how things were going and whether the board would be able to hire someone quickly. Cribiore dismissed Fleming's entreaties airily, saying everything was under control, but Fleming began to think Cribiore was enjoying his perch at the top of Merrill Lynch a little too much. Maybe it was just paranoia, but Fleming feared that Cribiore might recruit some junior varsity player for the CEO job at Merrill, so that he himself could retain the chairman's title and all the trappings that went with it.

Those fears turned out to be misplaced. Cribiore was leading a two-track effort to identify the next chief executive officer of Merrill Lynch. He had engaged the firm Spencer Stuart, one of the top executive recruiting firms in the country, and the services of Tom Neff himself, the top banking recruiter at the firm.

Neff and his team at Spencer Stuart quickly put together a roster of some ten executives in the financial services industry whose credentials could be presented to Merrill's board of directors. The list was headed by BlackRock's Larry Fink. As a formality, Neff's team also included Fleming and Bob McCann, head of Merrill's private client business, on the list.

At the same time, Cribiore started down a parallel track, without the aid of an executive recruiter, in pursuit of a superstar candidate who would instantly restore credibility to Merrill's sagging franchise. He was convinced that John Thain, a former top executive at Goldman Sachs who had engineered a brilliant turnaround at the New York Stock Exchange, would be perfect for the job.

For years, Cribiore had been fascinated by Goldman Sachs, its astounding ability to earn outsized profits each year, and the equally astounding bonuses it paid out to its top people. When O'Neal used to drop by his office at Brera for a cup of coffee, the men would often plot about ways in which they could transform Merrill Lynch's business model into something with a closer resemblance to Goldman Sachs.

Cribiore reached out to John Weinberg, a vice chairman at Goldman Sachs and a friend of Thain's, and asked him to place a call to the NYSE chief on behalf of Merrill's board. Thain was receptive to the overture.

So convinced was Cribiore that Thain was the right candidate that even before Stan O'Neal was officially out, the Italian financier informed him he was making an overture to Thain. Then Cribiore visited the New York Stock Exchange chief at his office in the famous palace of capitalism at the corner of Broad Street and Wall Street in lower Manhattan.

This was the moment John Thain had been waiting for. He had enjoyed a stratospheric rise at Goldman Sachs, the legendary investment bank, becoming co-president in his early forties. But after several years of waiting for his turn to get to the top job, he jumped to the NYSE at the end of 2003, at a time when the Big Board was mired in a scandal over former CEO Dick Grasso's $187 million pay package and needed a white knight to restore its reputation.

Among the many things he had learned from his experience at Goldman Sachs, Thain knew enough to play his cards close to the vest, and not to exhibit any undue enthusiasm over the opportunity being dangled before him. He told Cribiore he was quite happy in his current position.

"Really?" Cribiore asked in his deep baritone. "Are you going to be wedded to the New York Stock Exchange forever?" The Big Board is a prominent institution, a global brand that symbolizes capitalism, but as a business, it was a smallish enterprise. Thain missed the world of large, powerful Wall Street banks.

"I am very happy here," Thain insisted. "At the same time, I have succeeded at what I came here to do." In less than four years, Thain had modernized the NYSE's trading systems for the electronic age and globalized the company through mergers and acquisitions.

"Exactly," said Cribiore. The Merrill Lynch chairman said he would like to visit Thain himself the following weekend to discuss the matter in more detail. Thain agreed.

The next Sunday, November 4, Cribiore drove out to the affluent suburb of Rye, about twenty-five miles from Manhattan. He picked up his fellow board member, Ann Reese, who also lived in Rye, before turning into Thain's residence.

Even by the standards of Rye, filled with with million-dollar homes, Thain's abode stood out: a baronial estate featuring a mansion perched at the highest point of a ten-acre property, walled off from public view by an imposing stone fence. As Cribiore and Reese drove up to the gated entry, the mansion loomed before them. It was like the estate of an English country gentleman or a European nobleman, not a big house in the New York suburbs.

Thain greeted the two Merrill Lynch directors and showed them inside. Before being recruited onto Merrill's board of directors by Stan O'Neal, Cribiore and Reese had both worked at Clayton, Dubilier & Rice, the private equity firm. They themselves moved in affluent circles and yet both were impressed by the elegance and taste of Thain's residence.

Cribiore laid out the facts concerning Merrill Lynch, describing its strengths as an investment bank, a stock brokerage firm, and most of all, as a wealth manager to private clients. Merrill's network of financial advisors, totaling 16,000, was the envy of the industry. The $1.5 trillion in assets under management—and the revenues those assets generated— gave Merrill Lynch a buoyancy during the downturn that other banks did not enjoy.

Cribiore and Reese showed Thain the internal presentation that had been made to the board a few weeks earlier, laying out the disaster that had befallen the firm in mortgage-related securities and other debt-related products. Cribiore, like O'Neal before him, was both enamored and fascinated by Goldman Sachs's success. Cribiore knew that in 1994, when Goldman hit a bad patch in the markets, John Thain, the thirty-eight-year-old chief financial officer, had helped reorganize the investment bank's risk-management operations and turned them into the envy of the industry.

As Thain offered his views on what could be done to improve Merrill Lynch, the directors sized him up. It was clear that he "got it," and understood the murky and destabilizing effects of mortgage-trades gone bad. His off-the-cuff observations about Merrill also seemed on the mark.

There was something else, too, not quantifiable on a résumé or through Thain's responses to their questions. He *looked* like he was the right guy for the job. Just over six feet tall, square-jawed and with his erect, athletic bearing, this was someone who could lead men and women into battle. This was a general among soldiers.

Thain wore glasses, which seemed to magnify the bright hazel hue of his eyes. They also added to the Clark Kent–Superman aura that had attached to Thain during his successful turnaround of the New York Stock Exchange. A competitive wrestler at MIT, Thain earned a degree in electrical engineering from the school and was one of the few applicants accepted directly into Harvard Business School. With this gold-plated academic background, he was hired by Goldman Sachs.

The firing of Stan O'Neal resulted not just from Merrill Lynch's sudden losses, but from O'Neal's panicked reaction to those losses. Instead of fixing the problem and raising fresh capital, he wanted to sell Merrill Lynch to a larger bank. Cribiore put the question directly to Thain: Did he think it was possible to turn Merrill Lynch around, or would it be necessary to find a buyer?

It could absolutely be turned around, Thain said. First of all, assets that lost their value during market downdrafts rarely went to zero. Instead, they rebounded once the market began to bounce back. As long as there were no other fundamental problems on Merrill's balance sheet—and Thain insisted on looking at Merrill's mortgage book—the problem was fixable.

Cribiore agreed completely and came away from the meeting

convinced that Thain was the right man for the job. His background, his strengths, and most of all his confidence in being able to fix Merrill Lynch were exactly what the chairman was looking for.

As Cribiore and Reese departed from Thain's estate, it was clear that they had been in the presence of someone who had succeeded brilliantly at everything he'd done. Thain wasn't desperate for the job—and the opulence of his lifestyle indicated that he didn't need the money—but he seemed intellectually stimulated by the challenge it posed. Cribiore had to make this happen.

THE MERRILL LYNCH CHAIRMAN soon realized that signing his dream candidate for the top job could prove difficult. Like Merrill Lynch, Citigroup had also committed far too much of its balance sheet to assets backed by subprime mortgages, announcing $11 billion in losses in early November.

Citi's CEO, Charles "Chuck" Prince, had been general counsel of the bank before Sandy Weill, his predecessor, tapped him for the top job in 2003. At the time Weill picked Prince as his successor, state and federal regulators were investigating Citi for a wide variety of shoddy practices. Putting a lawyer in the top job made sense.

Once the regulatory issues went away, Prince faced the daunting challenge of running the most complex global banking franchise in the country—a sprawling institution that combined standard depository banking with capital markets businesses, an investment banking franchise, and a network of wealth management advisors through its Smith Barney unit. Citi's cost structure was bloated and nearly unmanageable, but when Prince learned of the money that could be made through mortgage securitization—and Citigroup could originate many of the mortgages itself—he allowed the bank's fixed-income unit to ramp up production of CDOs and similar products.

Following Citi's admission of losses, Prince's tenure seemed close to the end. Sure enough, over the same weekend that Cribiore and Reese visited Thain, Citi fired Chuck Prince and launched its own search for a CEO.

Cribiore suspected that Citi would likely be interested in Thain as well, so he accelerated the interview process, arranging one-on-one interviews for the candidate with most of Merrill's directors, starting with Finnegan and Codina.

Tom Neff, the Spencer Stuart headhunter leading the official search process, interviewed Fleming and another inside candidate from Merrill, Bob McCann, the forty-nine-year-old head of Merrill's thundering herd of financial advisors. Fleming knew he would not get the job, and that the board was merely showing him a courtesy, so he spent most of his time during the interview with Neff pushing for his favored candidate, BlackRock's Larry Fink, whom Fleming considered to be a friend.

When Fink interviewed with Neff, the BlackRock CEO asked about other candidates for the job. Neff told him that based on everybody he had interviewed, Fink was clearly the lead candidate at that point. Fink started making plans, advising his board of directors that he was on the short list of candidates for the CEO position at Merrill Lynch. He also discussed the future management structure at Merrill Lynch with Fleming, saying he wanted him to remain as president, and join Merrill's board of directors. Fleming was excited by the prospect of working with Fink, being given a seat at the board level, and becoming the odds-on favorite to be CEO in five or ten years, after Fink had turned Merrill around.

AS EXPECTED, CITIGROUP'S BOARD of directors did contact Thain about the top job. If there was one thing that everyone learned early on at Goldman Sachs, it was that the price of an asset always went up when there were rival bidders. In this case, Thain himself was the asset and the fact that Citi was interested in him increased his bargaining power with Merrill Lynch.

Thain made it clear to Cribiore that Citi was in the hunt, so the Merrill Lynch chairman accelerated the interview process. He left nothing to chance and sat in on Thain's "one-on-one" interview with Aulana Peters. Joe Prueher, a retired Navy admiral, met with Thain at the offices of Brera, Cribiore's fund. Carol Christ, president of Smith College, interviewed Thain by phone. As a former SEC commissioner, Peters was taken aback by Cribiore's presence during her interview with Thain, which suggested that the chairman didn't trust her.

Once he had secured the tentative approval of the entire board, Cribiore wanted to make Thain an offer. He and John Finnegan, the head of Merrill's compensation committee, met Thain for dinner in Manhattan where they discussed what kind of financial package might make the job attractive enough to accept.

Thain talked about the size of the bonus he would be giving up if he left the NYSE and the size of his stock holdings, which hadn't vested there, and the need to be made whole. The group eventually reached a general agreement involving a onetime signing bonus of $15 million, $33 million in stock, and options for another $34 million worth of shares, depending on whether Merrill's share price increased or decreased over the next several years. The stock and options awards were spread out over three years. Thain expressed no interest in having a change in control clause, which removed a potential sticking point with the board.

On Saturday, November 10, Greg Fleming and his wife, Melissa, were invited to dinner at the home of Chip Montgomery in Rye. Montgomery's wife, DeeDee, had been friends with Melissa since their days at Colgate (where Melissa had also met Greg). There was a third couple, neighbors in Rye, whom the Montgomerys wanted the Flemings to meet: John and Carmen Thain.

Fleming had no idea that Thain was already deep into negotiations with Merrill's board of directors, but the men hit it off reasonably well. Thain sat next to Melissa Fleming and was pleasant and talkative throughout the evening. As the group broke up that night, Thain and Fleming exchanged good-byes.

"I think we'll be seeing more of each other," Thain said.

OVER THE NEXT FEW days, Cribiore's presence at Merrill's offices became even more grating to Fleming. No matter what time of day, it seemed, or with whom he was on the phone, Cribiore would barge into Fleming's office to interrupt him about the smallest matter. In response,

Fleming would push back by asking Cribiore about the CEO search, hectoring the chairman about doing something quickly.

Those exchanges, tiresome to both men, ground to a halt on Wednesday, November 14, at 1:00 p.m., when Cribiore marched into Fleming's office to announce that the next chief executive of Merrill Lynch would be John Thain.

Fleming was surprised, but heartened by the speed with which Cribiore had gotten the job done. Then he thought of Larry Fink, who was under the impression that he was the lead candidate for the job. "Have you told Larry?"

Cribiore said no, he hadn't informed him yet. Fink's name had been surfacing on CNBC, the business cable channel, as the favorite for the job, much to Cribiore's annoyance. Larry Fink would find out at 3:59 p.m., Cribiore said, just before the board announced Thain's appointment to the world.

"That's a big mistake," Fleming warned him. He had seen Stan O'Neal blow himself up with his board a month earlier by not cluing them in to his decision to enter into discussions with Wachovia. And now here was Cribiore, about to antagonize Fink, one of the most important executives in the Merrill Lynch firmament. Merrill's investment in the firm had grown in value from $10 billion to $13 billion in just a year and a half.

Fleming insisted that Cribiore call Fink and let him know personally, before the announcement was made. Cribiore brushed off the suggestion. Thain had accepted the job and the last thing he was going to worry about was Fink's bruised ego. Fed up with Cribiore's meddling presence at Merrill's offices, Fleming angrily told the chairman that he would make the call himself.

Fink had already gotten wind of the news before Fleming phoned him. As expected, the BlackRock CEO was irate. Someone working on Fink's behalf leaked word to CNBC that Fink had turned down the offer of becoming the next CEO of Merrill Lynch because the bank's board wouldn't allow him to examine its balance sheet. It gave Fink some cover for the public embarrassment of having been passed over for John Thain, especially after he'd informed his own board that the job was virtually his.

Cribiore called up Fink to demand an explanation for the CNBC story, but instead got an earful from the BlackRock chief, who abruptly terminated the conversation with the cosmopolitan sixty-two-year-old Italian banker.

"Go fuck yourself!" said Fink, hanging up.

CRIBIORE REFUSED TO LET Fink's outburst sour his coup: the announcement that afternoon that John Thain would become the twelfth chief executive of Merrill Lynch. The news provided a great source of comfort at Merrill's headquarters, since Thain enjoyed a terrific reputation, and the fact that he had accepted the job indicated his own belief in the viability of the firm.

Thain visited Merrill's headquarters that afternoon, just a few blocks away from his job at the stock exchange. He was greeted warmly by the board and senior executives, including Fleming. Thain appeared before an impromptu meeting of Merrill Lynch's management committee, about thirty people, and took questions from anyone who wanted to know where he stood on various issues.

One of the first questions involved Merrill's top executives and whether Thain was planning to bring in a new team of managers.

"Let me say something about that," said Thain. "I have a good friend in Rye, where I live, and he's been telling me for a while that there's this 'great guy' I have to meet, and last weekend, my friend hosted a dinner party and I finally got to meet the guy he was talking about—Greg Fleming. And my friend turned out to be right. Greg Fleming really is a great guy and I can tell you honestly that I'm looking forward to working with Greg and everyone here at Merrill Lynch."

Dan Sontag, who was Bob McCann's deputy in the financial advisory business, told Thain that one of Merrill's top FAs, as the advisors are known within the company, was hosting a cocktail party upstairs, on the thirty-third floor. Sontag asked Thain if he cared to drop by and introduce himself.

Thain had done his homework, and knew that in addition to the problems on Merrill's balance sheet, Stan O'Neal had caused morale problems in the ranks of Merrill's financial advisors by ignoring them. O'Neal viewed Merrill's private client business as a mundane and relatively low-growth business, a hindrance more than a help in his attempt to transform Merrill Lynch into a high-octane investment bank.

"This is a client-oriented business," said Thain. "I'd be happy to meet some of Merrill's clients." Cribiore was beaming as Fleming escorted Thain upstairs.

Thain's arrival at the cocktail party on the thirty-third floor sent a charge of electricity through the gathering of well-heeled Merrill Lynch customers, who got to meet *the* John Thain, savior of the New York Stock Exchange, face-to-face. Word quickly passed through the sales force that Thain "got it."

It didn't matter to Merrill's thundering herd of 16,000 brokers that Thain would also be the first outsider hired to take over the reins at the firm. Starting with Charlie Merrill himself, almost every chief executive of the firm had worked his way up from a starting position as a financial advisor, helping affluent Americans make prudent investment decisions. Even O'Neal had run the private client business for an eighteen-month spell.

From a public relations point of view, Thain's hiring was a big success. The news was broadcast across the country that evening and was a top story in every major newspaper the following day. Unlike other Wall Street firms, Merrill Lynch was a well-known brand name across the U.S. For most Americans outside New York, Merrill Lynch was synonymous with Wall Street, and the news in recent weeks that Merrill Lynch was bleeding money because of bad investments affected the public perception of the marketplace in general.

The announcement that Merrill Lynch—the firm that advertised itself as "bullish on America"—had hired a Wall Street superstar to be its next CEO was reason enough for most investors to be bullish once again on Merrill Lynch.

The fact that the once proud company was in such dire straits that it had to hire a former competitor to right the ship was lamentable but unavoidable.

Dan Tully, who served as Merrill's chief executive in the 1990s, told one newspaper, "Charlie Merrill would turn over in his grave if he knew we hired someone from Goldman Sachs." But he added: "Let's give him a chance."

IN THE WEEK BETWEEN the announcement of Thain's impending arrival at Merrill and Thanksgiving, the future CEO asked Fleming if he would be staying. Fleming said he'd be happy to, as long as Thain wanted him around. "I do," said Thain.

Before handing the reins over to John Thain, there was one final piece of housekeeping that Fleming needed to attend to: the *Wall Street Journal* article. On Monday, November 26, after the long Thanksgiving weekend, the *Journal* printed a retraction:

"On Nov. 2, the *Journal* published a page-one article on Merrill Lynch & Co. that was based on incorrect information that the firm had engaged in off-balance-sheet deals with hedge funds in a possible bid to delay the recognition of losses connected to the firm's mortgage-securities exposure. In fact, Merrill proposed a deal with a hedge fund involving $1 billion in commercial paper issued by a Merrill-related entity containing mortgage securities. In exchange, the hedge fund would have had the right to sell the mortgage securities back to Merrill after one year for a guaranteed minimum return.

"However, Merrill didn't complete the deal after the firm's finance department determined it didn't meet proper accounting criteria. In addition, Merrill says it has accounted properly for all its transactions with hedge funds."

Fleming didn't like the fact that the retraction was buried at the bottom of page two, while the original 1,300-word article had been splashed across page one, but he was jubilant over the outcome nonetheless.

That day he sent out a triumphant e-mail to all 60,000 employees, blowing up the retraction in large letters for all to see, and reiterating his message from the town hall meeting earlier in the month: Merrill Lynch was an upstanding, ethical business and everyone should be proud to work there.

There was another reason to be proud as well. Fleming wrote that the arrival of John Thain as CEO on December 3 was an additional reason for people to look forward, not back. Fleming assured employees that Thain had high regard for Merrill's people and its culture. "He is a seasoned and decisive leader with deep knowledge of our industry who has tremendous respect and admiration for our franchise," Fleming wrote.

CHAPTER 6

THE ADVENTURES
OF SUPER-THAIN

ON THE MORNING OF Saturday, December 1, 2007, just two days before he was to show up at the offices of Merrill Lynch for his first day on the job, John Thain stopped at a liquor store in Rye to pick up some wine for an evening event, when he was accosted by a stranger.

"You're John Thain, aren't you?"

"Yes," Thain responded, flattered and nonplussed at the same time.

"That's great! I just started at Merrill, too," the man said, adding how happy he was that Thain was coming on board.

The new CEO thanked him. It seemed like an auspicious start to a new era.

JOHN ALEXANDER THAIN'S EMERGENCE as a rock star on Wall Street was a most unlikely event.

The son of a family doctor in Antioch, Illinois—a local practitioner who charged $15 for a house call—Thain inherited the same smarts as his brothers, both of whom grew up to be physicians. A popular student in high school, Thain's favorite sports were activities that he pursued alone: He was a star on his high school wrestling team, and also joined the ski patrol at a local mountain. Thain also applied himself to his studies, and was named class valedictorian. His classmates weren't surprised when he was accepted by Stanford and the Massachusetts Institute of Technology. Thain opted for MIT and arrived in Cambridge, Massachusetts, in September 1973. For a high school kid from small town Illinois, the sudden move to Boston was a heady change of pace.

Thain immersed himself in all aspects of student life at MIT, majoring in electrical engineering, joining the Delta Upsilon fraternity, and continuing to wrestle. The Delta Upsilon house was located off campus, across the Charles River, in Boston's Back Bay. Unlike some of the "party hearty" frat houses, Delta Upsilon members tended to be more buttoned-down and focused on academics.

Thain took an early interest in organizing activities, serving as treasurer of his fraternity, and volunteering for several other campuswide committees. One of the highlights of his MIT years was a Christmas ski trip he organized during his junior year with a few fraternity buddies—including Joe Scire and Art Bieser—to Alta, the resort just outside Salt Lake City.

The group stayed at the base of the mountain, which is accessible from Salt Lake City only along a winding canyon road. During the week they were there, so much snow fell in the Wasatch Range that an avalanche shut down the access road, stranding the MIT frat brothers for another week at the ski resort. Thain and the guys found themselves in a snowbound paradise, skiing in waist-deep powder at a world-class resort that was nearly empty. The conditions were amazing. When one of the guys fell in the powder and lost a ski, it actually took a few minutes for him to dig out, retrieve the submerged ski, hoist himself upright, and resume his trip down the slope.

It was an era in which college students did not routinely carry credit cards, and the fraternity brothers pooled their funds to eke out every last day on the slopes. They finally hitched a ride back to Salt Lake City in the back of a fish truck and, penniless, camped out at the Delta Upsilon chapter of the University of Utah until they could catch a flight back east. By the time they made it to Cambridge, Thain and Scire—two pillars of the wrestling squad—had missed a meet against Springfield College. Their coach chewed them out for being off skiing when he needed them most.

Within the context of MIT—where the student population was equal parts "nerd," "geek," and "brainiac"—Thain was something of a Joe College type, an affable Midwesterner in an intensely cerebral environment. Some things that were difficult for his classmates, such as finding an attractive date among the tiny female population at the school, came easily to him.

As an upperclassman, Thain volunteered to help with the annual "freshman welcome" picnic each September. It was there that he met Carmen Ribera, a year behind him at the school, who had also volunteered to work the picnic. Ribera was an exotic creature at MIT, an effervescent brunette from an affluent family who emigrated to the United States from Barcelona before she was born. An architecture major, Ribera played tennis, sailed on the open expanses of the Charles River, and was involved with college theater. She could have had her pick among hundreds of eligible upperclassmen at MIT, or surveyed the selection a mile up the road at Harvard, but she chose instead to date Thain, the good-natured young man from Antioch, Illinois.

Unlike his brothers, who would study medicine, Thain was attracted to the business world. Every year, Procter & Gamble recruited a select group of MIT students for a special management program, and when Thain applied, he was accepted. That summer, he shipped off to Cincinnati, where he supervised men who worked on the production line at P&G's Ivorydale facility, the factory where P&G's famous soap is manufactured. Thain learned a memorable lesson when he noticed a recurring problem at the factory: Whenever the conveyor belt stopped working, the men on the line stopped boxing the soap. Thain tried to explain to the men that they could keep boxing the soap and stack it in piles, so that when the conveyor belt resumed operations, they could place a large stack of boxes on the line. It would be good for them, he insisted, because they got paid by production volume, not by hourly wage. But the workers, mostly grown men without college degrees or the prospect of advancement, didn't care to listen to a college boy, especially a pencilhead from MIT. The dynamic changed when Thain himself volunteered to help out, lifting boxes of packaged soap onto the conveyor belt. The men joined in and, realizing that they'd earn more pay, kept the practice up.

Thain excelled at MIT and applied to Harvard Business School. Most business schools prefer applicants who had spent a few years in the workforce, but Thain's grades and application were impressive enough to put him in the one-fifth of the class admitted straight out of college. Between his first and second years at Harvard, Thain did a summer internship in Manhattan at EF Hutton, the research and brokerage firm, where he worked in corporate finance. The experience enthralled him and the people appealed to him, so Thain applied to one of the top Wall Street banks, Goldman Sachs, in his second year. In 1979, Goldman Sachs hired only six job candidates straight out of business school, and they were from six different schools. John Thain was the one applicant from the Harvard Business School offered a position that year at 85 Broad Street.

In 1979, Goldman Sachs was a private partnership, not a public company. Although it was a successful, well-regarded investment bank at the time, a venerable Wall Street institution, it was not the unstoppable and insatiable money machine it would become by the twenty-first century. There were only about fifty partners back then, fifty men who put their own capital at risk in the firm. These days, Goldman has nearly four hundred partners, but the designation is misleading, since Goldman, like all the other major Wall Street banks, converted from the private partnership structure to public ownership in 1999.

For most of the twentieth century, Wall Street banks were configured as privately held partnerships. They owed their success—indeed, their existence—to the stock market crash of 1929 and the financial reform laws that were passed during the Great Depression. One of the lessons learned from the crash was the danger posed by banks that invested their own capital in companies. Congress passed the Glass-Steagall Act in 1933, which separated commercial banking activies—such as making loans to businesses—from investment banking activities, which were inherently riskier.

The law created a bifurcated banking system consisting of depository institutions, which were supervised by a range of regulators, including the Federal Reserve, and investment banks, which enjoyed less onerous oversight. For investment banks, the risk-reward equation was much wider than for staid commercial lending institutions: They could invest their own capital in companies, which sometimes led to outsized returns, and occasionally to disaster.

Until the 1980s, most investment banks were privately held partnerships, like Goldman Sachs. Because the partners' own capital was at stake, the investment banks tended to manage their risks carefully. It was only after most of these investment banks went public that some of them pursued risky investments recklessly. After all, whether you're running a business or visiting Las Vegas, the same principle applies: It's always easier to gamble when you're using someone else's money.

John Thain, still the naive Midwesterner, moved to Manhattan with no money and no friends in New York, and rented the cheapest apartment he could find, a studio at Fourth Avenue and East 12th Street. The area today has been completely gentrified, featuring top-rated restaurants and fashionable cooperative apartments, but in 1979, when New York subway trains were covered with graffiti and the city seemed ungovernable, the neighborhood was in a decidedly wrong part of town.

Thain was entering the world of finance at an inflection point, at the end of the stagnant markets of the 1970s. Every industry has its transformational moments, when innovation does more than improve performance at the margins, it fundamentally changes the nature of the business. The Wall Street that John Thain entered in 1979 was perched on the edge of one of those transformational moments.

Financial innovators such as Michael Milken at Drexel Burnham Lambert were already creating a new market for high yield debt, more commonly known as "junk bonds." Advances in computer technology allowed traders to accelerate and simplify the process of buying and selling stocks and bonds, especially when using the analytic tools that would soon be found on Bloomberg terminals, the boxlike machines that started popping up on trading floors across Wall Street in the 1980s.

On the supply level, a huge generation of Baby Boomers, who were now funding their own retirements through 401(k) plans, sent a surge of new money into the mutual fund industry and Wall Street. Technology also accelerated the globalization of finance, making it easier for people on one side of the world to invest in other parts of the world. By the year 2000, the pool of money sloshing around in the capital markets was exponentially larger than what it was in 1979, when Thain started at Goldman Sachs.

Even before all that, the first lesson John Thain learned was that Wall Street takes care of its own. He took home about $50,000 in 1980, more than his father had ever earned in one year as a doctor. He also married his college sweetheart, Carmen Ribera.

Thain spent five years working for Goldman's investment banking division, not in the relationship end of the business, but in execution. Goldman Sachs partners, the investment bankers, would bring in financing deals for large clients and Thain was part of the team that figured out how to make the deals work. It was a plumber's introduction to the world of high finance.

Thain's hard work and keen mind caught the eye of Goldman's top partners, Steve Friedman and Robert Rubin, who tapped the young engineering major to help the firm enter into a new business area on Wall Street, the trading of securitized mortgages.

The securitization and trading of mortgages was one of the great innovations on Wall Street in that era, a business pioneered by Lewis Ranieri at Salomon Brothers. The idea was simple enough, to package mortgages of various durations and interest rates into tranches, then securitize those tranches and sell them like bonds, where buyers could look forward to receiving annual payments, or "coupons," on their investment.

Thain immersed himself in the business, learning the arcane details of mortgage trading, from the payment cycles and coupon rates to the special considerations of prepayment pools and the "negative convexity"—an inversion of the standard price/yield curve—that creeps into the valuations of mortgage portfolios.

Mortgage trading fell within Goldman's fixed-income trading division, and the leader of that business, Jon Corzine—who would eventually be elected U.S. senator from New Jersey and governor of the Garden State—took a special interest in Thain, a fellow native of Illinois. At Goldman Sachs, which employed only the best and brightest financial minds trained at the top business schools, everyone is smart, so a partner's rise in the organization comes from how much revenue he generates for the firm and whether one of the firm's top partners takes an interest in him. Propelled by Corzine's support, Thain moved quickly up the ladder, becoming partner in 1988 and treasurer a few years later.

There's a long tradition at Goldman Sachs of top partners leaving the firm to go into public service. In 1992, Robert Rubin felt that call. He contributed to the presidential campaign of Arkansas governor Bill Clinton, and helped the candidate formulate the program he would use to jump-start an economy mired in recession. The internal theme of the Clinton campaign—"It's the economy, stupid"—grew out of Clinton's conviction that voters wanted strong leadership in Washington in areas such as job creation, economic growth, and the balancing of the federal budget.

After Clinton's upset victory over President George H. W. Bush, Rubin left Goldman Sachs to become the president's economics czar and, eventually, his treasury secretary. Left alone at the top of Goldman, Steve Friedman wearied of the pressure and responsibilities of running the investment bank by himself and announced in 1994 that he was retiring.

The news shocked Goldman's management committee, which had successfully facilitated leadership transitions time and again at the organization, but was caught this time unawares. After intense internal debate, the management committee tapped Corzine as the lead partner, and named an investment banker from Goldman's Chicago office, Hank Paulson, to be Corzine's deputy.

Corzine rewarded Thain in 1994 by naming him chief financial officer and granting him a seat on Goldman's management committee, vaulting him into one of the most prominent positions on Wall Street, and placing him ahead of other rising stars, such as Lloyd Blankfein, a top trader. Thain also moved to London for several years to work in investment banking, part of the grooming process that would prepare him for even larger roles at Goldman Sachs.

In 1999, Goldman Sachs became a public company, selling a portion of its shares to the public. The public float put a dollar value on the ownership stakes controlled by the firm's partners. Thain and other top partners suddenly found themselves sitting on fortunes worth more than $100 million each.

A few months before Goldman became a public company, the firm's management committee ousted Corzine in favor of Paulson, the investment banker. Thain and John Thornton, another investment banker, both several years younger than Paulson, were named co-presidents, with the understanding that "the two Johns" would eventually succeed Paulson.

Thain's finest moment at Goldman Sachs had nothing to do with finance. On September 11, 2001, he was in a partnership meeting just before 9:00 a.m. when John Rogers, a Goldman partner, pulled him out to inform him that there had been a huge explosion a few blocks away. It wasn't even clear yet that a hijacked plane had been flown into the north tower of the World Trade Center, just that a huge cloud of smoke from the explosion was billowing through the Financial District.

Paulson, the CEO, was somewhere in an airplane over Russia, en route to China. Thornton, Thain's co-president, was in Washington, D.C.

Thain assumed operational control of Goldman Sachs. For the next seventy-two hours, he steered the firm through the chaos unleashed by the attacks by making calm, rational decisions in the face of hysteria.

Because he had been in charge of internal operations at the firm, he was familiar with the infrastructure of the building. He ordered the air-conditioning shut down, so ground pumice stone from the black clouds around the building wouldn't get pumped into the building through the air shafts. He also ordered everyone to stay inside 85 Broad Street, and not join the hordes of other workers stampeding out of lower Manhattan. Thain ignored the Goldman hierarchy and picked out the people he felt he could rely on, regardless of rank, to deal with problems as they came up, without ever exposing to ridicule the senior executives who were having trouble coping.

On the business front, Thain shifted the processes of clearing and settling trades from New York to the firm's largest international offices, in London and Tokyo. At a meeting at the New York Stock Exchange a few days after the attacks, he stunned people in attendance, including the CEO of Verizon, with his knowledge of the switching station that served lower Manhattan. His mastery of Goldman's backroom operations and calm demeanor helped hold a battered institution together in those first, most difficult days following the attacks.

In spite of this demonstration of his leadership abilities, he still got no closer to the top job, the one he'd been angling for. His frustration began to build.

Two years later, Thain was still in his role as co-president when a crisis struck the New York Stock Exchange. Members of the NYSE's board of directors, led by Thain's boss, Hank Paulson, pushed out the Big Board's charismatic CEO, Richard "Dick" Grasso, after the disclosure that Grasso had amassed $187 million in compensation for himself over his career at the exchange, a staggering figure for someone in charge of a not-for-profit entity that functioned as a glorified trading parlor.

The revelation was an embarrassment to Paulson and some of the directors, who claimed not to have been fully aware of Grasso's gargantuan compensation package.

On top of the pay scandal, the Securities and Exchange Commission had also launched an investigation into whether the NYSE's auctioneers, known as "specialists," were cheating investors out of hundreds of millions of dollars.

Having lost the support of Paulson and the rest of his board, Grasso stepped down and the NYSE brought in an outsider, retired Citibank chief John Reed, to assume control. Working for the nominal sum of $1, Reed quickly came up with a governance plan to impose more transparency at the exchange. The biggest challenge Reed faced was to find a permanent CEO who could do the hard work necessary to restore the NYSE to its former glory.

An executive recruitment firm had started the process of looking for a new CEO, but Reed had someone else in mind, someone he knew from MIT's board of trustees, which met four times a year. Reed attended a lunch at Goldman Sachs in late 2003 featuring German chancellor Gerhard Schroeder as the main guest. After the lunch, Reed approached John Thain with an idea.

"Don't say anything to me right now, but I want to say something to you," the former Citibank CEO told Thain. "There is a wonderful opportunity for someone to run the New York Stock Exchange. You've done extremely well here at Goldman, but what a boring life it would be to spend your entire career in one place. I'd like you to think about joining me at the exchange, where you would have an opportunity to do something important for your country, and for the capital markets. If you came to the exchange, you would have a much broader platform than you do here, and you would have career choices afterward, either in Washington or in the academic world."

Thain listened closely. He was, coincidentally, growing tired of laboring in Paulson's shadow. And as every year passed, his prospects for becoming CEO of Goldman Sachs dimmed. The head of Goldman's trading operations, Lloyd Blankfein, had emerged as a new rival for the top job, replacing Thornton as co-president. Blankfein was now responsible for generating the bulk of Goldman's profits and as such, his star was outshining Thain's.

"If you're interested, give me a call," said Reed before leaving.

The idea of public service resonated with Thain, as did the challenge of restoring a national treasure to its former glory. It was in line with a Goldman Sachs tradition in which senior partners left Wall Street for the halls of government. John Whitehead, who led Goldman Sachs in the 1980s, served as deputy secretary of state in the Reagan White House, and Rubin, who joined the Clinton administration, had won wide acclaim for his role in helping to defuse the Mexican peso crisis.

Based on his success in Washington, Rubin was recruited to Citibank in 1999 by Sandy Weill to serve as vice chairman, a position that gave him wide-ranging power and a substantial paycheck without the nagging concerns of day-to-day responsibilities at the bank.

A week after his conversation with Reed, Thain called his fellow MIT alumnus to discuss the NYSE opportunity further. It didn't take long before he accepted the job. In January 2004, Thain took over as chief executive of the NYSE, at an annual salary of $4 million, a fraction of Grasso's pay package, and an 80 percent haircut from the $20 million he made in his last year at Goldman.

When Thain called his first management committee meeting to order at the NYSE, he was met with a wall of silence. He asked about some of the challenges facing the exchange and was met with stares that were either blank or frightened.

"Well, I guess everything's perfect," he deadpanned, which helped break the ice.

It soon became apparent that he had walked into an organization that had been dominated by one individual, a chief executive who reigned over the NYSE like the Sun King or a totalitarian dictator. Richard Grasso had put himself at the center of an organization with some four thousand employees and his top managers did not push back on him at all; they acceded to his every wish and whim.

The extent of Grasso's micromanagement style became even more apparent a few days later when a subordinate approached Thain in his office and handed him a blue slip of paper.

"What's this?" Thain asked.

"It needs your signature," said the man, who explained that a mid-level manager at the exchange wanted to hire a secretary.

"Why are you bringing this to me?" Thain continued.

The subordinate explained that at the NYSE, Dick Grasso signed off on every hire.

"This is ridiculous," Thain said. "If someone needs to hire a secretary, they can go ahead and do it."

Despite the lack of initiative or independence among top managers at the NYSE, Thain identified some of the key people he wanted to keep on board, and began hiring selectively, from Goldman Sachs and elsewhere, to form his own management team. Among them was Margaret Tutwiler, who had deep connections with the Republican Party in Washington, D.C. She became Thain's head of corporate communications.

Tutwiler had worked for James Baker when he was chief of staff for President Reagan and later treasury secretary. When Baker became secretary of state under President George H. W. Bush, Tutwiler followed. A decade later, President George W. Bush appointed her ambassador to Morocco.

When Thain took over as CEO, there was no doubt that the NYSE was in crisis, but what Thain didn't have was a game plan or a strategy for fixing and improving the institution. In his first few months, he went on what his aides called a "listening tour," meeting with the NYSE's seat holders, for whom he worked, and also the Big Board's other main constituents: the companies that sold their stock through the exchange, and the big institutional customers that purchased and sold their stock through the NYSE.

In short order, Thain realized that the exchange couldn't revert to its previous business practices and remain competitive in a world where New York was no longer the sole focal point of the capital markets. It would have to embrace technology and merge with or acquire other exchanges in order to broaden its footprint.

Embracing technology would have its costs. The NYSE conducted most of its transactions through the open outcry—or live auction—system, organized around market makers, who were also known as "specialists" in various stocks. Thain worked hard to ingratiate himself with the specialists and listen to their concerns. He told them he was committed to electronic trading in the long term, which was a threat to their livelihood, but he insisted he wanted to work with them rather than against them.

Many of the NYSE specialists, who controlled the majority of share trading in open auctions, were wary of Thain because of his background at Goldman Sachs. Goldman, like most of the major Wall Street banks, would have preferred to convert the NYSE into a completely electronic exchange, where huge blocks of stock could be traded instantly between counterparties.

To these big banks, the NYSE specialist system seemed archaic and fraught with potential problems and conflicts. If, for example, a large institutional investor such as Fidelity, the mutual fund giant, wanted to sell a huge block of stock in a company—say, 500,000 shares of General Electric—the process of placing that order through an auctioneer could affect the price of the trade in the wrong direction.

The auctioneer, or specialist, would know that Fidelity was selling a large block, and the traders who normally bought and sold GE shares from that specialist would quickly figure out what was going on and sell their own GE stock before Fidelity could sell the entire load, thus driving the price of GE down while Fidelity was trying to execute its trade.

On an electronic exchange, such as NASDAQ, Fidelity could find a large counterparty willing to buy the 500,000 shares at a negotiated price—not as much as the shares were commanding on the open market, but enough to make the trade worthwhile at a reasonable discount. An electronic exchange provided speed and allowed for stealth.

One of the problems that undermined Grasso's position at the NYSE was a regulatory investigation into trading practices of the specialists themselves. As "market makers," the specialists had a duty to step up and buy or sell shares of their specific stocks when markets temporarily seized up, ensuring an orderly flow of prices up or down.

For years, institutional investors suspected that the specialists, who were allowed to trade in their own accounts, were using their own position to advantage themselves over their customers by stepping in between counterparties. For example, an investor who wants to buy IBM stock would place an order that gets referred to a specialist. If the last trade in the stock was at $102.50 per share, the specialist might step into the trade himself, buying shares at $102.52, and selling the shares immediately to the outside buyer at $102.54. The specialist thereby makes a two-cent profit per share on the trade, while the investor doesn't know that he or she has been forced to overpay, however slightly, for IBM.

Two cents isn't much. Even if the trade was for a thousand shares, the specialist nets a grand total of $20. But multiply these trades by the thousand each day, across a wide range of stocks, and put them together over a multiyear period, and each of the five dominant specialists wound up reaping tens of millions of dollars in profits through the practice.

That's what was going on under Grasso at the NYSE. Less then three months after Thain took over, the specialist firms reached a settlement with the SEC and the exchange, calling for them to disgorge $154 million in ill-gotten gains and pay a combined penalty of $88 million.

The settlement cleared the air of the suspicion that had taken root among investors that shady trading practices pervaded the NYSE.

It also paved the way for the transformational deal Thain sought, the one that would reposition the Big Board for the future. In 2005, Thain brokered an agreement for for the NYSE to acquire Archipelago, an electronic trading platform. The acquisition would give the exchange access to Archipelago's high-tech trading systems. More important, by acquiring a publicly traded company, the NYSE would itself become a publicly traded entity, ending its 213-year run as a private club and giving it access to a deep pool of investor capital and the ability to expand around the world.

Goldman Sachs, which had invested in Archipelago, served as the advisor on both sides of the deal, with one of Thain's close friends from 85 Broad Street, Peter Kraus, acting as lead banker. Goldman's position on both sides of the trade roused the anger of rival Wall Street firms—Merrill's Stan O'Neal was particularly critical—but Kraus helped steer Thain through the controversies generated by the transaction.

The Archipelago deal would probably not have happened during Grasso's reign. Archipelago's founder, Gerry Putnam, poked fun at the exchange in his company's advertising and public remarks, and Grasso—who had devoted his life to building and promoting the NYSE—did not take those barbs lightly. Thain, on the other hand, had no problem with the Archipelago founder and had even convinced Goldman Sachs to invest in the company a few years earlier. When the deal closed, in early 2006, it proved to be transformational for the exchange, as well as for its CEO.

At Goldman Sachs, Thain had been largely invisible to the outside world, an industrious but unheralded financial engineer. At the NYSE, he was suddenly a public figure. Shortly after accepting the job, people he didn't know would recognize him on the street or in the subway and say something, often wishing him luck in his efforts to turn around the embattled institution.

Thain also became a regular commentator on TV, especially on CNBC, the business news channel. His early interviews on the cable channel were choppy, evidence of his discomfort in the public eye. CNBC's reporter at the exchange, Bob Pisani, would give the Big Board chief feedback after their sessions and over time, Thain, ever the quick study, improved his on-air style.

Like Grasso before him, Thain evolved into a quasi-governmental figure, meeting with finance ministers from around the world during their visits to New York, or on his own trips abroad. In particular, Thain became a regular fixture at the annual World Economic Forum in Davos, Switzerland, where his appointment book would fill up quickly with meetings with foreign dignitaries.

Thain's plain looks, glasses, and modest Midwestern manners suggested Clark Kent prior to visiting a phone booth. After pulling off the Archipelago deal and bringing the NYSE public, Thain had indeed become Superman, at least on Wall Street. The cover story on the trade publication *Institutional Investor* summed up that opinion with its headline: "The Adventures of Super-Thain," complete with an illustration of Thain as a caped crusader taking flight.

Despite these Wall Street heroics, Thain remained logical, even bloodless. After the NYSE became public, he cut expenses relentlessly, eventually dismissing the big board's barber, a forty-three-year veteran of the NYSE who lived on a salary of $24,000 per year and tips. Even after offering to work only for tips, the old man was rebuffed by Thain and sent packing.

A year later, Thain followed up with another transformational deal, acquiring Paris-based Euronext, and creating an alliance of exchanges that spanned seven countries. The Euronext deal demonstrated Thain's newfound negotiating abilities. A rival bidder, Deutsche Boerse, was actually offering to pay more for Euronext, but Thain convinced the Parisian exchange that an NYSE marriage would make more sense.

Just as his predecessor, Dick Grasso, had become the embodiment of the old New York Stock Exchange, for better and then worse, Thain represented the new NYSE, global, electronic, and efficient.

Heeding Reed's advice, Thain had also begun to use his NYSE platform as a jumping-off point for his next move, signing on early as the chief fundraiser for Arizona senator John McCain's campaign for the Republican presidential nomination. Thain had first thrown his support behind the war-hero-turned-politician in 2000, when McCain surged to an early lead for his party's nomination before being overtaken by Texas governor George W. Bush. This time around, McCain stood a strong chance of winning his party's nomination, and Thain had the inside track in the race to become the candidate's man on Wall Street.

As 2007 drew to a close, Thain had a track record of accomplishments that he never would have achieved had he stayed on at Goldman Sachs. He had also severed another cultural tie that had impeded him at Goldman. The investment bank, with its partnership culture, was a "we" organization, not an "I" organization. From the moment when junior analysts are hired out of college and business school, they are trained at Goldman Sachs to work collaboratively and to share credit.

More than most areas of business, Wall Street is driven by ambitious, egotistical individuals who strive to make as much money for themselves as possible. In order to rise to the top of Goldman Sachs, and achieve partnership status at the firm, these ambitious strivers have to learn to subordinate their own egos for the good of the firm. Managing directors at Goldman Sachs who brag about their accomplishments and claim that "I did this" or "I was responsible for that" are usually drummed out of the bank in due course. At Goldman Sachs, people who say "we" are the ones who are recognized and rewarded.

John Thain, who displayed flashes of ego and ambition at Goldman, succeeded in the 1980s and 1990s because he kept those natural impulses in check and worked unremittingly for the benefit of the entire firm.

At Goldman, Thain was like a senior staff officer who stood at some remove from the fighting, providing support and direction to the troops to execute the firm's strategy. At the New York Stock Exchange, which was weak on management talent, Thain morphed into a battlefield general who led his troops into combat and won glory for the exchange, as well as for himself.

Now, having transformed the NYSE into a successful, global franchise, and having groomed a successor plucked from the ranks of Goldman, Thain was ready for his next challenge.

BETWEEN THE DATE THAIN'S hiring was announced—November 14, 2007—and his first official day on the job in December, the new CEO visited Merrill's offices frequently, getting briefings from Fleming and other top executives and formulating his strategy for the turnaround at the Wall Street firm.

Merrill's treasury department had begun preparations to raise capital from outside investors, putting together a "deck" of statistics showing Merrill's underlying health and growth potential with a fresh infusion of capital, but Thain didn't want to make any rash decisions. He told Eric Heaton, the firm's treasurer, not to move too far until he had a chance to look at all the alternatives available.

By the end of November, Thain made two of his most important hires, bringing on board a pair of people from the NYSE who would come to be identified closely with his tenure at Merrill Lynch: chief financial officer Nelson Chai and communications director Margaret Tutwiler.

The appointments raised eyebrows, not because anyone expected Thain to keep members of the O'Neal regime in place, but because neither Tutwiler nor Chai had a typical Wall Street background.

Tutwiler had extensive skills in political communications, a background that served her well at the NYSE, which had come to be viewed as a quasi-governmental institution. But she evinced no interest in or knowledge of Wall Street and the world of finance.

The forty-two-year-old Chai had been chief financial officer of Archipelago at the time of its merger with the NYSE. Thain then tapped him to keep the job with the combined organization. At Merrill Lynch, Chai would be responsible for a balance sheet of nearly $1 trillion, much of which was comprised of hard-to-value financial instruments.

Thain's selection of a relative unknown to handle one of the toughest jobs in finance suggested either that the new CEO intended to be the de facto chief financial officer himself, with Chai playing a supporting role, or that Thain did not think Merrill's balance sheet problems required the hiring of a high-profile, high-priced heavyweight.

At Thain's urging, Chai and Fleming had dinner in late November. Fleming talked a great deal about the financial challenges facing Merrill, and described some of the cultural damage O'Neal had wreaked on the organization through his purge of experienced old Merrill hands. Although Fleming had recommended that Thain tap Heaton or Todd Kaplan, another internal candidate, for the CFO job, Chai's modesty and lack of guile made a good impression on Fleming. Toward the end of the meal, Fleming confided in the newcomer, warning him about McCann, who was in charge of Merrill's network of financial advisors. "You should watch out for him," Fleming said conspiratorially.

THAIN'S HIRING DECISIONS AND lack of communications skills ruffled a few feathers on Merrill's board even before he showed up for his first day on the job.

In late November, Finnegan—who headed the management development and compensation committee—sent an e-mail to Cribiore, expressing disbelief at Thain's first two appointments and the lack of consultation that had taken place surrounding them. Finnegan also griped about the fact that Thain wasn't returning his e-mails or phone calls. Merrill Lynch was in dire trouble, facing untold billions in losses stemming from investments in exotic securities, and Thain had picked, as chief financial officer, a guy with a thin résumé, Finnegan wrote.

On top of that, Thain's other hire was a head of communications, a woman with no financial experience whatsoever, and he wanted her to have the title of *executive vice president.* There were only six executive vice presidents at Merrill Lynch, all of whom had vitally important responsibilities. To name Margaret Tutwiler as an executive vice president of Merrill Lynch would make a mockery of the title, and place her above dozens of senior vice presidents who were generating billions of dollars in revenue for the firm. Left unsaid was the oddity of hiring a PR executive whose job would be to tout the successful turnaround at Merrill Lynch before the presumed turnaround had even begun.

"In retrospect, the board cannot feel great about some of the personnel moves made during Stan's tenure," Finnegan wrote to Cribiore. "Over the last four weeks, we have bemoaned our lack of successors and the magnitude of the dysfunction in the organization. I thought our conclusion was that we had to be more involved in the organizational structure and moves going forward. We are off to a hideous start if that is our objective."

Cribiore, who was Thain's biggest booster on the board of directors, convinced his newly minted CEO to scale back Tutwiler's title to "senior vice president."

WHEN THAIN ARRIVED AT the office on Monday, December 3— his first official day on the job—Wetzel, one of the investment bankers called to New York by Fleming, presented him with several fundraising options, including the sale of Merrill's 20 percent stake in Bloomberg, and its 49 percent stake in BlackRock. Wetzel said he had already started conversations with Temasek, the sovereign wealth fund of Singapore, and Mizuho, the Japanese bank, about equity investments in Merrill Lynch.

"Great, let's go with those," Thain said, indicating he wanted to raise capital from outside investors, not sell off the stakes in Bloomberg or BlackRock.

A few days later, Thain had breakfast with Bob McCann, the head of Merrill Lynch's financial advisors, the business which set the firm apart from its competitors.

In his last few years, O'Neal had largely ignored the private client business, McCann told Thain. There was no better indication of that than the fact that McCann himself didn't report to the CEO. As he looked at the forty-nine-year-old McCann—a hard-charging, ambitious

Irish-American from Pittsburgh who seemed to embody the old Merrill Lynch culture—Thain agreed completely with McCann's assessment. McCann would now report directly to him, the CEO, and not through Fleming, the president. McCann left the breakfast impressed with his new boss's directness and decisiveness.

THAIN HAD LEARNED A good deal from Margaret Tutwiler and his stint at the New York Stock Exchange, particularly about the importance of appearances and symbolic acts. Without ever insulting his predecessor at the NYSE, Dick Grasso, Thain made a series of symbolic gestures early in his tenure at the exchange to show how different he was. He brought the same game to Merrill Lynch, where ill will toward O'Neal permeated the organization.

Over the years, O'Neal commandeered one of Merrill's jets nearly every summer weekend to fly to his home on Martha's Vineyard. Other senior executives, including Fleming and McCann, also used the planes for personal travel when available.

Thain sold off one of the bank's two corporate jets and banned the personal use of the remaining corporate jet by senior executives. (His own contract precluded him from using the corporate jet for non-business purposes.)

In addition to the jets, Merrill Lynch owned a helicopter, which appeared to exist only to ferry O'Neal to select golf courses in Westchester or the Hamptons, the tony seaside retreat of Manhattan's wealthiest people, located at the far eastern end of Long Island. Thain put that on the block, too.

Then there was the special elevator. On December 3, after his driver deposited him out front of Merrill's headquarters in lower Manhattan, Thain entered the building and was guided to an elevator bank on the ground level. He was whisked up to the thirty-second floor. The same thing happened later in the day, when he was leaving: He caught an elevator on the thirty-second floor which took him directly to the bottom of the building so he could walk out to meet his car and driver.

On the afternoon of his second day, Thain needed to go down to an intermediate floor, so he paced out of his office and pressed the down button at the elevator bank. A car arrived, mostly full. When everyone on board saw Thain entering the car, they began stepping out.

"Why are you all getting off?" Thain asked.

"We're not supposed to be on the elevator if you're here," responded one of the employees.

Thain couldn't believe it.

"This is nonsense," he said. "Get back on and we'll all go down."

Thain now realized why an elevator car had been waiting for him when he arrived at the base of Four World Financial Center in the mornings, while other employees had to ride an escalator to the second floor and pass through a turnstile with a corporate ID in order to get access to the building. Stan O'Neal, as CEO, never had to ride in an elevator with the regular employees of Merrill Lynch.

As of day three, Thain himself took the escalator up to the second floor and passed through the turnstile alongside thousands of other Merrill employees.

O'NEAL STILL CAST A long shadow at his former place of employment. Every small gesture of openness on his part as the new CEO, Thain soon realized, won him massive amounts of goodwill from the old guard of Merrill Lynch.

Within a week of starting on the job, at Fleming's suggestion, Thain invited several of O'Neal's predecessors, and other senior executives from the pre-O'Neal era, to lunch at Merrill Lynch headquarters. Former Merrill Lynch chief executives Dave Komansky and Bill Schreyer attended, along with Win Smith, son of one of the firm's original founders, and Launny Steffens, who had been in charge of the thundering herd of brokers for most of the 1990s, until he was displaced by O'Neal.

Thain talked about his respect for the culture of Merrill Lynch. He noted that the teamwork mentality that used to be the firm's hallmark had disappeared under O'Neal, replaced by silos of people who sometimes worked at cross purposes. Because so many senior people, such as Jeff Kronthal, had been pushed out during the O'Neal era, Thain explained, he would need to go outside the organization to hire top talent in areas like risk and debt trading.

Thain also remarked on the excesses and waste under O'Neal. According to the log, the primary purpose of the Merrill Lynch helicopter was to facilitate golf outings. Since he didn't golf, Thain joked, he had no alternative but to put the chopper up for sale.

On a more serious note, Thain described the severe damage that had been done to the firm's balance sheet, and his plans to raise capital.

The former Merrill Lynch executives talked about the importance of the Merrill Lynch culture and how O'Neal had made it his mission to rip that culture apart. The retired executives left the meeting grateful to have had a sympathetic hearing with Thain, and impressed with his respect for their views and the old culture of Merrill Lynch.

Of all the attendees at that meeting, Win Smith had become the most outspoken critic of Stan O'Neal. Smith stepped down from the firm in 2001, after refusing to join in the effort to push Komansky out of the CEO job ahead of schedule. In a speech to a class of business students at Duke University's Fuqua School in September 2003, Smith criticized O'Neal's lack of regard for what Merrill Lynch once stood for. After Smith's speech and its specific criticisms were reported in a newspaper, O'Neal voiced his displeasure. A few years later, when Merrill's financial problems exploded into public view in October 2007 and O'Neal was fired, the cofounder's son gave a long interview to CNBC in which he blasted the former chief executive.

Bill Schreyer, who was CEO from 1984 to 1993, took Smith aside after the meeting with Thain to praise him for going on TV to air his views.

"You were at your best, and your father would have been proud," said Schreyer. Smith was flattered by the praise, especially since it came from a man who did so much to put O'Neal into the CEO's chair in the first place.

THERE WAS ONE OTHER contrast Thain would draw between himself and O'Neal, and it involved his predecessor's corner office on the thirty-second floor, with a commanding view of the Statue of Liberty, New York Harbor, and the Hudson River.

The first time he saw the décor of O'Neal's office Thain cringed reflexively, and couldn't imagine receiving the firm's most important clients and investors there. He had been particular about his office at Goldman Sachs, to the point of paying for special furnishings out of his own pocket. (Those were the rules at Goldman Sachs: People got paid spectacularly well, but the firm was tight on personal expenses.) Now that Thain was in charge of a global investment bank, he would have an office commensurate with his stature. His wife, Carmen, who had worked as a merchandiser at Pottery Barn and Bloomingdale's early in her career, came by to inspect the premises and agreed that the whole thing needed a renovation. They hired Michael Smith, an interior designer to the rich and famous, to redo the three-room suite.

Tutwiler, who was hypersensitive about her boss's public image, didn't think the renovation sent the right message. She suggested discreetly at one point that Thain pay for it himself, but was ignored. It was a decision that would come back to haunt him.

After Michael Smith inspected the premises, the famous designer came up with a plan for an office of European elegance, chock full of valuable antiques. But before construction on the new office could begin, Thain had to preapprove all expenses. The bill that came in from Smith included the following items:

MAHOGANY PEDESTAL TABLE:	$25,000
GEORGE IV DESK:	$18,000
NINETEENTH-CENTURY CREDENZA:	$68,000
RUG FOR CONFERENCE ROOM:	$87,000
AREA RUG:	$44,000
GUEST CHAIRS:	$87,000
COMMODE ON LEGS:	$35,000
CUSTOM COFFEE TABLE:	$16,000
CHANDELIER FOR PRIVATE DINING ROOM:	$13,000
DINING ROOM MIRROR:	$ 5,000

The list went on. The biggest charge was for labor and renovations, which, along with an $80,000 fee to Michael Smith, totaled $800,000. The sum total was $1.2 million.

Thain called down to an executive in the global corporate services department to review the bill. The CEO said he wanted to remove one item on the bill, something for the reception area, which would have cost $15,000. Otherwise, the bill was approved.

TUTWILER INHERITED THE OFFICE of O'Neal's former PR chief, Jason Wright. In contrast to her boss, she made it clear to her new subordinates that the furniture and trappings of her predecessor's office were fine with her. The implied message, which was not lost on Merrill's public relations team, was that the previous leadership of the firm had squandered shareholder funds on the trappings and perks of executive life. It didn't seem to matter that Thain's own office renovation undercut that message.

Chai took an equally spartan approach to his new office. The workers who helped clear out the effects of Chai's predecessor as chief financial officer, Jeff Edwards, had left Post-it notes on the walls to mark where Edwards's pictures had hung. From Chai's first day on the job, those Post-it notes remained in place.

In recognition of Merrill's dire financial condition, Chai and Tutwiler frequently ate downstairs in the company cafeteria, ordering the same daily specials as regular employees. Fleming and other investment bankers preferred the executive dining room on the thirty-third floor, which had been transformed into a high-end restaurant by Fakahany, a wine enthusiast. But neither Tutwiler nor Chai wanted anything to do with the overt luxuries held over from the O'Neal regime.

Fakahany had also been responsible for stocking the common areas of the thirty-second floor with massive flower arrangements, which were replaced every week and cost up to $200,000 per year. Under Thain, the lavish flower budget disappeared.

BOB McCANN WENT OUT of his way to greet Thain's new hires. He had vacated his own office on the thirty-second floor of the firm's headquarters for more space in an adjoining tower, where most of Merrill's private client operations were housed. He called Chai early on to say hello, and eventually dropped by the younger man's office for a handshake and a chat.

As he settled into a chair in Chai's office, with commentary from CNBC droning on from a TV monitor in the background, like a continuous soundtrack, McCann welcomed the new executive to the organization and mentioned his own long history at Merrill Lynch. An affable colleague and consummate people person, McCann told Chai that if there was anything he needed, from guidance about how to navigate Merrill's distinct culture, to practical advice about how the place worked, to feel free to ask. It would also be smart, McCann continued, for Chai to keep his eyes open. Fleming had wanted to put one of his own people in the chief financial officer position, so he advised Chai to be wary of Fleming. "You can't trust him," McCann said.

In general, Chai had little use for small talk, and at a time when he felt inundated with the daunting task of grappling with Merrill's financial condition, he was in no mood to let McCann drag him into the muck of Merrill Lynch politics.

"I'm pretty busy right now doing some things for John," said Chai. "My primary focus will be on working with him."

McCann got the message: Chai was close to the CEO and didn't need to waste his time chitchatting with a division head.

SHORTLY AFTER ACCEPTING HIS new position, John Thain reached out to Stan O'Neal and arranged to meet him at a neutral location, the office of O'Neal's attorney in Midtown Manhattan.

"What do you think happened at Merrill Lynch?" Thain asked.

"I don't think I'm the right person to explain that," O'Neal replied.

Thain asked him about other matters, such as how the overall wealth management business had functioned and how the investment banking business had performed. He also asked about individual executives he was inheriting from O'Neal.

The former CEO spoke positively about Rosemary Berkery, the

general counsel he had appointed to replace Steve Hammerman in 2001. O'Neal also provided a mostly positive assessment of Greg Fleming's skills. When Thain asked about Bob McCann, O'Neal was more measured.

Thain also asked about the board of directors. O'Neal was tempted to give him a lengthy discourse on the topic, but thought better of it.

"You will form your own relationship with them," he said.

Thain closed the meeting by praising the former CEO for taking the aggressive cost-cutting measures he had initiated in October. O'Neal thought Thain was patronizing him, and wondered whether his successor understood the magnitude of the problems that remained on Merrill's balance sheet.

THE LOSSES GROWING ON the balance sheet of Merrill Lynch every month meant the firm needed fresh capital to fill the hole in its capital base. In the longer term, Thain had a choice to make: sell the CDO positions at a loss or hold them for a while until the market rebounded. One problem was that Merrill Lynch didn't even know what its CDO holdings were worth, which is why Jeff Kronthal had been brought back as a consultant.

Over the first few weeks of December, a team of bankers from Temasek, the sovereign wealth fund of Singapore, studied Merrill's financials and consulted frequently with Thain and Wetzel. Wetzel, who didn't want the parade of outside investors to be seen by scores of Merrill's own employees, designated the boardroom on the thirty-third floor as the place for sensitive fundraising meetings. During these meetings, Thain articulated his vision of the new Merrill Lynch.

Thain told the foreign investors about how he would reorganize Merrill's internal reporting lines so that the people in charge of risk management, who had been shut out of the decision to load up on CDOs between August 2006 and April 2007, would have direct access to him, the CEO. With this new structure, Merrill would never again find itself in a position where a few people could wreak such enormous damage.

Other potential investors, such as J. Christopher Flowers—a former colleague of Thain's from Goldman Sachs who had left in the late 1990s to form a private equity fund—also studied Merrill's books.

Most of the CDOs had a similar structure. In most cases, as much as 90 or 95 percent of the product consisted of "super senior" tranches of mortgages that had been given an single A, double A or triple A rating by the credit rating agencies. The rest of the product consisted of lower quality mortgages and paid a much higher rate of return. Because Merrill Lynch retained only the higher quality portions of the CDOs, there was an assumption that even in a slower market, the assets would retain most of their value.

The traders who structured these deals had no incentive to pay attention to internal traffic cops who warned of the inherent risks embedded in those securities, which could plummet in value if the economy changed. The traders didn't care. They made money based on what happened in the moment. If the subprime-related securities blew up down the road, it was not going to be their problem.

Merrill Lynch had stumbled for essentially the same reason that all banks stumble: by taking imprudent risks with its capital in an attempt to ramp up profits. As long as there have been banks, bank failures have occurred because lenders made too many loans, not too few loans. The more loans a bank makes, the more profit it earns, until it makes so many bad loans that defaults erase profits, and the bank's own capital shrinks. The ability to manage that risk, to discern the fine line between a loan worth making and the one that might blow up, distinguishes successful bankers from the foolhardy.

For investment banks, risk management is an even more important discipline, since they are allowed to make investments with their own funds. Until the repeal of the Glass-Steagall Act in 1999, depository banks were not allowed to invest directly in businesses they advised. They could only make loans, which generated lower returns on capital. Investment banks, like venture capital firms, could deploy their capital in businesses they supported, with the prospect of hefty returns. When times were good, especially during the swelling of the real estate bubble from 2004 through 2006, investment banks dove into the subprime-mortgage business, generating record profits from securitization and sale of mortgage-backed assets. But of the great investment banks, only Goldman Sachs heeded the warnings of its own internal risk managers, who began sounding the alarm in late 2006.

THAIN'S VISION WAS THAT Merrill could improve its internal controls and pay bonuses to employees based on the overall success of the firm, not just the success of individual units within the firm. It was the lure of outsized bonuses that drove the fixed-income people to keep stockpiling CDOs after the market for those products cooled off. Those organizational improvements would make Merrill more like Goldman Sachs, the most successful investment bank on Wall Street.

Temasek, the Singapore wealth fund, liked Thain's vision, as did Davis Advisors, a Manhattan investment firm. On Christmas Eve, less than four weeks after Thain arrived, Merrill Lynch announced that the firm had raised $6.2 billion from Temasek and Davis Advisors.

That the new boss had already flown to his vacation home in Colorado for a few days of skiing at Christmas did not matter to his new charges at Merrill, who were delighted to have received the votes of confidence from outside investors.

The speed with which Thain had clinched the deal solidified his credibility in the marketplace. In a statement distributed to the media, Temasek, which would put in $5 billion of the $6.2 billion, expressed full confidence in John Thain's ability to move the Merrill Lynch franchise forward. There was only one catch: The Singapore fund insisted on a "reset" clause surrounding its investment, so that if, within a one-year period, Merrill Lynch had to raise more capital by selling equity at a lower price than the $48 per share Temasek was paying, the bank would have to make Temasek whole on the difference. In other words, no future investor would be able to buy in to Merrill Lynch at a lower rate during 2008 without Temasek being compensated for that price drop.

Fleming had urged Thain to cut a deal that didn't involve a reset, while Wetzel—who was the primary contact with the Temasek people—insisted that without that protection, the Singapore fund would not put any money into Merrill Lynch. Instead of doing battle over that one issue, and perhaps getting Temasek to drop its insistence on a reset in return for a significantly lower share price, Thain decided it was better to get the deal done than to haggle. Besides, the reset clause was hardly a worry now, as Thain's arrival had already brought the steady erosion of Merrill's share price to a halt.

CHAPTER 7

THE SMARTEST GUY
IN THE ROOM

WITH THE CHRISTMAS EVE announcement of a $6.2 billion capital raise, even Fleming was able to relax for the first time in months.

For Eric Heaton, Merrill's treasurer, the holiday ended too quickly. On December 31, when the final numbers came in from the firm's fixed-income trading division, the trading marks resulted in a nasty surprise: Merrill's losses would be almost twice what his team had predicted just a month earlier.

There were two forces driving the increased losses. Like other large Wall Street investment banks, Merrill Lynch held hundreds of billions of dollars' worth of assets on its balance sheet.

But the problem with Merrill Lynch's balance sheet was that it contained more than $30 billion of collateralized debt obligations and billions more in other arcane investments, the underlying value of which was difficult to determine. The CDOs may have been worth an aggregate $30 billion at the time they were securitized, but there was no way they were still worth that amount.

As 2007 came to a close, the U.S. real estate market was in free fall. The epicenter was the subprime mortgage market, where unqualified buyers were walking away from mortgages underwritten by profligate lenders, particularly in such overheated markets as California, Arizona, Nevada, and Florida.

With home foreclosures spiking to unprecedented levels, the values of securities backed by subprime mortgages also plummeted, generating losses on the balance sheets of Wall Street investment banks.

At Merrill Lynch, scores of investments in CDOs and other illiquid investments had to be marked down at the end of the quarter, causing the bank's losses to balloon by several billion dollars.

Thain, Fleming, and others knew that Merrill Lynch wasn't done raising capital on Christmas Eve. Fleming himself spent part of Christmas Day on the phone with bankers from Mizuho in Japan, where there was no holiday. Merrill's fundraising team had kept the lines of communication open with other potential investors.

And yet, on December 31, with some trepidation, Heaton took the elevator up from his office on the twenty-second floor to Thain's office on thirty-two, the executive floor. Since Thain's office was being redone, the CEO was working temporarily out of Bob McCann's old office.

Heaton explained how the losses were worse than expected. Thain was slightly exasperated by the news, and by Heaton's recommendation that the firm would need to raise more capital than what the CEO was already planning to drum up in January.

"Have you talked to Nelson about this?" Thain asked, referring to his CFO, Nelson Chai. Heaton said he had.

"Okay, go ahead," he said, giving Heaton the green light to expand Merrill's fundraising activities.

Companies hire CEOs not just because of their résumés, which in Thain's case was sterling, but also on the candidate's vision for the future of the enterprise. Stan O'Neal had been forced out because he thought Merrill Lynch had to align itself with a large commercial bank, such as Bank of America or Wachovia. The board was angered that O'Neal didn't seem to be willing to fight his way out of the mess he'd created, that he wasn't willing to raise capital and turn the company around. The power of Thain's name in the marketplace was such that other investors still wanted in, as evidenced by the capital Merrill had been able to raise by Christmas Eve.

IN MID-JANUARY, JUST IN time for the year-end earnings release, Thain announced an additional infusion of $6.6 billion in Merrill Lynch from sovereign wealth funds in South Korea and Kuwait, as well as Mizuho, the Japanese bank that had worked closely with Wetzel. Since Merrill's stock price was above $50, there was no need to compensate Temasek for the additional capital raise.

Such was the appetite among investors for the opportunity to buy in to a Wall Street bank at a bargain rate that Thain could have raised as much as $25 billion or $30 billion in fresh capital. But the new CEO didn't want to dilute the existing shareholders any more than was necessary. And by drawing the line where he did, Thain was sending a strong signal of confidence to the marketplace that Merrill's financial problems were already under control.

For Fleming and other top executives at Merrill, who had witnessed the implosion of Stan O'Neal just a few months before, it was clear that Thain enjoyed the credibility and clout that his predecessor had lost by the end. Thain exuded confidence. There was a feeling around Merrill's headquarters at Four World Financial Center that, with Thain on board, the brokerage firm was finally being run by "the right guy."

AT THE MANAGEMENT MEETING where final details of the additional raising of capital were discussed, the talk turned to the smallest of the new investors, the state of New Jersey. Merrill Lynch was raising billions of dollars from the Koreans, Kuwaitis, and Japanese. But when Wetzel told Thain, with a chuckle, that the state of New Jersey, with its tiny investment fund, wanted in, Thain weighed the prospect seriously and told Wetzel to follow up.

At this time, a number of major banks, particularly Citigroup, had reached out to sovereign wealth funds for a lifeline during the turmoil.

The prevalence of the foreign investors had sparked populist opposition, as some politicians questioned why U.S. banks were ceding so much ownership to overseas potentates, so when Thain heard that a U.S. state wanted to participate in the latest raising, he encouraged Wetzel to take the bid seriously.

Eventually, the New Jersey division of investment did sign on for a small slice of the new $6.6 billion funding. At the final management meeting to discuss details of the project, one of Wetzel's colleagues suggested Thain travel to the Garden State for the ceremonial signing to mark the investment.

Wetzel, who owned a home in New Jersey and kept it during his years in Tokyo, offered to shepherd Thain around his state. "Yeah, Paul, why don't you bring John to your weekend home in Trenton?" cracked one of his colleagues.

"You have a weekend home in Trenton?" Thain asked, generating more laughter.

"No," said Wetzel, also warming to the conversation. "But you should go to the signing, John," he told Thain. "Who knows? You might run into your friend Jon Corzine," a reference to the state's governor, who had been Thain's boss at Goldman Sachs a decade earlier.

After the laughter subsided, Thain stood up, looked at his lieutenants, and said, "Now we have to go make money." With that, the meeting broke up, and Thain's management team left the office feeling energized by the call to arms.

It was only later that Chai called Wetzel to say that Thain and Corzine weren't really "friends." Thain's involvement in Corzine's departure from Goldman nearly a decade earlier had created some lingering ill will, Chai explained.

EVERY JANUARY, MANAGERS IN Bob McCann's financial advisory group held an off-site meeting, usually at a golf-friendly resort, to reward top performers and motivate them to improve their performance in the year ahead.

On January 15, 2008, the private client managers descended on

Scottsdale, Arizona. For most of the group, this would be their first opportunity to meet their new CEO John Thain in person.

Members of the thundering herd were not full-time employees, or officers of the company. They were entrepreneurs, men and women who earned their paychecks by advising their clients, and helping those clients invest wisely. The vast majority liked working with Merrill because it was the best brand name in the business.

The O'Neal regime had done great damage to the franchise. He didn't like mixing with the advisors or glad-handing them at events such as this. Besides, he believed the private client business was a middling performer that would never match the profitability of the sales and trading desk, where shrewd bets with large pools of capital generated enormous profits.

As head of the unit in 2000, O'Neal fired more than six thousand support staff, closed unproductive offices, and shunted Merrill's smallest clients—the ones with less than $100,000 in assets with the firm—to call centers in New Jersey, so that the brokers could focus on bigger fish. Although the moves improved the unit's bottom line, they didn't endear O'Neal to the thundering herd.

From 2004 through early 2007, Merrill's profits soared, so O'Neal's critics didn't have much ammunition to use against him. But in the second half of 2007, when it became apparent that O'Neal had mortgaged the future of the firm for short-term profits in the risky area of subprime products, all the antagonism that had built up over the previous years spilled forth.

Nowhere was this antagonism more keenly felt than among the advisors. After a month on the job, Thain knew this. And so he made it a priority to show up at the Scottsdale event.

THAIN ARRIVED THE EVENING before his speech, in time to attend a cocktail party for the advisors, sporting a name tag, no less, which humanized him in comparison to the imperial O'Neal, who viewed such gatherings as trials to be endured.

The next day, Thain addressed the assembled group.

"Now I'm going to talk a lot about the wealth management business," he began, "but I want to start out by saying we also have great strengths across all of our businesses. Our investment banking franchise, our equity franchise, and actually most of our fixed-income businesses are very strong.

"But no business at Merrill has a greater tradition or a greater pride than the wealth management business. And I certainly saw that last night when I got to talk to a number of you. You are the most visible in the world. You are the face of Merrill Lynch in our communities. And you represent our brand across America and the Americas and throughout the world.

"And even though we are a global company, you are what make us local because it's the relationships with our clients that sets us apart. And I believe [what] differentiates us from our competitors is our client focus. It's different at Morgan Stanley, it's different at Citi and it's certainly, I can tell you, different at Goldman Sachs.

"So I am very excited about leading this franchise. I think the Merrill Lynch franchise has been built over a hundred years. The more I learn about what Charlie Merrill said the more I appreciate what a great financial statesman he was. He was a visionary, he was a pioneer, he had a bold view, but he was also a realist. He understood that the success of Merrill Lynch would always rest upon the success of our customers; that we must always put our customers' interests first.

"And he was devoted to a life with one ambition—that Merrill Lynch would stand for the best in financial services."

Thain explained what he was trying to do at headquarters, drew some laughter with a few well-aimed one-liners, and took questions afterward. He connected with the group. Rather than rush back to New York following his presentation, he basked in the afterglow and stayed around to listen to the next speaker, Fleming.

Despite his association with the O'Neal regime, and his pedigree as an investment banker, Fleming had now become accepted as a true "Merrill guy." Even before he began his speech, one member of the audience stood up and paid tribute to the new management team.

"What you did back in November was courageous," the audience member said aloud to Fleming, referring to the arduous town hall session on November 2, the day of the *Wall Street Journal* story. "We now have a new CEO, and we have you as well! I feel really good about Merrill Lynch and its management team."

The praise was an unexpected tonic to Fleming, who had tried to banish the memory of November. Beaming, he acknowledged the kind words and looked over toward his boss, who was sitting in the front row. Thain's eyes narrowed slightly.

Over his years as an investment banker, Fleming had evolved into a good public speaker. He launched into a talk about how Merrill Lynch was poised to take advantage of the current economic turmoil and would emerge stronger than before. The speech, which he had given on other occasions, generated a big round of applause. Afterward, Thain approached him.

"That was very good," he said.

ON JANUARY 17, Merrill announced its earnings for the fourth quarter of 2007. Given the sinking values of its subprime-related securities, the bank posted a $10.3 billion loss in the quarter, wiping out the profits of the first half of the year and saddling the firm with a net loss of $8.6 billion for 2007.

But the loss was expected, and grew out of bad bets made during O'Neal's tenure. Merrill's new chief executive had already raised almost $13 billion in fresh capital to cover for the expected losses. The outlook for the U.S. economy in 2008 was worsening, dragged down by the declining real estate market, but for the first time in six months, executives at Merrill Lynch felt some control over their destiny.

At the end of every quarter, when earnings were announced, Merrill Lynch held a conference call for investors, analysts, and the media, the purpose of which was to describe in more detail the underlying performance of the firm. It was an opportunity for analysts who follow the stock to drill into specific aspects of the firm's performance.

The last earnings call of the O'Neal era had gone poorly, with the chief executive admitting that he and his finance team had screwed up, and the CFO sounding uncertain about the depths of Merrill's problems. Skeptical analysts asked probing questions about Merrill's mounting losses, and neither O'Neal nor his lieutenants were capable of explaining what was going on.

By contrast, Thain's performance during his first conference call as chief executive of Merrill Lynch was strong. After less than two months on the job, he demonstrated a thorough command of the bank's balance sheet and its business, and a confidence in the firm's future that had evaporated under O'Neal. He announced several initiatives designed to bring Merrill's cost structure down, including a layoff of several thousand employees.

With the infusion of almost $13 billion in new funds, Thain said, "We're very confident that we have the capital base now that we need to go forward into 2008 and beyond."

Across the firm, jaws dropped at this gaffe. Yes, Thain had just raised an impressive amount of fresh capital, but it was foolhardy to claim that the problem was now solved. It was as if a driver had filled his tank with gas and, on the verge of driving into a desert, declared that he had enough gas to make it to the other side, without knowing whether the desert was 200 or 2,000 miles across.

It was a breathtaking statement of certainty on a subject that was inherently unknowable. If the economy worsened in 2008 there was no way Merrill would be able to avoid further losses in its CDO positions. And Thain had now boxed himself into a corner. If Merrill's trading positions led to further losses, Thain would have to eat his words and raise more capital, prompting questions about whether he actually knew what he was doing.

FOLLOWING THE EARNINGS CALL, Thain took the elevator down to the fifth floor, Merrill's equity trading room, for an interview with CNBC's anchor, Maria Bartiromo, and the opportunity to discuss the situation at Merrill Lynch.

Because this was Thain's first earnings announcement at Merrill, at a time when investors were eager for information about his plans to turn the company around, it would not be an ordinary interview. Margaret Tutwiler, Thain's head of communications, thought that staging the interview on the trading floor would reinforce the message she was trying to get out about the new Merrill: The troubled brokerage firm was back in business, and Thain was firmly in control.

Prior to the interview, Tutwiler had painstakingly orchestrated the stage and the backdrop so that images of her boss would appear in front of Merrill's insignia, featuring the beloved bull. In lighter moments, Tutwiler, an Alabama native who retained her distinctive southern drawl, would playfully refer to Merrill's emblem as an "old cow," but when it came to communications, she took the image of the bull seriously.

"Our businesses are doing really, really well," Thain told Bartiromo. "One area that's the problem is the CDO and subprime area. Our goal has been to write off as much as we can, to be as conservative as possible and go forward into 2008 with a much stronger balance sheet and capital base and a great earnings prospect."

Given that Merrill had announced another big write-down of its subprime-based assets, Bartiromo asked, "Can you categorically say there will not be another write-down next quarter?"

"No one can ever say that," Thain replied. "We have a big balance sheet. We have other mortgage-related securities. The answer is no. You can never say there's no risk. We're in a trading business. Trading businesses take risks. That's okay. It's making sure we really understand it."

Another question involved Merrill's stake in BlackRock, and whether it would make sense for Merrill to sell it in order to raise more capital.

"No," Thain declared. "That's a strategic stake and it's important to us going forward. It fits very well with our high net worth business."

FROM A MERRILL LYNCH point of view, the interview was a success. Thain projected an image of authority in what amounted to "the trenches," the place where Merrill had lost money under O'Neal and would now make money under Thain.

The interview also showed that under Tutwiler, who had learned her craft in Washington, D.C., with the "A team" of Republican Party communications experts, public relations would be handled differently from the way it was handled at other Wall Street banks, where the focus tended to be on the institution first, then the CEO.

When subordinates came in to her office to seek advice or direction, Tutwiler shared her philosophy, which was modeled on the political strategies she learned in the nation's capital. Tutwiler's role was to support the top executive, John Thain. Positive media exposure for him was positive media exposure for Merrill Lynch. It was that simple.

An appearance on the evening news, an interview on CNBC, or a photo of Thain in a newspaper article all enhanced the image of the chief executive and therefore of Merrill Lynch as well.

When Tutwiler worked for James Baker in the 1980s, the strategy was perfect. Baker was a master of his material and his frequent TV appearances, showing him near the insignia for the White House and then the Treasury, cast a positive light on the institutions he led.

In Thain, Tutwiler had another superstar client. She didn't have to coach him on how to say things—Thain was a brilliant numbers guy and a strong strategic thinker. All she had to do was focus the media's attention on Thain and the Merrill Lynch image of the bull, and get everyone and everything else out of the way.

Greg Fleming learned this early on. Shortly after Thain arrived, Fleming felt as though he had been misquoted in a story about the firm. He went into Tutwiler's office and said he wanted to contact the reporter to set the record straight, but Tutwiler told him not to worry about it. "John Thain is the public face of Merrill Lynch," she declared.

Fleming recoiled at the statement, and its obvious relegation of him to second-class status.

"No, Margaret. Merrill Lynch is 60,000 employees around the world who get up every day trying to help their clients. I know you're new here, but Merrill Lynch is an institution in this country, going back almost a hundred years. It's not about one person and never has been. It's about every financial advisor in every town across the country, and every one of those FAs work with real people, people who want to retire, or save for their kids' college funds. Those advisors are what Merrill Lynch is."

Tutwiler cast a weary look at Fleming. "That's all very wonderful, Greg. But John Thain is still the public face of Merrill Lynch."

NOT EVERY MEMBER OF the management committee shared Fleming's sensitivity on the matter of whether John Thain alone represented Merrill Lynch. Heaton, the treasurer, felt that Thain's high profile translated into fundraising power for the firm.

But some of the hagiography surrounding the new chief was off-putting. In a article about the Merrill Lynch CEO published in the February 2008 issue of *Bloomberg Markets* magazine, Nelson Chai talked about Thain in glowing terms.

"When you're the smartest guy in the room, which he typically is, you come at things from a different altitude," said Chai, describing his own role as Thain's eyes and ears on the ground. The "smartest guy in the room" description of Thain may have been true at the New York Stock Exchange, an organization closer in size to a country club than a Fortune 500 company, but at a global investment bank and brokerage firm the size of Merrill Lynch, which had its share of smart people, Chai's gushing praise didn't go down well.

If Thain was indeed the "smartest guy in the room," his repeated statements about Merrill being well capitalized did nothing to support that reputation. Just the opposite. During a tour of Europe in March, Thain declared Merrill's fiscal fitness several times over. In an interview with a French newspaper, Thain said, "Today I can say we will not need additional funds. These problems are behind us. We will not return to the market."

That same month, he told a Spanish newspaper, "We have more capital than we need, so we can say to the market that we don't need more injections. We can confirm that we have tackled the problem."

The statements had become an embarrassment at the firm. Fleming asked Thain to back off, and Nelson Chai suggested to his boss that he shouldn't be making declarative statements about Merrill Lynch's capital position. Even Paul Critchlow, who had transferred into Merrill's municipal bond business from public relations four years earlier, approached Tutwiler and insisted that she get Thain to stop making those statements. She rebuffed him.

THE DAY THAIN ARRIVED at Merrill Lynch, the firm needed more than fresh capital. It needed to rebuild a whole layer of executive management. One reason the board had to look outside the organization for the next CEO was that O'Neal refused to let any of his direct reports rise to a sufficient level of stature and experience to step into his job.

It had cost a lot of money to sign Thain from the NYSE, but one of the reasons for hiring someone of Thain's stature was the belief that an executive with his contacts would attract an entourage of seasoned players who actively wanted to participate in his turnaround efforts. After being ousted from Citigroup a decade earlier, Jamie Dimon bided his time until the opportunity to run Bank One in Chicago emerged. Once Dimon took the Chicago job, several of "his guys" followed him to the new job. Eventually, JPMorgan Chase acquired Bank One because William Harrison, the CEO, recognized in Dimon a strong candidate to succeed him in the corner office. By the time Dimon returned to New York, a gang of his people from the Citigroup days had reconvened to work with him once more.

The people who were closest to Thain at the NYSE, Chai and Tutwiler, signed on immediately at Merrill Lynch. When Finnegan, the head of the management and compensation committee of the board, questioned Thain about Chai's fitness for the job, Thain assured him that Chai could handle the work. Besides, Thain countered, it would take more than six months to pry a respected veteran such as David Viniar away from Goldman Sachs.

But when it came to other hires, Thain was in less of a rush. Goldman Sachs was in the process of encouraging some of its seasoned executives, such as Thain's friend Peter Kraus, to move on. Thain thought Kraus and Tom Montag, a top trading executive who was also on his way out, would fit in well with his long-term plans for Merrill Lynch.

In late December, Thain met with Rohit D'Souza, the head of Merrill's equities trading business. D'Souza had been recruited by Dow Kim in 2004 to rebuild and upgrade Merrill's equities trading operations, which had been the envy of the industry in the 1980s, but had fallen behind technologically from the 1990s onward. D'Souza had proven himself to be a strong leader in that division.

D'Souza urged Thain to move quickly and put someone in charge of Merrill's sales and trading operations, which had been rudderless for almost a year. Thain nodded and asked D'Souza if he'd be willing to play a larger role in Merrill's sales and trading operations. D'Souza readily agreed.

In general, Thain was not overly impressed with the talent he encountered at Merrill Lynch. O'Neal had eliminated some of the strongest players from the team, such as James Gorman, who had been head of the financial advisory business until an unceremonious demotion spurred him to accept an offer from Morgan Stanley.

Fakahany, the co-president, had been O'Neal's top lieutenant, and the man ultimately responsible for risk management. After a brief transition period, he would leave. Thain weighed whether to give D'Souza the additional challenge of running fixed income. For now, the business was headed by David Sobotka, who had been thrust into that role after the purge of Semerci. Sobotka had established himself in commodities, but he didn't have the breadth of experience across a broad range of debt securities and derivatives to prepare him for the job.

Rosemary Berkery was Merrill's general counsel, the top lawyer at the firm. Thain accepted her, but didn't see her as a candidate for advancement at Merrill Lynch beyond her current position.

Bob McCann, who replaced Gorman as head of the thundering herd of financial advisors, had aspirations of becoming CEO of Merrill, but Thain didn't think he was up to the job. McCann personified the old Mother Merrill culture that Stan O'Neal tried to eradicate. McCann worked hard, was an excellent salesman and strong motivational speaker, but Thain felt he spent too much time promoting himself.

Fleming had potential. He was obviously a competent investment banker, Thain thought, and had promise as an executive. But compared to some of the Wall Street veterans Thain had worked with at Goldman Sachs, Fleming seemed young and untested.

Thain was in frequent touch with Kraus about building an A-team of management at Merrill Lynch. The best way to achieve that goal, Thain ultimately decided, was to bring Kraus and Montag over from Goldman Sachs.

AFTER THE JANUARY 17 announcement of fourth-quarter earnings, and the CNBC interview, Thain spoke to a pair of reporters from *The Wall Street Journal*.

The reporters asked whether Thain was trying to recruit Montag, who was also being courted by Morgan Stanley, UBS, and Bear Stearns. "He is a very popular guy," Thain responded. "I can't speculate on my chances, but I am hopeful he will join us."

Was there a risk that hiring another executive from Goldman Sachs might send the wrong message to his employees at Merrill? "I am not bringing in that many people from Goldman or anywhere," he said. "But I need more senior trading talent. Tom Montag is not the only guy. He is just a particularly good one."

Other traders and executives wondered about Thain's public airing of his recruitment efforts. To them, Thain's statement undercut all the right things the new boss had been saying about Merrill Lynch since accepting the job two months earlier.

On multiple occasions, including his appearance in Arizona just two days earlier, Thain had talked about all the talented people at Merrill and how important the firm's culture was. Now, with one statement in a newspaper interview, he had reinforced the notion that Merrill's own executives weren't good enough to assume leadership roles in his turn-around of the company.

. . .

IN THE LAST WEEK of January, Thain and Fleming headed to Davos, Switzerland, for the annual World Economic Forum, where leaders from business and government gathered each year to discuss the global economic situation.

The greatest minds of the economic world debated by day whether the recent downturn in the U.S. economy and the collapse of the real estate bubble would have a wide impact. The general consensus was that the global economy was in for a rough 2008.

In the evenings, a select group of companies hosted parties. Merrill Lynch held its reception, as always, at the Belvedere Hotel. In recent years, owing to Stan O'Neal's aversion to the gathering, Fleming had been the primary host. This year John Thain was the star attraction. Thain held forth at the Belvedere as visiting dignitaries, such as George Soros or Henry Kissinger, dropped by to say hello. In the media, Thain was omnipresent: Tutwiler had orchestrated a series of interviews, in print and on TV, that put Thain and Merrill Lynch at the forefront of the entire forum.

In contrast to other prognosticators at Davos, who were warning of a long, difficult recession, Thain expressed guarded optimism about the economy, suggesting that 2008 could turn out better than expected.

FOR AN EXECUTIVE WHO had a reputation for decisiveness, Thain seemed oddly passive during his weekly management meetings. In contrast to O'Neal, who could ice someone who spoke out of line with a chilling stare, Thain welcomed every opinion and encouraged debate. But over time, these meetings, featuring about twenty executives from various parts of Merrill Lynch, took on an unusual dynamic of their own.

Thain presided over these gatherings, but remained aloof from the Merrill Lynch executives who participated. He welcomed the views of his subordinates, and took them under advisement, but rarely set the tone for a meeting or articulated a path he wanted to pursue. And he almost never made a decision on the spot. Rather, the meetings would end with some general agreement that the firm would be better off selling its problem assets, but without any specific action plan for making sure that happened.

There was something else that was odd about Thain in these meetings. Usually, after a month or so on a job, a senior executive develops a feeling for the people he likes and doesn't like, for those he trusts and doesn't trust. Thain remained oddly passive in this regard, betraying no special trust in or connection to anyone on his management committee.

Jeff Kronthal, who had been pushed out of Merrill after Semerci was promoted in 2006, had known Thain for almost twenty years, from the time they were both starting out as mortgage traders in the 1980s. He attended the management meetings and found it strange that Thain kept his distance from even him, the guy who was supposedly brought in to help solve the CDO problem.

On March 31, the dynamics changed further when a new woman appeared at the table a few minutes before the weekly gathering began. First Greg Fleming, then a few others, said hello to the woman. When Thain arrived, he was teased about not introducing his newest hire. Thain apologized and asked everyone to say hello to May Lee, a former colleague from Goldman Sachs, who had just joined Merrill Lynch as his chief of staff.

Lee, an Asian-American in her early forties, said her job would be to act as Thain's eyes and ears at Merrill Lynch, communicating with his direct reports and managing the flow of information to the CEO.

Lee herself seemed sharp and trustworthy, but for a group of executives who had watched Stan O'Neal morph from a hands-on, get-it-done leader into an isolated presence insulated from direct contact with the troops by Fakahany, her arrival didn't bode well. The previous version of this movie had ended badly.

Another dynamic was now common in the management meetings: a noticeable friction between Fleming and Bob McCann. Early on, Thain promised McCann that he could report directly to him, the CEO. Fleming, a tenacious infighter when it came to protecting his turf, objected to losing oversight of such a large chunk of Merrill's business and convinced

Thain to keep the private client unit within his purview. As a result, McCann wound up in a position where he reported to two people, Thain and Fleming, without feeling loyalty to either one.

Fleming's territorial nature had become a matter of discussion among Thain's hires, as Lee found out on her first day. Making her rounds on the thirty-second floor, Lee introduced herself to Margaret Tutwiler and Nelson Chai, who were chatting.

"I'm going to be John's chief of staff," Lee said.

"We work for John, too. Everybody else in this building seems to work for Greg Fleming," said Tutwiler with a laugh.

CHAPTER 8

PROFIT INTO LOSS

PAUL WETZEL WAS TURNING into a permanent resident of the Embassy Suites hotel across the street from Merrill Lynch headquarters at Four World Financial Center. He had flown to New York from Tokyo the previous fall and, when Fleming called, immersed himself in capital-raising activities for the next ten weeks.

After following Thain from the NYSE to Merrill Lynch, Nelson Chai wanted to do more than simply be CFO. At his request, Thain allowed Chai to take over responsibilities for strategic planning, which had been part of Fleming's domain. Then Chai approached Wetzel and asked him to move back to New York permanently and become head of global strategy for Merrill Lynch.

Financially, it would be a step backward for Wetzel, since investment bankers make a lot more than corporate executives, who don't produce any revenue. Fleming urged him to keep his job in Tokyo because that's where he needed Wetzel, and Fleming didn't want to see a player from his team defect to another unit. But there was a new CEO at Merrill Lynch, and his hand-picked chief financial officer had offered Wetzel a job at headquarters, where he'd have access to the boss and much more influence than he'd had in Tokyo. Not only did Chai encourage him to take the job, but Thain lobbied him as well. Wetzel accepted the offer.

During his first two months working with Thain's team, Wetzel had become popular with his new colleagues. With his dry humor, he talked matter-of-factly about the strange doings he witnessed after hours in his usual haunts around Merrill Lynch headquarters. Thain's team couldn't believe that an executive with Wetzel's expense account actually lived in a small quadrant bordered by the office, the Embassy Suites across the street, the Applebee's around the corner, and SouthWest NY, a casual-dining restaurant. Tutwiler in particular thought he was overstating his middle-class tastes. "Applebee's? No one eats there," she said.

Before going back to Tokyo to begin the process of moving his family to New Jersey, Wetzel squired Tutwiler, Chai, Heaton, Lisa Carnoy, and others to his two favorite haunts. Yes, the manager at the SouthWest NY confirmed that Wetzel ate there every Sunday night, and he showed the group Wetzel's regular table. After dinner, it was over to Applebee's for a nightcap, where the Merrill team could meet, in person, the Russian manager, a woman who often supplied the punchlines to Wetzel's funniest stories.

It was the upside-down world of Paul Wetzel, the only investment banker on Wall Street who dined at Applebee's.

BY MARCH, A CONSENSUS had formed at Merrill Lynch about Nelson Chai: He was a nice guy, but he needed help in his role as CFO. Time and again, people from Merrill's internal finance and audit departments would have to walk Chai through some of the more complicated elements of the firm's financial statements. Gary Carlin, John Fosina, and Dave Moser—the internal compliance guys—helped Chai with his presentations before they were circulated widely at the firm. Heaton and Tosi also spent a significant amount of time with Chai, walking him through various dimensions of the firm's complicated balance sheet.

One habit of Chai's that annoyed Tosi was the CFO's attachment to CNBC. Chai had a large screen TV in his office permanently tuned to the cable news channel, and during meetings he would glance sideways at regular intervals so as not to miss anything of import. Over time, Tosi made a point to park himself directly in front of the TV screen during meetings so that the CFO would have no choice but to focus on what he was saying.

In early March Chai showed Tosi a presentation he was planning to make to Merrill's board of directors, indicating Merrill Lynch on track to record a profit for the first quarter, with a return to profitability through the remainder of the year.

"No way!" Tosi said. "We're going to lose more money." He explained what was happening on the seventh floor, with Merrill's fixed-income positions. Given the harsh climate, every time the firm extricated itself from a sticky debt position through a sale, the transaction generated a loss. It would be virtually impossible, with a regular stream of losses building up each week, for Merrill Lynch to report a profit in the quarter, Tosi said. Chai thanked him for his input, but said he and Thain believed that the worst was over in the capital markets. At a board meeting in London in early March, Chai presented his plan, which indicated a profit for the quarter.

About two weeks later, one of Merrill's primary competitors disintegrated. Bear Stearns, one of the five giant investment banks on Wall Street, collapsed in late March when concerns over whether it had enough cash on hand to continue its operations sparked a run on the bank.

For years, Bear Stearns had funded itself through the sale of overnight commercial paper—short-term loans backed by the firm's assets. But in the early months of 2008, as Bear stumbled to deal with the losses generated by exposure to subprime assets, management tried to quell rumors that the firm was running low on cash.

Alan Schwartz, Bear's newly installed CEO, went on TV in mid-March to declare that the firm had plenty of liquidity, but the statement backfired and led to massive withdrawals by hedge funds that used Bear for prime brokerage services—the clearinghouse for their buying and selling of stocks and other securities. By the end of the month, Bear Stearns had been sold to JPMorgan Chase for the bargain-basement price of $10 a share (a year earlier, the stock had hit $170), in a transaction managed by treasury secretary Hank Paulson, Federal Reserve chairman Ben Bernanke, and New York Fed president Timothy Geithner.

BY APRIL, PAUL WETZEL had returned from Tokyo to begin his new job as head of global strategy when Thain called him to discuss an idea. "Is there a way for UBS and Merrill Lynch to come together?" Thain asked him.

UBS, the large Swiss bank, had just announced a loss of $12 billion for the first quarter, along with plans to raise $15 billion in fresh capital to fill the hole in its balance sheet. Thain wondered whether the combination of UBS and Merrill Lynch could generate enough savings through cost cuts to make both banks healthier.

There were some interesting possibilities in the deal: Merrill's investment banking and wealth management businesses, which were predominantly U.S. operations, would get an enormous boost in Europe from access to the Zurich bank's super-wealthy private client base. In America, UBS also owned the Paine Webber franchise of wealth managers, a second-tier network compared to Merrill's franchise but one that, combined with the thundering herd, could put Merrill miles ahead of competitors at Smith Barney and Morgan Stanley Dean Witter.

Best of all, because UBS's longtime CEO had been ousted just months before, in much the same way Stan O'Neal and Chuck Prince had been fired, Thain would clearly emerge as the CEO of the entire enterprise.

It was important, Thain told Wetzel, for the board of directors to be comfortable with the idea. Thain knew that Stan O'Neal had lost his job not just because he tried to sell to Wachovia, but because he had begun the process without consulting his directors. Thain wanted Wetzel to put together a simple deck—a series of slides—that would show the board how a combined Merrill Lynch–UBS operation would work.

In order to sell the idea, Thain continued, Wetzel should also include a list of other potential banking partners. That way, the directors could see how UBS made much more sense than the other options.

At the New York Stock Exchange, Thain's signature achievements were to convert the not-for-profit organization into a public company through the acquisition of Archipelago, and globalize the NYSE through a merger with Paris-based Euronext.

At Merrill Lynch, he wanted to pull off a similar type of transformation. Fixing the problems on Merrill's balance sheet and changing the culture of the place would take time. But a blockbuster deal that reconfigured the financial services industry would be an immediate achievement.

AFTER ONE MANAGEMENT MEETING, Thain asked Bob McCann if he had a moment to talk. When everyone else had cleared out, Thain told McCann that he wanted him to meet Peter Kraus, a top partner from Goldman Sachs, who would be joining Merrill Lynch in a senior capacity, probably to run investment banking. Kraus had just left Goldman Sachs, where he had been in charge of asset management.

Days later, McCann and Kraus met for breakfast at the firm's executive dining room on the thirty-third floor. Kraus, a bearded man in his early fifties, colorfully dressed, dominated the conversation during the meal, pausing only to take a pair of phone calls. Toward the end of the meal, a staff waiter came in and handed McCann a note, saying John Thain wanted him to walk Kraus down to his office on thirty-two when they were done.

Kraus dismissed the request with a wave of his hand.

"John can wait," he said, picking up his train of thought where it had been interrupted. "You and I will continue to talk."

As McCann walked Kraus down to Thain's office after the meal, he couldn't help but think the reason for the breakfast was so that he could meet his future boss.

• • •

DURING HIS FIRST FEW weeks on the job, Kronthal started working with Donald Quintin, the lead trader on the mortgage desk, to come up with an improved methodology for valuing Merrill's mortgage-based assets, particularly its CDOs. Once that was done, Kronthal's primary job was to find someone—anyone—who might be willing to buy these assets from Merrill Lynch.

In March, he contacted representatives of Lone Star Funds, a private equity firm that specialized in buying distressed real estate assets. Merrill's book of CDOs wasn't a neat box of similar products that could be valued easily. There were more than sixty different deals, each worth hundreds of millions of dollars, within that portfolio. Each deal consisted of a mountain of legal paper defining the underlying assets, the payment terms, and other details. The Lone Star people spent several weeks combing over Merrill's CDOs before telling Kronthal that they would be interested in talking deal, but insisted they would only be bidding pennies on the dollar. Kronthal forwarded the offer to Fleming and Chai, who took it to Thain.

IN EARLY APRIL, THAIN traveled to Japan to meet with clients. While there, he gave an interview to a local media outlet in which he said, "We have plenty of capital going forward, and we don't need to come back into the equity market."

After returning to New York, Thain reiterated his view to his top reports in their regular weekly meeting. The moment Thain left the meeting, near his office on the thirty-second floor, Nelson Chai shrugged and said, "I wish he didn't say that."

Within hours, CNBC reported Chai's quote on its website, suggesting that Thain and his protégé disagreed over whether Merrill would need more capital. For both men, the fact that something said in confidence at an executive committee meeting would be leaked almost immediately increased their mistrust of their Merrill colleagues. Thain suspected that McCann was the leaker, but ultimately it didn't matter: The leak reinforced a notion among Thain's people—Chai, Tutwiler, and May Lee, the newly hired chief of staff—that the old-line Merrill people, particularly McCann and Fleming, were not to be trusted.

On April 17, Merrill reported a $2 billion loss for the first quarter of 2008. During the conference call to discuss the results, Thain emphasized what most investors already knew: The losses resulted from the steady erosion in value of assets already on Merrill's books, exacerbated by the demise of Bear Stearns. Merrill's operations actually performed well in the quarter, but not well enough to make up for the billions of dollars in write-downs associated with those toxic assets.

Thain told analysts in the conference call that "we do not have any plans to raise any additional common equity and Nelson actually agrees with that."

IT DIDN'T TAKE LONG for word to get back to Jeff Kronthal that Thain had no interest in pursuing discussions with Lone Star about the CDO sale, especially at such a lowball price. If Merrill did unload the portfolio, it would have to recognize billions of dollars in losses, necessitating an embarrassing change of direction for Thain, who would be forced to raise more capital.

As of late April, Merrill's share price had rebounded from a temporary swoon brought on by the failure of Bear Stearns a month earlier. The stock traded in the $48 range, exactly the level where Merrill Lynch had sold shares to Temasek when it first raised capital the previous December.

If Merrill Lynch did sell its CDO position at that point, and take a multibillion-dollar loss, its $48 share price would protect it against the reset provision in the Temasek contract. That deal, struck on December 24, stated that if Merrill were to sell more stock within one calendar year of Temasek's investment, at a price below $48, the bank would have to make Temasek whole on the difference between the price it paid and the price subsequently given to later investors.

Given his generally optimistic view on the economy and the markets, Thain had no inkling that the most advantageous time to unload the CDOs, take the losses, and raise more capital was at that moment.

If Merrill's stock ever sank below $48 per share, then Thain would face a hard choice: pay a penalty to Temasek and the other investors who put money into the firm in January or try to hold out until January 2009, by which time the reset clauses would have expired.

PAUL WETZEL CAME UP to Thain's office on the thirty-second floor to show him the package he'd put together concerning a UBS–Merrill Lynch combination. Thain flipped through the deck Wetzel had created and said he was impressed with the breakdown of the Swiss bank's businesses and how they would match up with Merrill's.

"If you pulled this off, John, you'd have to move to Zurich, you know," said Wetzel.

"I'd have no problem living over there," said Thain.

As they stood in the hallway outside Thain's office, the CEO glanced through some of the supporting materials Wetzel had also worked into the presentation, concerning other banks and how they might match up with Merrill Lynch.

"Why is Bank of America on this list?" Thain asked suddenly, pointing to a section of the report concerning the Charlotte bank.

"They fit into any group of banks that we'd consider aligning ourselves with," Wetzel replied.

"No, no. I don't want to talk about them."

"Why? It's only logical that they would be included on this kind of list."

"Paul, if we were to combine with Bank of America, we wouldn't be running it. We wouldn't be in control." The idea of merging with another bank only made sense, apparently, if Thain was going to end up being the CEO.

"I didn't understand that issue to be part of the criteria," Wetzel said.

Thain leaned his head down toward Wetzel, who was a few inches shorter. "Paul, do you want to work for Ken Lewis?"

ON THURSDAY, APRIL 24, Merrill Lynch held its annual shareholder meeting in the third-floor conference room. At the board meeting that took place afterward, on the thirty-third floor, several directors, including John Finnegan, wanted to know how the collapse of Bear Stearns might affect Merrill Lynch.

Merrill's business was fundamentally healthier than Bear Stearns's, Thain said, because the wealth management business managed by the firm's herd of 16,000 financial advisors provided a steady stream of income. That private client business would help Merrill weather any future storms.

"Are you sure that would be enough to protect us?" Finnegan asked.

"Bear's real problem was lack of liquidity," Thain explained, referring to the importance of having excess cash on hand. "They were long on commercial paper and their prime brokerage business held $30 billion, while their cash on hand was only $18 billion."

As always, Thain projected an air of complete confidence. During his first few board meetings, especially at the dinners that kicked off business, Thain would make broad declarations of fact concerning everything from politics to finance, with the air of someone who harbors no doubt of the truth of his words. During what was shaping up to be an interesting presidential campaign, for example, Thain remarked several times on the self-evident correctness of Republican positions, interspersed with criticism of Senator Hillary Clinton, then a candidate for the Democratic nomination. It was clear he wasn't soliciting input in order to have a discussion about politics. Nor had he considered whether any board members were Clinton supporters.

ABOUT A WEEK LATER, at a meeting with his top executives, Thain mentioned that some senior people were about to join the firm, former Goldman Sachs colleagues Tom Montag and Peter Kraus. McCann moved quickly.

"John, we've resolved all the issues surrounding investment banking," said McCann. "What are you thinking of hiring Peter Kraus for?"

Thain avoided direct eye contact with McCann, and said that Kraus could be helpful to him in a variety of ways.

. . .

LUNCH WASN'T SCHEDULED UNTIL noon, but Paul Wetzel invited Nelson Chai down to the twenty-second floor a little early, at 11:45, to tell him about his expectations for the meeting.

Having commuted back and forth from Tokyo for two months, Wetzel was now in charge of forty-five people in the strategy department, and ready to go. Wetzel had invited Chai down so he could meet the strategy team face-to-face. It would be a good morale boost for the team, Wetzel explained, if Chai himself would come down and have sandwiches with everyone.

After a few minutes of discussion, Wetzel began to escort Chai out of his office toward the conference room where lunch with his team was waiting.

"Hold on a minute, Paul," said Chai hesitantly. "I'm no longer going to be your boss."

"What do you mean? I just moved back."

"Eric likes the idea of you doing strategy, it's a perfect fit. John likes you too, you're perfect."

"So, what are you telling me?"

"Peter Kraus is coming in."

"What's he going to do?" asked Wetzel.

"It's not entirely clear yet. John would like him to do this."

"I don't understand."

Chai explained that Thain needed to find a temporary place for Kraus in the organization, and that a decision had been made to install the ex-Goldman executive as head of strategic planning for Merrill Lynch. That was the title and position that Chai and Thain had talked Wetzel into taking just two months earlier, and Wetzel had begun the process of uprooting his family after accepting the job. Now Thain had given the job to one of his Goldman buddies and Wetzel's new role would be to work for Kraus.

"Kraus will be doing something else eventually, but it's going to take some time," Chai said. "The best way to get Kraus into this place is for you to work for him. You have to trust John on this."

"You've got to be kidding me!"

Chai and Wetzel then went through the meaningless exercise of having sandwiches with the staff of the strategy and business development department.

About a week later, when Wetzel was back in Tokyo, he received a call from Thain, who was in Boston.

"Paul, nothing has changed," Thain assured him. "You're going to be doing the same stuff, and dealing directly with me. I'm bringing Peter in, but it's not really to do strategy and business development. There's no way I'm paying him what I'm paying him just to run that!"

Wetzel wasn't sure which stung worse: the demotion or the implied put-down.

BECAUSE TOM MONTAG WAS going to be one of the top five Merrill Lynch executives when he joined the firm later that year, his compensation package was disclosed on May 2 with the SEC. According to the terms of his contract, Montag would receive an annual salary of $600,000, in line with what other senior executives at the firm received. On top of that, he was *guaranteed* a bonus of $39.4 million for 2008, no matter what his performance turned out to be.

As Merrill's incoming head of strategy, Peter Kraus would not be in the top tier of executive officers and therefore his compensation did not have to be disclosed. But word soon seeped out that his salary and bonus were almost as high: He would also receive a salary of $600,000, and his guaranteed bonus for 2008 would be $29.4 million, bringing him up to $30 million. On Wall Street, compensation is correlated closely with how much revenue someone produces for his firm. If Montag excelled in his job, he could help generate billions of dollars in trading revenues for Merrill Lynch. The head of strategic planning, however, brings in no revenues: He's an on-staff management consultant. And yet Thain was willing to pay Kraus $30 million for the privilege of receiving his advice.

In December and January, Thain had dazzled the Merrill Lynch staff and board of directors with his ability to pick up the phone, call the heads of sovereign wealth funds in Singapore, Korea, and Kuwait, and convince them to place a multibillion-dollar wager on *him*, John Thain, and his ability to turn around Merrill Lynch.

But back in New York, on Wall Street, in Thain's own neighborhood, the people who knew him best—his friends from Goldman Sachs—weren't taking any such risks. Leadership on Wall Street is sometimes measured by how much pull an executive has with his peers. When a charismatic leader departs from one bank and lands at another, a trail of people from that leader's senior team usually follows. In Thain's case, the people who followed him to Merrill Lynch were Tutwiler and Chai, whose experience on Wall Street and salaries were limited. The heavy hitters—Montag and Kraus—only followed when Thain removed all economic risk from the equation.

Both men had been asked to leave Goldman Sachs, not for performance-related reasons, but because the firm's continuous drive to develop young talent meant that a steady stream of senior executives, usually in their early fifties, were amicably shown the door each year. The pay level at Goldman Sachs is so high—top executives can reap tens of millions of dollars each year—that senior partners who leave at age fifty usually don't have to keep working on Wall Street.

Because Montag and Kraus were going to work for a competitor, however, they would forfeit the restricted Goldman Sachs stock they had accumulated in their last three years at the firm. Merrill Lynch would have to make them whole on the value of the Goldman shares they were leaving behind. In Montag's case, the total was about $84 million, while for Kraus, it was approximately $49 million, most of which would be paid out in Merrill stock.

IN HER FIRST MONTH on the job, May Lee scheduled appointments with most of John Thain's direct reports, as well as some other senior people who interacted with Thain on a regular basis.

In every meeting, Lee's message was the same: Her job was to act as John's eyes and ears, sitting in on meetings below the top management level, so she could keep her boss posted about what was happening one or two rungs down in the organization. Earnest and direct, Lee explained to people that her role was "to help."

Most Merrill Lynch executives, having survived the Machiavellian intrigue of the O'Neal regime, were wary of Lee and interacted with her cautiously. Almost alone among the firm's top executives, Bob McCann embraced her. His relationship with Thain was almost nonexistent, so Lee provided him a form of access to the corner office.

The worst experience Lee had in her first month was with the one person most important to her job: Greg Fleming. Throughout April, she scheduled several meetings with the firm's president, whose office was just down the hall, and every time, his secretary would cancel just ten or twenty minutes beforehand, saying "something had just come up." The first time, she understood, and also the second time. But the third, fourth, and fifth cancellations convinced her that Fleming had no interest in ever sitting down for a meeting.

BY LATE MAY, AFTER being on the job for almost six months, the near universal popularity that Thain enjoyed at Merrill Lynch started to ebb, at least among the business executives who interacted with him on a regular basis.

His deliberative approach to the job, which involved taking in information from all sides and then going off to weigh his options at greater length, frustrated many of his Merrill Lynch subordinates. Thain's general view that the economy had reached a low point early in the year and was poised for a rebound had yet to play out.

If the larger economy had stopped contracting and started growing again, Thain's laissez-faire approach to managing Merrill Lynch would be working. The private client business and the investment bank were churning out solid revenues, and even the sales and trading operations were performing reasonably well. But as long as some of the worst assets sat on Merrill's balance sheet, deteriorating in value because the housing market continued to decline, massive losses would wipe out the firm's earnings every quarter.

In April, Thain had rejected out of hand Lone Star's bottom-fishing offer to talk about the CDO portfolio. But by May, Thain changed his mind and decided to sell the toxic assets.

Since the day Thain joined Merrill Lynch the previous December, Fleming, Heaton, Kronthal, and Tosi had encouraged him to sell the CDOs as soon as possible, no matter what the losses were. In recent months, even Nelson Chai joined the effort. But Thain paid no mind. It wasn't until April, when Thain was finalizing the agreements to bring Montag and Kraus on board, that the CEO's view changed. That was because Montag and Kraus insisted, as a final condition of their agreements to join Merrill Lynch, that Thain clean up the balance sheet and sell the CDOs before they showed up for work. Such was the power of Goldman Sachs. When Kronthal, Fleming, Heaton, Tosi, and Chai recommended the sale of the CDOs, Thain took their opinions under advisement. But once Montag and Kraus told him to sell the CDOs, Thain got serious about it.

Now that he was on board with the idea of selling the CDOs, even at a steep loss, Thain would have to raise more capital. He could do that by returning to the equity markets, as he had done in December and January. There were also assets that Merrill Lynch could sell, which could generate billions of dollars in ready cash. The firm owned a 20 percent stake in Bloomberg, the financial information system and news service. Preliminary discussions to sell that stake in late 2007, which Thain halted upon his arrival, had centered around a price tag of about $5 billion. There was also Merrill's 49 percent stake in BlackRock, Larry Fink's asset management business, which was also worth billions.

Fleming opposed selling Merrill's stake in BlackRock, on the grounds, he said, that it meshed well with Merrill's own wealth management business and provided a steady stream of profits. But Fleming's view on the subject was peripheral. Peter Kraus had recommended selling the BlackRock stake, and Thain adopted Kraus's view.

ON MAY 21, AN INVESTOR named David Einhorn gave a speech at a conference in New York in which he challenged the accuracy of the values that Lehman Brothers had placed on its own assets. Einhorn was not just any investor, but a short seller, someone who looks for companies that are overvalued in the market and bets against them, borrowing shares at current prices and promising to sell those shares at a future date.

Across corporate America, short sellers are generally viewed as parasitic creatures who target healthy companies with "dirty tricks" political campaigns designed to frighten investors into selling shares, causing the target company's stock price to decline and the short seller's profits to soar.

While some short sellers do engage in unscrupulous practices, others have exposed companies that cooked their books and fooled investors. It was Jim Chanos, a short seller, who first called attention to questionable accounting practices at Enron in 2001. In 2000, after studying Enron's financial statements closely, Chanos concluded that the Houston energy company's profits were a mirage and that its stock price, which had hit $90 a share, was unsustainably high. Over several months, he accumulated a large "short" position in the stock. When some of the company's dubious accounting practices came to light in October 2001, investors panicked and sold the stock all the way down to one dollar. The company filed for bankruptcy protection in December 2001 and its shareholders were wiped out, but Chanos and other short sellers made a fortune.

Now Einhorn was accusing Lehman of similar gimmickry in the way it marked its illiquid assets. Einhorn had correctly diagnosed problems at other companies in the past, so his latest volley caused Lehman's share price to plunge. The issues he raised in his speech, and the specificity of his accusations, led investors to question the asset values at other Wall Street banks as well.

Merrill Lynch's share price, which had been at $52 in early May, dropped to $43 by the end of the month. At that level, any attempt to go to the capital markets to raise new funds would require a "make-good" payment to Temasek and other recent investors.

Over the years, ever since Kraus helped him put together the NYSE's acquisition of Archipelago, Thain had come to rely on his Goldman Sachs friend for advice on a variety of topics. Now that Kraus's hiring had been announced, Thain came to depend on him ever more heavily. Kraus's counsel to Thain was, by necessity, held closely between the two men, since the Goldman executive was technically on "garden leave" through August and thus barred from working for a competitor. During this period, Goldman Sachs still paid Kraus's salary. Nevertheless, Thain consulted with him almost daily on questions of strategic significance, like whether to sell the BlackRock stake. On that matter, Kraus was firm: Thain should sell it.

Up until this point, Fleming deferred to Thain in matters on which they disagreed. As president of Merrill Lynch, he viewed his role as providing counsel, if asked for by Thain, and in executing the CEO's plans for the firm. But on the matter of BlackRock, Fleming was unusually direct with his boss, arguing that the asset management giant was of enormous strategic importance to Merrill Lynch and should not be sold. In February 2006, Merrill had exchanged its own asset management business—which was constrained in its growth by being part of an investment bank—for 49 percent of a company that, after the transaction, was worth $28 billion. By June 2008, BlackRock's market capitalization had grown to $42 billion.

Thain recommended that Kraus and Fleming meet for lunch.

The two met off-site, and Kraus spent the entire lunch talking about his vision for Merrill Lynch, where he felt it could grow and what needed to be done to fix things. Kraus also told Fleming that holding on to BlackRock simply didn't make sense in the long run for Merrill, and that John Thain's mission was to fix Merrill Lynch for the long run.

For an outsider to speak with such certainty about what Merrill's problems were and what it should be doing to grow struck Fleming as arrogant. Conversely, Kraus came away from the meeting less than impressed with the Merrill Lynch president.

Thain sided with Kraus and had his finance team begin the process of negotiating the sale of Merrill Lynch's position in BlackRock.

THROUGHOUT THE SECOND QUARTER, business picked up for Merrill and across Wall Street. The collapse of Bear Stearns, which had raised the prospect of an industry-wide meltdown, had caused surprisingly few ripples. Investors seemed to like the changes that Thain was bringing to Merrill Lynch.

At Lehman Brothers, it was a different story. Lehman had avoided the massive write-downs that plagued Citigroup, Merrill, and even Morgan Stanley in the fourth quarter of 2007, but David Einhorn's recent criticism had led to growing skepticism about the value of the assets on Lehman's books.

Lehman executives fought back against Einhorn, maintaining that their marks were accurate, and pointing out that short sellers such as Einhorn had a financial incentive to talk down stock prices, since they stood to benefit the most.

On June 9, the argument was settled in Einhorn's favor when Lehman announced a surprise loss of $2.8 billion for the quarter. In response, Lehman CEO Richard Fuld demoted his longtime lieutenant, Joe Gregory, and his newly installed CFO, Erin Callan.

Lehman's losses gave a boost to the short sellers who had bet against the stock, and encouraged more doubters to pile on. Lehman's shares were now under enormous pressure, spurring credit rating agencies to review the bank's status. At Merrill Lynch, Thain and his team also knew that Lehman's problems would not be contained, but threatened to spill over onto them.

ON JUNE 11, two days after the Lehman losses were announced, Thain spoke to investors on a conference call hosted by Deutsche Bank analyst Mike Mayo. Mayo asked Thain whether, under certain circumstances, he would reconsider his position against selling the firm's stakes in BlackRock and Bloomberg.

Thain explained that in late 2007, he looked at various fundraising options, including the sale of Merrill's stakes in those entities. "And if we were to raise more capital, we would continue that process of evaluating what alternatives we had and what made the most sense for us to do from a capital efficiency point of view."

Thain's admission that Merrill was looking at ways to raise

money—after insisting for months that the firm's capital position was fine—sparked a sell-off of shares in Merrill Lynch.

Merrill's shares declined in part because Thain had been so adamant that the firm's capital position was fine. Investors also worried that if Merrill Lynch sold its stake in BlackRock—which provided a steady stream of income—the firm might be exposed to a downgrade from the big credit-ratings agencies, Moody's and Standard & Poor's. Any downgrade would make it much more expensive for Merrill to borrow money.

As for BlackRock, the possibility that the company's biggest shareholder would unload its 49 percent stake meant that a huge parcel of locked-up stock would be dumped on the market, depressing the value of the shares currently in circulation. Larry Fink, BlackRock's CEO, was outraged when he heard what Thain had said.

Having lost out to Thain as a candidate for the top job at Merrill Lynch, Fink wasn't fond of his rival. But as a member of the search team that had recommended Thain for the top job at the NYSE a few years earlier, Fink had held Thain's quantitative skills in high regard.

Now, with Thain blurting out the possibility of Merrill selling its stake in BlackRock, even while negotiations to find a buyer were quietly under way, Fink was appalled at what he perceived to be the man's lack of judgment, which was crushing him in the market.

On June 10, the day before Thain's remarks, BlackRock stock had been trading at $212 per share. A week earlier, it had been at $223. Over the next several weeks, BlackRock shares swooned below $170. The drop not only hurt Fink's shareholders, but it eliminated close to $3 billion in value that Merrill's treasury team calculated the firm could capture through a successful sale. Instead, by the end of the month, with BlackRock's depressed price, it wasn't worth it for Merrill to consider the sale.

Bloomberg, however, was a different story. Thain and Fleming agreed that Merrill Lynch should begin the process of selling the company's 20 percent stake in the financial information media company, preferably back to its founder, New York City mayor Michael Bloomberg.

To that end, Thain met the mayor for breakfast in Midtown Manhattan. As mayor, Bloomberg had recused himself from the business operations of Bloomberg L.P. But as its founder and principal owner, the decision as to whether the company would want to buy back the Merrill Lynch stake was entirely up to him. At the end of the breakfast, Mayor Bloomberg told Thain that when Merrill Lynch wanted to move forward with the transaction, his advisor at Quadrangle Group, Steve Rattner, would be ready to negotiate.

AT SOME POINT IN MAY, hoping to get a better offer for its CDO portfolio than what Lone Star had been prepared to put forth, Thain got in touch with Steve Mnuchin, a former Goldman Sachs colleague who ran Dune Capital, a firm that specialized in buying distressed assets.

It might seem strange that any investor would even consider buying Merrill's toxic assets. But the history of the financial services industry in the U.S. has shown that fortunes can be made by investors willing to buy banks and degraded properties on the cheap.

The reason is simple: Markets are cyclical, and very few financial products ever go all the way to zero in value. The only question is whether an investor thinks the value of a security has hit bottom, and is about to turn upwards, or whether the asset is still overpriced.

In the 1990s, gutsy investors who purchased the remains of failed savings and loans reaped financial windfalls when the U.S. banking industry bounced back to robust health. That lesson was not lost on the market in 2008. It was just that the severity of the credit crunch and the collapse of Bear Stearns suggested that this downdraft might be more severe than others in recent memory.

Traders and investors are always on the lookout for bargains in the financial markets. They're also wary of trying to "catch a falling knife" and miscalculating on when a stock or other type of asset will turn around.

CHAPTER 9

TERMINATED WITH
PREJUDICE

AT BANK OF AMERICA, Brian Moynihan embodied all the attributes
of the old NCNB culture: He was completely dedicated to the Charlotte
bank, a tireless worker, and he executed every order he received from on
high. He had never served in the armed forces, but when it came to his
career at BofA, Moynihan was as loyal and dedicated as a Marine.

Moynihan had been a senior executive at Fleet Financial when the
Boston bank was acquired by BofA in 2004. At the time of that acquisition, community leaders in Massachusetts complained about the sale
of the region's prized bank to an out-of-town organization, and the loss
of jobs that would ensue. In order to appease local concerns, BofA chief
Ken Lewis structured the deal in such a way that Chad Gifford, who had
been CEO of Fleet, would be chairman of Bank of America and retain an
influential role in doling out philanthropic grants in New England. BofA
also agreed to keep a significant part of Fleet's workforce in place at its
Boston headquarters.

Another critic of the Fleet sale to BofA was Barney Frank, the Massachusetts congressman who was the ranking Democrat on the House Financial Services committee. Lewis hated dealing with Washington and with Congress. When Lewis and Steele Alphin, his top advisor, learned that Fleet's marketing and public relations team, headed by Anne Finucane, had longstanding ties to Frank and other figures on Capitol Hill, they decided to keep that team in place. Finucane became president of the bank's northeast operations.

After the deal closed, a number of senior Fleet executives, starting with Eugene McQuade, who became president, joined BofA's management structure. But one by one, each senior Fleet executive left. McQuade reached an agreement to commute back and forth between his home in Rhode Island and Charlotte, but Lewis shut him out of any significant management discussions at headquarters. Then, after consulting with Alphin, who didn't like exceptions being made for selected individuals, Lewis told McQuade that he could no longer commute. The CEO wanted him to move to Charlotte. McQuade promised to think about it over the coming months, but Alphin peppered him with questions about when he was moving to Charlotte and McQuade finally gave up and tendered his resignation.

Over time, other senior Fleet executives washed out of the organization. By 2007, the only top Fleet people who retained significant roles at the Charlotte bank were Moynihan, president of the bank's global wealth and investment management business, and Finucane.

Despite his formidable work ethic and his embrace of the Charlotte culture, Moynihan had difficulty cracking the inner circle of the organization. The innermost core of power at BofA consisted of Lewis and Alphin, who were bound together at an atomic level. Lewis, as the CEO, made all the decisions, but Alphin, like an electron furiously spinning around a proton, balanced Lewis and defined his power.

The next layer of closeness consisted of Amy Brinkley, the chief risk officer, and Greg Curl, head of strategy. Brinkley, a graduate of the University of North Carolina at Chapel Hill, was a close friend of Alphin and

Lewis. A decade younger than the CEO, she was perceived as Lewis's heir apparent. Curl, who was nearly Lewis's age, joined BofA in the 1990s, when NationsBank, under Hugh McColl, acquired Boatmen's Bank of St. Louis. McColl had plugged Curl directly in to his management structure and the newcomer fit.

Then there was Joe Price, the CFO who had been promoted from the treasurer's position when Al de Molina quit in a huff in December 2006. Unlike de Molina, a hot-tempered executive who had developed his own following among investors and analysts and who dared to challenge Lewis over some issues, Price could be relied upon to follow orders.

Two other members of Lewis's management team, Barbara Desoer and Liam McGee, had joined the organization from the old San Francisco–based Bank of America in 1998. McGee headed BofA's consumer banking operations, a highly visible perch at the biggest retail bank in the U.S., while Desoer was chief technology and operations officer. Both were well-regarded professionals, but neither could be described as a true Charlotte insider.

Moynihan's orbit was even further away from the core. He still lived in Boston, where his wife was raising a young family. Starting in October 2007, when he replaced Gene Taylor as head of the company's investment bank, Moynihan began commuting to New York.

Taylor had been installed as chief of the investment bank in 2005 with a mandate to grow the business. Moynihan's brief was just the opposite. Lewis considered Bank of America to be a pristine, well-managed business. The losses generated at the investment bank in 2007 disgusted him and only served to confirm his negative view of investment bankers and traders as self-important cowboys who took wild risks with the bank's hard-earned money. Lewis told Moynihan and Curl to conduct a "strategic review" of the investment bank to determine where its costs could be pared back.

Curl and Moynihan considered the various operations within BofA Securities. Like most investment banks, it had an advisory business that helped companies with mergers and acquisitions. There was also a sales and trading business, which generated most of the investment bank's revenue. But just as had been the case at Merrill Lynch, the sales and trading desk invested in CDOs and other subprime-related assets that tanked in value throughout 2007, causing the losses at the investment bank.

In the end, Curl and Moynihan ignored the CDOs that continued to fester on the bank's balance sheet and decided to pursue quicker, easier fixes for the bank's problems: They would fire people and sell off parts of the business. In general, that's how BofA dealt with most of its issues, by finding the quickest, near-term solution and lunging in that direction. Bank of America was not an organization that had the patience for deep, strategic thinking. It was an opportunistic company that preferred action of any kind to inaction.

In January 2008, following the strategic review, Moynihan announced a layoff of 650 people, including some of the stars in the research department, since the analysts didn't bring in any revenues directly. Moynihan also announced the bank's intention to sell the prime brokerage unit, which catered primarily to hedge funds.

Of the seventy-two analysts in BofA Securities's research department, Moynihan targeted about fifteen for dismissal, including the top researchers in important segments such as energy, banking, and media. They were given two weeks' notice, with a termination date of February 13, which sparked outrage at the unit. Bonuses for 2007 would only be paid out to employees who were still with BofA on Febuary 14, so the timing of the mass firing seemed designed to save some $20 million in bonus payments on top of base salaries.

Executives who worked in BofA's equities trading business implored Moynihan not to fire the analysts, because the research was a significant reason why BofA's clients did business with the bank. But the strategic review put together by Curl and Moynihan didn't account for such gray areas, so the layoffs were executed according to schedule.

As for the proposed sale of the prime brokerage unit, competitors were puzzled but intrigued. In February, JPMorgan Chase emerged as the most serious bidder for the BofA unit, which employed more than three hundred and generated $400 million in revenues each year. The bank—headed by CEO Jamie Dimon—sent a team of nearly sixty over to BofA's offices to comb through the books of the operation. In preliminary discussions about price, Dimon's team indicated that they might be willing to pay $1 billion.

But the proposed sale got off track in late March, when Bear Stearns—which had its own substantial prime brokerage business—tottered on the edge of bankruptcy. Over a weekend, Dimon swooped in, and with the support of federal regulators bought the failing investment bank. Originally, he offered $2 a share, but concerned that Bear's shareholders might reject the offer, Dimon eventually raised the bid to $10, which was accepted. As a result of that deal, Dimon received two valuable assets—Bear Stearns's new Manhattan office building, just across the street from JPMorgan Chase's own headquarters, and Bear's prime brokerage operations, one of the best on Wall Street. Following the Bear Stearns windfall, JPMorgan Chase dropped out of the bidding for BofA's prime brokerage business.

Running a prime brokerage business for hedge funds on Wall Street is like running a luxury hotel for business travelers. The prime broker executes trades and handles a wide variety of logistical issues for the hedge funds, while charging an exorbitant fee for each little service. Because prime brokers also hold a large chunk of collateral from the hedge funds, they can shut down any client that falls behind on payments. Once a prime broker establishes a critical mass with hedge fund clients, the business throws off a regular stream of low-risk revenues.

Savvy hedge fund managers took note of what was happening: Dimon—considered one of the sharpest bankers of his generation—was building up his prime brokerage operation, while Bank of America CEO Ken Lewis was trying to exit the business. In spite of his position at the top of the nation's largest bank, Lewis seemed to have no understanding of the prime brokerage business, likening the activity to "going out on the interstate to pick up a nickel."

Following the sale of Bear Stearns to JPMorgan Chase, Moynihan's attempts to sell BofA's prime brokerage business floundered. Moynihan himself got distracted by the blowback from his earlier decision to fire the best-paid research analysts. Several clients complained and by May, Moynihan had to go out and hire new researchers to replace the senior people he'd let go. Because of concerns over whether BofA was committed to its research group, Moynihan had to pay out even more to rebuild the unit than the savings generated by the firings early in the year.

Embarrassed by the retreat with the research group, Moynihan doubled his efforts to get rid of the prime brokerage unit, at any cost. Given the collapse of Bear Stearns, BofA's prime brokerage business could have benefited from a "flight to quality," the perception among hedge funds that it would be better to do business through a large commercial bank than a riskier investment bank. But Moynihan remained adamant about executing the plan to sell the business or, if a buyer couldn't be found, to shut it down and lay everyone off.

Several foreign banks kicked the tires of the operation, but only BNP Paribas, a French bank, seemed serious. However, BNP moved slowly, and Moynihan wanted the issue resolved before the second quarter ended in late June. He decided to shut the business down rather than continue the quest for a buyer, forfeiting any premium from a possible sale.

On June 4, BofA's HR apparatus swung into high gear in preparation for the shutdown of the bank's $400 million prime brokerage business and the mass firing of hundreds of employees. An announcement was crafted in Charlotte with help from the legal, PR and corporate planning teams: "In January, after completing a strategic review of global corporate and investment banking, we announced we would exit the prime brokerage business. After pursuing a sale process with multiple bidders, we do not believe we can find a buyer prepared to offer an appropriate value and structure for Bank of America and its clients. We will instead reshape the prime brokerage unit to meet our client, balance sheet, and risk objectives."

Hours before the announcement went out, Ciaran O'Kelly, the head of BofA's global equities unit, asked Moynihan for permission to offer the prime brokerage unit one last time to BNP or other possible bidders. Since BofA was going to shut the business down anyway, the transfer of the unit to a competitor would prove less disruptive to clients and would save a lot of jobs, he argued. Moynihan gave him permission for one more try and O'Kelly convinced BNP Paribas to take over the business. Plans for the mass firing were halted and a week later, BofA announced that BNP had acquired its business. The Charlotte bank would net several hundred million dollars if the unit hit certain performance targets.

JUNE 10 WAS A big day at BofA's New York investment bank. Not only was the sale of the prime brokerage business announced, but Ken Lewis would make his first official visit to the bank's new building at One Bryant Park. BofA's new building, a striking, beveled structure at the corner of 42nd Street and Avenue of the Americas, had won several awards for its distinctive architecture and as being the most environmentally friendly building in Manhattan. It relied on a "gray water" system to capture and reuse all rain and wastewater, maximized the effect of solar heating with floor-to-ceiling windows, and was constructed mostly of recycled materials.

For many bank CEOs, a visit to an office or a trading floor is part of a daily routine. Dimon, the CEO of JPMorgan Chase, loved to roam the floors of his bank, sitting in on meetings of subordinates, and mixing it up with employees. Part of Dimon's game was to make sure he still had a feel for what was going on within his organization, but direct contact with the CEO also provided a morale boost to employees at all levels, who could not help but conclude that the boss actually cared about them.

After seven years in the CEO job, Lewis had gone in a different direction. He had risen to the top of BofA because he was an excellent manager of consumer banking operations, not because he was an inspirational leader. With his elevation to the top job in 2001, he became less involved in the day-to-day running of the organization, ceding much of that responsibility to his management team and Alphin's HR department.

Because his interactions with regular employees were so constricted, it was of paramount importance for Lewis to be perceived as a flawless leader whenever he dealt with the bank's "associates." The stakes were even higher for his visit to New York, where he would show up on the trading floor to speak. Lewis understood BofA's retail banking system and its commercial lending business. Those were the areas in which he had worked. That business was in his veins. But he had little understanding of his bank's capital markets business beyond the impression that it was like playing with fire—sooner or later, you'd get burned. After his remarks the previous fall, about having "had all the fun" he could stand with investment banking, Lewis's lieutenants in Charlotte had lorded it over the investment bank employees in New York, letting everyone know they were suspect, and that Charlotte was running out of patience with the unit. Moynihan's actions reinforced those rough sentiments: The firing of the bank's top analysts and the near shutdown of its prime brokerage business sent a message that the entire investment bank was on thin ice.

And so, when Lewis decided to visit the trading floor at his bank's new building in New York, the HR people in Charlotte and the public relations people in New York worked themselves into a frenzy to make sure every move was choreographed and every statement was scripted. Lewis's advance team selected various leaders on the floor—people who could be relied upon—and gave them specific questions that they were to ask Lewis during the "spontaneous" question-and-answer session that followed his remarks. The CEO's scripted answers guaranteed that the whole production would come off as planned.

Prior to Lewis's arrival, a podium was set up on the floor, so that Lewis—who is of average height—would be above everyone in the audience. When the chief executive finally arrived, an occurrence presaged by the gaggle of handlers who preceded him, the energy of the room came to a halt.

Lewis shook a few hands, ascended the podium, and delivered a short speech, extolling the achievements of everyone in the room and claiming the bank was on pace to earn "record revenues" that year. For the traders in the room, Lewis's discomfort was apparent—he kept using the wrong words when referring to what they did. Most notably, Lewis flubbed one reference to his audience, praising their work on "rates," a reference to interest rates, which were traded on a different floor. Although the gaffe was minor, it caused several members of Lewis's PR team to blanch, and raised the possibility that one of them might be blamed for the imperfection. Following Lewis's speech, on cue, a few traders asked the questions that had been handed to them, and Lewis recited the appropriate responses.

At the end of the question-and-answer session, Lewis and his entourage left the trading floor and business returned to normal.

CHAPTER 10

FIRESALE

ON THE EVENING OF Friday, June 27, Greg Fleming and his wife flew with their three children from New York to Naples, Italy, and then made their way Saturday to a house they had rented for two weeks in the town of Massa Lubrense. The town is about thirty miles south of Naples, perched on a steep hillside at the westernmost tip of the Amalfi coast, within walking distance of the most beautiful beaches and picturesque harbors in Italy. On a previous visit, Fleming and his wife, Melissa, had become enchanted with the area, and they returned each year to the same house, with a porch overlooking the azure waters of the Mediterranean and the island of Capri.

After driving from the airport on Saturday and reorienting themselves on Sunday, the family spent a full day Monday relaxing and basking in the sun. As midnight approached, the children lay asleep and Melissa prepared for bed. Her husband sat out on the porch, looking out at the sea and letting his mind drift, like the boats that floated along the waters each day. He was exhausted, not by two days of frolicking on the

Amalfi coast, but from the previous eleven months of stress at his job, from which there had been no vacation.

One year earlier, Merrill Lynch closed the books on the second quarter of 2007, clocking an impressive $2 billion in earnings. He, Greg Fleming, the son of schoolteachers, from the village of Hopewell Junction, New York, had just been promoted to co-president at the youthful age of forty-four. If he played his cards right, he could emerge as chief executive officer of Merrill Lynch when Stan O'Neal stepped down in a few years. Life was good.

That was now a remote memory, from a distant era, before Merrill Lynch's year from hell. Only now, eleven months later, did Fleming feel comfortable taking his wife and family on an overdue and extended vacation. It was just last August that he was sitting in this very spot, overlooking Capri at the start of a two-week vacation, when the original discovery of losses on Merrill's own CDO portfolio forced him to uproot his family and fly back to New York to sign off on a letter prepared by Fakahany to Merrill's board of directors.

It seemed like a lot longer than eleven months ago, he thought, and the midnight breeze felt wonderful.

The phone rang.

"Hi, Greg. . . . It's Eric." Heaton, the treasurer, was on the line. It was just after 6:00 p.m. in New York. "Sorry to call so late."

Fleming had no idea why Heaton was calling, except that something had to be wrong.

"We have the revised estimates for the quarter."

"This better be good," growled Fleming. "It's midnight, and we just got here."

"We've known each other a long time," said Heaton. "I wouldn't have called unless it was important."

"What is it?"

"The preliminary numbers are a lot worse than what we expected. The losses have increased, by somewhere between $2 billion and $4 billion."

Fleming was incredulous. When he left New York the previous Friday, all signs indicated a decent quarter, with a manageable loss. This would look far worse than Lehman's losses.

"How is that possible?"

Heaton explained that the marks on some of Merrill's assets, which seemed fine the week before, had dropped yet again. The losses at Lehman spooked the market in late June, slowing down trading in a wide variety of debt products, driving the marks on Merrill's assets—especially the CDOs—down even further than the conservative estimates that Heaton's group had been able to capture the week before.

"Does Thain know about this?"

"No," said Heaton.

As treasurer, Heaton reported directly to Nelson Chai, the CFO, who in turn reported to Thain. By calling Fleming directly, Heaton was short-circuiting that process, and Fleming knew why.

The magnitude of Merrill's new losses, when announced July 17, meant the investment bank would have to raise billions of dollars, quickly. If the bank didn't have the money to fill the hole by then, investors would think Merrill was in worse shape than Lehman Brothers.

After seven months of working for Thain, Heaton and Fleming knew that the CEO did not arrive at decisions quickly, or even firmly. If they turned the problem over to Nelson Chai, there was no guarantee that the CFO would be able to move Thain quickly enough to hit the July 17 deadline.

"We have limited time, and I know you'll get it moving," said Heaton.

"I'll take care of it," said Fleming, in a tone halfway between disgust and resignation.

Fleming could no longer see the twinkling lights of Capri. He took a deep breath and called Thain, who was at his vacation home not far from Saranac Lake in the Adirondacks.

His boss sounded like he was in high spirits.

"How are you, Greg? Hey, what time is it over there?" And then a short pause. "Why are you calling?"

"I'm hearing that the loss is going to be much larger than you and I were told," said Fleming carefully. "It could be anywhere from $2 billion to $4 billion worse than what we heard last week."

"How is that possible?" asked Thain, his lighthearted tone now gone.

"I don't know. I'm not close to it. But it sounds like this is where it's going. You should call Nelson."

There was a pause as Thain absorbed the news.

"If this is the case," Fleming continued, "we're going to have to accelerate things."

"Other than letting me know, what do you want?" demanded Thain, as the purpose of the call dawned on him.

"I want to accelerate the process of selling the Bloomberg stake right now."

Thain had already put the Bloomberg sale in motion following his breakfast with the New York City mayor. But he wanted the best possible price, and that would only happen if Merrill Lynch could get several bidders to compete against each other.

"We should test the market," Thain said, floating the idea that Merrill could find an outside buyer willing to buy the 20 percent stake in Bloomberg L.P.

"No, we can't do that," said Fleming. "The mayor's not going to put up with that kind of move."

Thain pressed his point, insisting that only by testing the market could Merrill get the best possible price.

"There is no market to test," Fleming said, exasperation in his voice. Bloomberg was a privately held company, with no market capitalization, and no significant chunks of ownership changing hands. "Besides, the mayor has the right of first refusal. It's part of our agreement with him."

Thain remained unconvinced.

Fleming tried another tack. They weren't dealing with some private equity hustlers who could be fooled with a quick fake or a hidden-ball trick. "This is Michael Bloomberg. He is a serious and accomplished man," he told Thain. "We have to do this straight up."

Thain agreed.

Then it was on to the next contentious issue, BlackRock. Thain still wanted to sell Merrill Lynch's 49 percent stake in the asset management company. Fleming countered with the arguments he'd used before: Selling BlackRock would hurt Merrill's earnings, jeopardize its credit rating, and, given the decline in BlackRock's share price in recent weeks, result in much smaller gain than the stake was potentially worth. After another extended back-and-forth, Thain relented.

Finally, Fleming suggested, it might be a good time to sell a stake in Financial Data Services, a processing business catering to high net worth individuals housed within Merrill's wealth management unit. Todd Kaplan had brought FDS to Fleming's attention in April, when the Merrill Lynch president was brainstorming for ideas on how to raise capital without selling more shares.

Among other things, FDS marketed a software product that allowed big-ticket investors to retrieve historical prices of all kinds of stocks, making it easier to place a value on their portfolio. It was not a glamorous business, but it was extremely useful for Merrill's well-heeled clients, and Fleming figured he could get several billion dollars from selling a stake in it.

Thain paused. "Let me sleep on it," he said before hanging up.

Not for the first time, it occurred to Fleming that Thain was putting off a difficult decision until he could discuss it with his Svengali, Peter Kraus, who was still on the Goldman Sachs payroll and wouldn't be joining Merrill Lynch for two months.

It was now 1:30 in the morning, local time. Fleming called Steve Rattner, principal of the Quadrangle Group, who would serve as Bloomberg's primary negotiator on the sale of Merrill's stake.

Rattner, who early in his career was an up-and-coming reporter for *The New York Times* in Washington, D.C., and London, left journalism to become an investment banker in the 1980s. He made a name for himself at Morgan Stanley and then Lazard Freres as a top dealmaker in the world of media. In 2000, he struck out on his own with three colleagues to form Quadrangle. In early 2008, when Mayor Michael Bloomberg was considering a run for the presidency, Rattner was named to handle the billionaire media mogul turned politician's investments.

Bloomberg decided against running for president, and Rattner became a big supporter of Senator Barack Obama. After Obama's victory, Rattner would become the president's "car czar" in 2009, responsible for the turnaround of General Motors and Chrysler, which were rescued from bankruptcy with taxpayer funds. Andrew Cuomo, the New York attorney general, would eventually bring charges against Rattner's firm, Quadrangle, for providing gifts to the New York State Comptroller in return for getting a piece of the state's lucrative pension investment business.

But in July 2008, well before any of this, Fleming called the Manhattan financier from his vacation retreat on the Amalfi coast.

"Steve, we're going to move forward with the sale of our stake in Bloomberg," said Fleming. "We'd like to have it done by July 17."

"That's a very quick timetable, Greg."

"Yes, it is. I will move everything on my side to make this happen."

"We'll do everything we can," said Rattner, aware that Fleming was calling in the middle of the night from Italy and that Merrill had to be desperate for the timetable to be so aggressive.

Just as Fleming had explained to Thain, that the best way to make this deal happen was to take the high road, the Merrill president now made his pitch to Rattner accordingly. "We're not going to try to go in a different direction on this," he said. "The mayor has the right of first refusal. We're not going to try to bring any leverage. What I'm asking of you is to not take advantage of us in the other direction."

The mayor felt the same way, said Rattner.

As to price, that would take a while to sort out. "It's a very difficult time in the markets right now," said Rattner.

"Yes," countered Fleming, "but it's a very valuable stake."

After agreeing to get the negotiation process on track the next day, the conversation ended. Fleming then called and e-mailed several of his lieutenants—Todd Kaplan, Stuart Kaperst, and Pete Kelly—to apprise them of the accelerated Bloomberg plan. He also told the three of them to get ready to move on an FDS sale.

Fleming contacted Heaton and Paul Wetzel, and organized a conference call for the next day. Then he lined up Rodgin Cohen, the lead partner at Sullivan & Cromwell and one of the top merger and acquisition lawyers in New York, to represent Merrill Lynch in the transaction. Finally, before dawn arrived, Fleming knocked off for the night.

THE NEXT DAY, MERRILL'S Bloomberg team started the process of figuring out how much the company's 20 percent stake in the financial media company was worth. After organizing a battle plan, one member of the group asked Fleming if they should also start down the FDS track, which would potentially be a more difficult task.

Fleming said he needed sign-off from Thain first, and that he would speak to the CEO later that day. As the hours wore on, Thain didn't call, so Fleming called him. Thain still wasn't convinced he should sell FDS, and said he wanted more time to think about it.

When Fleming reconvened later that day with his group—it was afternoon in New York and evening in Italy—Kaplan pressed him on FDS. The decision could not wait much longer. Fleming begged off, saying he needed more time with Thain.

The following day, Thursday, July 3, sitting in the sun on the porch of the house on the Amalfi coast, Fleming was facing down a rebellion among his own people: Pete Kelly said they had to find out about FDS that day for anything meaningful to happen in time for the earnings call two weeks later. Every one of them knew that once the July Fourth weekend began, it would be far more difficult to locate and coax prospective buyers to the table. Fleming vowed he would get a response from Thain sometime that day.

When he did finally reach Thain, the CEO didn't share his sense of urgency and still wasn't ready to pull the trigger. Fleming pleaded with him to at least allow the process to start, otherwise they would not be able to pull it off by July 17. All he wanted was permission to *explore* it, Fleming said.

Thain finally relented, but not without a warning: "I'm not sure I'll go ahead and do it. This is just an option."

"I'm not telling you we're going to sell it," Fleming replied, betraying some frustration. "I just want to be able to move down that road so we have the *option* to sell it."

"Okay," said Thain. "But remember, I just want this to be an option."

It was pointless to go on in semantic circles, Fleming thought. He had gotten the permission he needed, however conditional. After he hung up the phone, he couldn't tell whether his frustration with Thain was less than, equal to, or greater than Thain's annoyance with him, which was obviously growing with each confrontation.

For Fleming, the day in Italy was shot, but at least the kids had made it to the beach. He would fly back to New York the next day, but instead of dragging his family along with him, as he had the previous year, they would stay on for the full two weeks.

BY MID-JUNE, THAIN WAS fully committed to the sale of Merrill's package of toxic CDOs, which he wanted off the books by the time Montag arrived for work in August.

Thain had reached out to Steve Mnuchin at Dune Capital in part because of their shared history at Goldman. Thain had a higher level of comfort dealing with Goldman people, but by late June, it wasn't clear that Dune would actually be there when Thain wanted to pull the trigger. Donald Quintin, the mortgage trader who was in charge of the CDO book following Kronthal's departure, had reopened discussions with Lone Star. On July 4, as Quintin was driving up to Vermont for the weekend, he received a call from Thain, who gave him the authority to move ahead and strike a deal with Lone Star.

Merrill's CDO book consisted of about sixty-five separate deals, which varied in size, from $150 million at the low end to about $800 million on the high end. But by early 2008, those "notional" values shed no light on what the underlying value of the securities was. Through the winter, Kronthal and Quintin devised a "home price appreciation" model, which was an attempt to tie the CDO's carrying value to the actual package of mortgages underlying each derivative.

Eventually, Kronthal and Quintin calculated that the total amount of CDO assets sitting on Merrill's balance sheet was $30.6 billion. Of course, the market value of those assets was nowhere near that amount.

BY LIMITING HIMSELF TO one buyer—Mayor Michael Bloomberg—Fleming had tied his hands at the negotiating table. Merrill would have to accept whatever Bloomberg's people wanted to offer. In late 2007, both sides were discussing a deal worth approximately $5 billion. That was then. In the current environment, following the collapse of Bear Stearns and with Lehman on shaky ground, $5 billion was no longer realistic, in Rattner's view.

Bloomberg, a hardnosed businessman who charged full value for his ubiquitous information terminals, did not become a billionaire by being a soft touch. Nevertheless, there was a long history between him and Merrill Lynch going back to the 1980s, when he was launching his business.

Michael Bloomberg started his career as a trader at Salomon Brothers, where he managed the firm's internal computer systems. In 1981, he was fired and given a $10 million severance. With that as his grubstake, Bloomberg devised his own computerized system for figuring out complex valuations of bonds and other financial products and began peddling his idea on Wall Street.

In 1982, Merrill Lynch became an early investor when Ed Moriarty—whose son was a top executive in Merrill's risk-control department by the time Thain arrived—took a chance on Bloomberg's business, agreeing to install twenty of the electronic boxes on Merrill's trading floor and putting $30 million into the start-up business.

True to his word, Rattner didn't crush Fleming over price. Instead, the two sides held numerous meetings about ways in which Bloomberg could maximize its business opportunities within Merrill. The bank pledged to rent so many terminals—which cost upwards of $1,500 per month—that some members of Fleming's team began to joke that they'd have to have Bloomberg machines put in their showers at home, and in their cars, in order to use up their new allotment.

Merrill had spent hundreds of millions of dollars developing its own electronic platform to be used by its thundering herd of brokers. But that plan was now scrapped for a pledge to use Bloomberg terminals exclusively throughout the system.

In the end, Fleming got $4.425 billion from Bloomberg for Merrill's stake. The costs associated with that price—hundreds of millions of dollars in guaranteed business for Bloomberg and financing for the deal—effectively brought the price down to $4 billion, about $1 billion less than the stake might have fetched some six months earlier.

AS FOR FDS, WETZEL and two other members of Fleming's team, Todd Kaplan and Stuart Kaperst, took the lead on identifying a possible buyer and fleshing out the framework of a deal quickly.

Midway through a July Fourth getaway weekend with his wife to New York City (the couple lived in New Jersey), Wetzel received a call back from Tim Hurd of Madison Dearborn, a Chicago investment fund that had co-invested with Merrill Lynch on other deals. Bolting from his hotel into Central Park to take the call, Wetzel quickly outlined the situation regarding FDS.

Hurd listened, then said it might be of interest, depending on certain conditions, such as a minimum rate of return for his fund, but that overall, it could potentially work as an investment for Madison Dearborn.

Kaplan, who lived in Chicago and had to abort his own family vacation to work on the Bloomberg and FDS deals, holed up in a New York apartment and immersed himself in the minutiae of both projects. Kaperst also dropped everything to work on the deals, as did Pete Kelly, the deal lawyer, and Eric Heaton, the treasurer.

Every day the group held conference calls with Fleming. Conspicuously absent from these efforts were Thain, who continued his sojourn in the Adirondacks, and Nelson Chai, the company's chief financial officer. Thain stayed up at his vacation home, touching base with Fleming once a day throughout the process. Chai volunteered to help out with the deals, and was included in some of the conference calls. On more than one occasion during the frenetic days of early July, the capital-raising team would assemble for a conference call, and only after the call had begun would Wetzel or Kaplan or Heaton realize that someone had forgotten to alert Chai and include him in the meeting, not out of an attempt to exclude him, but because he was not an integral part of the effort.

After two weeks of nonstop activity on the projects, involving two full weekends and the busted vacations, the pressure and strains of the helter-skelter asset sales began to show. Kaplan found himself in the offices of the law firm working with Steve Rattner on the Bloomberg transaction, at 7:00 p.m. one evening, gulping down his ninth cup of coffee of the day. He had a splitting headache, hadn't had a full night's sleep since late June, and after taking a swig of his coffee, put the cup down and said to no one in particular, "This is insane."

Fleming and every member of his team knew that this entire exercise, the desperate firesale of Merrill's assets done in pell-mell fashion to meet the July 17 earnings announcement, could have been avoided with some foresight from the top. Wetzel's group had presented the sale of the Bloomberg stake as an option back in December, only to be rebuffed by Thain. Kaplan had raised the idea of the FDS sale, brought to him by Russ Stein, a former treasurer of Merrill Lynch, back in April. Thain wasn't even aware that FDS existed, a sure sign of how unimportant it was to the CEO's vision for the company, and yet he told Kaplan not to start doing any due diligence on FDS at that point, since it might disrupt the subsidiary's operations.

Now, three months later, Fleming, Wetzel, Heaton, and the rest were all paying the price for that lack of preparation, working frenetically through early July to sell these assets. Worse, Merrill Lynch was getting a lower price on both properties because the buyers knew that the company had no alternatives and was under extreme time pressure. Given a few months, Merrill might have found several bidders for FDS, or raised the possibility with Bloomberg that an outside party would be willing to pay $5 billion for a 20 percent stake in the company.

But no. The company was boxed into this corner. The opposite of

Thain's declarations that Merrill Lynch had enough capital and would not need to raise more turned out to be true. Over his thirty-year career, Thain had lived through several major downdrafts on Wall Street, and every time the markets came roaring back. Thain had positioned Merrill Lynch to take advantage of this market's inevitable, buoyant return, but in doing so had left himself little room to tack in case his forecast proved not to be as positive as he'd hoped.

On Sunday before the July 17 earnings announcement, some of the pent-up tensions surrounding the sales boiled over in a conference call. Details were still being worked out, but by now it was clear that Bloomberg would buy back its 20 percent stake for at least $4 billion. As for FDS, Merrill would be able to get Madison Dearborn to sign a letter of intent that placed a value on the business of $3.5 billion.

Thain told everyone on the call that later in the week, to coincide with earnings, Merrill would announce proposed sales of assets with a combined value of $8 billion. Kaplan spoke up, telling Thain it might be safer to say the combined total was between $7 billion and $8 billion. Thain insisted that $8 billion would be the number. "Then why stop there?" demanded Kaplan. "Why not just go ahead and say $10 billion?"

Later, the discussion turned to details surrounding FDS. Unlike the Bloomberg transaction, which was a straight-up purchase of Merrill's stake, the FDS negotiation was complicated. The business was somewhat easier to sell off since it had its own financials, audited separately from Merrill's numbers. But it was a business that had only one customer: Merrill Lynch. No outside party would contemplate any kind of investment in FDS without a guarantee that Merrill would keep using the business not for years, but decades.

The unit's dependence on Merrill as a customer raised thorny accounting issues, since it was to some extent a "captive" business and not a freestanding entity.

Thain listened as Wetzel outlined some of the vagaries of the accounting questions involved. Thain had been frustrated with Fleming's inability to run a proper auction for the business, and he bored in on a question of the tax treatment for the current proposal. He felt there were several hundred million dollars' worth of tax benefits that could be generated from the FDS sale.

Wetzel countered, saying it wasn't like that, but Wetzel's own understanding of the tax rules wasn't definitive. Kaplan stepped in to explain the accounting details. Merrill's own internal accountants would not approve the aggressive treatment that Thain wanted, Kaplan said. The accounting rules were clear on the matter.

Thain cut him off abruptly. "I'm sick and tired of this stuff," he vented. "You guys don't know what you're doing. You're supposed to tell *them* how to do it, not have them tell *you* how to do it!"

"Nelson," Thain barked to his deputy, who was also on the call. "You get the accountants on the phone. I want this fixed!"

Wetzel was appalled at Thain's outburst, in part because of the abusive treatment doled out to Kaplan, who had run himself ragged over the previous two weeks, and because of Thain's low regard for the advice given by Merrill's internal accountants.

At the office the next day, Thain's chief of staff, May Lee, who was also on the call, tried to explain her boss's position to Wetzel. "Paul, you just can't accept what these people say," she told him. Wetzel also spoke to Chai, who assured him that the matter would get sorted out properly.

Down on the twenty-second floor, members of the strategy team and treasurer's office discussed Thain's intransigence on the issue, trying to figure out how someone who had been chief financial officer of Goldman Sachs could have such a dim grasp of basic accounting issues.

"You've got to remember," said one member of Heaton's team, "when Thain was CFO of Goldman, it was a private company."

For several people in the room, it was an interesting point. Thain had never been chief financial officer of a publicly traded company, forced to adhere to rigorous disclosure and accounting rules overseen by the Securities and Exchange Commission. When a company is private, the only people who matter are the owners, who, in the case of Goldman Sachs, were the partners. Before it became a public company, Goldman could have used any accounting treatment it wanted to manage its books, as long as its partners were satisfied.

. . .

ON JULY 17, after an arduous two weeks of nonstop negotiations, Merrill Lynch announced a loss of $4.7 billion, along with the sale of its Bloomberg stake for $4.425 billion, and a letter of intent to sell a majority stake of FDS in a transaction that valued the enterprise at $3.5 billion, more than compensating for the hole created by the losses.

The successful replenishment of capital kept Merrill Lynch from getting drawn into the choppy waters in which Lehman Brothers was foundering, at least for the time being. Meanwhile, Lone Star representatives said they were ready to buy the CDOs for almost $7 billion, as long as Merrill Lynch could handle the financing.

Thain was finally ready to pull the trigger, even though the deal would force Merrill to recognize another $5 billion in losses. Merrill Lynch would have to raise yet more capital, this time in the public markets, and it would cost the firm dearly. But Thain wanted those corrosive, toxic assets off his balance sheet.

Merrill Lynch's share price was now in the $30 range, well below the $48 level at which Temasek had demanded protection. The funds that bought "mandatory preferred" shares in Merrill in January—Korea Investment Corporation, Kuwait Investment Authority, Mizuho corporate bank, TPG-Axon Capital, the Olayan Group, T. Rowe Price—were also guaranteed similar treatment.

The reset clause seemed like a minor component of the previous winter's capital-raising efforts, but now emerged as a huge hurdle to get over before Merrill could go out and sell shares of common stock.

Donald Quintin, Merrill's top mortgage trader, became the lead negotiator with Len Allen of Lone Star. Fleming's team, including international bankers Andrea Orcel and Fares Noujaim—an ex–Bear Stearns banker who had just joined Merrill—would pitch in on the effort to exchange convertible preferred shares held by the January investors for chunks of common stock. Chai, who had originally brought the Korea Investment Corporation into the fold, worked with Noujaim on those discussions, and Thain himself spent time with Temasek, the largest of the new investors, to convince them to go along with the plan.

Thain coordinated daily conferences with all of these bankers to determine when Merrill could close on a sale of the CDOs. When the CDOs were sold, Merrill would have an opportunity to buy out the hedges it had purchased as insurance on some of the assets. Those hedges cost billions, and if Merrill could renegotiate the terms, the firm would realize some form of cash payment. On top of that, Merrill Lynch had to have its equity raising plan in place in order for the CDO sale to close, and that topic now sparked discussion among members of the special committee working on this project.

Despite the internal tension that had developed between Thain and Fleming over previous issues, the CEO seemed to have newfound respect for his top lieutenant. During that period, whenever Fleming was late for a conference call to discuss all these matters in late July, Thain declared to the group that he would not commence discussion "until Greg gets here."

The sale of a massive new amount of shares in Merrill Lynch was a huge undertaking. Because of its size—Merrill needed to raise more than $8 billion—Thain and Lisa Carnoy, head of equity capital markets, thought it would make sense to do a "road show" for investors, traveling the country over several days to meet with large institutional buyers, and make the case face-to-face for why it made sense to buy in to the "new" Merrill Lynch.

Based on what he had heard from investors—that the outstanding stock would get killed during the road show, dampening interest—Fleming recommended against that approach, saying that the bank ought to price the shares, then put them up for sale as quickly as possible. Unlike the heated discussions that took place between the men earlier in the month, Thain was open to Fleming's arguments and decided to follow that course, with a quick sale of stock into the marketplace.

Lone Star had now made a firm offer to Quintin: For $6.7 billion, it would buy out Merrill's CDO package, which at one time was valued at $30.6 billion. Thain assigned Pete Kelly, the lawyer who worked closely with Fleming, the task of drawing up the legal documents that would finalize the transaction.

On Friday, July 25, Kelly started negotiating the thorniest part of the deal, the financing for the CDOs, which would give Lone Star a fallback position if the portfolio ever sunk to zero.

Over that weekend, Kelly called Thain several times, but never heard back, so he kept at it, and reported in on Monday, July 28, just before 5:00 p.m., that he had signed off on a deal to sell Merrill's CDOs for $6.7 billion, some $4.4 billion less than the level at which Merrill was carrying them on its books.

When Kelly finally got through to Thain, he wondered what the reaction would be to the complicated financing contract he had committed the firm to as part of the sale. Instead, there was almost no reaction.

"Do you want to go through it?" Kelly asked.

"We'll go through it on the board call," said Thain.

Kelly appreciated the confidence Thain showed in him. At the same time, to allow one lawyer to go off and negotiate a complicated deal in a seventy-two-hour time frame, without any guidance or feedback, and then fly blind into a board of directors meeting—surely, this wasn't the way things were done at Goldman Sachs.

ON MONDAY, JULY 28, Merrill Lynch announced the sale of the CDOs to Lone Star for $6.7 billion, the termination of the CDO hedges, the plan to issue $8.5 billion in common stock, an agreement to allow Temasek to purchase $3.4 billion of stock, and the exchange of the reset preferred shares into common stock.

The next day the bank went to market and sold 320 million shares of stock at $22.50 each in the largest secondary offering ever conducted for a U.S. financial institution.

It was an amazing performance by a wide variety of executives under pressure. The timing and coordination of the capital raises, asset sales, insurance restructuring, and equity offering reflected a team of people, across multiple disciplines, working in unison.

All told, the recapitalization of Merrill Lynch and the restructuring of its balance sheet in July 2008 was one of the largest reconfigurations of an investment bank in history. Compared to what Lehman Brothers and its CEO had done in the same month—virtually nothing—John Thain had now shown some leadership on Wall Street, putting many of the problems from the O'Neal regime behind him and positioning Merrill Lynch for a comeback.

And he had done it in large part by cutting loose a band of legacy Merrill Lynch employees who had become the butt of jokes on Wall Street. The losses which first appeared in October 2007 had revealed an amazing ineptitude in management at Merrill Lynch, and raised questions about the competence of everyone at the firm. Now, some nine months after Merrill's problems first emerged, executives at the firm had taken dramatic, meaningful action to right the ship.

Despite the dramatic fundraising efforts, support for Thain among his biggest investors was now eroding. The restructuring of the balance sheet had come at great cost—there were no more assets that could be sold off to raise cash. Merrill's shareholders had witnessed the value of their holdings diluted by the massive issuance of new shares, starting with the previous December's deal with Temasek. As for the managers of the sovereign wealth funds that had bet on Thain's ability to turn Merrill around, their patience was growing thin. After their original investments, Thain had assured them and the rest of the world that Merrill Lynch was well-capitalized. Those assurances, in hindsight, had been premature. The equity sale of late July only exacerbated their concerns about Thain's leadership.

CHAPTER 11

THE CHAIRMEN'S GALLERY

EVERY YEAR, STAN O'NEAL would have a presentation put together for Merrill Lynch's board of directors, a strategic review of the financial services landscape and how it had shifted in the past twelve months. These reviews showed which banks had merged, which financial services firms had gotten into new business lines, and whether those new business lines were growing. A regular feature of these presentations was a list of which banks would be the best fit with Merrill Lynch, should the firm ever pursue a strategic combination.

Given the collapse of Bear Stearns and the turmoil at Lehman Brothers, one of the directors, John Finnegan, asked John Thain over the summer if the board could have an updated version of this presentation, with an emphasis on whether investment banks such as Merrill Lynch and Lehman could survive without being attached to a large commercial bank.

In particular, Finnegan told Thain he wanted the presentation to include a list of institutions Merrill Lynch could merge with, in case the environment for investment banks became so harsh that the firm could no longer go it alone. "We've escaped this, John, but truthfully, as a standalone, is an investment bank really a viable entity?" Finnegan asked.

Thain turned the assignment over to Paul Wetzel, who was not only head of strategy, at least until Kraus arrived, but who also had an extensive background in the global banking industry. Over several weeks in July, Wetzel and members of his strategy team constructed an overview of the banking landscape, and identified eleven financial institutions which would be logical acquirers of Merrill Lynch.

PRESENTATIONS TO THE BOARD of his own company were rare for Wetzel, so he prepared meticulously for this one. He'd been asked to predict the future of the investment banking industry and consequently the future of Merrill Lynch.

The boardroom at Merrill Lynch headquarters was located on the thirty-third floor, one level above the executive suite. To access it, Wetzel got off the elevator and entered a large reception area, known as the "chairmen's gallery," located on the north side of the building.

To the left was the entrance to the executive dining room; the hall to the right led to the boardroom. Directly ahead, through the windows, the skyscrapers of Midtown Manhattan looked closer than they were, appearing to rise out of the city's bustling streets just a few blocks away, when they were in fact more than two miles uptown.

Along the walls framing this reception area hung a series of portraits depicting the ten chief executive officers in the firm's history prior to Stan O'Neal, from Charlie Merrill up to David Komansky.

Over at one end hung the image of Merrill himself, a bemused, slightly crooked smile on his benign visage, his light suit the only indication that he was a southerner, from Florida. This most unusual character, a combination of visionary businessman and thrice-married bon vivant, founded his eponymous investment firm in 1914. A year later he was joined by Edmund Lynch, and Merrill's firm thrived for fifteen years. Merrill believed in the concept of chain stores and their ability to grow along with the expanding middle class in the U.S. He helped bring Kroger, Kresge, and First National public, along with the chains that became known as J.C. Penney and Thom McAn. He founded the Safeway chain of supermarkets. Wary of the bubble-like characteristics of the stock market in 1929, Merrill withdrew most of his money from stocks and urged his clients to do the same, sparing himself from the consequences of the cataclysmic crash of 1929.

It would be more than a decade before Merrill returned to the markets, buying E.A. Pierce & Co., as well as Cassatt & Co., and unifying them as one network of stock salesmen, Merrill Lynch, E.A. Pierce & Cassatt, in 1940. That year, Merrill brought all these salesmen together for a summit at the Waldorf-Astoria hotel in New York, where his new business—designed to bring Wall Street to Main Street—was launched. Merrill didn't want a sales force pushing stocks on unsuspecting customers. He wanted his brokers to serve as trusted financial advisors to affluent and well-to-do households across the country. To demonstrate good faith with the customer base, Merrill's brokers would be paid straight salary, and not rewarded with commissions on sales of stock.

By extending the pool of Wall Street investors well beyond the province of the super-wealthy, Merrill Lynch increased the amount of capital that flowed into up-and-coming businesses, helping the U.S. economy grow at a faster rate. By focusing on the investment needs of average Americans, and not just the rich, Charlie Merrill had created something of enduring value, a business that would stand the test of time and flourish in the latter half of the twentieth century.

The success of Merrill Lynch spurred growth at competing firms, such as Smith Barney, Dean Witter, and Paine Webber, which further increased the flow of funds from average investors across the U.S. to Wall Street.

Next to Merrill in the chairmen's gallery hung a picture of Winthrop Smith, who took over operational control of what had become Merrill Lynch Pierce Fenner & Beane in 1944, after Merrill was slowed down by heart problems. Where Merrill was the bold visionary, Smith was the hands-on operational manager who kept the organization growing. He was rewarded for his service in 1958, when the firm's name was changed to Merrill Lynch Pierce Fenner & Smith.

In another part of the room hung a portrait of Donald Regan, chairman and CEO of Merrill Lynch from 1971 through 1980, and beyond doubt the greatest leader the firm had after Merrill himself. The son of a Boston policeman, Regan served in the U.S. Marine Corps from 1941 to 1945, rising to the rank of lieutenant colonel. He joined Merrill Lynch after World War II as a management trainee. Charlie Merrill liked recruiting veterans to his firm, since they tended to be serious-minded young men who could focus on goals and follow direction. Because of this predilection, Merrill Lynch ended up with a disproportionate number of Irish-Catholic recruits, an anomaly on Wall Street.

Regan could take direction, but only if those directions made sense. Brimming with self-confidence after his first posting in Washington, D.C., he was one of ten young men selected out of a thousand account executives to be part of a new sales promotion team being trained in New York. Listening to a long-winded lecture in that program, Regan raised his hand, interrupted the instructor, and complained that the presentation had little to do with the way things worked in Merrill's branch offices. Standing as witnesses to the incident at the back of the room, having slipped in quietly, were Charlie Merrill and Winthrop Smith. Merrill was impressed with Regan's backbone.

Regan's willingness to fight for what he believed in pushed him to the forefront of young executives poised for promotion. In 1951, following a scandal in the over-the-counter trading desk of Merrill Lynch, Regan was tapped to fix the mess. One success begat another and in the 1960s, he joined a small circle near the top of the company. In a culture focused on selling stocks to customers every day, Regan stuck out for his ability to look forward. In 1969, when he was president, he wrote a paper titled "Toward the 1980s and Beyond." The 1970s had not yet arrived, and Regan was already grappling with the challenges Merrill Lynch might face more than a decade down the road. He was named chairman and CEO, effective January 1, 1971.

In the mid 1970s, when most of Wall Street quivered at the loss of the fixed-commission system, which guaranteed brokerage firms a fat fee on every stock trade, Regan embraced the change. As CEO, he never tired of criticizing the hidebound practices of other Wall Street firms and used every deregulatory change in the industry as an opportunity for growth and innovation. The greatest of those innovations was the cash management account, which allowed Merrill Lynch brokerage customers to keep all of their financial products—mortgages, insurance, checking account, credit cards, and stocks and bonds—in a single account at Merrill Lynch. Under Regan, Merrill Lynch did business *with* Wall Street but was not *of* Wall Street.

A combative, sometimes bullying presence, Regan feared no one. In 1981, he was sworn in as President Ronald Reagan's treasury secretary, and in 1985 he became White House chief of staff. He was a top advisor to Reagan during the secret swap of arms for hostages that became known as the Iran-Contra affair. Although he was not intimately involved in the transaction, he was eventually called to testify before Congress about his role. During that testimony, Regan recalled his frustration over the amorphous negotiations between representatives of the U.S. government and the Iranian government, which led him, at one point, to declare to the President that the United States had been "snookered" yet again by the Iranians. "How many times do we put up with this rug-merchant stuff?" Regan demanded.

The chief of staff's refusal to bow to First Lady Nancy Reagan eventually led to his dismissal, but his fall from power in Washington did not silence him. In his memoir, *For the Record,* Regan created a firestorm of controversy when he revealed that Mrs. Reagan consulted an astrologer when scheduling public activities for her husband. This disclosure shocked Reagan loyalists, who viewed Regan's book as a heretical violation of trust, but came as no surprise to the thousands of Merrill Lynch employees who had worked with or for Regan during his Wall Street career. When it came to a fight, the former Merrill CEO did not know the meaning of the phrase "back down."

Regan's ten-year tenure as chief executive of Merrill Lynch marked a high point for the firm. Through his far-reaching vision, Regan had built Merrill Lynch into a powerhouse that could dominate its business for decades to come. But his departure for the Reagan White House in 1981 created a problem for Merrill Lynch, one which afflicts most companies that have been blessed with a larger-than-life CEO: Once the great man departs, it's almost impossible to find someone of comparable stature to fill his shoes.

Not far from Regan's portrait in the chairmen's gallery hung that of William "Bill" Schreyer, who was CEO from 1984 to 1993. Like Regan, Schreyer also worked his way up the Merrill management ladder, starting off as a broker in a regional office. A genial Pennsylvania native, Schreyer grew up in a Merrill Lynch household: His father was a financial advisor for the firm. He had neither Regan's incisive mind nor relentless drive. But faced with sudden challenges, Schreyer responded with vigor.

In 1987, Schreyer learned that Howard Rubin, a trader in Merrill's fixed-income department, had accumulated a massive, one-directional position in mortgage-backed securities, well beyond his limit, and that his directional bet had been wrong. The result was a loss of $377 million—a shocking sum at the time. For decades, Merrill Lynch had been protected from the volatility of Wall Street because its primary business was in managing the investments of its clients nationwide. Once Merrill Lynch started making bets on its own behalf instead of just servicing its clients, management learned the biggest danger of being a Wall Street trading firm: that one trader could destroy an entire company. Schreyer confronted the problem immediately, admitting to investors that Merrill Lynch had just lost the largest sum of money in Wall Street history. Then he commissioned a study to find out what happened and make sure it never happened again. Going forward, Merrill Lynch would stick with what it knew best: taking care of its clients across the U.S. Never again would the firm aspire to be the market leader in a business involving high-risk securities. It was a pledge that would be ignored at great cost two decades later.

A few months after the mortgage-backed securities blowup, Schreyer faced another crisis. On October 19, 1987, the Dow Jones industrial average of stock prices, which had been jittery for several weeks, sustained a near collapse, dropping 508 points, the largest single decline ever and the second largest percentage decline in history. At the time there were fears of a 1929-style rout in the capital markets.

Investors panicked, business leaders froze, and the threat of a general meltdown in the markets and the overall economy emerged as a real possibility.

Schreyer did something unusual, especially for a Wall Street leader. He taped a TV commercial, to be broadcast during the World Series that week, which dispensed with Merrill's usual images of bulls romping through fields or city streets. Instead, looking into the camera, he said: "I'm here for some straight talk about the stock market. It's important to everyone. It provides capital that creates jobs to make America grow. Emotions can run high during market turbulence, just when reason should prevail. We are confident in the markets. We've stayed active in them for all investors. America's economy is the strongest in the world, with great ability to bounce back. At Merrill Lynch, we're still bullish on America."

The commercial was an instant success, delivering precisely the right tone of confidence, infused with the gravity that the situation called for. Schreyer became a hero in the business world for speaking out in a situation fraught with risk. If the markets had continued to tank, he would have been a laughingstock and Merrill Lynch would have become the punchline in a never ending series of jokes from Johnny Carson on the *Tonight Show*. Instead, the markets steadied and bounced back and Merrill Lynch reaped the biggest benefits of having made the right call in the most public fashion possible.

After Schreyer retired, he was succeeded by his deputy, Dan Tully. Tully fit to the letter the Merrill stereotype of the Irish-Catholic firm targeting America's emerging middle class. Like Schreyer before him, Tully compensated for lack of strategic vision with a deep, almost devout belief in Merrill Lynch as an institution. As a veteran of Merrill's private client business, Tully had a gregarious approachability and "regular guy" manner that disguised sharp executive instincts. He was brilliant at managing clients and speaking extemporaneously in meetings about ways in which Merrill could help their business.

Schreyer used to say, partly in jest, that "the key to success is sincerity. If you can fake that, you've got it made." Tully was no match for his predecessor in this department, but he could make clients feel like they were Merrill Lynch's most important customers. On road trips, he would follow up client meetings with visits to the local retail branches of Merrill Lynch private client managers, where his glad-handing and banter weren't an act, but the expression of a man who actually cared about the firm's network of financial advisors.

Tully was smart enough to know what he didn't know. The capital markets of the mid-1990s were becoming more complex than anything he had dealt with earlier in his career, and the company needed a deeper bench of management strength to compete. When Schreyer finally stepped down, he sent Tully a crystal fashioned in the shape of a large stone, with a sword sticking out of it, a reference to Excalibur and King Arthur. "Congratulations," the accompanying note said. "Well deserved."

But on his first day in the big job, Tully turned to his executive assistant, Brian Henderson, and asked, in all seriousness, "Who's my replacement?" For decades, Merrill Lynch had relied on a steady stream of financial advisors from the private client business to grow into top management roles. That system no longer guaranteed that Merrill Lynch would have access to the best talent on Wall Street. The firm had acquired an investment bank, White Weld, in 1978, and beefed up its sales and trading operations to keep pace with its competitors. But even those infusions of new people didn't result in an abundance of top-tier executive minds.

Tully's highest ranking subordinates were Launny Steffens, who ran private client, and David Komansky, a lovable bear of a man who never went to college but whose people skills propelled him to success as a financial advisor in the Merrill Lynch system. Tully preferred Steffens as his successor, but Steffens loved Merrill's private client business and didn't want to rotate out of his job to learn other aspects of the company. Komansky did. Tully eventually designated Komansky as his successor, but insisted on pairing him with Herb Allison, a detail oriented manager.

Nearby on the wall hung a portrait of Komansky, who succeeded

Tully in 1997. Just as the decades of growth following World War II had eventually produced a leader of Don Regan's caliber to run Merrill Lynch, decades of managerial inbreeding following Regan had produced salesmen like Schreyer, Tully, and finally Komansky, the epitome of the old-school financial advisor: friendly and personable, a great cheerleader for a growing company, but lacking the technical skills needed for a downturn in the financial markets and the strategic vision to navigate the complexities of an interconnected world of capital markets and global finance.

Herb Allison, Komansky's deputy, possessed those skills. But Allison insisted on a culture of meritocracy at Merrill Lynch, and never wavered from his vision. His stubbornness on the subject of turning Merrill into an organization run on a set of fixed principles instead of a culture of promotion based on whom you knew led him to cross powerful people. His refusal to play favorites also incurred the displeasure of Schreyer himself. Tully used to rebuke Allison for his obstinate stances, asking him point-blank, "Would you rather be right, or do you want to make it to the top?" Allison's willingness to make hard decisions and ruffle feathers in the private client business and elsewhere at the firm made him few friends, but Tully and Komansky found that the Navy veteran could be quite useful. When Allison decided to shut someone down or cut costs in a business, his superiors were able to step back and let all the blame fall on him.

In the fall of 1998, after the meltdown at Long Term Capital, Allison's willingness to make hard decisions backfired. He downsized Merrill's bond trading desk immediately, getting rid of 3,500 people from the fixed-income desk. When the market rebounded smartly in subsequent months, Merrill's competitors were in a much stronger position to benefit.

A few months later, there was another issue. In early 1999, Komansky started talking with Walter Shipley, CEO of Chase Manhattan Bank, who suggested a possible merger between the two companies.

After bringing Allison along to a meeting with Shipley, Komansky said to his deputy, "These guys really want to merge. We should do it. I'll be number one and you'll be number two."

Allison argued against the deal, saying that a Merrill-Chase merger didn't make sense. A much better fit would be between Merrill Lynch and Citibank. Komansky had much less interest in a merger with Citi, which was not in need of a new CEO at the time.

In July, Komansky pushed Allison aside and set up a horse race to determine who would be his successor. The candidates at that point were Stan O'Neal, Jeff Peek, and Tom Davis.

O'Neal won the competition in part for his strong performance at running Merrill's private client business, and because of the support he received from an imposing group of people, including Schreyer; Tom Patrick, the CFO; and board member Bob Luciano, the CEO of Schering-Plough.

In July 2001, O'Neal was named president and heir apparent to Komansky, who still had several years left in his term as CEO. O'Neal didn't want to wait that long, and immediately set about forming his own executive team, which included Tom Patrick and a brilliant young trader, Arshad Zakaria.

After winning the battle, O'Neal set out to rid the firm of perceived enemies, starting with Peek. He told Critchlow he would make Peek "an offer he couldn't refuse" by leaving him off the organizational chart. Peek got the message and left.

Even before the attacks of September 11, 2001, Komansky was a weakened executive. Most of the board wanted O'Neal to take over. Then O'Neal suggested to Komansky that he wanted to run his executive committee meetings on his own, without the CEO around. Komansky agreed, further undercutting his own authority.

The CEO was about to be ousted by his own handpicked protégé when he received a call from Don Regan, who, even in his late seventies, liked to call in and chat with Komansky every once in a while.

"How's it going?" Regan asked, his voice aged but still full of pep and vigor. "I hear you're having some trouble with your president."

That's right, Komansky answered.

"What are you going to do about it?" Regan asked.

"There's nothing I can do," Komansky said. "He's got the support of the board."

"Fuck 'em all," Regan said. "Fire him. I fired four of my presidents."

Even at his advanced age, Regan still had that famous backbone, forged, it seemed, from pure steel. Komansky's was of a lesser alloy. He had no appetite to pick a fight with his board, and he hung on for one more year with the title of CEO, but the torch had been taken from him already, thanks mostly to the efforts of Schreyer and Luciano. Schreyer's full-throated support of O'Neal did not pass unnoticed. After taking over, O'Neal provided him with a car and driver for a period of time, courtesy of Merrill Lynch shareholders.

Noticeably absent in the chairmen's gallery was a portrait of O'Neal, the eleventh CEO in Merrill's history. Until 2007, O'Neal had been well on his way to a place of honor in this room for the amazing transformation he had overseen. Charlie Merrill was the brilliant visionary who launched the firm, Don Regan was the unstoppable dynamo who had made Merrill Lynch one of the most powerful financial franchises in the world. And O'Neal, up until 2007, had turbocharged Merrill's profits, transforming a company that was held back by the modest profits of its financial advisory network into an aggressive, risk-taking trading operation that placed billion-dollar bets in the capital markets. O'Neal's vision had been to make Merrill Lynch more like Goldman Sachs, the perennial profit machine of Wall Street, but like everyone who made the mistake of trying to copy Goldman, O'Neal was mesmerized by the profits and gargantuan pay packages for which Goldman was famous. O'Neal had no interest in replicating the foundation of Goldman's success, which was a culture based on restraint, teamwork, and self-discipline, where risk managers wielded more power than traders.

John Thain, the twelfth chief executive in the history of the franchise, was still putting his imprint on Merrill Lynch. On this day at the end of July 2008, as the Merrill Lynch board gathered to consider the future of the firm, it was too early to judge whether Thain's tenure would be a success or failure, too early to fill in anything but the most general outlines of his profile.

. . .

WETZEL ENTERED THE BOARDROOM, the same room where he had parked the outside investors from Temasek and Mizuho months earlier, and where he had made presentations to them showing what a solid investment Merrill Lynch would be under John Thain.

In the middle of the room was a rectangular table. By custom, Thain, as CEO, sat in the middle of one of the long sides. Most of the nine directors sat across from him, but several also sat to his right.

In addition to Wetzel, Fleming and Chai were called in to attend this part of the board meeting. The two executives sat to Thain's left, while Wetzel took the seat at the perpendicular end, nearest Chai, where he could make his presentation to the entire board. It was the same seat O'Neal had taken the previous October, when he issued his ultimatum to the directors, that if they didn't trust his judgment on pursuing a deal with Wachovia, he didn't want the job anymore.

Having finished the previous item of business, Thain moved on to the seventh item on the board's agenda that day, saying that Wetzel, head of strategy, would provide the board with an overview of the investment banking landscape, particularly in light of the credit crunch. Thain then directed the board members to look at the blue spiral books that had been handed to them, so they could follow Wetzel's presentation more closely.

The forty-eight-year-old executive, a native of Buffalo, began talking about how the banking world had changed in the past twelve months. Financial behemoths that were setting records for profits in 2005 and 2006 began crashing to earth at the end of 2007. The biggest banks in the United States and Europe lost, in aggregate, hundreds of billions of dollars. Market capitalizations of banking institutions—the number of shares outstanding in a company times the price per share in the open market, a measure of strength—had shriveled.

Broker dealers, such as Bear Stearns, felt the first effects of the crash, as had Merrill Lynch and Citigroup, but another wave of losses was coming, Wetzel warned. The big consumer banks, JPMorgan Chase, Bank of America, and Wells Fargo, would see ever-increasing losses as customers defaulted on home loans and car loans, and small businesses went belly-up. Regional banks across the country that relied heavily on the mortgage industry for growth would be in danger of failing.

Having a brokerage license, which is what differentiated the investment banks such as Merrill and Goldman Sachs from the depository banks, would no longer be an advantage, Wetzel argued, because the usual sources of overnight funding would dry up. Without funding, investment banks would not be able to use leverage to magnify the returns of easy, low-risk bets.

Investment banks would have to secure long-term funds, which cost more than overnight funding. The higher cost for money would cut into their profitability, pushing down their return on equity for shareholders. The whole reason investors bought shares in investment banks is that with the higher risk came a higher reward. Until the failure of Bear Stearns, the high risk of owning stock in an investment bank had disappeared. Like the real estate market, it had become an assumption of the marketplace that the profitability of investment banks would just keep going up.

Because of the bursting of the real estate bubble, Wetzel continued, and the collapse of Bear Stearns, it was more than likely that strict new regulations would come from Washington, D.C., restrictions that would further cut into the profitability of investment banks.

As investment banks looked around for new, more permanent sources of funding, it was inevitable that they would have to pair up with, or get bought by, large depository institutions. Goldman Sachs had dodged the worst of the subprime crash so far, by taking positions against the housing market, but even it would need to find new sources of funding.

"Eventually, we're going to be in this position," Wetzel said. With that, the head of strategy directed board members to look at the grand list of global banks, almost forty of them, that he had put together to see which would turn out to be the best match with Merrill Lynch.

The roster of banks was divided into several tiers. In one tier was a group of banks with which Merrill could partner in a "merger of equals." In many of these cases, the other banks had funding issues of their own. Another category included larger banks that could acquire Merrill, such as Mizuho, the Japanese bank that had invested billions of dollars already.

Wetzel, who had recently relocated from Japan, explained some of the cultural challenges that Merrill Lynch would face in trying to strike a deal with Mizuho or other Japanese banks. In general, Japanese banks were cautious and preferred to buy stakes, increasing those stakes incrementally over time. They were not likely to move quickly in an hour of need.

Finally, there were three banks that were big enough to buy Merrill Lynch, and nimble enough to move quickly on a deal: Bank of America, HSBC, and JPMorgan Chase.

Merrill could merge into BofA or JPMorgan Chase, Wetzel said, but HSBC, based in London, could pose some cultural challenges. A board member asked for a fuller explanation of what Wetzel meant by "cultural challenges."

"The people who run HSBC are like the Marines," said Wetzel. "The Marines take the best, strongest, most brilliant members of the corps and put them into the special forces. HSBC has a version of that. If they bought Merrill Lynch, it would be people from that group who would be parachuted in here to run this place."

The entire board listened closely, none more so than Joseph Prueher, a retired Navy admiral who had joined Merrill's board in 2001.

"If you're one of these guys, and you're sitting in Japan, and one day headquarters tells you to go to Brazil to take over that division, you don't ask, you go. It's run like the military."

Wetzel explained how the generally low levels of pay at HSBC, combined with its lack of a "star system," had impeded its efforts to build an investment bank. HSBC executives gagged at the idea of paying out $20 million bonuses to rainmakers. Wetzel talked about one deal that he was involved in, the sale of the Bank of Bermuda to HSBC in 2004. Instead of flying to Bermuda on a private jet, Stephen Green, the CEO of HSBC, traveled to New York and then Bermuda by coach on commercial airlines. He showed up late to the cocktail party and closing dinner in Bermuda to mark the deal because he'd been stuck at JFK, sitting in a terminal. No executive from any other comparable bank would ever deign to suffer the indignities of flying on a commercial airline.

"This is their culture," said Wetzel. "They fly coach, they carry their own bags, they're driven, and they love working for HSBC. They're the best and brightest."

Admiral Prueher smiled. "So you're saying that they wouldn't like a flashy, highly paid investment banker like you?"

"Exactly!" replied Wetzel with a self-deprecating laugh. "I'm not that guy."

Wetzel turned to the next potential acquirer, Bank of America. "This makes sense on the retail piece," he said, referring to Merrill's thundering herd of financial advisors, who could be unleashed on BofA's extraordinary roster of "mass affluent" customers across the U.S. Another good fit was the international business: Merrill had a strong network of overseas offices, but BofA was almost entirely a U.S.-focused bank. But there were problems with such a marriage, Wetzel said. BofA had started its own investment bank and built up its own trading operation in New York. Both had grown from small experiments into thriving midsized operations. "Bringing the two investment banks together would be pretty ugly, but ours would dominate," he said.

After he wrapped up his presentation, the matter was opened up for discussion.

"This is all very interesting, but I don't see why we need to spend a lot of time thinking about this," said Alberto Cribiore. "Merrill Lynch is an iconic brand and should remain independent."

Fleming, who'd heard this same speech from Cribiore before, in October 2007, challenged the Italian banker directly.

"We've got to be prepared for the worst," he said.

Cribiore disagreed, insisting that Merrill Lynch could and should remain independent, just as Goldman Sachs would always be independent.

Fleming didn't give up. He said that of the major banks on Wetzel's list, three were clearly superior in terms of being a strong match with Merrill: Bank of America, HSBC, and JPMorgan Chase.

"BofA is a strategic fit," Fleming said, "and so is HSBC, although it might be difficult to pull off. With JPMorgan, there's a lot of overlap among the business units, and Jamie Dimon would be very difficult to deal with." Fleming was referring to the hard bargain Dimon drove with federal regulators over Bear Stearns.

Cribiore rolled his eyes. "Bank of America is a bad idea!" he said. "How do we know they don't have more financial problems than we do? Why would we ever sell to a bank in Charlotte, North Carolina?"

Fleming would not back down.

"The following things are incontrovertible," he said. "We have a strong wealth management business. They don't. We have a huge investment bank and capital markets business. They don't. We have a strong international presence. They don't. There's almost nothing here that they don't need. It's as close a thing as there is to a perfect match."

Finnegan, who had instigated the exercise, joined in the general thanks given to Wetzel, but made no comment. Neither did Thain.

His presentation over, Wetzel excused himself from the boardroom and returned to his office on the twenty-second floor.

Later that day, after the board meeting ended, Thain called him.

"I think that went quite well," said the CEO. Wetzel, who knew by now that Thain almost never praised anyone directly, interpreted the remark as a compliment.

ON MONDAY, AUGUST 4, relaxed after a six-month garden leave and an extra few weeks off for a family reunion at Yosemite National Park, Tom Montag showed up at Merrill Lynch to take over as head of global sales and trading.

Since his bonus of $39.4 million, guaranteed, had been publicly disclosed back in May, a degree of resentment had already built up within Merrill Lynch toward him. And the fact that he was not around during the month of July, one of the most frenetic months of activity in the history of Merrill Lynch, only intensified that sentiment.

Starting at 7:00 a.m. on August 4, workers came down to the trading floor to set up a podium and microphone so Montag could speak to everyone, just as Thain had done on his first day the previous December. But after 8:00 a.m., the podium was taken down. Montag didn't want to deliver a speech, apparently. Instead, he wandered the floor, shook people's hands, and retreated to his office just off to the side of the trading area.

When Thain arrived the previous year, he went out of his way to "make nice" with the Merrill team in place, and encouraged people to talk to him about business issues they cared about. Montag had a different approach.

Practically from day one he was clear about the low regard in which he held much of Merrill Lynch's trading talent. Within days, he brought in a small entourage of his own traders.

At weekly meetings of Thain's management committee and risk committee, Montag was unsparing in his criticism of the talent he was inheriting. When he announced the hiring of traders he was bringing on board, he would describe them as "a big upgrade from what we've got now." Or when describing how a Merrill trader had put a poor trade on the books, he would add a personal insight, opining that the individual was an "asshole."

IN EARLY AUGUST, THAIN invited Fleming to join him onstage for a presentation to Merrill Lynch's top financial advisors at a hotel in Midtown Manhattan. It was rare for Thain to share the stage at such events.

"I thought we'd do this together," Thain announced to the advisors when introducing Fleming, "since we lived together for the last month."

The honeymoon didn't last long. A few weeks later, someone slipped Fleming a copy of e-mail correspondence that had been going back and forth between Thain and Michael Rubinoff, a Goldman Sachs investment banker who had joined Merrill's private equity business a year earlier.

Rubinoff, who was supposed to be reporting to Fleming, was providing Thain with a progress report on an effort to acquire Fortress Investment Group, an alternative asset management firm. Also copied on the e-mail were Tom Montag, who'd been at the bank for less than a month, and Peter Kraus, who was still on the Goldman Sachs payroll and would not join Merrill until September.

Fleming couldn't believe his eyes as he looked at the document. A group of former Goldman Sachs partners now running Merrill Lynch was hatching a plot to acquire Fortress, an investment group that was struggling with its own misadventures in real estate. Merrill Lynch had just unloaded $30 billion of the most toxic real estate–based assets in the marketplace, cleaning up its balance sheet considerably, and these guys were thinking of buying more distressed assets with the firm's newly raised capital?

And the e-mail, containing sensitive and confidential business information, had been copied to Peter Kraus, who had yet to join Merrill. To Fleming, it was weird. Then there was the Goldman Sachs connection, not only on the Merrill side, but on the Fortress side as well. Among others, Thain was negotiating with Peter Briger, a principal at Fortress and an ex–Goldman partner. The whole thing was a Goldman show. It was as though Thain was incapable of trusting or doing business with anyone who lacked a Goldman Sachs seal of approval on their forehead.

And the idea that Thain thought he could actually get a project like this up and running without Fleming finding out? That was ludicrous. Hadn't Thain learned anything in his eight months at the helm of Merrill Lynch, Fleming wondered.

Fleming called Rubinoff, his subordinate in the investment banking unit, and told him that from now on he wanted to be copied on everything. Then he went to see Thain, not to throw a fit but to ask him what he possibly could have been thinking.

Thain disliked confrontation, and when Fleming arrived he insisted that there had been no deliberate intent to ice him out of the negotiations. "We were going to get you in the loop," Thain said. "It's early."

Fleming shrugged. "I have to tell you, John. I think it's the wrong move."

"Why do you say that?"

"It's tautologically bad. This is not the time to be buying someone else's exposure. We don't know where the cycle is going here. We don't know whether we're catching their falling knife. We just got rid of our falling knife."

Thain pointed out that there could be a huge upside from the undervalued assets at Fortress.

"Is Finnegan or anyone on the board ready for this?" Fleming asked. Evidently not, according to Thain's body language.

KRAUS APPEARED TO BE the driving force behind the initiative to acquire Fortress. At several points throughout August, working from his apartment because he had not yet finished his garden leave, or from the offices of a Midtown law firm, Kraus called Wetzel and asked for research to be done on Fortress's assets, with an eye to determining what their value really was. Most of these requests were of the quick-turnaround variety, and Wetzel's strategy team would churn out the work in a matter of hours, before the final product was sent to Kraus's home.

Early on, Wetzel noted that there might be a significant roadblock to any deal with Fortress: Merrill's contractual obligation to BlackRock. As part of the BlackRock arrangement, Merrill Lynch was forbidden from investing in or acquiring any competing asset management business.

"Don't worry, Paul, I've already talked to John about it," Kraus told Wetzel. Fortress's asset management business was small compared with its private equity investments, so the deal wouldn't be problematic for BlackRock. "It works. It's not really a conflict."

Wetzel persisted. In addition to fulfilling Kraus's requests, he had the legal team research Merrill's contract with BlackRock. The lawyers located specific language in the BlackRock contract that forbade investment in any company that also owned and operated an asset management business, no matter how small.

Wetzel sent the contract to Kraus and followed up with a phone call. Once Kraus saw the specific clause in the contract, he grasped the problem immediately. "Oh, wow," he said to Wetzel. "John doesn't understand this, does he?"

TOWARD THE END OF AUGUST, Fleming took a few days off for a mini vacation with the family, making up, in part, for the aborted Italy break the previous month.

Over the Labor Day weekend, Peter Kraus was busy moving into his new office. Wetzel, who had been head of strategy, worked on the twenty-second floor, because he wanted to be near Eric Heaton, the treasurer. Wetzel thought it was so important to work closely with the treasurer on strategy issues that he took over Heaton's conference room and turned it into his office. That way, the discussions and meetings could flow easily between one office and the next.

Kraus would begin work after Labor Day, but, as Thain had pointed out to Chai and Wetzel months earlier, Kraus was far above the level of a mere strategist. Befitting his role at Merrill Lynch, Kraus would have an office on thirty-two, the executive floor, not far from Thain's.

Kraus was also above having a simple office. Just as Thain and his wife had recoiled at O'Neal's décor, Kraus was repelled by the contours and confines of a plain four-walled space with a desk.

An avid collector of modern art, Kraus knew exactly what he wanted to do with his space. Prior to his first day on the job, Kraus and his wife supervised a complete overhaul of the office, bringing in a roomful of his paintings and other objets d'art.

Most striking of these objects was a plasma screen that featured a group of French street cleaners sweeping sand in the desert. On a continuous loop, the figures swept the sand, forming small mounds. The sand piles would then be dispersed by the wind, forcing the figures to start sweeping all over again. The work, *Les Balayeurs du desert*, created by Su Mei-Tse, had won a prize at the Venice Bienniale. One of Kraus's colleagues on the thirty-second floor dubbed it "Futility."

Then there was "the bookcase." People entering Kraus's office immediately noticed the stunning art on the walls, and out of the corner of their eyes, they'd also note the fact that Kraus had a large bookcase, about thirty feet long by six feet high. But either while speaking to Kraus, or walking across the office, visitors would do a double take when they got to the bookcase and realized, upon closer inspection, that it was a piece of art itself and that the "books" were constructed from the same material as the "shelves."

Fleming ran afoul of Kraus one day when he dropped by for a casual chat and sidled up against the bookcase.

"Please don't lean on that," Kraus said.

"Why not?" asked Fleming. "It's a bookcase."

"No. It's art."

ENSCONCED AT HIS NEW space, just down the hall from Thain, Kraus immersed himself in the company's business. After work during his first week, he went down to the controller's office to dig into Merrill's finances, staying past midnight poring over the bank's funding contracts.

Although he was not in charge of Bob McCann's private client group, Kraus summoned McCann and some of the unit's top managers to a meeting to talk about international expansion of the unit through acquisition.

Despite the impression he had left on Fleming and McCann earlier in the year—that he was arrogant—Kraus impressed his new colleagues with his energy. Merrill's top tier of managers, most of whom had grown weary of Thain's reluctance to make hard choices about selling assets until his hand was forced, found Kraus's decisiveness and direction bracing, even if they disagreed with his views, which was often the case.

In many ways, Kraus was a perfect foil for Thain. The CEO could often seem removed, humorless, and methodical, while Kraus was engaging, keenly conscious of himself and those around him. Thain's wardrobe, if it could be called that, consisted of white shirts and dark suits. For TV appearances, he wore blue shirts.

Kraus, with piercing blue eyes and a neatly trimmed beard, donned pink and lavender shirts as well as ties sporting splashy colors and patterns. He wore plaid suits and a wristwatch that looked like it had come from the Museum of Modern Art. Just as he had transformed his office into a stunning aerie high above New York Harbor and the Hudson River, he also lavished great care and attention on his own presentation and appearance. He looked more like the creative director of a large advertising agency than an investment banker.

The women who worked directly for Thain—Margaret Tutwiler and May Lee—admired their boss's fierce intellect, but were absolutely taken with Kraus's presence. He was the epitome of urbane sophistication and taste.

Nelson Chai's office on the thirty-second floor was situated between

Thain's office, occupying the southwest corner of the building, and Kraus's space, which faced west overlooking the Hudson River and New Jersey. Unlike the offices that surrounded his, Chai's work area still resembled a makeshift space. No artwork decorated his work area, just the big TV monitor showing CNBC. The two Post-it notes on the walls of his office, covering the holes left by the pictures from his predecessor Jeff Edwards, were still there.

Chai was not a political animal. His absence of egocentricity, uncommon in the upper reaches of Wall Street, endeared him to his colleagues at Merrill Lynch, even those who felt he was not right for the role of CFO. Thain, too, prized this quality in his subordinate. But Chai's selflessness did not blind him to the realities of the thirty-second floor. He knew that for investment bankers, which is what Fleming and Kraus had been earlier in their careers, access to the CEO is as vital as oxygen. Kraus's arrival in the executive suite would cut down Fleming's access to Thain, which was sure to intensify an incipient rivalry.

KRAUS'S ARRIVAL ALSO TRANSFORMED the dynamic of Thain's management meetings. Since he started as CEO, Thain held meetings with direct reports every Monday at 8:00 a.m., and risk meetings every Wednesday morning. Over the summer, as Merrill was forced into emergency capital raises and Lehman's financial position worsened, Thain started holding liquidity meetings every morning at seven o'clock.

Once Kraus joined the meetings, the Goldman-versus-Merrill effect was magnified several times over. Thain would ask Ed Moriarty III or another legacy Merrill manager a question about a specific risk profile, or the bank's capital position or liquidity. If a precise answer wasn't forthcoming, Kraus would pounce, asking how it was possible not to know exactly what the firm's position was, and Montag would pile on, declaring that at Goldman Sachs, this would never happen.

The advent of Montag and Kraus emboldened May Lee, Thain's chief of staff. At times during her tenure, she felt like an emissary in enemy territory, holed up in her bunker on the thirty-second floor and making forays down below to interact with legacy Merrill people. Now, with two former comrades in arms from Goldman in place, she felt a greater degree of comfort and empowerment.

At one meeting, the discussion turned to a trading position that had the potential to cost Merrill Lynch a significant chunk of money if it wasn't unwound. One trader, Scott Brown, assured everyone that the position was properly hedged with a different trade, guaranteeing that Merrill would be protected. Montag would have none of it.

"I don't know why we're even listening to you," Montag told Brown in front of everyone. "You've been wrong for the last three weeks."

Thain never participated in such criticism, but his silence in the face of Montag's remarks to Brown was construed as support of his new colleagues' opinions.

TOWARD THE END OF the first week of September, concerns over the financial stability of Fannie Mae and Freddie Mac—the giant financing companies that purchased the vast majority of home mortgages from the nation's banks—reached panic levels. Over the course of the previous year, the collapse of the real estate market had led to speculation that Fannie and Freddie would suffer crippling losses. And yet, over several quarters, each institution reported small losses compared with those taken by Citigroup, Merrill Lynch, and other financial institutions.

The market presumed that Fannie and Freddie were sitting on huge losses, and despite the belief that the government would never let the two companies fail, investors sold off the stock of the two enterprises between July 2007 and July 2008, driving down Fannie from the $65 per share level to the low teens. When IndyMac, the largest savings and loan in Los Angeles and seventh largest mortgage originator in the country, failed in mid-July 2008, shares in Fannie broke through the $10 barrier into single digits.

Government guarantee or not, investors were fleeing the two finance companies, as they were fleeing the financial services sector in general.

In late July 2008, Congress passed a law allowing the Treasury Department to take over Fannie and Freddie should their losses exceed their capital. Although the law was intended to comfort investors, since it provided an orderly way for Fannie and Freddie to be wound down in case of an emergency, it actually generated the opposite reaction: Investors assumed that since the Treasury now had the power to take over Fannie and Freddie, wiping out shareholders, it was only a matter of time before such an action inevitably followed.

Shares in Fannie bounced back into the low teens by mid-August, but by the end of the first week of September, it was clear that Fannie and Freddie would not be able to raise the capital that they needed to stay solvent. On Sunday, September 7, U.S. treasury secretary Hank Paulson announced that the two mortgage consolidation companies would be placed in a conservatorship, effectively wiping out shareholders.

THAIN HAD MADE THE right call on Fannie and Freddie. At a meeting of his trading and risk teams late in the week leading up to the takeover of the two entities, he had talked about inevitable government intervention that was coming and said he wanted Merrill Lynch to remain absolutely neutral on any security associated with Fannie and Freddie. It was unclear whether the government would recapitalize the two corporations, so he forbade any long positions on the stock. He didn't want Merrill's traders gambling on the other side of the trade either, shorting Fannie's and Freddie's stock in the belief that shareholders would be wiped out. Thain also expressed his concern about debt issued by the two companies, lest a bankruptcy tie up any such investments for years.

Despite his prudent approach to the weekend, Thain received a nasty shock at his Monday-morning management meeting when it was revealed that a trader had purchased a large position in preferred shares of Fannie and Freddie, betting that government action would actually help the share prices of the two companies bounce back. The bet failed, costing Merrill some $500 million.

"That's unbelievable!" Thain shouted, startling everyone at the table. "I thought I was clear about this!" Displays of raw emotion were so rare with him that this outburst registered with everyone in the room.

Sales and trading were the responsibility of Tom Montag, but he was still new enough that the bad bet could be attributed to incompetence by a Merrill trader and the lack of rigid control systems and not his own management skills.

MERRILL HAD TO SWALLOW a half-billion-dollar loss from the weekend's events, but the government takeover of Fannie and Freddie also exacerbated the situation at Lehman Brothers. As of late August, Dick Fuld, Lehman's CEO, had been in talks with the Korea Development Bank about getting an infusion of as much as $6 billion in capital. In early September, as the talks became public, Lehman's share price hovered in the mid-teens, well down from the $44 per share level it traded at in May, before David Einhorn's speech and the bank's surprise second-quarter loss.

But on Tuesday, September 9, the Korean bank announced that the talks had broken off. The news that Lehman's one lifeline to fresh capital had been closed sparked a furious sell-off in the stock, which had closed the previous day at $14.15 per share. The share price itself, which had broken through the symbolic $10 barrier into single digits, caused Standard & Poor's, the credit rating agency, to warn of a possible downgrade in debt issued by Lehman, which only exacerbated the sell-off. At the end of the day, Lehman shares closed at $7.79 following an unprecedented surge in trading volume.

Executives at Merrill Lynch were transfixed by what was happening at Lehman. On the twenty-second floor, Heaton and Wetzel understood immediately that the downgrade from the credit rating agencies on Lehman was likely to put the investment bank into a death spiral, from which its only escape would be a sale to a competitor, or some kind of a government bailout. They also realized that if Lehman went down, which was now looking like a probability, not a possibility, Merrill Lynch would be next.

On the thirty-second floor, Thain rebuffed a request from Fleming that he call Ken Lewis, the CEO of Bank of America.

Instead, Thain called Hank Paulson, the treasury secretary, to ask whether the government was monitoring the situation at Lehman and to extend an offer of help in case Lehman's meltdown turned into another version of the Long Term Capital Management crisis a decade earlier.

Like his colleagues on the twenty-second floor, Fleming didn't believe that Merrill would be able to ride out the storm, even though it was now in a much healthier position than it had been just two months earlier. In the spring of 2008 Fleming had been quoted in a news story describing what was going on in the capital markets as something akin to a horror movie, in which an insatiable monster marauds across Wall Street, attacking leverage wherever it could find it. The monster, having destroyed Bear Stearns, was throttling Lehman and would soon be rumbling toward Merrill Lynch.

Over the past twelve months, every time it seemed that Merrill Lynch had freed itself from the entanglements of its balance sheet, new problems emerged, binding the firm and threatening its ability to raise capital. In July, a series of Herculean efforts had finally, definitively cleaned up Merrill's balance sheet and recapitalized the bank.

And yet, only a month later, Merrill was once again in trouble. If Lehman collapsed, the marketplace wasn't going to look at Merrill and pronounce it healthy. All investment banks were under siege, just as Wetzel had told the board a month earlier. But Wetzel estimated it would take two to three years for the investment banking model to fade out. It was happening now, just weeks after his pronouncement, and the banks seemed to have no control over their fates or the timing of this transition.

LEHMAN WAS NOT SCHEDULED to announce its third-quarter earnings until midmonth, but the loss of confidence in the marketplace forced Fuld and his top managers to rush out their earnings announcement early Wednesday, in order to remove an overhanging uncertainty that would surely build up in the days ahead. The bank announced a loss of $3.9 billion, driven largely by a write-down of $7.8 billion on real estate–related assets.

Late Wednesday, September 10, after the markets closed, Lehman CEO Dick Fuld announced a plan to spin off Lehman's problematic loans into a separate "bad bank," akin to what Tosi had suggested to O'Neal a year earlier. Although the idea made sense on paper, it was similar to other proposals floated by companies such as Citigroup earlier in the year, and like the Citigroup proposals, it didn't strike investors as credible.

The next day, Lehman's stock endured another precipitous fall, opening up almost $3 down from where it had closed the day before. More than 473 million shares traded hands that day and the stock closed at $4.22. The company was well into the red zone now and everyone on Wall Street knew that Lehman would not be able to survive as an independent entity, if it survived at all. The ending would be bad and would have to take place over the weekend. The only question was, how bad?

On Thursday and Friday, Thain and Fleming attended a special board meeting called by Larry Fink of BlackRock, held at the St. Regis Hotel in Midtown. Like everyone who worked in the financial services industry, Fink was following the Lehman news closely, and more than most, he was acutely aware of how closely Lehman's fate was intertwined with Merrill's.

To Fink, both Thain and Fleming appeared distracted during the two-day retreat, each man immersed in frequent conversations on his cell phone. Thain called Paulson again, to reiterate his offer of helping out with any government-sponsored initiative to prop up the failing bank. Paulson told him that there would probably be some kind of meeting that weekend, along the lines of what transpired a decade earlier with Long Term Capital Management.

Fleming was not aware of Thain's attempts to get information or direction from Paulson. Instead, he grew ever more frustrated at his boss's preternatural sense of calm in the face of impending disaster. Thain consistently brushed off Fleming's recommendation that he call Ken Lewis at Bank of America. It was now apparent that BofA was combing over Lehman's books, exploring the possibility of an acquisition on the cheap, an acquisition which, if it took place, would eliminate the one concrete possibility Merrill had for saving itself in an emergency.

Between boardroom sessions, Fleming spied an opportunity to speak to Fink privately, away from Thain and other attendees, and approached.

"Are there any circumstances under which you would consider acquiring Merrill Lynch?" Fleming asked.

Fink paused to let the question sink in. "Maybe," he answered, "at $11 per share." At the time, Merrill shares were trading at twice that price, although trending downwards. Fink had calculated the amount of Merrill's share price that was attributable to BlackRock, about half, and come up with the $11 per share figure. He was assigning zero value to the rest of Merrill's business.

Two years earlier, a huge investment bank with a market capitalization of $70 billion had acquired its 49 percent stake in Fink's smallish firm, with its own market capitalization of $5 billion. Access to Merrill's platform and customer base had helped BlackRock flourish over the two years, while Merrill's bad investments had brought the legendary brokerage firm to the brink of disaster. Now BlackRock's market capitalization had blown by Merrill's, and Greg Fleming, the man who helped put the deal together two years earlier, was the supplicant, seeking outside help for the mighty Merrill Lynch.

But $11? Not a chance, thought Fleming, who believed that anyone who wanted to buy Merrill Lynch would have to pay a premium.

As part of the two-day board session, Fink arranged for a dinner on Thursday evening. Fleming and Thain attended and did their best not to display any worries. As far as Thain was concerned, discussions about Merrill could wait until the next morning, when he would convene a conference call to apprise his own board of what was happening in the markets and on what he was planning for Merrill Lynch in the days ahead.

CHAPTER 12

A CALL TO ARMS

ON THE MORNING OF Friday, September 12, the nine outside directors of Merrill Lynch dialed in to a conference call hosted by CEO John
Thain. The group had shrunk by one with the departure of Alberto
Cribiore just a week earlier. Cribiore, who served as lead director and
chairman of Merrill Lynch during November 2007, had been the driving
force behind the hiring of Thain. He was moving to Citigroup, which
had offered him a full-time post in its international investment banking unit, the lucrative position that the Italian banker had sought a year
earlier.

In a statement issued by Merrill, Cribiore said, "I am delighted by
the excellent progress that Merrill has made under John's leadership over
the past nine months and have great confidence in the company's long-
term prospects in the hands of this capable board and world-class senior
management team."

The departure of Cribiore, a tireless proponent of Thain who was
adamantly opposed to any discussion about selling Merrill Lynch, altered

the dynamic of the board. Most CEOs, over the course of several years, have the opportunity to replace retiring directors with people of their own choosing, a situation that engenders deeper support for the top executive at the board level, because the new directors owe some allegiance to the person who recommended them.

Thain had not yet had that opportunity and with the departure of Cribiore, he lost his primary champion. Instead, on the September 12 call, he had to deal with the one director whose experience with the capital markets approached his own, John Finnegan, the CEO of Chubb Insurance.

Unlike O'Neal, who by the end of his reign could barely hide his contempt for some of Merrill's directors, Thain maintained a professional demeanor at all times in his interactions with the board. But even here, dealing with the only people who had authority over him, Thain's elemental lack of people skills came through. He began board calls and board meetings without the slightest greeting, not even a "hello, everyone" or a "good morning," and avoided the type of small talk and chitchat that normally serves as the transition between a greeting and the start of a business discussion.

Thain began the call by updating the directors on what was happening in the stock market, discussing the problems Lehman faced and telling everyone that Merrill was in much better shape than its unfortunate competitor.

Finnegan countered, politely but firmly: How would Merrill Lynch avoid the contagion that had brought Lehman Brothers to its knees? Thain reassured everyone, saying Merrill would be able to ride out this storm. Its stock could never plummet to the level of Lehman's share price because Merrill had several tangible assets: its stake in BlackRock and its thundering herd of financial advisors, each of which would prevent the share price from collapsing to zero. Thain estimated that those two assets alone would put a floor of $10 a share on Merrill's stock price.

Kraus, who had yet to work a full week at Merrill Lynch, leapt to support his boss, reiterating Thain's arguments about the intrinsic value of Merrill's assets.

Finnegan was unconvinced. Merrill's assets might provide a floor for the stock price in a normal market, but it was clear that investors were running away from Lehman in a panic. Rational arguments would not protect Merrill Lynch from a similar panic. As for selling a stake in Merrill's wealth management business, which might be worth as much as $30 billion, that would be no easy feat. It would take months of accounting work to separate the business—the most vital organ in Merrill's operations—from the company's investment banking operations and sales and trading divisions. Given what was happening with Lehman, Finnegan said, Merrill Lynch might not have that kind of time to prepare for an emergency.

Finnegan asked about the financial advisors, many of whom considered themselves migratory entrepreneurs who, if the circumstances got bad enough, could pull up stakes and move across the street to Smith Barney or Paine Webber. Thain turned to Bob McCann, head of the investment management division, and asked how his group was holding up under the pressure of the past few months.

Things were going well, McCann replied, with no significant drop-off among the advisors.

Finnegan persisted, asking whether there was any emergency plan in case Merrill Lynch could no longer survive as an independent entity. Finnegan and Fleming had spoken several times that week about the need for Merrill to initiate some kind of dialogue with Bank of America. Finnegan now made those arguments to Thain and Kraus, who was supporting his CEO at every point.

Thain wouldn't budge, insisting that Merrill Lynch would be fine.

Armando Codina, who had been a prime mover behind O'Neal's ouster, now weighed in, recommending that Thain keep his options open depending on what happened with Lehman, and with the markets in general.

To Fleming, Codina's neutral position made it clear that the board was not going to push Thain into opening up discussions with Bank of America, or force him down any other road. Fleming's stomach tightened as he realized that Merrill Lynch, the company where he had spent the last sixteen years, was about to go into the most turbulent weekend in Wall Street history without any kind of plan for survival.

THROUGHOUT THE DAY, LEHMAN'S share price floundered, sinking as low as $4, wiping out much of the capital cushion the bank would need to survive. For executives at Merrill Lynch, it was like watching a horrible car crash or train wreck play out in slow motion. There was the shock and sadness of what was happening to Lehman, coupled with the morbid inability to look away. Worst of all was the sense of foreboding, since many people at Merrill assumed that Lehman's fate would eventually be visited upon them.

Fleming kept after Thain, urging him to contact Ken Lewis at Bank of America, but the CEO refused. Nelson Chai also joined in, imploring his mentor to consider starting discussions with BofA. Thain assured Chai that he had a grip on everything, and warned the younger man of the dangers of starting to negotiate too soon. "Once you start down that road, you can lose control of your fate," Thain said.

It was now apparent that two banks had emerged as serious bidders for Lehman: Barclays Capital, the securities unit of London's Barclays Bank; and Bank of America. The news about Barclays's interest in Lehman did little to assuage Fleming, who was still fearful that BofA would pull the trigger on an acquisition. The prospect horrified him. In his mind, the Charlotte bank was the best possible acquirer for Merrill, and he briefly wondered if had made the wrong move earlier in the summer.

Just a month earlier, after the board meeting where he and Cribiore argued over whether BofA would make a good partner for Merrill Lynch, Fleming happened to speak with Ed Herlihy of Wachtell, Lipton, Lewis's go-to deal lawyer.

Herlihy—who had arranged the meeting between Stan O'Neal and Ken Lewis the previous September—wondered if Fleming was interested in having an informal chat with Greg Curl, the head of strategy at BofA, and the man who negotiated all of Lewis's deals. Fleming, who wasn't aware that O'Neal had ever met with Lewis, was intrigued. He knew that any kind of transaction with the Charlotte bank would be anathema to Thain, but Fleming also saw the North Carolina bank as the best possible match for Merrill in terms of stability, the most logical partner for his firm if the markets continued to erode. Fleming called Curl and set a date for a meeting.

But the moment he set it up, Fleming had qualms about the furtive meeting and its ramifications. He weighed whether he was doing something unethical, or at least sneaky and insubordinate, in meeting Curl on his own. At home that night, Fleming was tormented by the process he'd set in motion. Herlihy had assured him that just because he was meeting with Curl didn't mean the two men had to talk about a deal. It could be strictly a get-to-know-you affair, with no reference to an acquisition, the seasoned lawyer explained. But Fleming knew that wasn't possible. Any unilateral move like that would constitute a betrayal of trust in Thain. He had come to question the CEO's judgment, and no longer interpreted Thain's calm demeanor in times of crisis as a sign of strong leadership. Rather, Thain's eerie calm in the face of worsening market conditions had begun to strike him as a naive optimism that the markets were on the verge of getting better, an outlook not justified by the realities facing Merrill Lynch.

After getting advice from Finnegan, it became clear to Fleming that he could not proceed alone. He either had to give Thain a heads-up about what he was doing, or drop it. Fleming knew Thain would not support the meeting under any conditions, so he called Curl, apologized, and canceled. Curl said he understood, and the conversation ended, but the Charlotte banker, a veteran dealmaker, now had some important information to pass along to Ken Lewis: Someone high up in the Merrill Lynch organization was interested in a deal with BofA.

AS THE FRIDAY BLACKROCK board meeting dragged on, Fleming tried to find out what was going on between Bank of America and Lehman. He also kept in touch with Finnegan, who was sounding out other board members to determine their level of concern over Merrill's situation. Although Finnegan spoke to four or five different board members during the day, he did not find anyone who shared his level of anxiety over Merrill's situation. In general, the board felt reassured by Thain's confidence in Merrill's position.

As of 4 p.m., when its share price tumbled to $3.65, the market had passed its final judgment on Lehman Brothers, whose roots extended back to 1866 in Alabama. It was clear that the only people who were buying shares in the final days of that week in September were thrill seekers betting that the government would broker some kind of sale to a stronger bank. Just six months earlier, Bear Stearns had been sold to JPMorgan Chase at $2 per share and then, faced with a potential revolt among shareholders who threatened to block the deal, JPMorgan Chase CEO Jamie Dimon upped the price to $10 per share. Any comparable transaction involving Lehman could produce a similar windfall.

After the BlackRock meeting broke up, Fleming and Thain retreated to Merrill's Midtown office, just off Fifth Avenue, behind the Saks department store. It was there that Thain received a call from the office of Tim Geithner, president of the New York Federal Reserve Bank, asking him to come downtown that evening for a meeting at the bank, but divulging no details about the purpose of the meeting.

Fleming asked Thain if he wanted him to accompany him downtown. The CEO said no, and instead called Kraus, his closest confidant. To whatever extent Fleming had served as a trusted advisor to Thain over the previous nine months, it was now clear that Kraus—a man with less than two weeks' experience at the ninety-four-year-old institution—had supplanted him.

That dynamic had been apparent in the morning board meeting. Every time Thain made a statement about Merrill's strengths compared to Lehman's, Kraus seconded him. Kraus shared Thain's dream of transforming Merrill Lynch into a bigger, stronger bank than it had ever been. By contrast, Fleming had been a naysayer all year, warning Thain against declaring that Merrill Lynch did not need to raise any more capital, and urging the boss to move more quickly to sell assets. The breaking point had occurred the previous month when Fleming flatly declared his opposition to the idea of acquiring Fortress, the struggling investment fund.

In contrast to Fleming, who could become excitable and even petulant when he dug in on an issue, Kraus was smooth and never lost his composure.

Before heading to the Fed, Thain got some good news from Donald Quintin on the mortgage desk. Even as the world seemed to be crumbling, "DQ," as he was known, had found a buyer for Merrill Lynch's $2.5 billion portfolio of Alt-A bonds, a subprime position that had eroded dramatically in value, netting more than $1 billion in cash for the firm.

THE FEDERAL RESERVE BANK of New York is an imposing structure, built like a fortress, and wedged into the angle formed by Liberty Street and Maiden Lane in lower Manhattan. In addition to its seemingly endless corridors connecting ornate sitting rooms with conference rooms, it sits on one of the largest collections of gold bullion in the world. Because of its important role in crafting policy and its proximity to most of the nation's money-center banks, the New York Fed is a singularly important institution in the world of banking, the most powerful of the reserve banks outside of Washington, D.C.

Thain and Kraus arrived at the Federal Reserve around 6:00 p.m. The top executives of other Wall Street banks also bustled in around the same time. Lloyd Blankfein, chief executive of Goldman Sachs, and John Mack, head of Morgan Stanley, were there, as was Jamie Dimon, the top executive of JPMorgan Chase, along with Steve Black, Dimon's right-hand man. Citigroup CEO Vikram Pandit and the heads of Bank of New York Mellon and State Street, along with representatives of foreign institutions, including Deutsche Bank, Credit Suisse, and Société Générale, had all arrived. Dick Fuld, the CEO of Lehman, was not there, nor were Ken Lewis, Bank of America's CEO, nor Bob Diamond, head of Barclays Capital, the two banks negotiating with the government to acquire Lehman.

The only other time Thain had been called down to the Fed for an emergency meeting had been a decade earlier, in 1998, when the meltdown of Long Term Capital Management had threatened the stability of the entire banking system. By 1998, Thain already enjoyed a reputation as a brilliant quantitative mind, and his performance during the Long Term Capital crisis—in which he determined the amount of money that would be needed to bail out the fund—only enhanced that reputation. He and his mentor, Jon Corzine, worked closely at the Fed back then to guide the industry-led bailout.

Paulson was late arriving at the Fed from the airport. Neither Thain nor Kraus had been overly concerned about Merrill's prospects, even as pressure mounted on Lehman over the summer. But now, standing at the Fed on a Friday afternoon, with the heads of other major banks around them, and the treasury secretary himself due to arrive, the gravity of their own plight began to hit home.

While most of the other attendees worked their phones, maintaining contact with their top executives, Thain and Kraus slipped out of the building for a short walk. It was a gray, wet evening, following a gray, wet day, but there was still enough daylight for Kraus and Thain to saunter down to a small park.

"What do we do?" Thain asked Kraus, his friend of twenty-five years. Never at a loss for ideas, Kraus suggested that they might approach Bank of America or HSBC to see if either wanted to make an investment in Merrill. Neither man wanted to sell any part of the company, but offering a 10 percent stake to a large bank would bolster Merrill's capital position, shore up investors' faith in Merrill's ability to make it through the crunch, and leave the bank independent, in control of its own destiny, with Thain remaining in charge.

The two men returned to the Fed. Paulson had arrived from the airport and gone directly to the thirteenth floor to talk to Geithner. At about 7:00 p.m., Paulson, Geithner, and Christopher Cox, chairman of the Securities and Exchange Commission, came down to the first floor and entered the Liberty dining room, the largest open area on the floor. Before them had gathered the most powerful men on Wall Street, the top executives of the nation's biggest financial institutions, unified in their anxiety about what was going to happen not just to Lehman, but to their industry.

The regulators took their seats at the end of a large table, and Geithner opened the meeting by pointing out the magnitude of the crisis that everyone was facing. The failure of Lehman would be catastrophic to the markets, he said. Therefore, it was in the interest of every CEO in the room to work together to prevent such a failure. But Geithner's biggest statement, the one every CEO was waiting on, involved the government's position toward Lehman. In this he was clear: The government would not be putting up any money to bail the bank out.

Geithner, a brilliant thinker and student of finance, owed his quick rise in government to the Clinton administration, where he served in various capacities before being plucked in the 1990s by treasury secretary Robert Rubin for the position of undersecretary for international affairs. A few years later, at the age of forty-two, he was named president of the New York Fed.

Geithner's youthful looks and unassuming manner had been a plus for much of his career, but on this night, as the fate of the financial markets teetered on the brink of disaster, his youth undercut his message. Geithner's warning that the government would not step in to save Lehman was interpreted by some as being a bluff intended to get the bankers to put up some of their shareholders' money to save Lehman. The CEOs in the room—men who had worked their way to the top of the financial world through decades of tireless effort, mental toughness, Machiavellian intrigue, and the ability to force other men to submit to their will—were not about to be bullied by Geithner alone.

Then Paulson spoke. With his gravelly voice—he always sounded like he had a head cold—he reiterated Geithner's points. Unlike his younger colleague, Paulson had the gravitas to pull off the threat of Armageddon if the people in the room didn't come together to solve the Lehman problem. The fact that he had come up from Washington to deliver this message personally denoted the magnitude of the problem. A former football star at Dartmouth, Paulson stood well over six feet, his height accentuated by a large, mostly bald head and his tendency to bend over and peer directly at people he was talking to.

After working in the Pentagon in the early 1970s, Paulson served in the Nixon White House, working for John Ehrlichman, assistant to the president for domestic affairs. (Ehrlichman later served eighteen months in prison for his participation in the Watergate cover-up.) In 1974, Paulson joined Goldman Sachs, working out of its Chicago office. An investment banker who was relentless in working client relationships, Paulson rose quickly at Goldman, running the firm's Chicago operations before moving to New York as vice chairman in 1994 and becoming CEO in 1999 when the partnership became a public company.

Everyone in the room respected Paulson as a fierce competitor who had not only made it to the pinnacle of Wall Street, but had now become the most powerful cabinet secretary in the administration of George W. Bush. But of all the talent amassed in that room at the Federal Reserve that evening, no one looked up to Paulson as much as, or through as complicated a prism as, John Thain.

EXACTLY TEN YEARS EARLIER, in September 1998, Thain had been paired with Jon Corzine, the head of Goldman Sachs, to represent the firm in the bailout of Long Term Capital Management.

From a distance, the investment banks of Wall Street appear to be pure meritocracies. The executives who rise to the uppermost ranks, it is widely believed, are the ones who generate the most income for the firm. But that is only partly true.

The men who rise to the top of the biggest investment banks—and they are almost always men—are the ones who combine the ability to generate profits for the firm with the ability to lead others on a shared mission. The two traits are inextricably woven together: The more followership an executive can command among his colleagues, the greater the profits he can reap for the enterprise.

In his rise to the top of Goldman Sachs, Jon Corzine displayed both. He combined a masterful ability to generate profits on the trading floor with the popularity to develop a large following. When Steve Friedman, Goldman's senior partner, shocked the firm in 1994 by announcing his retirement, Corzine was voted senior partner and chairman, and Paulson, Goldman's top investment banker, was named president and vice chairman.

John Thain owed his rise at Goldman Sachs to Corzine. In the 1980s, Thain led Goldman's initial foray into the trading of mortgage-backed securities, at a time when Corzine headed up the entire fixed-income division. Corzine, a gregarious, bearded Midwesterner, took a liking to his fellow Illinois native, and moved him up the career ladder quickly, installing Thain as treasurer in the early '90s.

When Corzine ascended to the top job in 1994, he named Thain as his CFO and put his protégé on Goldman's powerful management committee.

For much of its illustrious history, Goldman Sachs has been led by two men sharing power, instead of the traditional one-man corner office. For the most part, the firm's attempts to pair two men together at the top have worked well. But starting in 1994, it was clear that Corzine and Paulson did not work well as a team.

The two men had been paired together because Goldman's management committee wanted Corzine's expertise in trading—where short-term decision making skills are paramount—to be leavened by Paulson's ability as an investment banker to cultivate deep client relationships and engage in long-term strategic planning. But Corzine and Paulson did not get along, and Paulson frequently complained about his boss, even threatening, in late 1997, to quit.

Corzine exacerbated the situation with Paulson with his tendency to act unilaterally, without seeking the consensus of the management committee. Members of that committee, including Thain, John Thornton, Robert Hurst, and Paulson, repeatedly reminded Corzine that he could not make commitments on behalf of the firm until the committee had agreed on a course of action.

"I don't understand this," Corzine said during one of these sessions. "Jack Welch doesn't have to ask permission to do something." The other partners reminded Corzine that Welch was the chief executive of General Electric, fully vested with the power to act on behalf of the board. As a private partnership, Goldman was different.

Corzine knew that Goldman Sachs would not be able to thrive in the global financial markets unless it expanded, either by merging with a large commercial bank or going public. His exploration of both courses of action sparked friction on the management committee, as Thain, Paulson, and Thornton remained adamantly opposed to an IPO.

Thornton, a colorful investment banker and a brilliant strategic thinker, was a natural partner for Thain. Like Thain, he had been posted to Goldman's London office in the mid-1990s and while there, Thornton had taken the measure of his colleague's strengths and weaknesses. By 1998, "the two Johns," as Thornton and Thain had become known, were positioned as the next generation of leadership at Goldman Sachs. But Corzine's plans to engineer a transformational change at the firm, either through a merger or an IPO, left both wondering what their futures would be.

In the spring of that year, the two approached Corzine and asked him to designate them formally as his heirs apparent at Goldman, to remove any doubt about who the future leaders of the partnership would be. Corzine refused, saying he wasn't ready to make that kind of commitment, especially with so much work to be done. Unlike Corzine, Paulson was more open-minded on the topic. In May of 1998, the management committee voted to elevate Paulson to the same level as Corzine, in the hope that as partners with equal authority, the two men would do a better job accommodating each other.

But it was no use. Corzine and Paulson continued to argue like children, even as Corzine prevailed in convincing the partnership as a whole that Goldman Sachs should become a public company. But as the bank geared up for an initial public offering in the fall of 1998, the collapse of Long Term Capital Management forced Goldman to back away, an embarrassing retreat for a firm considered to be the most elite of the investment banks.

By the time Corzine and Thain decamped to the Federal Reserve to lead the effort to bail out LTCM in September of 1998, the insurrection against Corzine was in full bloom. Paulson had secured the firm support of Thain and Thornton in part by promising to give the men the formal designation as heirs apparent. Corzine's role in the Long Term Capital bailout, and his agreement to put $300 million of the partnership's money to make the rescue effort work, played into Paulson's campaign to undermine him with the rest of the management committee. The postponement of Goldman's IPO, which was moved to the following year, increased Paulson's sense of urgency, because if Corzine succeeded with the offering, it would be virtually impossible for him to be removed as CEO of a public company.

Corzine recognized early in 1998 that Thain had come under the influence of Thornton and Paulson, but he felt confident that their long friendship, which included ski vacations together in Colorado, dinners out with the wives, and other activities, would endure the temporary ups and downs of work life. The men were so close that in his will, Corzine had entrusted Thain with the welfare of his children in the event of an untimely death.

Corzine misjudged his protégé. By the final days of 1998, Thain's personal ambition to run Goldman Sachs had overtaken his sense of loyalty to the man who had put him on the fast track at the firm. While Corzine was off skiing in Telluride over the Christmas holiday, Paulson convened the other three members of Goldman's five-member management committee—Thain, Thornton, and Bob Hurst—and the group voted to strip Corzine of his power.

On Corzine's first day back after New Year's, Thain called and asked if he could drop by his office on the thirtieth floor of Goldman's headquarters at 85 Broad Street. Of course he could, Corzine said. A few minutes later, Thain entered the room and sat down across from his boss. Corzine had always prized Thain's calm under fire, his single-minded focus on issues and his directness. But now those attributes had been turned against him, and Corzine began to tear up as Thain coldly relayed the information that the management committee had voted him out.

SPEAKING BEFORE THE ASSEMBLED CEOs of Wall Street, Paulson declared that Lehman was in deep trouble and that its fate needed to be sorted out over the weekend. Unlike Bear Stearns, which had benefited from a government pledge to cover most of its losses if JPMorgan Chase acquired it, Paulson said there would be no bailout for Lehman.

The notion of an industry-led bailout did not sit well with these captains of the financial services industry. It was clear that they would be asked to use their own shareholders' funds to prop up a deal that would benefit either Bank of America or Barclays Capital, both of which were negotiation to acquire Lehman's good assets. Fresh in everyone's mind was the sweetheart deal struck six months earlier, in March 2008, when the government stepped in to help JPMorgan Chase buy Bear Stearns. Bear Stearns had a potential hole of $30 billion on its books, but Paulson and Geithner protected JPMorgan Chase, putting it on the hook for the first billion in losses, and assuming responsibility for the next $29 billion.

It was a nonstarter, and despite the warnings from Geithner and Paulson, many attendees thought, as the meeting drew to a close, that by the end of the weekend, the government would figure out some way to prevent Lehman's failure.

When the meeting broke up, sometime after 9:00 p.m., Thain called Pete Kelly, the deal lawyer, and told him to be at the Fed the next morning at 8:00 a.m. to be part of his team. Thain also called Fleming to inform him of what had gone on at the Fed.

"It's not good," Thain told him. "It's not clear they're going to save Lehman."

"We need to start thinking about our position, John," Fleming said, pressing the case again for Bank of America.

Per usual, Fleming was getting all hot and bothered, Thain thought. The CEO urged him to calm down about the Bank of America discussions. "We'll talk tomorrow," he said and hung up. Thain's driver took him to a restaurant in Greenwich, Connecticut, where his wife and another couple had been waiting for hours to meet him.

FLEMING, AT HIS HOME in northern Westchester County, fretted over the lack of urgency in Thain's voice. He called Finnegan yet again, around 11:00 p.m., and told him that Thain still didn't seem convinced of the need to reach out to Bank of America. Finnegan reported that his efforts to round up support among other directors for such a move had fallen flat.

"The board's not going to convince him to do that," said Finnegan. "It's up to you. Good night."

And with that Finnegan hung up, leaving the task of getting Thain to the table with BofA squarely on the younger man's shoulders.

Around 11:30, Fleming went to bed, but he couldn't sleep. He tossed and turned for much of the night, disturbing his wife, Melissa. At about 2:30, she asked what was wrong. Friday was usually the one carefree evening of the week that her husband had for sleeping, and here he was, twitching in the wee hours.

"This is not just any Friday," he told her. "The next week is going to be historic in this business."

CHAPTER 13

THE LONGEST DAY

AROUND 5:00 A.M. ON Saturday, September 13, unable to sleep, even fitfully, Fleming got out of bed and started preparing notes for his first conversation with Thain that day. He drew up a list of bullet points to focus his thinking. He wanted to call Thain immediately, but held back out of concern for disrupting Thain's family. The minutes ticked by slowly. He paced around his home in the distant suburbs, animated by negative anticipation. Around 6:00, he called Heaton.

By 6:30, Fleming figured, the CEO would be awake, so he called. Thain was just getting out of the shower. He told Fleming to call him back in a half hour or so, when he was en route to Manhattan. Around 7:15, Fleming called again, as Thain sat in the back of his Yukon, being driven to the Federal Reserve in lower Manhattan.

Fleming implored his boss to reach out to Ken Lewis, the BofA chief executive, before the Charlotte bank got too entangled with Lehman. Thain urged calm, saying he doubted BofA was going to do the Lehman deal. Fleming persisted, arguing that even if BofA walked away from any deal with Lehman, Merrill Lynch couldn't afford to have its stock price sink the same way Lehman's had in the past week.

"If we wait and things get very difficult, it will be very hard for us to get anything done," Fleming pleaded. "Our stock will drop like Lehman's, the ratings agencies will downgrade us, and then where will be be? If we start talking now, we have the whole weekend in front of us. Remember, we have an obligation to our shareholders, our clients, and our employees."

"You're panicking," said Thain, with an edge to his voice, reflecting some resentment at the suggestion that he did not have the interests of shareholders, clients, and employees at heart.

"I don't think so," replied Fleming.

"Well, I'm not ready to go there," said Thain, "You're ahead of things, and not in a good way. We'll talk later."

Fleming called Ed Herlihy, the lawyer who handled Bank of America's transactions, to find out whether BofA was proceeding with the Lehman transaction, and to encourage the Charlotte bank to think about Merrill. Herlihy didn't say anything about what was happening with Lehman, and told Fleming that BofA wouldn't even think of Merrill until John Thain called Ken Lewis to start the process.

THAIN ARRIVED AT THE FED around 8:00 a.m., where he was joined by Kraus and Pete Kelly. Geithner reiterated his stance from the day before, that there would be no federal bailout for Lehman and that it was up to the men gathered in the room to come up with a rescue plan. After the Friday night meeting had ended, Kraus had spoken with Dan Jester, a former Goldman colleague who worked for Paulson at Treasury, and suggested that the Wall Street bankers break up into several teams, with one group focused on Lehman's balance sheet and another looking at the exposures each bank had to Lehman in case of a bankruptcy.

That morning, Geither and Paulson did break up the group into several units, along the lines of Kraus's suggestion. Thain, whose experience with the Long Term Capital Management bailout the decade before had given him a fair degree of experience in such exercises, was part of the group responsible for figuring out the structure of an industry-led bail-out. Another group, including teams from Goldman Sachs and Credit Suisse, took the lead on figuring out the size of the hole in Lehman's balance sheet.

Work had barely begun when, at 8:30, Fleming called Thain again.

"You need to call Lewis," he said.

"We already had this conversation."

"You have to do it."

"You're starting to get on my nerves!"

"That's likely to happen again this weekend," Fleming snapped back.

The call ended. Fleming paced back and forth in his home. As coach of his son's soccer team he would have to leave shortly for a game. No way. He asked another parent to cover for him. Fleming called Herlihy to say he was still working on Thain and was hopeful of getting his boss to come around shortly. Herlihy was gruff and sounded like he was losing patience. But the lawyer didn't make any sweeping statements, such as "Don't bother," which Fleming interpreted as confirmation that BofA still had no deal with Lehman. That was good.

At 9:15, Fleming called Thain yet again. This time he gained some traction. Thain indicated he might be willing to meet with Lewis for a general discussion, though it sounded as if the response was designed as much to get Fleming off his back as to pursue any kind of deal. Fleming called Herlihy immediately to relay the news, but Herlihy was not interested in "might" or a "general discussions." He wanted an actual meeting, so Fleming committed to a 2:30 rendezvous.

Before hanging up, Herlihy, who had also arrived at the Fed with Lewis's top dealmaker, Greg Curl, and Joe Price, BofA's chief financial officer, said Thain would have to call Lewis in order for the meeting to happen. Herlihy and company were in the same building as Thain now, but in a separate part of the cavernous fortress. Unknown to Fleming, their mission was to tell Paulson privately that without government help, BofA had no interest in Lehman Brothers.

"Greg, I've been down this track before," said Herlihy. "We need to hear from John Thain."

Eric Heaton was coaching his own son's soccer team, just a few miles away from where Fleming lived. Sometime after 9:30, he received a call from Fleming on his BlackBerry. Heaton was part of a group within the Merrill Lynch finance department, including Nelson Chai, that believed Merrill Lynch would have no chance in the wake of a Lehman failure. He and Fleming had spoken several times the night before about the importance of getting Thain in a room with Lewis, and Fleming had called Heaton at 6:00 a.m. that morning as he worked himself up for his calls to Thain. Now Fleming had told him that he had set up Thain to meet with Lewis at 2:30, and that Heaton and other key people should be ready for action. Heaton left the soccer duties to his wife, and went home to change.

While he was at home, the phone rang again. This time it was Nelson Chai.

"I bet you've heard this already," said Chai, "but things are in motion. We've got to get everyone into the office. But we can't discuss it openly."

Fleming called Thain yet again, this time to urge him to make a personal call to Lewis. "Why?" asked Thain, aggravated that after agreeing to a 2:30 meeting, he had to take the additional step of calling Lewis on the phone.

"He wants to hear from you!" said Fleming. "It doesn't matter what you say. Just call him and tell him the weather in New York is good. But you *have* to call him. He's not coming up unless he hears from you."

"I don't want to do that," said Thain. "We'll be at a tactical disadvantage."

Fleming nearly exploded. "Are you kidding!? These guys are going to be our partners. How can you talk about 'tactical disadvantage'?"

Thain hung up. Fleming shook his head in disbelief, then called him back.

"You're really annoying me," said Thain.

"Look, John, you have to call Lewis, then get back to me and let me know."

Sometime after 10:30, the group comprised of people from Goldman Sachs and Credit Suisse returned from their brief examination of

Lehman's balance sheet. The CEOs of the two banks, Lloyd Blankfein and Brady Dougan, then made a brief presentation to the assembled group, and the news was shocking. It would take at least $20 billion to fill the hole in Lehman's books.

Thain recalled how excruciatingly painful it had been ten years earlier to get a bunch of Wall Street banks to put up $250 million to $300 million each to fill the $4 billion hole at Long Term Capital Management. There was no way this group of banks, most of which had toxic assets on their own books, could be expected to pony up a grand total of $20 billion.

When the presentation ended, and the size of Lehman's problems had been outlined, it was clear to those in the room that the federal government was now prepared to let Lehman fail.

Bob Kelly, CEO of Bank of New York Mellon, said, "We have to figure out how to organize ourselves and how to do something, because we're toast if we let this thing go."

Paulson kept to a hard line. "I'm just going to say bluntly that you need to help finance a competitor or deal with the reality of a Lehman failure," he declared.

Vikram Pandit, the CEO of Citigroup, asked Paulson out loud whether, given Lehman's impending failure, his bank should start cutting its credit lines to Merrill Lynch, the next investment bank destined for the emergency ward.

At that moment, the gravity of the situation hit Thain fully. Suddenly he became nervous, shaken. As he huddled with his colleagues from Merrill, Pete Kelly asked, "What's going to happen?"

"I don't think they're going to make it," Thain said slowly, referring to Lehman. After another minute or two talking to Kraus and Kelly, Thain took out his phone and dialed Lewis's number in North Carolina.

"Ken, this is John Thain," he said in a quiet, numb voice. "We ought to have a discussion."

"Yes," said Lewis, waiting for Thain to take the next step and propose a meeting.

"Yes, we should have a discussion," Thain said hesitantly.

"Well, maybe we ought to have a meeting, don't you think?" Lewis continued.

"I guess so," said Thain distantly.

Lewis said he would fly up to New York and meet Thain at the corporate apartment in the Time Warner Center at 2:30 that afternoon.

Thain wasn't the only CEO who now grasped the severity of the situation and the danger it posed. A few minutes later, John Mack, the chief executive of Morgan Stanley, the next investment bank up the food chain from Merrill Lynch, ambled over to Thain and said, casually, that perhaps the two of them should talk. Thain agreed immediately. He feared having any kind of conversation with Ken Lewis without an alternate plan in place. One of the cardinal rules Thain learned at Goldman Sachs was to keep as many options as possible open before committing to a course of action. In any negotiation, you needed leverage, you needed some alternative that would force the other party to make the highest bid possible. That way, you could strike the best deal.

After his conversation with Thain, Mack came over to Kraus to ask what they should do next. They agreed to speak again in an hour or so to arrange a meeting. Thain and Kelly had departed in a car taking them to Merrill's downtown headquarters just a few blocks away.

On his way back to Merrill headquarters, Thain called Fleming, reported that he'd set up the meeting with Lewis, and told him to come into the city immediately.

At last, Fleming's moment had come. The bank's president, who had spent a miserable, sleepless night worried about Merrill's fate, and an excruciating morning harassing his boss and the top lawyer representing BofA, felt a surge of energy on hearing the news. There were numerous obstacles to getting a deal done, Fleming realized, but at least Merrill Lynch would now have a chance to survive. Adrenaline rushing, Fleming threw some clothes into a bag and told his wife he'd see her on Monday.

AT MERRILL'S HEADQUARTERS, Kelly, Kraus, and Michael Rubinoff started working on preparations for a discussion with Morgan Stanley. Nelson Chai's team, including Heaton and Sara Furber of investor relations, were already up to speed. Fleming called Rosemary Berkery, the general counsel, for a briefing and to ask her to join him later at Wachtell, Lipton, Bank of America's law firm. Merrill could not go to Rodgin Cohen at Sullivan & Cromwell, its usual outside law firm, because Cohen was representing Lehman, so Berkery called Shearman & Sterling, the firm where she used to work.

Thain was driven to Merrill's Midtown office, where he would have a pre-Lewis meeting with Fleming around 1:30, to go over the parameters of the conversation. Chai tracked Wetzel down in Lehigh, Pennsylvania, where he was visiting his daughter. Wetzel said he'd come into the city immediately.

When Fleming arrived at the Midtown office, he and Thain started talking about Bank of America. Just then, John Mack called to set up a meeting that evening at the apartment of Walid Chammah, one of Morgan Stanley's top executives, on the Upper East Side of Manhattan.

This was the first Fleming had heard of any talks with Morgan Stanley. Thain asked him if he wanted to attend, but Fleming said he'd rather see how Thain's meeting with Lewis went. Besides, Morgan Stanley had its own set of problems on the balance sheet. Fleming wanted to focus exclusively on Bank of America, which he viewed as the only real solution for Merrill.   ·

Thain explained his strategy for the meeting with Lewis: He'd offer to sell a 10 percent stake in Merrill Lynch to Bank of America in return for a line of credit.

"I don't know, John. He's going to say he wants to buy the whole thing."

AT 2:30, THAIN ARRIVED at the Time Warner Center on the southwest corner of Central Park, wearing slacks, shirt, and blazer, but no tie. He went up to the Bank of America apartment and was ushered into a reception area, where Ken Lewis was waiting for him. Thain hadn't eaten a proper meal that day, and there would be no food here. Lewis offered him a Diet Coke, and they sat down at a table.

Despite their divergent backgrounds and careers, the two men shared certain characteristics, including a distaste for small talk and false bonhomie.

"I'm interested in selling a 10 percent stake in Merrill Lynch," Thain said, in his typically direct manner. "In return, we would like a multi-billion-dollar line of credit."

Lewis, fully aware that he had the stronger hand, said he didn't want a 10 percent stake. "I'm interested in buying the whole company," he declared.

"I didn't come here to sell the whole company," Thain replied.

Lewis, for all his introversion, had been down this road before, as CEO of Bank of America since 2001 and as the top lieutenant to Hugh McColl, who had taken NationsBank from its humble North Carolina roots and transformed it into BofA, a financial colossus striding over the entire continent. McColl had built the bank through serial acquisitions, many of which began with conversations just like the one Lewis was having with Thain right now, with a man who did not want to give up the independence of his bank or his job as CEO. Lewis knew Thain's reluctance to sell more than 10 percent was simply the opening of the chess match, and he had a series of moves he was prepared to play in order to capture his quarry.

Over the next forty-five minutes, Lewis talked about the strategic beauty of a combination between Merrill Lynch and Bank of America. Marrying the biggest and best army of financial advisors with the top retail bank in the U.S. would generate business opportunities on both sides. BofA could refer its commercial clients—the people who took out business loans—to Merrill Lynch advisors to handle their personal investments. Merrill's advisors, on the other hand, could refer their clients—many of whom were successful entrepreneurs and businesspeople—to BofA when their businesses needed financing. In laying out his vision of a vibrant financial supermarket, Lewis invoked the phrase that McColl had used so often in his successful acquisitions, imploring Thain to see "the wonder of it all."

Thain loathed the idea of giving up his job as CEO of Merrill Lynch, and felt revulsion at selling to a company that proudly proclaimed itself to be the "Walmart of banking." But he prided himself on not letting his emotions get in the way of making a rational decision. It was clear to him that on paper, at least, a combination between Merrill Lynch and Bank of America made sense. Before leaving the corporate apartment, he and Lewis agreed that negotiations should proceed and be handled by the "two Gregs," Curl and Fleming, starting at 5:00 p.m.

Lewis suggested that he and Thain also meet up at 5:00 at the law firm, where they could oversee the negotiation process. Thain declined, and said he had some other matters to attend to, which Lewis interpreted as a sign that the Merrill Lynch CEO was also negotiating with someone else.

Lewis closed the conversation by urging Thain to keep the discussions quiet. Thain said he felt uncomfortable about carrying on a negotiation with Lewis that might undermine Hank Paulson's attempts to get BofA to save Lehman.

"You can tell Hank," said Lewis. "We're not pursuing Lehman. We've sent all our bankers back home to Charlotte."

After leaving the Time Warner Center, Thain called Fleming. "Lewis wants to buy the whole company," he said.

To keep an eye on what was happening with Lehman, and so as not to arouse too much suspicion, Thain, Kraus, and Kelly returned to the Federal Reserve for the afternoon discussions.

The negotiations between the "two Gregs" would take place at Herlihy's law firm, Wachtell, Lipton, on 52nd Street, just off Sixth Avenue, a short walk from Merrill's Midtown offices. Fleming would have an entire floor for his team, the thirty-fourth floor, and Curl's BofA group would occupy the floor below.

Fleming immediately went over to Wachtell to meet with Curl. He told the BofA executive, who was about fifteen years his senior, that he wanted to have something in place to announce on Monday morning.

"That's a very aggressive timetable," said Curl, who added that he wouldn't even begin to discuss price until his team had had a chance to do "due diligence" on Merrill's books. That is, BofA wanted to look at every substantial asset on Merrill's balance sheet, and review every pertinent fact about the company, from the number of financial advisors it employed to its derivative trading positions in the European mortgage market.

Fleming said he understood, and would supply anything and everything that Curl wanted to see. It would take several hours to get Merrill executives in New York and around the world suddenly engaged in this effort to produce information for Bank of America's team, but it would also take BofA several hours to get its team of internal accountants and business leaders in place to review Merrill's books.

Dozens of BofA people had spent the last few days in Manhattan going over Lehman's financials. Earlier on Saturday, when Lewis decided he didn't want to make a bid for Lehman, the entire team, except for Curl, had been dispatched back to Charlotte.

BofA owned a fleet of corporate jets—mostly G4s and G5s—and five were used to ferry its accounting staffers from Teterboro Airport in New Jersey back to Charlotte. One of the planes was scheduled to take off around 1:30 p.m. A dozen BofA passengers who were waiting at the Teterboro terminal to board that plane noticed something unusual: They saw Ken Lewis, their CEO, arriving just as they were preparing to leave. As he passed through the small terminal, Lewis ducked into a rest room to avoid further contact with his acquisition team.

Just before 5:00, after the fifty-plus members of BofA's acquisition team had returned to Charlotte, several received an all-points-bulletin e-mail from David Belk in corporate planning: Put the troops together and return to New York immediately.

HAVING SETTLED IN AT Wachtell, Fleming called Mark Patterson, head of Merrill's real estate portfolio, reaching him at a diner on Long Island. Fleming told him to get into the city immediately and that no one should know what he was up to. If Patterson had to tell his wife, that would probably be okay, but it would be best if no one knew. Just get into the office, Fleming said. Then he called David Gu, head of currency trading, who was based in London. Gu was getting ready for bed, but after Fleming spoke to him, Gu knew there would be no sleep that evening.

There were scores of calls that needed to be made, so Fleming put Sara Furber, the head of investor relations, in charge of the due diligence. In rapid-fire succession, Furber made dozens of calls to people who needed to be brought to headquarters. She either told them to come in or handed them over to Fleming so he could explain what was needed.

Meanwhile, down at the Federal Reserve fortress, where meetings progressed throughout the afternoon, Kraus was approached by two former colleagues at Goldman Sachs: Gary Cohn, the co–chief operating officer, and David Viniar, the CFO. Kraus had been encouraged to leave Goldman less than a year earlier, as part of Goldman's annual cull of fifty-something partners. There had been no acrimony, as Goldman was always moving older partners out of the way to make room for the up-and-comers. In the end, the ties that bind at Goldman endure longer and outlive most of the uncomfortable moments that occur.

Such was the case now.

"How can we help?" asked Viniar and Cohn.

"We need a credit line," said Kraus. "And if you're serious, you could buy a 10 percent stake," he added, reprising the idea he'd floated to Thain the evening before. "It would kill the shorts," or short sellers, who had been reaping a windfall betting against Lehman's shares and would soon be out in force on Merrill's shares. Cohn and Viniar said they'd be in touch.

When Thain rejoined Kraus at the Fed, he told his colleague about the meeting with Lewis. Neither man was keen on the "nuclear" option, selling the entire company. And for Thain's part, it wasn't just about not wanting to lose his job as CEO. Kraus argued convincingly that the markets were going through a temporary downdraft, and if there were some way to get through the next few weeks intact, there would be a tremendous upside for Merrill Lynch during the inevitable recovery.

Kraus described the conversation he had just had with his former Goldman colleagues, which was more promising than the idea of linking up with Morgan Stanley. Either option was certainly preferable to an outright sale to Bank of America, Kraus said. A merger with Morgan Stanley, whose CEO was approaching sixty-five years of age, could position

Thain for the top job or result in him getting the top job right away. Or a 10 percent investment from Goldman Sachs, along with a line of credit, might be just enough to help Merrill get through the next month or so.

To some of the people closest to him that weekend, Thain was a man torn between two diametrically opposed advisors. On one side was Kraus, one of his oldest friends through a relationship forged at Goldman Sachs, whispering in his ear that with a little strategic dexterity, Thain could navigate his way through this rough patch and maintain Merrill's independence and his own job. In the other ear, Thain heard Fleming's voice, not a whisper at all, but an urgent, pressing, even nagging insistence that selling the company to Bank of America was the only solution. Thain wanted to follow Kraus's reasoning, but he couldn't ignore Fleming's view.

Thain and Kraus were planning to meet John Mack and his two top lieutenants that evening. The next morning, Kraus would head down to Goldman Sachs, at 85 Broad Street, with Pete Kelly, to discuss the nature of Goldman's investment. To prepare for the Goldman meeting, Kraus scheduled a visit to Merrill's treasury department, on the twenty-second floor, to find out, in granular detail, what the bank's liquidity situation was. Kraus needed to know how much cash the bank had on hand, and whether it had access to other sources of cash in the near term.

Eric Heaton, the treasurer, was keenly aware of how quickly Merrill's capital base would erode if the bank didn't find a savior over the weekend. If Lehman declared bankruptcy, the contagion would move directly to Merrill Lynch. The company's $70 billion in available cash on hand would disappear in two to three days, maximum, as people pulled their money out and counterparties stopped doing business with Merrill.

Heaton had been in constant touch with Fleming over the previous twenty-four hours about the latter's efforts to push Thain into a meeting with Ken Lewis. Kraus contacted Heaton and told him about the possibility of an investment from Goldman Sachs, and then scheduled a visit to his floor later that evening for a briefing on Merrill's liquidity situation. Heaton surmised that Kraus had effectively convinced Thain that a sale to BofA was not necessary and that, armed with a few facts, Thain's top lieutenant would be able to fashion a less drastic solution to Merrill's problems, one involving his old friends at Goldman Sachs.

He called Fleming and told him about the Kraus presentation. Heaton and Fleming—the two men had worked closely together for fifteen years—had reached a point where neither man had to spell out exactly what he was thinking in order to communicate a thought.

The first wave of BofA bankers had now completed the return trip from Charlotte and Fleming wanted Heaton to be there, at Wachtell, to answer questions. Fleming thanked Heaton for the heads-up about the Kraus presentation and hung up. The fact that Kraus wanted to get a briefing on Merrill's cash balances and its ability to hold its own during a challenging environment could only mean one thing: Thain was desperately looking for an alternative to the BofA deal, and the best alternative was selling a 10 percent stake to Goldman. The only reason Kraus was having a briefing with Heaton's team would be to bolster the argument for the Goldman option.

Once again, Thain seemed to be embarking on a major initiative without even asking for his advice. No matter: To Fleming, the Goldman option was wacky, just like the notion of buying Fortress a month earlier. And just like the Fortress idea, this one had to be nipped in the bud. Fleming thought for a few moments, trying to figure out what he should do, and the solution occurred to him: Paul Wetzel.

"PAUL, I NEED YOU to do something for me," said Fleming when he'd reached Wetzel at the office.

"Sure. I'm heading up to Wachtell now."

"No, don't. There's a team of us up here. I need you to stay back for now. Kraus has asked for a presentation from the treasury department tonight about our liquidity situation. John Thurlow and Marlene Debel are going to walk him through our situation. I'd like you to be there, too."

"All right. Why?"

"Kraus and Thain have this idea that if they can get Goldman to buy a stake in the firm, and give us a line of credit, we'll be okay. It doesn't make sense at all."

"I'm glad you convinced them of that," said Wetzel.

"They're not convinced, Paul. They actually believe that will solve the problem. I can't tell you what to say, but you know how serious the situation is. Thurlow and Debel will provide all the detail and expertise that's needed, but they might present this from a very narrow point of view. I need someone there who can explain to Kraus where we are *right now* and what could happen next week. This can't be spin and there's no room for sugarcoating. Someone's got to stand up to Kraus and lay it on the line."

There was a pause. "Can you do this, Paul?"

"Yeah."

NELSON CHAI, ERIC HEATON, and Sara Furber sat down in a conference room at Wachtell. Across from them were Joe Price, Bank of America's CFO, and Brian Moynihan, the head of BofA's own investment bank. Chai reviewed Merrill's financials, explaining in detail what the team had done in July to clean up its books. He described Thain's successful efforts at raising capital since his arrival last December, and how Merrill's balance sheet appeared now compared with what it looked like a year earlier. To Chai's surprise, neither man across the table asked about the forecast for Merrill's fourth quarter.

AT THE FEDERAL RESERVE, Paulson sent word to Thain that he wanted his former Goldman colleague to come up to the thirteenth floor for a meeting with him and Geithner around 5:00 p.m.

Thain arrived, but Geithner had to leave the room to take a call, so Paulson proceeded with his former deputy one-on-one.

After the September 11 terror attacks, when Paulson was stranded in the air halfway around the world, Thain had proven himself as the interim leader of Goldman Sachs, remaining calm in the face of an emergency and holding the firm together through its most difficult physical challenge.

This was different. A kind of financial 9/11 had been unleashed in the capital markets. Instead of employees being frightened, fleeing their offices in lower Manhattan to get home on foot, it was investors who were panicking and bailing out of the markets.

Paulson was now the one with the steady hand in times of crisis, and Thain was feeling the pressure. The treasury secretary warned his former subordinate that once Lehman collapsed, the situation for Merrill Lynch would be dire, and that he should consider selling the firm.

Thain said he was on top of the situation, that a meeting had been scheduled for that evening to discuss a merger with Morgan Stanley, that he'd already begun discussions with Bank of America, and that their old firm, Goldman Sachs, had expressed an interest in shoring up Merrill.

Paulson said the Morgan Stanley merger idea seemed like a non-starter: The firms had too many similarities, and the match was unlikely to restore confidence in Merrill Lynch among investors. Thain acknowledged Paulson's point.

Then Paulson started talking about Bank of America and how it was by far the most logical partner for Merrill. He urged his former subordinate to consider selling Merrill to BofA. Thain avoided a direct answer, but appeared uncomfortable at Paulson's suggestion.

BACK AT WACHTELL'S OFFICES, the due diligence activities were beginning to happen. The next wave of bankers and accounting people had arrived from Charlotte, and now various teams of people from Merrill Lynch—representing credit, treasury, and other areas—paired off with their counterparts from BofA in smaller conference rooms.

To some extent, BofA's attempts to wrap its arms around Merrill's complicated balance sheet—a process that would normally take at least a full week—was aided by Merrill's recent capital raises. In order to reset the share prices of its big sovereign wealth fund investors, and then raise capital through the sale of common stock in July, Merrill Lynch had to organize its financial presentations, complete with underlying documentation. Most of this work was still fresh and suitable for reuse two months later.

On the thirty-third floor, BofA general counsel Tim Mayopoulos had already begun considering the ramifications of a Merrill acquisition on his department. The investment bank had a huge staff of lawyers and a general counsel, Rosemary Berkery, who had been unsuccessfully recruited by the Charlotte bank on several occasions in recent years.

Mayopoulos knew that before he got the job, BofA management wanted Berkery for his position, so he raised the point with Ken Lewis that evening and said he'd understand if, once the deal went through, Berkery was put in charge of the entire legal department of the combined entity.

Lewis assured Mayopoulos of his support. "Tim, you're my general counsel," Lewis declared. "I'm happy with you."

SHORTLY BEFORE 7:00 P.M., Thain, Kraus, and Montag arrived at the apartment of Walid Chammah, Morgan Stanley's co-president, on Manhattan's Upper East Side. Also with Chammah were John Mack, the firm's CEO; James Gorman, the firm's other co-president; and Cordell "Cory" Spencer, Chammah's top deputy.

Chammah's apartment—an exquisitely appointed "bachelor pad" that the London-based banker kept in Manhattan—was chosen as the site for the meeting in order to assure some level of convenience and privacy. Mack, like Thain, lived on a sprawling estate in Rye, a wealthy Westchester suburb. Chammah's neighbors included Larry Fink of BlackRock and Mayor Bloomberg, but Fink was not in the city and Bloomberg, fortunately, was out on the town when the guests arrived.

Two sofas were set up across from each other, where the deputies would sit, accompanied by a single chair on each end, where the principals could face each other for the conversation. About fifteen minutes after Chammah and the Morgan Stanley contingent arrived, John Thain came, with Kraus and Montag in tow.

Thain and Mack exchanged greetings; the two men knew each other reasonably well as competitors and from Thain's tenure as CEO of the New York Stock Exchange. Gorman, who had spent six years at Merrill Lynch running the private client business before falling out of Stan O'Neal's favor, greeted the three men politely. As he sized up Thain, Kraus, and Montag—and their combined lack of experience at

Merrill—he wondered why Thain hadn't brought any longtime Merrill executives—such as Fleming or McCann—with him for a discussion about selling or merging the franchise.

Chammah greeted Montag warmly. He had tried to recruit the Goldman trader to Morgan Stanley before Thain landed him earlier in the year. Chammah had met Thain only once before, when Thain tried to recruit him to Goldman in 1987 from First Boston, but Peter Kraus was new to him.

After brief opening remarks from Thain about why the two investment banks should think about consolidation, Peter Kraus began explaining how certain parts of each firm's business would mesh with each other. There were synergies, since Merrill had a stronger presence overseas than Morgan Stanley, and areas of common interest, such as private client business, where Merrill's thundering herd could be combined with the old Dean Witter network of advisors, now under the Morgan Stanley flag.

Other parts of the firms' businesses, such as institutional securities, duplicated each other and would lead to a bloodbath of job cuts. Although he'd only joined Merrill Lynch two weeks earlier, Kraus spoke authoritatively about each of his firm's businesses while Thain and Montag looked on.

After some ninety minutes of discussion, Thain summed up Merrill's position: He needed to do something that weekend. There were "other options" for Merrill Lynch, which he did not describe, but his preference was a merger with Morgan Stanley.

The Morgan Stanley executives hid their unease with Thain and this desperate lurch for a solution to Merrill Lynch's problems. Politely, John Mack said the idea was intriguing, and that he'd bring it up with his board of directors Monday evening, but there was no way that Morgan Stanley was going to do anything as drastic as a merger over a weekend, and without proper due diligence.

Thain was not pleased. The Morgan Stanley group could tell from his body language, and that of Kraus and Montag, that Thain had set his hopes on making this transaction happen.

After Thain and his crew left, the Morgan Stanley executives went out to dinner to discuss everything they had just witnessed. Gorman in particular felt a profound sadness that the firm that had been run by stalwarts such as Schreyer, Tully, and Komansky—men who devoted their lives to Merrill Lynch—was now being shopped around by three men on loan from Goldman Sachs who had no feeling or understanding of the sacredness of the place, the sanctity of Merrill Lynch as an institution.

PETER KRAUS ARRIVED FOR the meeting with Heaton's people on the twenty-second floor of Merrill's offices downtown around 10:00 p.m. He wasn't alone: He had come with Tom Montag and Michael Rubinoff, forming a kind of Goldman Sachs alumni committee.

They gathered in a conference room near Marlene Debel's office, and after everyone had settled in, Kraus started the meeting.

"I want to understand better what our liquidity situation is, and how it's likely to be impacted next week, depending on what happens with Lehman."

For about fifteen minutes, Thurlow and Debel took turns explaining Merrill's plight. They described its cash on hand, and the value of the most liquid securities—government bonds and such—that the bank owned. They also described some of the problems that faced Merrill if the company needed access to cash quickly. Merrill did own a small bank, chartered in Utah, where it held billions of dollars in deposits. But banking rules restricted how those deposits could be used.

Another important part of Merrill's operations, and the operations of other investment banks, was the overnight funding market. Merrill Lynch relied on a balance of approximately $100 billion per day to keep its widespread operations going. It didn't *go through* $100 billion per day, but it used, invested, and profited *from the use of* $100 billion every day.

Merrill used to borrow funds from other banks for periods of thirty to ninety days. After Bear's collapse, such funding was more difficult. Merrill could now borrow for only the shortest periods, either overnight or for a week.

The failure of Lehman Brothers would probably restrict Merrill from accessing the overnight market for liquidity, and reduce the willingness of counterparties to trade with it.

Investment banks needed access to overnight funds in much the way that people need oxygen. Once that access is restricted, the vital organs start shutting down, precipitating a death spiral.

The question in Kraus's mind was whether a $10 billion line of credit from Goldman Sachs would provide enough oxygen to withstand a short-term convulsion of the markets, which was what was going on now. Again, Thurlow painted a blunt picture of what a post-Lehman world would look like for Merrill Lynch.

When the presentation ended, Thurlow and Debel left the conference room, and Montag began to saunter out. Rubinoff lagged slightly, while Wetzel came over to Kraus, with whom he'd worked closely in the past month, to have a private conversation.

"So if we got fresh equity, and a line of credit of $10 billion, or better, $20 billion, would that be enough?" Kraus asked.

Wetzel began to shake his head, but Kraus persisted. "If Goldman puts this money into us, their seal of approval in the marketplace, that could give us the credibility to get through this."

Now they were alone. "I understand what you're saying," Wetzel began. "You think there's a good chance we can make it through with this amount of money. I agree with you. The odds are we could make it, and if we do make it, the upside is spectacular. Our stock is at $17 a share. On the other side, it could eventually get to $100.

"But let me tell you what. In the environment that we're in right now, companies disappear in days. You just can't stop it. Once there's a crisis of confidence, you're done. Investment banks don't fail because of capital. They fail because of liquidity.

"I don't know what the probability of that happening here is. Is it 50 percent? Maybe not. Maybe it's only 20 percent. Let's say it is 20 percent, which means there's an 80 percent chance that an investment from Goldman will get us through. Even if there's just a 20 percent chance that we'll fail, you have to remember that you're gambling with 60,000 jobs."

Wetzel paused to let the point sink in.

"This is an all-or-nothing bet," he continued, boring in on Kraus. "I don't know how you do that. I don't know how you roll the dice in this situation. It's reckless. There's just too much at stake."

Kraus listened carefully, taking it all in.

BY 10:00 P.M., MOST of the fifty or so members of Bank of America's diligence and acquisition team had reassembled at Wachtell to pore over Merrill's financials and interview the firm's key executives. Among the BofA bankers, this process was a world apart from the diligence that had been done on Lehman over the previous few days.

With Lehman, the process had been perfunctory. Representatives from Lehman's treasury department came in to the offices of Sullivan & Cromwell (Lehman's law firm) with carefully prepared "decks" or presentations highlighting the bank's significant assets. Another group of BofA people sat in a room at Sullivan & Cromwell, interviewing Lehman executives one-on-one with a checklist, but without asking any questions off script, even along the lines of "how's your business?" or "what's happening in your area?"

By Friday evening, it was so clear to BofA's diligence team that the Lehman deal wasn't going anywhere that most of them, visiting from Charlotte, slipped out by 9:00 p.m. to enjoy a sit-down dinner at a restaurant, a pleasant change of pace from the food deliveries that were the norm during any serious acquisition process.

On Saturday night, BofA's diligence team felt the kind of pressure from top management that suggested this deal was going to happen. J. Christopher Flowers, a former Goldman banker who had become a billionaire private equity investor, took a separate room to review Merrill's balance sheet. Flowers, a close friend of Greg Curl, BofA's top dealmaker, had looked at Merrill's books the previous December, with an eye toward investing in Thain's vision of a new Merrill Lynch.

Among the most important members of the Charlotte bank's diligence team were Neil Cotty, chief accounting officer, and Jeff Brown, the treasurer. Both men reported to Joe Price, the CFO, and their mission on this accelerated diligence process was to comb through every detail of Merrill's balance sheet looking for any hidden "nuclear weapons" that might blow up the deal.

EVEN AFTER MIDNIGHT ON Saturday evening, Fleming wasn't doing anything resembling negotiating. He and Furber were still calling Merrill executives around the world and putting them in touch with BofA people at Wachtell for phone interviews and requests for more information about Merrill's worldwide operations.

Kelly, Heaton, and Wetzel each floated from one ad hoc meeting with Bank of America people to another, producing information about Merrill and answering questions about Merrill's business. Kelly also met with BofA's general counsel, Tim Mayopoulos, who wanted to get a sense of how many lawyers worked there, and what their duties were. The Merrill executives could sense that BofA was quickly getting the information they wanted from various departments, meaning that negotiations over price, which would only take place after due diligence, would begin sometime Sunday morning.

After 2:00 a.m., Fleming asked Wetzel—who had gone to Wachtell after his meeting with Kraus—to return to Merrill headquarters and compile information about Merrill's share price, and how the market had valued investment banks in recent years. This information would help Fleming support his arguments as to why Bank of America should pay a premium for Merrill Lynch.

Kelly and Heaton, separately, began to notice that a lack of sleep and increasing tension were taking a toll on Fleming. The investment banker was wandering around the thirty-fourth floor of Wachtell, where the Merrill people had gathered, with a distant look. He'd see a colleague and immediately fasten on to that person, asking for information or giving directions. The conversation over, he'd revert to a disengaged state.

Around 3:00 a.m., Kelly brought Fleming into a conference room, where they could speak privately, away from the chaotic, haphazard group meetings that were coming together and dissipating on a regular basis.

Kelly talked about some of the issues that would come up the following day, and about the importance of writing an airtight "material adverse change" clause into the deal. Fleming agreed.

Then Kelly, a veteran of many similar transactions, brought up the topic that was foremost in his mind: price. He had worked with Fleming on countless occasions, knew him to be not only energetic but excitable, and had the feeling that on a deal of this magnitude—the sale of Merrill Lynch itself, the place where they both had spent their careers—Fleming might let emotions get in the way of cold, hard facts.

Sure enough, after Kelly asked Fleming what price he had in mind when the negotiations began in earnest, Fleming said he was going to ask for a "three-handle," investment banking jargon for a price at or above $30 per share.

Shares in Merrill Lynch had closed on Friday afternoon at $17.05 apiece, the lowest level in years. In the previous two weeks Lehman's share price had plummeted from the 20s to just over $3 per share. If Lehman failed that weekend, an outcome that now seemed likely, Merrill's share price would crater over the next few days.

In Kelly's mind, Merrill Lynch had no negotiating leverage. Asking BofA to match the $17 share price would be a stretch.

"Stop thinking you're going to get $30," said Kelly. "These guys are Machiavellian. They're going to come back to us tomorrow and offer $5 a share. You've got to prepare John and the board for this."

Fleming, who considered himself a master at managing expectations and handling boards of directors, was taken aback, especially hearing this from someone he'd worked with so closely for so long.

"You've got to have a little more faith in me," he said.

"It's not about you. It's about the 60,000 employees who work at this company."

"Stop giving me all this," said Fleming, growing agitated. "I can get this done."

Kelly shook his head. "You've got to start preparing. When that number comes down, you have to manage your constituencies. I love you. I have faith in you, but stop throwing this three-handle around."

Once again, Fleming was taken aback at his words. "Don't doubt me on this," he said, shaking his head.

"You're overwrought," Kelly barked. "And you're going to blow it for all of us."

"I'm not overwrought! I know the dynamics here, and I know I can get this done."

Kelly moved closer, getting into Fleming's space. "There is no way that Bank of America is going to pay $30 a share for Merrill Lynch," he growled. "Our job is to prepare for the worst-case scenario, not the best. If the offer on Sunday afternoon is $3, we do that deal!"

"No, you don't understand," Fleming shot back. "If I don't get $30, Thain's not going to do this deal!"

Exasperated, Kelly moved away from the table. "I can't have this conversation anymore," he said, leaving the room.

Not long afterward, Heaton approached Fleming and took him aside for a private conversation. Kelly, who had started his career on the trading floor before becoming a deal lawyer, didn't flinch at the idea of confrontation, an unusual trait at Merrill Lynch. Heaton, who had been an investment banker before becoming treasurer, had a gentler manner, and even when he argued, he made his points smoothly, without giving offense.

How were things going with price? Heaton asked. Did Fleming have any idea what he'd be asking for later that day? Heaton had been heavily involved with the reset of shares owned by the sovereign wealth funds from Korea, Kuwait, Temasek, and other investors in July, when Merrill entered into a complicated arrangement that priced their shares at $22.50 apiece. In a perfect world, Bank of America would make an offer at that level, which would leave Merrill's biggest investors whole. Instead, Fleming shocked him by saying he wanted to get at least $30 a share.

Heaton paused and absorbed the information. "Greg, you've been doing an unbelievable job," he said. "Everybody supports you and what you've done to get us to this point. But maybe you should let someone else get involved here. That's a big risk, asking for that price."

Fleming looked directly at Heaton. "I know they want it," he said. "They can taste it. You've got to trust me on this."

"Greg, maybe you should get some sleep. This whole thing has been weighing on you."

"You guys have to stop this," said Fleming, practically spitting the words out of his mouth. "If they see any of this negative body language, we're done. We all have to hold it together."

THE CONVERSATIONS WITH KELLY and Heaton startled Fleming and began to undermine his confidence. He decided to go to the hotel for a few hours of sleep, so he would be ready for the negotiation session with Curl later that morning.

On his way out of the office, someone at the law firm asked if he needed a car to his hotel, the Mandarin Oriental, near the Time Warner Corporate Center, about ten blocks away. Fleming opted to walk.

It was about 4:00 a.m., and the office buildings in every direction were shrouded in darkness. The streets of Midtown Manhattan, normally jammed, were empty, the traffic lights continuing their rotation from green to yellow to red in the void.

As he made his way along the broad sidewalks, Fleming wondered whether his two colleagues were right. This wasn't just another deal. The fate of 60,000 employees was in his hands. If he was stubborn about getting the highest price possible, Greg Curl might just walk away from the table and call his bluff, letting Merrill Lynch and its share price twist in the wind for several days until the company collapsed. And that would be his fault, Greg Fleming's fault. He had built a wonderful career at Merrill Lynch, he had been promoted to the doorstep of the CEO's office, but if he overreached in this negotiation, he'd forever be remembered as the guy who destroyed it all by acting like a pig at the negotiating table.

Throughout his career, when he negotiated deals, he was always the agent working on behalf of the client. Fleming had earned a law degree from Yale, and when he put a deal together, he acted like a lawyer arguing on behalf of a client. He always served the client's interest and wanted his client to win, but ultimately he was representing someone else, and Merrill Lynch was benefiting from his efforts and the investment banking fees he brought in.

This was different. Merrill Lynch was the client. Heaton and Kelly and Wetzel and Furber and 59,996 others were his client, and if he miscalculated by the smallest margin, asked for a dollar beyond what Curl and Ken Lewis were willing to pay, it could all fall apart, employees would lose their jobs, and in many cases their lifetime savings. And it would be his fault.

CHAPTER 14

SUNDAY BLOODY SUNDAY

PAUL WETZEL WAS STILL in his golf shirt and slacks, the same clothes he was wearing more than twelve hours earlier when he was having lunch with his daughter in Lehigh, Pennsylvania. It was approaching 4:00 a.m. as he moved quickly through the twenty-second floor of Merrill Lynch's headquarters at the World Financial Center, gathering books of information that had been compiled earlier in the summer to show prospective investors in Merrill Lynch what the company's prospects were.

He reviewed the material, making sure he had everything that Greg Fleming would need for his negotiations a few hours later. He checked his watch. He had two hours, enough time for him to take a car to his home in New Jersey, shower, change, and come back in to meet Fleming at 6:00 a.m. at Wachtell.

AS WETZEL WAS LEAVING the building, Pete Kelly was arriving from Wachtell. Kelly joined a team of lawyers on the twelfth floor, reviewing Merrill's plans in case of a Lehman bankruptcy. Merrill Lynch, like every other Wall Street bank, had hundreds of trading positions with Lehman, each of which would have to be unwound in the now likely event of bankruptcy.

After an hour or two there, he would check into a hotel in lower Manhattan to shower and shave and be ready for an 8:00 meeting at Goldman Sachs with Peter Kraus.

Even though he hadn't slept, Fleming found himself refreshed after a shower at the Mandarin Hotel. On his walk back to the offices at Wachtell, around 5:30, he stopped at a Starbucks. It was still dark, but there was a hint of daybreak in the east. Unlike his earlier walk, in which he was weighed down with doubts about what he was doing, on this stroll he was focused and convinced of his reasoning.

He went over every negotiating point he had in his favor: Bank of America had just spent several days combing over Lehman's books, and Merrill's balance sheet was demonstrably better, less cluttered with toxic assets; Merrill's private client business—its army of financial advisors— was the envy of the industry, generating billions of dollars in revenues every year; and the stock had recently been trading well above $30 per share.

Fleming also had an important piece of information that he could use to his advantage. Over the previous month, he had learned about a discussion that took place a full year earlier between Ken Lewis and Stan O'Neal. In September 2007, before the damage from subprime mort- gages had begun to spill onto Merrill's income statement, spawning bil- lions of dollars in losses, Lewis had invited O'Neal to BofA's corporate apartment in the Time Warner Center and offered to buy Merrill Lynch, which was trading at $76 per share, for more than $90 a share.

Fleming knew that Ken Lewis wanted Merrill Lynch more than any other Wall Street bank, and if Lewis was willing to pay $90 a share just a year ago, a deal for $30 a share would look like a bargain. Besides, BofA's modus operandi was to pay full price. It had grown into the nation's largest retail bank not by penny-pinching and bottom-fishing for acquisi- tions, but by paying top dollar for the best properties. Merrill Lynch was the best franchise in the financial advisory area, and Ken Lewis was not going to let a few dollars per share deprive him of achieving the vision that he and his predecessor Hugh McColl had dreamed of.

Fleming entered Wachtell's office building on 52nd Street, passed through the lobby and into an elevator, and pressed the button for the thirty-fourth floor. "I'm right, and I'm going to close this out today," he told himself.

A LITTLE AFTER 6:00 A.M., Wetzel arrived at the law firm to meet with Fleming. He laid out Merrill's presentation books, as well as some graphics showing the share prices of other investment banks compared with Merrill, and Merrill's competitive position in several of its businesses.

Fleming asked Wetzel what he thought a fair price for Merrill would be, based on the data. A few hours earlier, Fleming had endured a good cop/bad cop routine in his conversations with Pete Kelly and Eric Heaton. Kelly had gotten his Irish up, badgering Fleming about his sky-high asking price. Heaton had taken a gentler approach, like a parent talking down to a wayward teenager.

"I'd like to get 30 bucks," said Fleming.

"You're nuts," said Wetzel. "If you can get market price," which was $17 a share at Friday's close, "you're a hero."

"Paul, John thinks it's worth $40."

"Greg, if you can get the market price, I will carry you around the floor on my shoulders. But face the facts. You have to take whatever they offer."

SOMETIME AFTER 7:00 A.M., as he was being driven back into the city, John Thain called Rosemary Berkery, the general counsel of Merrill Lynch, to discuss the company's position in the event of a Lehman bankruptcy. If Lehman went down, the legal issues surrounding the firm's trading positions with every other Wall Street bank would be staggering and Thain wanted to make sure Berkery and her team would be prepared for the onslaught of legal work that might ensue.

Thain and Berkery also agreed that Merrill Lynch should hold a conference call with the board at noon to give directors an update as to what was going on.

SHORTLY BEFORE 8:00 A.M., Fleming sent word downstairs to see if Curl was ready to start talking price. Not quite yet, Curl said. Chris Flowers's team, which had begun scouring Merrill's balance sheet around 5:00 the previous afternoon, was just finishing up its work, and Curl was still briefing Ken Lewis on what the team had learned about Merrill Lynch in the previous twelve hours.

IN THE DECADES LEADING UP to its transformation from private partnership to public company, Goldman Sachs always enjoyed a reputation as being a unique institution on Wall Street. Like an elite Ivy League college, it was able to attract the best and brightest talent in part because of its reputation as the place where the best and brightest wanted to be. Its exclusivity only added to its mystique.

After going public in 1999, Goldman had to disclose its earnings every quarter. But rather than puncture the myth about Goldman's profitability, the earnings disclosures, showing stunning profits every year, only added to the mystique. By 2007, when other investment banks began to stagger under the weight of billions of dollars in subprime mortgage–related assets, Goldman stunned the market with obscene profits, generated in part by its recognition that the housing market had headed south, and a subsequent series of bets it had placed against the mortgage industry.

Befitting its focus on business, Goldman's headquarters, just down the street from the New York Stock Exchange, were plain and unassuming, almost drab. It was here, outside the entrance to 85 Broad Street at 8:00 on Sunday morning, that Pete Kelly waited, whiling away the minutes until Peter Kraus showed up.

When Kraus arrived, the two men took the elevator to the thirtieth floor, the executive suite, where Hank Paulson's office had been until 2006 when he left to become secretary of the treasury, and where his successor, Lloyd Blankfein, now kept his office.

The two men entered a conference room and were joined by several of Goldman's top people, including CFO David Viniar, David Solomon, and Stephen Scherr.

The dynamic of the meeting was the opposite of the awkward discussion that had taken place the previous evening at Walid Chammah's apartment between team Merrill—consisting of Thain, Kraus, and Montag—and John Mack, CEO of Morgan Stanley. The lack of chemistry at the Saturday night meeting lent a sense of awkwardness.

Here at 85 Broad Street, the vibe was different. There was a comfort level between Kraus and his former colleagues that permeated the conference room. Kelly felt like the odd man out as Kraus, Viniar, Solomon, and Scherr asked each other about their families, inquired about the wives, and exchanged small talk about where they had gone on vacation the previous month.

The pleasantries concluded, Kraus turned to the general parameters of a deal. As Kraus had told Cohn the day before, Merrill was interested in selling a 10 percent stake, at the right price, as long as Goldman was willing to extend a $20 billion line of credit. What the Goldman executives needed to figure out was how much Merrill Lynch was worth, so they could calculate the cost of that 10 percent stake.

It soon became apparent that if Goldman's bankers wanted to place a value on Merrill Lynch, they would have to conduct a close examination of the bank's assets, including its sensitive trading positions.

Like many of Goldman's competitors on Wall Street, Kelly had a visceral distrust of the bank. He was convinced that the firm boosted its profits by "front running," or trading ahead of its own clients. That belief—the dark side of the Goldman mystique—grew out of the firm's uncanny consistency in making better trades than its rivals. Kelly, who thought Goldman would eventually have to confront looming problems on its own balance sheet, did not believe the fabled institution actually wanted to make an investment in Merrill Lynch. Rather, he suspected that Goldman simply wanted to see Merrill's trading positions so it could trade against them. As the conversation between Kraus and Goldman's executives approached the point where they would ask to see Merrill's crown jewels, laid out in a briefing book that Kraus and Kelly had brought along, Kelly's sense of dread increased.

But just before that crucial moment arrived, Kraus smoothly side-stepped the subject, saying he'd get in touch with "John" to determine how they should proceed. Like Kraus, Thain also had a long history with the men in the room, so a reference to his first name was enough.

At about 8:45 a.m., Jon Winkelried, one of Goldman's co-presidents, came into the room. Kraus chided him good-naturedly, saying he'd have to catch up on everything he had missed another time, since they all had a 9:00 appointment up at the Federal Reserve building.

The most logical next step, Kraus summed up, was to arrange for a proper due diligence session. That way, Goldman's bankers could get an accurate idea of the value of Merrill's assets. With that, the meeting was over, and Kraus and Kelly left the building, got into Kraus's car, which had been waiting outside, and made the short drive to the Federal Reserve, where they would reconnect with Thain.

WHILE KRAUS AND KELLY were at 85 Broad Street, Thain returned to Bank of America's corporate apartment at the Time Warner Center.

The pressure of the weekend was taking a toll on him, a man reputed to have ice water in his veins. He had barely been able to eat dinner the evening before, after the meeting with Mack at Chammah's apartment. He had had no breakfast this morning. Ken Lewis simply greeted him and gave him a cup of coffee.

As a face-saving measure for Thain the day before, Lewis had said he'd keep an open mind about Thain's suggestion that BofA buy only a minority stake, 10 percent, in Merrill Lynch. Now, with the clock ticking on Lehman, Lewis spoke bluntly: Bank of America was planning to buy Merrill Lynch outright, not make an investment.

Thain was not surprised, but it was not what he wanted to hear. He issued a warning of his own, saying he had no intention of selling Merrill Lynch, a ninety-four-year-old institution, at a discount.

"You can't do it on the cheap," he told Lewis as he was leaving the apartment. "Otherwise we won't do it."

As he was being driven from Central Park down to the Federal Reserve for the day's meetings, Thain checked in with Kraus, approved the idea of proceeding with due diligence on the Goldman Sachs front, then reviewed the options before him.

First, everything depended on Lehman. As of the previous night, it appeared as though Barclays Capital might buy the firm, backed by a pool of funds put up by a consortium of Wall Street banks. If the Barclays-Lehman deal came off, Merrill might have a chance. Its balance sheet was much healthier than Lehman's, based on the presentation given at the Fed the previous day. In that case, an investment from Goldman could be enough to get Merrill Lynch through this short, turbulent period.

That was another assumption that Thain had to make: that this current spasm of fear on the part of investors was temporary and that business would return to "normal" at some point in the near future. That assumption, which he had carried with him since the day he accepted the job at Merrill Lynch, had been proven wrong again and again. In January, after raising $13 billion in capital, the worst seemed to be over. Then Bear Stearns collapsed in March. In July, Merrill had finally gotten over the hump, unloading its entire position of toxic CDOs and raising more capital, but now Lehman was failing and everyone thought Merrill was next. The reality was that Merrill was in far better shape, but it was the perception that mattered, Thain had come to realize. Here he was, ten months into his job, and the world still hadn't returned to "normal."

The other branch of the decision tree was predicated on a failure at Lehman, a bankruptcy. That would be disastrous for Merrill Lynch. If Lehman folded, an outright sale of Merrill Lynch to Bank of America, the "nuclear option," might be necessary.

And yet, a Lehman failure could end up helping the firm, Thain thought. After all, if Lehman fell, then it wouldn't be just Merrill Lynch in trouble. Morgan Stanley and Goldman Sachs would also be under siege. Assuming that to be the case, if he decided to play a high-stakes game of "chicken," the government would probably save Merrill Lynch, because it would have to save Morgan Stanley and Goldman as well, or risk Armageddon in the capital markets.

Such was the calculus facing Thain as he arrived at the Fed and met with Kraus and Kelly. Kraus and Thain had already spoken, as had Kelly and Fleming. As much as Kraus and Thain believed that Goldman Sachs could help them through their problems, Kelly and Fleming believed the market would see the move as a desperate ploy to put off an inevitable day of reckoning. Over the phone, Kelly reiterated his conspiracy theory about Goldman, telling Fleming that the gold-plated investment bank simply wanted the chance to look at Merrill's trading positions.

"You don't think they want to invest?" Fleming asked him.

"This is the wild goose chase of all wild goose chases," Kelly said. "These guys are salivating to see our books."

At the same time, Kelly forwarded Kraus's request that Fleming hive off a portion of Merrill's team at Wachtell and send the group down to work on the Goldman Sachs proposal.

"I can't do that now," Fleming responded. "We need everyone here."

AS THAIN AND KRAUS milled around the dining area at the Fed that had been converted to a large conference room, mingling with other Wall Street executives, they began to hear rumors about the Barclays bid for Lehman running into trouble with British regulators. That would be a negative development, for Lehman and Merrill.

It was now more urgent than ever to have Goldman Sachs start the due diligence process on Merrill Lynch, Kraus knew. The ex–Goldman banker pressed Kelly to contact Fleming once more and arrange for half the Merrill team to leave Wachtell and head downtown so they could open up the firm's books to Goldman's bankers.

Kelly called Fleming again.

"Kraus wants you to send a due diligence team," he said.

"No. I can't spare anyone."

"What am I going to tell him?"

"Just tell him I can't do it right now."

"You are foreclosing the Goldman option," Kelly said. "You need to prepare everyone for alternatives."

"I'm going to get $30 a share."

"I can't keep having this conversation," said Kelly, hanging up.

Kelly relayed the information to Kraus, who was not happy. Kraus insisted he push harder, stressing the fact that "John wants this."

Kelly tried Fleming again, but couldn't reach him.

IT WAS ALMOST 10:00 A.M., and still no word from Curl downstairs. So far, Fleming had been able to rebuff the requests from Kraus to break up the team he'd assembled at Wachtell, in order to pursue a parallel track of negotiations with Goldman Sachs downtown. He didn't know how long he could keep Kraus and Thain at bay.

Fleming wanted to begin negotiations, but he also knew how the game was going to be played. Curl was an old pro. Nagging him and pushing to start the process before Curl was ready would send the wrong message, Fleming kept telling himself. He had to wait until Curl was ready downstairs, and when Curl was ready, he'd send word. That was the right play.

Just after 10:00, Curl called for him. Fleming walked down the stairs to the thirty-third floor, BofA's floor, and he and Curl went to a small conference room with a broad view of Central Park and the northern half of Manhattan. Neither man looked out the window. Instead, they sat down, facing each other across a table. The door was closed. They were alone.

"We're not selling this cheap," said Fleming. "Merrill Lynch is not going to get sold unless you're willing to pay what it's worth."

With that, Fleming launched into a description of Merrill's component businesses, using the list that Wetzel had provided him earlier that morning.

"Our wealth management business is unparalleled. No one in the industry can touch us, in terms of quality, size, or brand. You've seen the revenues it produces every year, including this year. Can you imagine how powerful our wealth management business will be when it's combined with BofA's customer base? That's worth $35 billion by itself, without anything else.

"We have a 49 percent stake in BlackRock. That's an incredibly safe business, even in an economic downturn. At the rate they're growing, that's worth $15 billion. We have a global banking footprint, which your bank doesn't have. We're in China, Russia, and India. How much would it cost you to build that on your own? That's worth $10 billion. Altogether, that's $60 billion of value, not counting all the capital we just raised."

Curl, sixty years old, had come to BofA, then known as Nations-Bank, in the 1990s when the upstart Charlotte bank purchased Boatmen's Bank of St. Louis. He didn't run any line of business at BofA, but instead held the title of chief strategist. When it came to deals, he was Lewis's closest advisor, a consigliere to the boss.

His was the definition of a poker face. Curl had been with Bank of America for more than ten years, and yet few people really knew him. A former naval intelligence officer, he presented himself as an exceedingly careful man. His office was devoid of any paperwork, since he was obsessive about destroying any memos, documents, or e-mails that came his way. It was widely believed by the bank's top managers that Curl had been selected for naval intelligence because his psychological tests in the military indicated an unusual ability to free himself from emotional connections to anyone or anything. He was a man without feelings or concerns, or so it seemed.

As Lewis's top dealmaker, he'd sat across a table like this many a time. He'd heard variations of the rap Fleming was giving him before, from executives at other banks Lewis had acquired.

"Your stock closed at $17 on Friday," said Curl matter-of-factly. "It's a difficult market, and there are not a lot of other buyers."

"This is a great company," insisted Fleming. "It's only going to be sold once. There's a fundamental value here. My shareholders have to get paid for this, for ninety-four years of work that went into building this institution. We just raised $8 billion in equity in July, at $22.50 a share. We have to treat those investors properly."

Fleming urged Curl to look at the long-term value of Merrill Lynch and not to get hung up on the turbulent conditions then prevailing.

After almost forty-five minutes of similar back-and-forth, Curl suggested they take a break. He wanted to discuss the matter with Lewis. Thain wasn't around, so Fleming huddled with Heaton.

DOWN AT THE FEDERAL RESERVE, the news was bad. British regulators had invoked a rule forbidding public companies from making acquisitions of a certain size without allowing shareholders the right to vote on it. In an emergency situation such as the one involving Lehman, Paulson and Geithner had assumed that the British would be supportive and allow the Barclays acquisition of Lehman to proceed, since it would benefit capital markets around the world. But the British weren't playing along.

Around 10:30, Paulson and Geithner broke the news to the Wall Street executives on the first floor. The group had been in the process of hammering out a $30 billion pool to support the Barclays deal, but the update from the regulators changed the dynamic in the room. Paulson returned upstairs, while Geithner urged the bankers to keep at it, in case the Barclays deal did come off. But he made it clear that Lehman was not going to be bailed out with federal money.

Kraus and Kelly kept running into executives from Goldman Sachs who wanted to know when the Merrill due diligence team was going to be ready to work. Frustrated, Kraus pushed Kelly to call Fleming again.

"I can't," Fleming told Kelly. "Everyone's tied up here. I'll send some people down as soon as I can."

"Things are breaking apart down here," warned Kelly. "If Goldman is not going to happen, then you need to get this trade done. Now is your time to deliver."

"I'm on it," Fleming assured him. "It's going to happen."

A minute later, Fleming's phone rang again. This time it was Kraus. Goldman Sachs was sending its bankers over to Merrill headquarters, and it was imperative that Fleming send a delegation.

"We need some people down there, Greg."

Fleming had kept his temper in check throughout the morning, but now began to lose it.

"If we send people down there, and Bank of America finds out, then they walk away from this deal and the company blows up. Is that what you want, Peter?"

"We don't know what Bank of America is willing to pay," Kraus responded calmly. "What if they offer $12 a share? We need to keep this option open." He paused before playing his trump card. "John wants this."

"If John wants it, John can call me," Fleming shot back.

"Look, I think you're making the wrong decision, but you're the president of the firm," said Kraus. "It's your call."

"Yes, I am the president," said Fleming. "I have made the call. Is there anything else?"

Kraus hung up.

Less than two minutes later, Fleming's phone rang again. This time it was Thain. No greeting.

"Send the people," he said in a steely voice.

"John, that's a bad idea. Let me tell you why."

The silence on the other end of the line suggested to Fleming that he could continue with his argument.

"We're on contiguous floors here. If half the people up here suddenly get up and leave, BofA could pull out."

Still no response on the other end of the line, so Fleming continued. "I don't believe the Goldman Sachs thing is for real. I don't believe they'll be there if we really need them, even if they're down there now."

"We need options," Thain repeated. "I hear those arguments, but we need options and I want people down here."

"I can't send all those people," pleaded Fleming.

"Then send a few," Thain said, coldly.

"I'm trying to get this done in time for the board meeting tonight," said Fleming.

"You're really getting on my nerves," said Thain.

"I'm doing everything I can to make this happen," said Fleming.

"You can afford two people."

"Okay. I'll send two people."

Thain hung up, just as Kraus had. No "good-bye," no "good luck" with the rest of the negotiations, not even an inquiry about how things were going with BofA on price.

AS THE PROSPECT FADED of Barclays acquiring Lehman, Thain and Kraus knew that Merrill's situation would become desperate. Around 11:00 a.m., as the two men strategized in the common dining area, which was now clogged with bankers and executives from across Wall Street, one of the many "admins" on hand to help facilitate the meetings approached Thain with a message: Secretary Paulson wanted to see him. Upstairs.

The request, in the middle of the hubbub and tumult developing on the first floor, suggested something ominous.

Thain detached himself from Kraus and Kelly and walked along the tiled hallway, past the wrought ironwork that still framed the original teller windows of the bank from its earliest days, through the front reception area to the elevator bank. He entered an elevator car and pressed thirteen.

How many buildings in Manhattan had a thirteenth floor? Practically every hotel and office building in the city used the thirteenth floor for heating and air-conditioning units, or simply labeled it "the fourteenth floor" to assuage the anxieties of the superstitious.

At the Federal Reserve Bank of New York, there had been a twelfth floor with huge ceilings that formed the penultimate level of the building. In order to accommodate the Fed's recent growth, architects had split the vast space occupied by the twelfth floor and created a thirteenth tier, housing the work areas of the top officials.

Thain exited the elevator car and saw more of the ironwork, which served as gates for the entrance to the hallway. By using the iron bars from deep below, the designers of the refurbished thirteenth floor hoped to create the feeling of a vault, but the bars also suggested a prison and Thain was going in.

Thain took a right down the hallway and proceeded to Room 17, the last door on the left.

The weight on his shoulders was crushing, but Thain did what he always did under pressure. He kept moving forward, putting one foot in front of the other. He was going to see Hank. It would be all right. Over the course of his career he had had hundreds of meetings with Hank Paulson, mostly about business issues when they worked together at Goldman Sachs.

But some of those meetings were more important than others. When Thain ran the NYSE, Paulson had helped him swing the deal with Archipelago that transformed the Big Board into a public company.

And then there was that other meeting a decade earlier, of the Goldman Sachs management committee, where Thain cast the deciding vote against Corzine. "It's for the good of the firm," he was told, and it would also be good for him. Paulson assured Thain and Thornton—Thain's charismatic, extroverted alter ego—that they would become co-CEOs just a year or two after the firm went public. But that never happened. The deal didn't work out right—CEOs never gave away power voluntarily, of their own free will.

Thain had cast the vote that *made* Paulson the CEO of Goldman Sachs, and now Paulson was Treasury Secretary of the United States of America. Thain had finally worked his way up to the corner office of Merrill Lynch, one of the greatest banking franchises in the world, and he did it the hard way, on his own, without Hank Paulson's help. And now Paulson was going to push him to give that job up.

Thain passed through the outer office of Room 17, and entered Paulson's lair. The arches from the two-story windows that framed the twelfth and thirteenth floors of the Fed peeked above the floor of the room, affording the occupants a constrained view of Wall Street and the Financial District, and creating the feeling that they were hidden away in the turret of a castle.

"Have you done what I recommended and found a buyer?" Paulson asked.

"Hank, I'm not thick! I heard you. I'm doing what I need to do."

Paulson kept it short. He knew Thain had been talking to Bank of America and he urged him to strike a deal. Then Paulson sent Thain on his way.

FLEMING WENT BACK DOWNSTAIRS for his second one-on-one meeting with Curl. Ken Lewis had come over to Wachtell that morning to consult with his group and meet key members of Merrill's management team, including Bob McCann, head of the private client business. Fleming knew that Lewis's presence meant one thing: He wanted this deal to happen. He also knew that at a minimum, BofA would be willing to pay a premium on the Friday closing price of $17. Now Fleming had to make sure Bank of America's offer was so good that Thain could not refuse it. Thain and Kraus clearly preferred a friendly arrangement with Goldman Sachs to an outright sale of the company. Fleming couldn't allow Thain to walk away from the Bank of America deal simply because of price.

Back at the negotiating table, Fleming finally started talking numbers.

"In order to make this work," said Fleming, "your offer's got to have a three-handle on it."

Curl didn't blanch.

"We have an optics problem here," the older man said. "Thirty dollars a share would be a huge premium, and we can't do that."

"I have an optics problem," countered Fleming. "I'm selling a hundred-year-old company at a distressed price."

"The premium is way above what the market can bear," said Curl.

"Don't get caught up in the short term," urged Fleming. "I'm looking at the fundamental value of this company, and ninety-four years of history."

The session only lasted ten minutes.

Fleming took heart from the fact that, after broaching the $30 figure, Curl didn't gag. He was in the right ballpark.

• • •

FLEMING RETURNED TO THE main conference room upstairs, where Heaton, Wetzel, and Sara Furber were sitting. "We need to get some people downtown," he said, referring to the Goldman Sachs due diligence request.

"Greg, this is nuts!" said Wetzel.

"Paul, just calm down and stay focused on what you're doing," said Fleming.

Thain had wanted Heaton and Furber to come down to Merrill Lynch headquarters, but Fleming felt he could not afford to lose Furber.

"You need to go downtown and start this process," he told Heaton.

"Do you understand what will happen here if they find out we're trying to do something with Goldman Sachs?" Heaton asked.

Fleming nodded. "If you don't show up down there, I'm not working tomorrow."

Heaton grabbed a few briefing books and left the building as discreetly as possible.

NOT LONG AFTER HIS meeting with Paulson, Thain left the Federal Reserve and returned to Merrill Lynch headquarters a few blocks away, where he would host a conference call to update his directors on what was happening.

Paulson was squeezing him from above, urging him to sell Merrill to Bank of America. Fleming was pushing him from below, undermining the Goldman Sachs option before it could even turn into a real offer.

One of Thain's attributes was his ability to remain calm in the face of adversity. At noontime, back on the thirty-second floor of Merrill's headquarters, Thain projected that calmness and confidence during the conference call.

After all the directors were on the line, Thain told them what he had learned down at the Fed—that the Barclays bid for Lehman had failed and that it was now likely that Lehman would have to file for bankruptcy protection. The consequences for Merrill Lynch would be serious, he added. Thain then launched into a description of the three strategic options he had set in motion to protect Merrill. He told the directors about the merger discussions with Morgan Stanley, but suggested those discussions were unlikely to lead anywhere; he said he had initiated merger discussions with Bank of America, which were being handled by Greg Fleming at that very moment; and he was also exploring the possibility that Goldman Sachs might make a strategic investment in Merrill Lynch.

Several board members asked for more detail about the Bank of America negotiations, particularly about how long the negotiation process might take.

"So we might get a merger agreement to look at sometime early in the week?" asked one director.

"No," said Rosemary Berkery, the general counsel. "We're going to need to have a fully negotiated agreement completed within twelve hours, before the markets open in Asia."

"Is that actually doable?" another director asked.

"If that's the path we take, it will have to be," said Berkery.

At least one director was operating with more information than his peers. Earlier in the day, Fleming had briefed John Finnegan on the progress of talks with BofA. Fleming had also cast doubt on whether the Goldman option would solve Merrill's problems. Finnegan seemed inclined to agree, but said nothing on the conference call with the other directors.

AT NOONTIME, WALID CHAMMAH pulled into the driveway of his ex-wife's home in Greenwich, Connecticut, to collect his daughter, Isabella. It was her eighteenth birthday and Chammah had brought her a gift. As soon as Isabella got into the car, his phone rang. It was Tom Montag.

"Listen, Walid, if you guys are serious, your John has to call my John in the next hour or so," said Montag.

"Tom, I'm not authorized to speak on behalf of Morgan Stanley, but let me tell you what I think," said Chammah. "First, if you want to do this, *your* John has to call my John. Second, if Thain thinks he's going to be the CEO, I don't think so. It's going to be John Mack. Third, if we do it, we'll only do it after proper due diligence. And finally, we're not going to pay a premium. The highest offer possible would be $17 a share."

. . .

SHORTLY AFTER NOON, the Merrill Lynch contingent at the Federal Reserve stepped outside the fortress for a break and to formulate a plan for the afternoon. Kraus told Kelly and a group of Merrill traders who had been summoned to the Fed that he would go back to headquarters and they should stay.

Over the weekend, most of the executives going to and coming from the Federal Reserve accessed the building from the parking garage and the employee entrance in the rear, on Maiden Lane. To accommodate requests for media access, the police designated an area across Maiden Lane as a special zone for cameramen and TV producers as well as reporters.

As the Merrill Lynch group made its way slowly out of the rear of the Fed onto Maiden Lane, Kraus noticed the photographers. He took out his phone, as if he were answering a call, and walked toward the media scrum. He paused in front of the photographers and stared ahead into the distance, portentously, as though contemplating an issue of great significance, one that could affect the course of financial history. A dozen or so photographers snapped pictures furiously, capturing this indelible image of Wall Street, poised at the brink.

Slowly, Kraus turned away from the photographers, put the phone back in his pocket, and rejoined his colleagues from Merrill Lynch.

AFTER NOON, THE ACTIVITY at the Federal Reserve became disorganized, as bank CEOs struggled to figure out where a Lehman failure would leave them. At one point, the group tried to bring traders from all of their representative firms into the building to unwind each other's positions with Lehman and minimize the impact of that bank's looming bankruptcy.

Pete Kelly remained as Merrill Lynch's top representative, to look after the firm's interest in any substantive matters that arose.

Jon Winkelried, the co-president of Goldman Sachs, approached Kelly. By now, the Goldman executives seemed to have concluded either that Merrill Lynch wasn't serious about an investment from them, or they'd learned through other channels—and Goldman always seemed to be better than its peers about sniffing out sensitive market information—about the negotiations with Bank of America. Either way, Winkelried was clued in to the fact that the plans for due diligence had evaporated.

"This isn't going to move forward, is it?" he asked.

"No," said Kelly with an air of resignation. "It's not going to happen."

MEMBERS OF BANK OF AMERICA'S due diligence team continued to pore over Merrill's trading books and assets at Wachtell, Lipton and BofA's One Bryant Park tower. They were constantly in contact with Lewis's inner circle, which was using the corporate apartment in the Time Warner Center as a temporary base of operations. Every time the due diligence team found something of import, they would call it in to Lewis's camp.

Shortly after 1:00 p.m., one of the bank's number-crunchers called Lewis's group at the corporate apartment to relay an important finding. As the information was being passed along, the caller heard a loud cheer in the background. Charlotte's NFL team, the Carolina Panthers, had just scored an early touchdown against the visiting Chicago Bears, and Lewis and his crew were whooping it up in front of the TV. The due diligence effort, apparently, was on hold.

AROUND THAT TIME, Curl sent word up to Fleming that they were to resume talks.

Bank of America was willing to pay $29 per share in stock for Merrill Lynch, Curl said. The poker face had dropped somewhat. Fleming could tell that this number was at the far end of what BofA could do, possibly beyond what Curl had recommended.

"Your market cap is below $30 billion right now," said Curl. "This offer allows you to announce a $50 billion deal. If you accept, Ken will take it to his board. But don't ask for any more. We won't go a nickel above that. If you ask for more, the deal is at risk."

Fleming had done enough deals to know that this threat was real. It was the absolute maximum that BofA would pay. Betraying nothing, he said he'd bring it to Thain.

It was all he could do to restrain himself from sprinting up the stairs to the thirty-fourth floor. He didn't say anything to his colleagues, who would be elated at the price.

Instead, he headed straight into a small conference room. Once he got inside and shut the door, Fleming pumped his fist. He'd done it! Kelly, Heaton, and Wetzel had warned him that he would have to accept whatever meager offer BofA made, but Fleming believed he could get $30, and $29 was close enough. *Touchdown,* and the extra point is *good*!

He called up Thain, brimming with excitement.

"John, I've got $29 a share!" Fleming said, practically shouting.

"Okay," said Thain, devoid of emotion. "Well, that's not bad."

Fleming listened, incredulous, as silence filled the line.

"All right," Thain finally said. "I want thirty."

"Thirty?" said Fleming. "You've got to be kidding!"

"I want thirty. It's a good, round number."

"John, at $29 a share, it's a $50 billion deal. That's a good round number!"

"I want thirty. See if you can get thirty."

"John, this is the drop-dead offer. If I try to push this, it could blow the whole deal. Believe me when I tell you this, we're not going to get any more out of Curl. He doesn't even want to do this. If I ask for another dollar, they might decide we're pigs and just walk away. Curl gave me his word. You're talking about a pro that I've dragged all the way to twenty-nine. You think he kept a nickel in his pocket? We can't push it any further."

"I want $30," said Thain.

"John, I'm not comfortable doing that. If you want to call Lewis yourself, go ahead. Curl and I have been looking at each other across the table. If I ask for the dollar, it'll infuriate him, and I don't want to do that. He won't support the deal. He'll walk away. If you want to try Lewis on your own, do it, but I can't go back to Curl after all this and ask for one more dollar."

FLEMING WANDERED INTO A different conference room, where Wetzel and Furber were. Wetzel asked what was going on, and Fleming said Bank of America was willing to pay $29 a share.

"Greg, that's remarkable," said Wetzel. "Let's get this thing signed!"

"No, I'm going for $30 a share."

Wetzel was stunned. "That's insane. You've got to be dreaming!"

"John wants $30."

"Greg, just stop! The worst thing that can happen is for this not to get done today. If we don't do this today, then when the market opens tomorrow we're toast."

"I've got to ask for $30."

Wetzel was beside himself.

HEATON OPENED HIS EYES, and it took him a moment to get his bearings. He was in a cab, on a cross street in Midtown Manhattan, sitting in traffic. After being told by Fleming that he had to head downtown, he'd left Wachtell and flagged a yellow cab. He told the driver he was going to Goldman Sachs, at 85 Broad Street, and then drifted off to sleep in the rear seat.

He checked his watch. It was almost a half hour after he'd flagged the cab, and he was stuck in traffic near Lexington Avenue, just a few blocks from Wachtell. The Tudor City Festival had congested the area, leading to gridlock on the streets intersecting Lexington Avenue. He shouldn't even have been on this side of town. He should have been going down the West Side Highway to Merrill Lynch headquarters, not heading east to the FDR Drive, which would take him to Goldman.

He told the driver to change course, but it took almost fifteen minutes for the cabbie to extricate himself from the mess, and by the time Heaton arrived at Merrill's headquarters downtown, more than an hour had passed since Fleming had dispatched him.

Heaton checked in on the twenty-second floor and learned that there were no Goldman Sachs bankers in the building. He rode the elevator up to the thirty-second floor and looked around. The entire executive suite seemed vacant. Heaton wandered through the hallways, which were quiet and empty. In the distance, on the other side of the floor, he thought he heard Kraus speaking to someone, not in a pleasant tone. Heaton approached the corner office, where he found Thain. The CEO was alone in his office, sitting at his desk.

Heaton entered, still holding a sheaf of paperwork he'd brought with him from Wachtell, and plopped down on a couch.

Thain picked up the phone and dialed. From the tone and subject of his conversation, it was apparent to Heaton that the call was to Fleming.

"If they're agreed on twenty-nine, I'll take it to the board," he said in a subdued tone.

Heaton remained in the office for some time, reviewing the paperwork he'd brought and answering specific questions from his boss.

Not long after agreeing to sell the company for $29 a share, Thain received a call from someone at the Federal Reserve. His countenance brightened. After hanging up, he told Heaton that the Fed had decided to expand the types of collateral that securities firms could post in order to access the discount window for cash. Wouldn't this allow the firm to survive on its own?

Heaton said no. Access to the Fed's discount window would not stop a run on the bank, the refusal of counterparties to do business with Merrill, and the negative spiral of the stock price.

BACK AT WACHTELL, FLEMING had told Curl that Thain would bring the offer to Merrill's board of directors later that day. The two negotiators knew there was still plenty of work to be done. Most important, since the deal would probably close by the end of the year, they had to negotiate the parameters of a bonus pool that Bank of America would allow Merrill to pay its employees. By buying Merrill Lynch, BofA was in essence buying the services of 60,000 employees, so it was important to lock down as much of that talent as possible with the promise of a financial reward for sticking around and remaining at work.

The other important issue that remained to be sorted out was an agreement over the language of a "material adverse change" clause. Any agreement reached later that day would not be executed for several months. Both sides wanted to protect themselves in case the world changed dramatically between September and the end of the year.

Among Merrill executives, Paul Wetzel was the most vocal about the importance of nailing down every contingency with the MAC clause. The language had to be airtight, to lock BofA in to the deal, even if the market continued to crumble, he said.

After Thain accepted the offer and said he'd take it to the board, there was another administrative matter associated with all mergers and acquisitions. Merrill Lynch would need approval from a "fairness committee" consisting of several senior bankers not involved with the deal. Wetzel said he'd bring the $29 per share offer to Merrill's fairness committee.

"I don't think I'll need you for this!" he told Fleming with a smile as he left Wachtell and headed downtown.

AT THE FEDERAL RESERVE, most of the Wall Street CEOs were still camped out, trying to prepare the industry for the unpredictable fallout of the failure of Lehman Brothers the following day.

As the top executives from Goldman Sachs, Credit Suisse, Citigroup, JPMorgan Chase, Bank of New York Mellon, Deutsche Bank, and Société Générale huddled with their people in the Liberty dining room, word came in that Merrill Lynch had just agreed to be sold to Bank of America for $29 per share.

Several executives were astonished that Merrill, which would have failed within days, had fetched such a whopping price.

"Who pulled that fucking rabbit out of the hat?" asked Jamie Dimon, CEO of JPMorgan Chase.

AS THE AFTERNOON WORE ON, Heaton left Thain's office to return to the twenty-second floor. Kraus came over to see how Thain was doing.

The two men went back almost twenty-five years, to the days when they were both ambitious up-and-comers at Goldman Sachs, bucking for the coveted title of partner. They had both succeeded, and when the firm went public in 1999, both men had become fabulously wealthy. Thain had advanced further up the hierarchy than Kraus, by dint of Corzine's strong support, but the two men had fashioned fantastically successful careers on Wall Street in tandem.

Kraus, who was keenly attuned to his friend's aspirations and a shrewd reader of his emotions, knew that Thain would be in a low mood.

They spoke for a while, quietly, about what lay ahead, and then Thain reflected on what had just happened.

"I really didn't come here to sell the company," he said. This crisis was only going to last for a few more days, he told Kraus. If they had only cut a deal with Goldman Sachs, they'd be able to get through the worst of this temporary market panic and emerge on the other side as a formidable investment bank. There was so much potential for the business, for this franchise. Thain hated to see it unloaded in a firesale to that gang in Charlotte.

Kraus commiserated, saying he shared his friend's belief that they could probably have stuck it out.

"If this was just you and me, John, we could take that chance," Kraus said, explaining that the odds of Merrill Lynch surviving on its own were probably as high as 80 percent. "But this isn't just about you and me. There are 60,000 employees at Merrill Lynch. We don't have the luxury of gambling with their future. We can't just roll the dice with that at stake."

It was the same message that Wetzel had given to Kraus the night before, repeated almost verbatim.

FLEMING, KELLY, AND MERRILL'S outside lawyers continued to work on the MAC clause and other issues with Wachtell during the afternoon. Around 5:00 p.m., Thain called Fleming with another issue to be included in the merger agreement, saying Lewis had agreed to let Merrill's top executives convert their most recently granted stock options into shares of Bank of America. Both sides had a general understanding that

Merrill Lynch would be able to pay all of its employees some kind of bonus for 2008, but this issue was a sweetener for top executives like Fleming, McCann, Chai, and other members of Thain's management team.

No problem, said Fleming, who didn't mind receiving some added value for his efforts over the past year.

AT THE SAME TIME, in a different room at Wachtell, Ken Lewis had convened a meeting of his own board of directors via conference call.

For the past decade, Bank of America had been one of the country's largest and most influential banks, and yet its board, a patchwork of holdovers from various acquisitions, seemed at times to be overwhelmed by its responsibilities.

The majority of the board consisted of men and women with deep regional ties to the South, starting with Temple Sloan, a Raleigh auto parts magnate who served as the lead director, and Meredith Spangler, the septuagenarian wife of one of the biggest investors in what had once been North Carolina National Bank, or NCNB.

A few directors, such as Walter Massey, former president of Morehouse College in Atlanta, had been on the board of the old Bank of America, prior to its acquisition by NationsBank. A large faction had joined in 2004 when BofA bought Fleet Financial, the Boston-based bank that dominated the industry in New England.

In recent years, the board had rubber-stamped such questionable acquisitions as BofA's $21 billion cash purchase of LaSalle Bank in Chicago. In January 2008, as a wave of foreclosures swept across the country, BofA's board approved the $4 billion purchase of Countrywide Financial, at one time the country's largest mortgage originator. Now, just two months after the controversial Countrywide deal had finally closed, Ken Lewis would once again ask for approval to complete the deal of a lifetime, the acquisition of Merrill Lynch.

Tom May, one of the directors who came over following the Fleet acquisition, had received word that there would be an important board meeting in the afternoon. Since he had been given no background briefing on what was going on, he assumed that BofA was going to acquire Lehman Brothers, and was shocked to learn—when he dialed in to the conference call—that his bank was planning to buy Merrill Lynch instead.

But another former Fleet director, Chad Gifford, quickly grasped what was going on. Brian Moynihan was among the few senior Fleet executives to survive at Bank of America, and Lewis used him like a mechanic, dispatching him to fix various problems at the bank. Lewis would funnel important information to his lead director, Temple Sloan, but was otherwise sparing in what he passed along to the rest of the board. Moynihan, however, worked his connections with the Fleet directors aggressively, and was frequently in touch with them. As for Gifford, he also had close ties to the Federal Reserve Bank in Boston.

Sensing there might be some resistance, Lewis asked Chris Flowers to attend the board meeting. Flowers's role would be to vouch for the relative health of Merrill's balance sheet, compared with Lehman's, and to advise the board that if BofA didn't move quickly, Merrill might pursue other options, such as an investment from Goldman Sachs. No one on BofA's board could go toe-to-toe with Flowers.

Lewis called the meeting to order and set forth his plans. Bank of America had agreed to buy Merrill Lynch, the legendary wealth management company and investment bank, in an all-stock deal. Lewis told the board he had looked at Lehman, but Merrill was a much better strategic fit for his bank. To his surprise and discomfort, several board members had questions about the deal.

Retired general Tommy Franks, who had joined the board after stepping down from the U.S. Army, asked about the strategic rationale behind the deal, and how Merrill would fit in with Bank of America. That question was relatively easy to answer, but Tom Ryan, the chief executive of the CVS pharmacy chain and a legacy Fleet director, expressed some reservations about the timing of the transaction.

"Why are we doing this now?" he asked. "Don't you think, given what's going on the market this past week, that it would make sense to wait a few days?"

Lewis referred the query to Chris Flowers, who said that Goldman Sachs was preparing to buy a 10 percent stake in Merrill Lynch and give the company a line of credit. There was no guarantee that Merrill would not make it through the week on its own, and then this opportunity to acquire it would be gone forever.

After a few more minutes, Gifford spoke up, asking about the due diligence, and whether there had been enough time to figure out whether Merrill had any lingering problems on its balance sheet. Visibly irritated, Lewis again referred the question to Flowers, who said that Merrill's books were much better marked than they had been the last time he looked at them, in December 2007. Eventually, the board voted unanimously in favor of the deal.

THE MERRILL LYNCH MIDTOWN conference center, consisting of several floors in a skyscraper at 50th Street, just off Fifth Avenue, was evidence of how well things had been going for Merrill Lynch just two years earlier. Former CEO Stan O'Neal signed a lease for the space in 2006, at the height of the market for office space in Manhattan, to give the company a convenient location for Midtown meetings.

Toward 6:00 that evening, several New York–based members of the Merrill Lynch board of directors arrived at a conference room on the thirty-fifth floor. Out-of-towners such as Virgis Colbert, Admiral Prueher, Carol Christ, and Judith Mayhew Jonas—who lived in Britain—were connected to the room via speakerphone.

By the time the meeting had started, most of the directors were aware of what was happening. Thain greeted them, and then described Bank of America's offer, an all-stock transaction by which each share of Merrill Lynch would be exchanged for 0.8595 shares of BofA stock. Since BofA stock had closed above $34 a share Friday, the offer pegged a $29 per share value to Merrill Lynch.

Rosemary Berkery spoke about the duties of the board, and the need to look at all aspects of the offer to determine if accepting it would be in the best interests of shareholders. Thain explained the strategic rationale behind the deal, and how it would protect Merrill Lynch shareholders at a time of great uncertainty.

As Thain spoke, Fleming and other members of the team that had been working at Wachtell trickled into the room, standing back from the table where the directors sat. After more than an hour of discussion, but no real debate, the time arrived for a vote.

One by one, each director said he or she was in favor of the transaction. When all ten, including Thain, affirmed their support, it was done. The mood among the directors was one of sadness, but great relief. Given what was going on across town at Lehman, the group knew that the sale was the right move for Merrill Lynch and its shareholders. Several shook Thain's hand and congratulated him; others saluted the efforts of the entire team, including Fleming.

And so, the board of directors of Merrill Lynch, the company founded in 1914 by Charlie Merrill, an energetic stock promoter from Florida, voted unanimously to sell the company to Bank of America. Merrill's vision of bringing Wall Street to Main Street, put in place in the 1940s, had succeeded beyond his wildest expectations as stock ownership in the U.S., either directly or through mutual funds and retirement plans, became commonplace. The company he founded created opportunity for ordinary Americans to participate in the stock market. It also created the opportunity for an Irish-American underclass to establish itself, and for a time dominate, a Wall Street bank.

Coincidentally, the vote to sell this institution—which was cofounded by a Lynch and built by people with names like Moriarty, O'Sullivan, Regan, Burke, O'Connell, Kelly, Kinney, Kenny, McCarthy, McCabe, McCann, Magowan, and Tully—took place in a room overlooking one of the great monuments to Ireland in the Western Hemisphere, St. Patrick's Cathedral.

AFTER THE VOTE, as the directors dispersed, Thain and his top executives walked the short distance from the conference center to Wachtell's office in the Eero Saarinen–designed building known as Black Rock on

52nd Street. They went up to the thirty-third floor, BofA's floor, to await the ceremonial signing of the merger agreement by Thain and Ken Lewis, which would be followed by a champagne toast.

But the contract wasn't ready to be signed, according to the outside lawyers for the two banks. The wording for the MAC clause was still being hammered out, and a variety of other contractual details, involving warranties and indemnifications and various mundane legal matters, remained.

There was also the matter of Merrill Lynch stock options, granted a year earlier, that needed to be converted into Bank of America shares. While the more routine matters were being handled through lawyers, Fleming and Curl took the lead on negotiating the conversion of Merrill options, which were worthless at Merrill's current share price, into something of real value.

But after several minutes of discussing the stock options of the top five executives at Merrill Lynch, Curl stopped Fleming.

"Ken says this is about Thain's options, no one else's," he said.

"Okay," said Fleming. "He's my boss, so let's keep at it."

THERE WAS ALSO ANOTHER issue that was kicking sand into the gears: Merrill's agreement in principle to sell a majority stake in FDS, negotiated in haste in early July, and now in limbo because of the larger transaction.

Peter Kraus zeroed in on this matter with the zeal of a company founder, demanding protection from BofA for the contract, which was worth a few billion dollars. If Bank of America tried to get out of the deal by invoking the material adverse change clause, the Charlotte bank should be required to post several billion dollars on Merrill's behalf. Some of Kraus's new colleagues at Merrill Lynch were impressed by the passion he brought to the subject. Others didn't get it.

"I can't believe he's fighting for FDS," Wetzel said to Heaton. "If BofA drops the bomb on this deal, it will be like Japan in 1945. There won't be anything left."

. . .

THE WACHTELL TEAM HAD brought in several bottles of champagne for the celebratory toast, but as the negotiations crawled forward through the evening, the lawyers managed to find one potential problem after another.

Curl returned after one brief visit with Lewis and said his boss was growing annoyed with the matter of Thain's stock options.

Fleming shrugged. "What do you expect me to do, Greg? John's my boss."

THAIN AND LEWIS SAT awkwardly together in a conference room, waiting for the deal to get done, so they could sign the proposed merger agreement. Montag and Kraus sat near Thain, while Lewis was accompanied by several BofA executives: Steele Alphin, the chief administrative officer; Anne Finucane, head of marketing and communications; Joe Price, the CFO; Brian Moynihan, who headed BofA's own investment bank; and Amy Brinkley, the chief risk officer.

As everyone sat and chatted, the Bank of America people tried to figure out the unusual dynamics of the Merrill team. Periodically, the "two Gregs" would enter the room. Curl would confer with Lewis while Fleming would tear through furiously, like a tornado, barking out orders. He'd disappear just as quickly, back to the various negotiations he was supervising.

Then there was Peter Kraus. When Fleming was gone, he filled up the room, sharing his views on the deal with Alphin and other BofA executives, and peppering Lewis with questions about Bank of America's financial health. Kraus kept his BlackBerry holstered in a bright, Kermit the Frog–green rubber sheath, and brought it out regularly to make calls and check e-mails.

Thain sat stiffly nearby, impervious to what was happening around him. Fleming would slow down just long enough to tell him that the business about the stock options was starting to generate some friction, but Thain insisted that Fleming keep at it, even though it was obvious that Lewis, sitting a few feet away, was growing irritated.

Off to the side of all this was Tom Montag, who sat quietly, talking matter-of-factly, but unobtrusively, about trading.

It was only at midnight, as other matters finally got sorted out, that Fleming gave up on the business of the options, accepting a vague letter of intent on the part of BofA to do its best to make Thain and his team whole on their grants from the previous year.

At about 12:30 a.m., the top people from Merrill and BofA, flanked by their outside lawyers, entered a large conference room on the thirty-third floor to put their names on the "agreement in principle" for the merger. Thain signed. Then Lewis, who was fed up with all the delays, also signed and left the room abruptly.

When the Merrill team adjourned to a larger conference room for the champagne toast, Lewis was conspicuously absent. Only after repeated urging from Curl and Brian Moynihan did he return, raise a glass of flat, warm champagne, pretend to smile, then bolt from the building, accompanied by Alphin and a small coterie.

Thain left shortly after, and his driver took him to his home in Westchester County. He was disappointed at having to sell Merrill Lynch, but took some comfort in the fact that the interests of the firm's shareholders would be served.

Outside the building, Lewis and Alphin were jubilant as they looked up into the Manhattan night.

"We win!" said Lewis triumphantly, to no one in particular, and everyone. The little Charlotte bank that could had conquered Wall Street.

"We've chased the comet for so many years," said Alphin, who was almost giddy. "We finally caught the tail!"

Lewis returned to the corporate apartment, where he poured himself a drink—Johnnie Walker Black—and went over to the window, where the dark expanse of Central Park lay before him, framed by lights from the buildings of upper Manhattan. The first time he'd come to New York City, three decades earlier, he couldn't get approval for a mortgage. Now the city was his. He'd just bought Merrill Lynch.

. . .

IT WAS CLOSE TO 1:00 a.m. by the time Fleming took the elevator down to the lobby. As he had done almost twenty-four hours earlier, he passed up a ride to the Mandarin Hotel, and walked instead. He took the same route had used the night before, but all the worry and anguish he bore the previous day—the self-questioning about whether he might ask for too much and blow up the deal—had evaporated. His spirit sagged under the emotions that were churning inside him. Fleming had spent sixteen years at Merrill Lynch. He had come within one rung of making it to the corner office, his dream job, only to wind up pushing for a sale of the legendary institution to which he had devoted his career.

The exhaustion which consumed his entire body numbed him to the sadness of what had just transpired. Like someone who was under the influence of anesthesia or alcohol, he was conscious that the pain he was not feeling at the moment was indeed real and would eventually catch up with him and sting.

Fleming was drained, physically, emotionally, and mentally, but relieved. He walked on the empty sidewalks of Midtown Manhattan in a daze, like an athlete leaving the arena after a bruising, enervating, do-or-die contest, groggy from the fight yet serene in the knowledge that there wasn't one ounce of effort that had not been expended on the field of play. But there was no cause for celebration. He had lost. Selling Merrill Lynch to Bank of America was not a victory. All Fleming had done was help secure an acceptable defeat, averting an unmitigated disaster.

Fleming shuffled into his hotel room, still too wired to sleep, cracked open a beer, and turned on the TV. He watched Nick at Nite until he faded from consciousness.

CHAPTER 15

THE CHARLOTTE MAFIA

ON MONDAY MORNING, SEPTEMBER 15, the tectonic plates beneath Wall Street had shifted. The world awoke to learn that Lehman Brothers had filed for bankruptcy protection, and Merrill Lynch—a name that symbolized an American faith in the stock market—would be acquired by a bank in Charlotte, North Carolina.

After dawn, thousands of Lehman employees came to the company's office tower, just north of Times Square, to clear out their belongings. Downtown, at Merrill Lynch's offices, thousands of employees came to their offices stunned but grateful. Lehman's employees were not only out of their jobs, but their stock holdings—which for many comprised the vast majority of their life savings and net worth—had been destroyed. Lehman's creditors would get first crack at whatever funds could be salvaged, but the shareholders were wiped out.

At Merrill Lynch, people still had jobs. Thousands would be laid off as a result of the merger, but everyone's company stock still had value.

Most of Merrill's employees, it seemed, listened to the 8:00 a.m.

conference call with the analysts in which Lewis and Thain discussed the deal. Thain went to BofA's new building at One Bryant Park to speak on the call alongside Lewis. Afterward, riding a wave of euphoria, Lewis took Thain on a tour of his bank's third-floor trading operations. BofA traders—most of whom knew their days were now numbered—watched as Lewis paraded Thain around as though he were a trophy, an exotic creature captured on safari who would now be on display at the bank's headquarters, complete with a Latin description of the species, *bankerus wallstreetiensus.*

After the tour of the trading floor and other parts of the building, the two executives went to the second floor auditorium for a joint press conference that would be telecast to both banks' offices around the world.

Lewis and Thain took the stage, shook hands for the cameras, smiled, and then sat down to discuss the merger of the two companies. Any rancor from the evening before had dissipated as Lewis beamed about the opportunities presented by combining Merrill Lynch's thundering herd of financial advisors with Bank of America's broad customer base. He went so far as to describe the private client business as the "crown jewel" of Merrill Lynch.

Thain said all the right things, talking about the synergies in the transaction and how the new Bank of America–Merrill Lynch would be a model platform for the financial services company of the future.

Lewis paid tribute to Thain, saying this was the first transaction he had been involved in where the CEO of the acquired company never asked once what his role would be in the combined organization.

For Lewis, the acquisition was a moment of triumph, up there with some of the great achievements of his predecessor Hugh McColl. It was the final victory in the forty-year campaign waged by a hearty band of Carolina bankers against the money-center banks of New York. It was Gettysburg and Appomattox, reversed.

The last time Lewis had been on a stage of this magnitude in New York was a decade earlier, in April 1998, when the merger between NationsBank and Bank of America was announced across town at the Waldorf-Astoria hotel.

McColl had been the star of that press conference, sitting at the middle of a long table shared with Lewis, CFO Jim Hance, and several top executives from BofA: Mike Murray, Mike O'Neill, and CEO David Coulter, who was designated as McColl's heir apparent.

The table was less crowded at this press conference, and Lewis and Thain took turns describing why the deal made sense. In particular, Lewis defended the price he was willing to pay, explaining that in the long term, BofA's acquisition of Merrill Lynch at $29 per share would seem like a bargain.

After the press conference, Thain left the building and headed downtown to Merrill Lynch's headquarters, where he would address his company's employees in an internal broadcast held at Merrill's third floor conference room.

At the appointed hour, hundreds of employees jammed into the low-ceilinged space and the firm's top executives—Kraus, Montag, Chai, Fleming, McCann, and others—sat in the front row, awaiting the CEO's arrival.

Around 11:30, Thain took the stage and received a standing ovation as he walked up to the center of the platform. When the applause died down, he spoke.

"I joined this company a little less than ten months ago. I came here because I first, believed in the strategy, the combination of the world's best wealth management business with a world-class investment banking, sales, and trading business. I came here because I like the culture. I came here because I thought we had a great brand, and I came here because I like the people and all those things are still true."

Thain explained why he had accepted Bank of America's offer: because it was in the best interests of employees and shareholders.

"Now for me personally, this is a sad day, but for the company, for the shareholders and for us going forward, it's going to be good." Thain choked up slightly at this point, showing a side that few Merrill Lynch colleagues had seen.

After a few more minutes, Thain opened up the floor to questions, but the employees, all of whom shared a sadness about what had happened to their company, sat quietly.

"I'll be amazed if there are no questions," Thain said good-naturedly. Still, the hundreds of people sitting in the auditorium remained quiet.

A moment later, one hand in the front row shot up. It was Peter Kraus, wearing a fluorescent yellow shirt. Thain looked at his friend and shook his head. "You can't ask a question," he told Kraus.

But there were no other questions and Kraus persisted, standing up finally. "John, I think that you talked a little bit about strategy. Can you just give us your view of, going forward, what some of the things that this combined organization can do that would be truly unique in the market?"

To those who had gotten to know Kraus in the two weeks that he'd been on the job, it was another reminder that their new colleague enjoyed playing a leading role in any meeting, no matter the size or the context. While most of the employees were mourning the death of John F. Kennedy, Merrill's newest executive was already asking about the "truly unique" opportunities that lay ahead in a Lyndon Johnson administration.

Kraus succeeded at his primary purpose, which was to spark a series of questions from employees in the audience and those hooked up by phone. One after another, the questions began to flow in, and Thain handled them with ease until one caller, "Ed," a financial advisor based in New York, asked him about management under the new ownership. There had been a story in that morning's *New York Times* suggesting that Bob McCann would most likely be put in charge of the combined unit's advisory business, and "Ed" said the advisors really liked Bob and hoped that the story was true. "There's a lot of respect for Bob in private client."

The question clearly rubbed Thain the wrong way. "I think Bob was the one talking to the press," said Thain. "Only kidding."

Something about McCann's blushing reaction to Thain's barb seemed to confirm in the CEO's mind that McCann had been the source for that nugget of information in the newspaper. Stressed from a long weekend of negotiations and grueling decisions, and increasingly agitated by what he perceived to have been a steady stream of leaks from

McCann or his followers over the previous ten months, Thain couldn't let the matter go.

"I've got enough problems," McCann said with a smile. "Do I get a rebuttal?"

"No," said Thain. "For those of you who can't see, Bob's asking, can he respond. I said no." Thain continued to discuss wealth management for a moment before another caller asked a question related to compensation for the financial advisors. McCann stood up near the front, gesturing that he wanted the microphone to respond.

"I'm not going to let Bob get to the mike, but you can talk to him afterward about that," said Thain.

After fielding about a dozen other questions over the next fifteen minutes, one caller asked when the financial advisors would be able to cross-sell products to Bank of America customers.

"That's actually a great idea, *and Bob in his new role as combined head of this organization* can work on that," said Thain with a sarcastic edge to his voice. "Bob got that, so he'll follow up on that. I didn't say *self-proclaimed.*"

McCann by now was seething with rage, his forehead turning a deep shade of red.

"Bob's not happy, for those of you on the phone," Thain said.

Candace Browning, Merrill's head of research, sat beside McCann, and kept her face staring straight ahead while her eyes turned sideways at the squirming executive. Thain continued to ignore McCann's attempts to speak and when someone asked about Bank of America's management team, Thain singled out Fleming, and asked him to talk a bit about the Charlotte bankers.

Fleming felt embarrassed for McCann, even though he didn't particularly like him. He got up, took the microphone from Thain and spoke for a minute about his respect for the Charlotte bankers before slinking back to his seat.

After a few more questions, "Kevin" from Media, Pennsylvania, asked when the retention package for the financial advisors would be discussed.

"That's an excellent question for you to talk *to Bob* about," Thain said, inserting another jab at McCann. "You know, I'm tempted to say, 'you know, when he's not talking to the press.' By the way, the truth is, I don't think Bob talked to the press, but now I'm teasing him about it."

After the meeting broke up, McCann called May Lee and vented his fury, demanding to know why he had been publicly humiliated. Lee, who had developed some rapport with McCann, said her boss's comments were most likely meant as humor that didn't come out quite right.

LEWIS RETURNED TO CHARLOTTE, and Bank of America's formidable transition team—a group of several hundred people who do nothing but bring newly acquired organizations into the system—was unleashed on Merrill Lynch.

Andrea Smith, one of the top HR executives at the bank, was among the first to arrive. She immediately befriended May Lee and came to rely on her for guidance around the office, and in personal matters, such as finding a place to live where her children could attend good schools. Lee, who had grown tired of battling a dysfunctional Merrill system that never trusted or opened up to her, extended a big welcome to her new colleague.

Back in Charlotte, high up on the fifty-eighth floor of the Bank of America tower, a building that dominates the city's skyline, Lewis received one of the most gratifying salutations in his career. Hugh McColl himself had dropped by with a note congratulating Lewis for the deal to acquire Merrill Lynch, describing it as "our best ever." McColl was not in the habit of dishing out praise to his successor, so this tribute impressed Lewis in a way that no other outside congratulatory calls could.

The next day, Lewis and Alphin started making decisions about the top jobs at their soon-to-be-acquired jewel.

Like their predecessors at NationsBank, Lewis and Alphin had always harbored a general dislike toward New York investment bankers and their stratospheric bonuses. Instead of hiring the best and brightest graduates of Ivy League business schools by waving the prospect of seven-figure and eight-figure pay packages, BofA preferred hiring aggressive young men and women from less prestigious schools, who were willing to roll up their sleeves and get their hands dirty on behalf of the bank, not for the promise of an obscene amount of money.

To Lewis, no bank epitomized Wall Street's out-of-control compensation system more than Goldman Sachs, the pristine jewel of investment banks, which populated its ranks with the best and the brightest students from the most elite schools. Lewis had spent his career battling against that elitism and there was no way, now that he was about to have his own Wall Street investment bank, he would allow that ethos to infect Bank of America.

It was clear to Lewis that the "Goldman guys"—Thain, Kraus, and Montag—had been in the process of taking over Merrill Lynch when he struck the deal to buy the Wall Street bank. One thing both men knew for sure: Based on his performance at Wachtell on Sunday evening, when he turned himself into the center of attention in the conference room by talking nonstop and continually flashing his bright green BlackBerry, Peter Kraus would not fit into the organization.

The BofA board of directors took an immediate dislike to Thain. Most of them watched the joint press conference that the Merrill CEO had given with Lewis in the morning. Temple Sloan, the lead director, was especially wary, seeing in Thain a representation of all the things that BofA didn't like about Wall Street.

The second-largest faction on the board consisted of a group of directors who joined BofA after the 2004 acquisition of Boston's Fleet Financial Group. This group was headed by Chad Gifford, the former CEO of Fleet who sold his bank to Lewis, and then watched helplessly as a half dozen senior executives tried and failed to integrate into the parent bank and eventually quit. The only senior executive left over from the Fleet acquisition was Brian Moynihan, who had been put in charge of BofA's own New York investment bank a year earlier.

Over the decades, a significant part of NationsBank's success came from the tribal solidarity shared by the Charlotte executives, and the collective chip they carried on their shoulders toward the New York bankers who looked down on them as small-time hillbillies. If there was one part of the country that was even more tribal, that carried an even bigger collective chip on its shoulder toward New York, it was Boston, which had been eclipsed by the Big Apple in the nineteenth century and consigned to second-tier status by New York in the twentieth century, in every endeavor from banking to baseball.

Gifford and the other Fleet directors realized immediately that the acquisition of Merrill Lynch—led by John Thain, the quintessential "golden boy" of Wall Street—could spell the end of Moynihan's rising career at BofA.

LATER THAT WEEK, ALPHIN visited Thain at his office in lower Manhattan to discuss general issues, and to get to know him better. As head of HR, an important part of Alphin's job was to size up talent and make a judgment as to whether an individual would be a good cultural fit with Bank of America. At BofA, raw intellect was all very well, but if an executive did not fit into the organization, or play well with others, it didn't matter how smart he or she was. They had a saying in Charlotte that the smartest guy in the room wasn't always the most effective guy in the room.

To Thain's surprise, one of the first topics Alphin wanted to address was his new colleague.

"We have concluded that Peter Kraus is not going to be part of the team going forward," declared Alphin.

"What do you mean?" asked Thain. "He's my closest advisor."

"There's no negotiation on that."

"You mean that decision has already been made?" asked Thain, incredulous.

"Yes."

"But that doesn't make any sense."

"He doesn't fit our culture," said Alphin, with an emphasis on the last word.

"Peter Kraus was one of the top investment bankers at Goldman Sachs," implored Thain. "He can run asset management, the private client business. He's a brilliant strategic thinker."

"We're fully aware of his background, his activities," said Alphin, with some frost in his voice. "We don't see him being part of our bank going forward."

"But you have no idea of what kind of a talent he is," insisted Thain.

"John," said Alphin, raising his voice. "He cannot be part of the team!"

Thain was startled by Alphin's vehemence on the matter and his outright refusal to consider any compromise, but quickly shrugged it all off as one of the bizarre foibles he would have to learn to manage in dealing with Charlotte.

Thain decided to let the matter go for the time being. Once his new Charlotte colleagues got to know Kraus, Thain told himself, they'd come to like and appreciate him. As for Alphin, he was, ultimately, just an HR guy.

FOR MERRILL LYNCH, the agreement to be acquired by Bank of America did not protect it from the violent repercussions unleashed in the capital markets by Lehman's bankruptcy. In the days following Lehman's collapse, investors took hundreds of billions of dollars out of the marketplace, selling stocks across the board, particularly financial stocks.

Government regulators discovered that AIG, the huge insurance company, had enmeshed itself in the center of the subprime-mortgage market by insuring financial companies against the risks embedded in securities backed by dodgy mortgages. The company's financial products group had become a profit center at AIG in recent years, selling insurance policies to Wall Street banks that wanted protection against the remote likelihood that various classes of securities, such as CDOs, would lose a significant amount of their value.

To executives in AIG's financial products group, it was easy money, as if people who built their homes in a dry flatland had been asking to buy flood insurance. The company obliged, selling as much flood insurance as it could to these flatlanders, without ever figuring out why the people in those homes felt it necessary to have that protection. If they'd done some research, they would have found that the flatlanders had been settling in what was a floodplain, and even though the floodplain had been dry for decades, these residents had some natural concerns about a worst-case scenario.

Sure enough, when that worst-case scenario arrived with the collapse of the real estate market, AIG—a company that existed to protect other people from financial risk—was massively overexposed by all the CDO insurance policies it had written and was in danger of going broke.

On Tuesday, September 17, the Federal Reserve effectively nationalized AIG, investing $85 billion to acquire 79 percent of the company's stock. The move wasn't enough to protect the remaining two investment banks, Morgan Stanley and even the mighty Goldman Sachs. Shares in those firms sank to historic lows as the week wore on. Regulators pushed both firms to align themselves with depository banks, as Merrill had done with BofA, but there were no logical fits. Instead, over the weekend of September 20–21, both banks were allowed to be reconstituted as bank holding companies, which put them under the direct supervision of the Federal Reserve. As bank holding companies, Morgan Stanley and Goldman Sachs would no longer be able to take on the same degree of risk as they had when they were investment banks. And just like that, less than two months after Paul Wetzel had predicted that the independent investment banking model would eventually go away, it had disappeared, at least among the nation's largest financial institutions.

WITHIN A DAY OR TWO of the merger agreement being signed, Tom Sanzone, head of internal operations at Merrill Lynch, had cleared out the entire sixteenth floor of Merrill's headquarters for BofA people from Charlotte to set up their own base camp.

For about two weeks after the deal, John Thain seemed slightly less engaged than normal. He showed up at management meetings, and responded to requests from subordinates, but the energy and focus that had marked his tenure since the previous December had dimmed.

Merrill's management meetings now featured a new face: Andrea Smith, Alphin's top deputy, who had moved to New York full-time to supervise the HR aspects of the transition. Much as the arrival of May Lee had surprised Thain's management team six months earlier, Smith's presence on the thirty-second floor and her attendance at every meeting Thain held surprised members of the CEO's inner circle, who had never considered human resources to be a vital part of any bank's operations.

SMITH BECAME THAIN'S day-to-day Bank of America contact. But by the end of September, Thain figured out that the real power behind the throne in Charlotte was her boss, J. Steele Alphin, who was now coming up to New York on a weekly basis.

Among the many unusual aspects of Bank of America and its culture, Thain was struck by the amount of power wielded by Alphin. As chief administrative officer at Bank of America, Alphin's title carried a measure of authority, but from the frequency with which Andrea Smith and Ken Lewis had invoked his name, Thain realized that he played an outsized role on the BofA management team. Alphin appeared to be closer to Lewis than any of the other senior executives on the CEO's team, including Amy Brinkley and Greg Curl. His title, chief administrative officer, didn't do justice to his importance in the BofA world.

Tall, athletically fit, and sporting a full head of prematurely gray hair, Alphin embodied the attributes that most people associate with patriotic southerners: supreme loyalty to country combined with an unswerving obedience to the commanding officer. In Alphin's case, the loyalty was to his company, Bank of America, and his obedience was to Ken Lewis, a man he'd worked for, on and off, for almost thirty years.

A native of the Virginia tidewater region and son of a sharecropper, Alphin worked nearly full-time on the family farm through high school. He went to Purdue on a football scholarship, and was just acclimating himself to the shock of living among thousands of other students—the largest gathering of people he'd ever seen—when he blew out his knee, ending his football career. The scholarship over, he transferred to the University of North Carolina in Chapel Hill, where he studied military history, graduating in 1974. After graduation, he returned to work on the family farm, but after two months he'd had it, and went north, where he found work in Princeton, New Jersey, selling customized packaging to pharmaceutical companies. He and his wife, Debbie, made lots of friends in Princeton, and Alphin was able to play rugby, despite the knee, but among the northerners, he and his wife stuck out. At various gatherings, the couple's friends would call on them to speak, just so everyone could hear their southern accents, which struck the northerners as being extremely funny. The Alphins eventually headed back to North Carolina.

In 1977, Alphin landed a job at NCNB's Chapel Hill branch. Three years later, he moved to the bank's headquarters in Charlotte, where he shifted away from banking operations and into human resources, specializing in compensation.

It was there, in the early 1980s, that he first crossed paths with Lewis. They had a nodding acquaintance in the hallways of the old NCNB headquarters, on Tryon Street, until one warm summer evening when a group of the bank's younger executives went out for dinner and some drinking. Alphin and Debbie hit it off with Lewis, who was a few years older and more senior in the organization. Around 10:00 p.m., someone in the group thought it would be a good idea to find a swimming pool. Alphin and Debbie were game, so the couple hopped into his 1965 Mustang convertible. After Alphin shifted into reverse, he heard a loud thud in the back of the car, and turned to see Lewis landing on the backseat, having vaulted over the trunk from the rear bumper of the vehicle. "Let's go!" he said to Alphin, and they were off.

The two men began working together in Florida in 1985, where Alphin had been serving as regional personnel director in Tampa. McColl sent Lewis down to the Sunshine State to improve NCNB's patchwork of banking operations there. The personal bond between Alphin and Lewis became a professional one. By the end of the decade, Lewis was given a much bigger job, running NCNB's newly acquired Texas bank, while Alphin returned to Charlotte.

After NCNB's acquisition of C&S/Sovran, Georgia's premier bank, in 1991, Lewis moved to Atlanta. The NCNB name, by now, had becoming confusing in the wake of the bank's serial mergers, so the company adopted a new name that would stretch with it, NationsBank.

Alphin was also reassigned to Atlanta, where he was reunited with Lewis. In order to create a sense of unity among the bank's new employees in Atlanta, Alphin and other members of the HR team helped arrange for a large off-site meeting in Braselton, Georgia, about forty miles outside of Atlanta. The purpose of the gathering was to instill a spirit of belonging at NationsBank among the C&S/Sovran people, who were now working for an institution they had long considered an enemy.

The meeting took place at the Chateau Elan, a winery and resort just off Interstate 85, which connected Charlotte to Atlanta. Outside the hotel, beyond a cow pasture, the organizers had erected a large tent. Shortly after moving to Atlanta, Lewis learned that the C&S/Sovran employees dreaded joining the NCNB system because it was so rigidly controlled by rules, like the military.

Lewis got up to speak and addressed that point. "At our bank, we don't have a rule for every single thing," Lewis said, firing up the crowd like an old-school preacher on a Sunday. "And we don't hide behind business operations. We get things done, and you can, too. You now have the freedom to act!"

T-shirts were circulated among the crowd, so that everyone could wear a shirt with the slogan FREEDOM TO ACT emblazoned on it.

"If we have a bad policy about something, you come to me and tell me about it," Lewis thundered. "If we agree with you, that the policy is bad or needs fixing, we'll do that. It's just paper. That's what policies and rules are, just paper. If they're wrong, this is what we'll do," Lewis shouted, as he picked up a big sheaf of papers and tossed them into a bonfire that had been started nearby. The crowd roared.

A lightbulb went on as Alphin saw for the first time Lewis's leadership potential. Over the next few years, Alphin arranged for Lewis to go all over the country, to places where NationsBank had significant operations, and speak to groups of 400 to 500 people, often doing question-and-answer sessions. The public speaking engagements helped Lewis improve his delivery and increase his profile at the bank, and helped strengthen the working relationship between the two men.

After Lewis succeeded McColl as chief executive, Alphin rose to the position of corporate personnel executive, BofA-speak for director of human resources. Throughout Lewis's reign, Alphin acquired more power. In 2006, he became chief administrative officer, consolidating more duties in his portfolio. Anne Finucane, the legacy Fleet executive who headed up marketing and communications, recommended that her group be shifted over into Alphin's domain. It was the first time any business manager had actively volunteered to report to Alphin, and he quickly accepted the offer, extending his range of responsibilities. Alphin even moved his way up the new skyscraper that dominated Charlotte's skyline, ascending from the fifty-sixth floor, where the "band one" executives had offices, to the fifty-eighth floor—the "c-suite"—where Lewis reigned supreme.

Now, sitting in John Thain's tastefully furnished office on the thirty-second floor of Merrill Lynch headquarters, Alphin asked Thain about compensation, and about how much he intended to get paid.

"As you might know," Thain began, "I had no change-of-control clause in my contract, so I didn't get anything for selling this company."

"I do know," said Alphin carefully. "That's good. At Bank of America, we don't like change-of-control contracts."

He then asked what kind of bonuses were being planned for Greg Fleming and Bob McCann.

"They'll get somewhere in the $20 million range," said Thain, noting that neither of the men received any cash bonus the year before, in the wake of the Stan O'Neal meltdown.

Alphin nodded slowly. "And what about you? How much are you expecting?"

"My board is going to pay me somewhere around $25 million this year," said Thain.

Quite a lot of money, Alphin said. After a pause, he continued: "John, going forward in our company, that's not the kind of pay you should expect if you want to consider a role, that's not what it's going to be. That's not our philosophy of paying, and we won't do that."

Thain insisted that $25 million was fair, especially considering what he had done with the merger. "I think I've done exactly what my board asked me to do. I tried to clean up the problems here and I delivered a $29 stock price to the shareholder. I've done my job."

"In our company, we don't pay people for the merger," said Alphin. "Ken's never been paid for a merger the year it's done or in advance. So in our company, you would be paid when this is successful, when the share-. holder benefits from it."

"Well, I really think I deserve it. An executive of my caliber, with my background, has an absolute value on Wall Street. I'm worth $25 million."

"I can't make that decision," Alphin said. "That's not my decision to make. But I can tell you, going forward that's not the type of compensation you're going to see if you want to be part of Bank of America, particularly next year, which is probably going to be a very difficult year."

AFTER HIS FIRST MEETINGS with Thain, Alphin developed a sense of the Merrill CEO's skill sets and leadership potential. Bank of America's board had been turned off by Thain's stiff bearing during the September 15 press conference, and by the general assumption that he was just another self-absorbed Wall Street egomaniac who measured his self-worth by the size of his annual bonus.

Alphin saw something different. During their conversation in the corner office, Thain interrupted the meeting to take a phone call from one of his four children. There were pictures of his wife and kids on his desk and elsewhere throughout the office.

Alphin had two daughters, so there was something in common with Thain, whose family consisted of two sons and two daughters. Alphin loved sports cars, and belonged to a Porsche racing club in Charlotte. Thain, an engineer by training, favored BMWs, and had bought several for his children.

Alphin had played football in high school and his first year of college, while Thain had been a wrestler, so they had common ground there as well.

The two men had dinner at a top-rated Italian restaurant in lower Manhattan where Thain was greeted by everyone—from the maître d' to the waiters and staff—as "John." As the men spoke, Alphin realized Thain was not at all like the stereotypical Wall Street banker that was so loathed in Charlotte. The Thains were private people, and during the summer retreated to a lakeside home in a remote part of the Adirondacks, where they never ran into other Wall Street families. The typical Wall Street go-getter owned a home in the Hamptons, the trendy retreat for New York's hyper-rich on the eastern end of Long Island.

The Thains enjoyed hiking, canoeing, waterskiing, and other woodsy sports that appealed to the Appalachian mindset.

Upon his return to Charlotte, Alphin spoke to Lewis about Thain, and eventually met with Temple Sloan, BofA's lead director. Sloan expressed doubts about Thain's character, but Alphin insisted that the Merrill CEO was different from the rest of the Wall Street crowd.

"He could run the company one day," said Alphin.

"You're seeing something I'm not seeing," replied Sloan.

"He has the capability to change," said Alphin. Thain's an outdoorsman, he added, so he couldn't be all bad.

"Why don't you see if John will go hunting with us?" said Sloan.

IN LATE SEPTEMBER, KEN Lewis invited Thain and select members of his top management team to Charlotte for the day, so that the heads of Merrill's business units could meet their counterparts at Bank of America. In his invitation, Lewis told Thain specifically that he wanted to talk about the Merrill CEO's role in the organization going forward.

That morning, Thain flew down to Charlotte on the company's new Bombardier jet with a platoon of top Merrill Lynch executives, including Bob McCann, Greg Fleming, May Lee, Tom Montag, Noel Donohoe, Ed Moriarty III, and Tom Sanzone. After the ninety-minute flight to Charlotte, the Merrill executives attended a series of meetings, including one-on-ones with Steele Alphin, designed to introduce them to Bank of America and the way it operated.

More important, the roster of attendees provided a clear indication of which Merrill executives were deemed to have a future at BofA. The fact that Rosemary Berkery, the general counsel, was not on the trip indicated that she would probably not be offered a comparable position after the merger closed. Nelson Chai was also conspicuously absent. Thain had promised his protégé that he would figure out a role for him in the new order, but it was clear from the start that Lewis's own CFO, Joe Price, would remain in place after the merger closed.

AROUND 5:00 P.M., the group gathered in the bar of Sonoma, a restaurant at the street level mall connected to Bank of America's headquarters. From the treatment that Lewis and his team received, it was apparent to Thain and the rest of the Merrill contingent that BofA's top people were regulars.

Lewis ordered a Johnnie Walker Black, his cocktail of choice, and Alphin had a Grey Goose vodka on the rocks. Amy Brinkley, who hovered near the men, sipped a glass of wine. Thain ordered a glass of white wine.

On the periphery of that central group, the Merrill executives drank and chatted with their BofA counterparts, including Greg Curl, Andrea Smith, Joe Price, Neil Cotty, Jeff Brown, Liam McGee, Barbara Desoer, and Brian Moynihan. Most of the BofA executives wore their "spirit" pins, featuring the bank's red, white, and blue "flagscape" logo, something the Merrill Lynch executives found vaguely cultish.

Thain enjoyed a glass of wine or two with dinner, but he was not a recreational drinker, the way his new "teammates" were. For the past two weeks, he had been trying to figure out why some people at BofA held such senior jobs. After a couple of sessions with Alphin, Thain was beginning to understand the chief administration officer's importance and how he came to accrue so much power. But Thain was puzzled by other members of Lewis's team. The men and women at the bar, who took turns hovering in close to Lewis to exchange a comment or wisecrack, all seemed nice enough, but none of them struck Thain as standout performers. And then it hit him: Ken Lewis surrounded himself with drinking buddies. It was as though the Beverly Hillbillies had taken over the largest bank in the country, and Elly May Clampett and Jethro Bodine were on the management team.

After about an hour of general socializing, Lewis and Thain retreated to the rear of the restaurant and sat down for a private dinner. A curtain was drawn so that the men were no longer visible to the rest of the group, and one of Lewis's bodyguards stood watch at the entrance to the area.

The rest of the executives broke into smaller groups, by business, and went out to dinner separately. Tom Sanzone and May Lee, who would lead the transition from the Merrill Lynch side, had dinner with Brian Moynihan and Andrea Smith, BofA's top executives on the transition.

Behind the curtain at Sonoma, Thain saw a different Lewis from the one he had dealt with a few weeks earlier. This Lewis, sixty-one years old, expressed concern about the future of the combined organizations and the importance of making the merger work. Looking Thain directly in the eye, Lewis conceded that he had not done a great job grooming a successor for his job as chief executive. If he, Thain, would stay on as head of Bank of America's global banking operations—essentially the same job as the one Thain had at Merrill Lynch—then in one year's time, if Merrill's business performed well, Lewis would name him president of Bank of America, establishing him as Lewis's clear successor.

"I'm not promising anything," Lewis reminded Thain. "You'll have to earn it, but the opportunity is there."

Once again, Lewis turned the conversation to the potential of the combined organization and explained how Thain would be the perfect man to lead the world's most powerful financial institution over the next decade. The opportunity before them was enormous, Lewis explained, and so was the responsibility to get it right. He needed the Merrill Lynch CEO on board to make this thing work.

Later, after the separate groups had finished their dinners, they reconvened at Sonoma, where Lewis and Thain were still having dinner. Several ordered a nightcap as they waited for the two chief executives to emerge from behind the curtain. When the men reappeared, Thain and his Merrill entourage were driven to the airport for the flight home.

On board the private jet, small talk disguised some of the anxiety felt by many. It was clear that Lewis had made an offer of some kind to Thain, an offer the Merrill CEO had taken under advisement, but did not discuss on the plane. Whether or not Thain accepted that offer would impact the future of almost everyone on board the flight.

The exception was Greg Fleming, who was confident he would have a place in the new organization. Kraus was no longer a threat, and as for Thain, it wasn't even certain he'd accept Lewis's offer. Fleming decided to mend some fences. He approached May Lee, whom he had rebuffed for much of the year. Knowing how much she liked Peter Kraus, Fleming admitted to Lee that he had misjudged the former Goldman banker. There had been cross words between them over the weekend of the BofA deal, Fleming said, and silly spats about the differences between furniture and art, but if only he had had more time to work with him, Fleming was sure he and Kraus would get along fine. May Lee had already written Fleming off for being insubordinate to Thain and insensitive to her, so this sudden show of concern for Kraus, slathered with what she felt was Fleming's unctuous sincerity, made her skin crawl.

ON OCTOBER 2, Bank of America announced that John Thain would remain with the organization after the acquisition of Merrill Lynch, as president of global banking, a division that encompassed all of Merrill's legacy businesses, including the financial advisory division, investment banking, and sales and trading. The bank also announced that Brian Moynihan, who had been in charge of BofA's comparable business unit, would move into a new global role with the company after the acquisition was completed. Until then, Moynihan would coordinate the transition between BofA and Merrill Lynch.

The news about Thain's appointment did not go down well in Boston. Just before 9:00 in the morning, Graceann Sullivan, assistant to Chad Gifford—a BofA director who had worked with Moynihan for years—sent an e-mail containing the Thain announcement to Gifford's wife, with the comment, "Perhaps you knew about this, but personally, I hope our buddy Brian is okay . . ."

Gifford's wife replied: "Ugh . . . Chad was worried about this."

. . .

DAYS AFTER THE THAIN announcement, Paul Wetzel had lunch with Margaret Tutwiler, Thain's communications chief.

"What are your plans?" Tutwiler asked him as they sat and ate. "Are you going to stay here?"

"I'm probably going to leave," Wetzel said. "It's time to do something else."

"Why would you do that?"

"I don't see a big role for me in the new organization."

"But John likes you, and he's going to be running the whole place," Tutwiler replied.

"I wouldn't count on it."

"What do you mean?"

"Once they take over, they're in charge. After the first slipup of any kind, John's going to be gone."

"Why do you say that?"

"Ever hear of David Coulter?"

Perplexed, Tutwiler shook her head.

DURING HIS EIGHTEEN YEARS as chief executive, Hugh McColl acquired dozens of large banks across the country, building NationsBank into one of the largest in the U.S. In every deal, it was clear who held the power: McColl ran the bigger, more powerful bank and his team would swallow up the smaller bank. There was never any question of whether the top executive of the acquired bank would play a large role at NationsBank. The fact that McColl could buy that executive's bank usually indicated that the CEO of the acquired entity had underperformed or was ready to retire.

McColl was willing to pay full price to fund his acquisitions, betting—most often accurately—that the combined savings of the deal and market share gains would make up for the extra dollar or two per share he usually paid to win in an auction. If he needed to sweet-talk the chief executive of a particularly valuable property into selling, he'd offer a seat on his bank's board and a lucrative financial package, overflowing with perks. When McColl wanted a bank, he had no qualms about the price he'd have to pay, or the golden parachute he'd attach to convince a reluctant CEO to sell.

Nowhere was this more evident than the deal to acquire Barnett Bank of Florida, in the summer of 1997. NationsBank already had a strong presence in the Sunshine State, and had extended its reach to Texas and up through Virginia. But Barnett was the biggest bank in the state and when its CEO, Charlie Rice, decided it was time to sell, McColl eagerly joined the silent auction to acquire Barnett.

In a silent auction, every participant formulates his own bid in private, then submits it in writing at the appointed deadline. There's no chance to renegotiate if it turns out that a competitor has placed a bigger bid, so the trick is to figure out how much the strongest rival is likely to pay, then try to top that.

In this auction, NationsBank was pitted against the two other powerhouse banks in Charlotte—First Union and Wachovia—as well as Banc One of Columbus, Ohio, and Sun Trust of Atlanta.

As the NationsBank team strategized about how much they should bid, they figured that the healthiest bank among their competitors, First Union, could reasonably afford a $68 per share bid for Barnett. Considering that First Union would probably up the ante by a few dollars, McColl's team discussed the prospects of bidding as much as $75 per share, or $15 billion, for a bank with $44 billion in assets. On its face, such a bid seemed outrageously high to several of McColl's subordinates, and the NationsBank management team could not reach a consensus. It was Ken Lewis who finally carried the day, breaking up a logjam by saying, "The question is simple. Would you want to wake up Monday morning and find that First Union had bought them?"

McColl embraced Lewis's position, and NationsBank won the auction with a bid of $76 per share. On top of that, McColl made Charlie Rice, Barnett's CEO, the chairman of the board of NationsBank and promised to keep most of Rice's management team in place.

On the basis of Barnett's earnings, NationsBank had overpaid. But the acquisition gave the Charlotte bank a market capitalization larger than any other U.S. bank, including Bank of America in San Francisco.

In 1998, a few months after the Barnett transaction closed, McColl learned that BofA might be interested in a merger, a prospect that excited him like no other deal. Unlike his previous acquisitions, however, BofA was large enough that any combination would have to be a merger, not a buyout.

McColl met several times with David Coulter, the chief executive of the San Francisco bank, to discuss how the deal would work. Since it would be a real merger, price was not an impediment. Rather, the major stumbling block centered on what are known in the mergers and acquisitions business as the "social issues," such as who gets to be boss, which also determines which group dominates.

Prior to McColl's negotiations with Coulter, he had his head of human resources, Chuck Cooley, draw up a psychological profile of the man he'd be negotiating with. Coulter had humble roots, the son of a Pennsylvania truck driver. He started his career at Bank of America in 1976 as a financial analyst, and worked his way up over the next two decades through hard work and keen analytical thinking.

Coulter was not a chief executive who gloried in the limelight (unlike McColl, who relished the image of the brash, acquisition-minded Carolina banker painted of him by magazines such as *Fortune* and *BusinessWeek*). He was more of a technocrat, described by one analyst as a Mr. Fixit who had moved from division to division within BofA, solving problems and spurring growth, without calling undue attention to himself.

The background profile of Coulter made McColl realize that he would have to negotiate the social issues on a rational basis rather than an emotional one. He would have to convince Coulter that the combined bank should be based in Charlotte because it made business sense, not because it was the sacred duty of every Confederate son to fight for the region's soil. Likewise, McColl would have to convince Coulter that the combined board of directors should be weighted in Charlotte's favor because NationsBank was larger, in terms of market capitalization, not because McColl wanted to lock in the upper hand for his team.

For his part, McColl conceded important territory. He agreed to let NationsBank, the beloved name he had created for NCNB, be rechristened Bank of America, since the San Francisco institution's brand was more indelibly fixed in consumers' minds, and since the name itself, "Bank of America," resonated more powerfully with consumers than the name "NationsBank."

The other concession was an agreement in principle that Coulter, who was more than a decade younger than McColl, would take the top job when the CEO retired within a year or two. The agreement stipulated that it was "the present intent of the boards of directors for Mr. Coulter to succeed Mr. McColl."

When the deal was announced in April 1998 it stunned the banking world and meant that Charlotte, North Carolina—not New York or San Francisco—would be home to the biggest bank in the United States. Coulter, who acceded to McColl's insistence that the new bank be headquartered in Charlotte, eagerly embraced his new role and worked hard in the months leading up to the completion of the deal to sell its benefits to disappointed colleagues and civic leaders in San Francisco.

In the months after the deal was announced, Coulter immersed himself in the ways of the Charlotte bank. A consummate team player, he never tired of extolling the virtues of the deal to his colleagues in San Francisco, and traveled several times to North Carolina to flesh out his understanding of NationsBank.

On one visit, Hugh McColl's predecessor Tom Storrs feted Coulter at a Charlotte country club. Coulter thanked Storrs and worked the crowd, introducing himself to all the local power brokers in attendance. McColl wasn't there. When it was time for a celebratory toast, everyone raised their glasses in honor of Coulter. Then one woman, an attractive, middle-aged doyenne of Charlotte society, giggled and asked her husband if she could make a toast. He rolled his eyes, in approval of something he knew could not be avoided.

"Here's to when," the woman said with her lilting southern accent, raising her glass. "And not to how, 'cause I've known how since I was ten!"

IN AUGUST 1998, weeks before the merger became official, the collapse of the Russian ruble that had sparked the meltdown at Long Term Capital Management also inflicted damage on other hedge funds, including

D.E. Shaw. Bank of America, under Coulter's watch, had invested $1.4 billion in Shaw's hedge funds, and as the financial crisis detonated by the ruble's decline became more widely understood, McColl learned that the Shaw exposure would lead to hundreds of millions of dollars in losses for the combined bank.

The investment in D.E. Shaw didn't catch anyone in Charlotte by surprise. McColl had his treasury team combing over Coulter's books for months, looking at every asset on BofA's balance sheet. Once the Shaw investment began heading south, McColl watched it like a hawk, asking for frequent updates on its status.

At one point during the throes of the crisis, McColl summoned a finance executive up to his corner office for an update on the D.E. Shaw position. What was the maximum it could lose? About $1 billion, came the answer. The finance executive took the elevator back down to his office in a lower floor of the tower. The moment he arrived, the phone rang. It was Ken Lewis. "So," Lewis asked, "do you think it's okay for the next CEO of this bank to lose $1 billion?"

In October, the deal closed and Hugh McColl was now CEO of a banking colossus that stretched from coast to coast. He had fulfilled the dream of his predecessors, Addison Reese and Tom Storrs, who envisioned creating a bank that could beat any other bank out there, from New York to California.

McColl had the power, and now he had the ammunition to make sure that the power stayed within the Charlotte family. After earnings were reported, in which a loss of $372 million associated with the hedge fund was disclosed, McColl convened a meeting of the executive committee of his board in Charlotte. Coulter wanted to be on hand, in case anyone asked for an explanation about the D.E. Shaw situation, but McColl specifically told him not to attend.

William "Hootie" Johnson, best known as chairman of Augusta National Golf Club, which hosts the Masters tournament every April, was a longtime friend of McColl's and one of the NationsBank directors who carried over to the combined BofA board. McColl and Johnson decided that Coulter should be penalized for the losses.

On Thursday, October 15, Johnson flew out to San Francisco to meet with Coulter. The next morning, over breakfast at the Mandarin Hotel, Johnson informed the CEO-in-waiting that the bank's board thought he was a decent fellow, but the D.E. Shaw losses, which resulted in a $372 million write-down, could not pass without response. "We think the captain of the ship needs to step up and take responsibility for this," Johnson said. "We, the board, have decided that you should leave."

Coulter was stunned. He actually believed in the merger and had fought hard with his own people to pull it off. Now he felt that McColl had strung him along with lies all summer.

If Coulter did the right thing and resigned, Johnson continued, he would be able to keep the generous benefits and the golden parachute that the board had already approved for him. If he resisted, he'd lose every cent of his pension and he'd be at war with the bank. Financially and professionally, the gang in Charlotte would ruin him if he did not comply.

With that, Johnson, ever the southern gentleman, thanked Coulter for his time and his service to the bank.

ON TUESDAY, OCTOBER 20, 1998, four days after Johnson's visit to San Francisco, Coulter announced his resignation from Bank of America. Subsequent filings with the SEC showed that Coulter would receive a combined salary and bonus of $3.75 million for the next five years, along with 300,000 shares of stock and annual pension benefits of nearly $5 million for the remainder of his life.

The enormous payout to Coulter vilified him in the eyes of his San Francisco employees, many of whom felt they had been sold out. By demonizing Coulter, the payout also helped bind together employees of both banks, who now had a common enemy to root against. It was the peculiar genius of Chuck Cooley, McColl's head of human resources, to know that a golden parachute for Coulter would eliminate any feeling of sympathy for him within the bank, particularly on the West Coast. With Coulter out of the way, McColl eventually recommended that he be succeeded in the corner office by his own NCNB protégé, Ken Lewis.

CHAPTER 16

PROJECT PANTHER

ON THURSDAY, OCTOBER 2, the same day of the announcement that Thain would stay on board after Bank of America completed its acquisition of Merrill Lynch, Ken Lewis, Joe Price, and Jeff Brown, BofA's treasurer, placed a call from the fifty-eighth floor of BofA headquarters in Charlotte to Ciaran O'Kelly, head of global equities at BofA's investment bank in New York.

The bank was thinking of raising some capital, Price said, and the management team in Charlotte wanted to get a sense from O'Kelly as to whether the capital markets would be receptive to an offer of new shares from BofA.

The earnings for the quarter turned out to be worse than expected, Price said, and the bank was planning to pre-announce its earnings, which were originally scheduled for mid-October, and cut the dividend to its shareholders as part of a cash conservation effort. JPMorgan Chase and Goldman Sachs had recently raised money from the markets, and the two men wanted to know O'Kelly's views on a similar move by BofA.

"Makes perfect sense," said O'Kelly, a forty-year-old native of Dub-
lin who came to the U.S. in the 1990s to work on Wall Street. "We can
get working on that. What are your thoughts on timing?"

"If you could work on this through the weekend, we want to make
the earnings announcement on Monday," Price said.

"Ahhh, okay," said O'Kelly. "Who's in the loop on this?"

"You, me, J.B., and Ken," said Price, referring to Brown, the treasurer, who had been recommending a capital raise for months.

"How about Brian?" O'Kelly asked, referring to his boss, Moynihan.
Silence on the line.

"How about our friends at Merrill Lynch, Thain and Fleming?"
More silence.

HAVING OPERATED FOR YEARS on the assumption that Bank of
America's balance sheet was an impregnable fortress, Lewis had suddenly
come to the realization that BofA's capital base had slipped to danger-
ously low levels. Lewis saw his bank's preliminary earnings numbers for
the third quarter and recognized that loan losses across all categories were
spiking. Just a few weeks earlier, on Sunday, September 14, when the
Merrill agreement was signed, Lewis had told Thain and Kraus he was
optimistic about the U.S. consumer, but his bank's earnings for the quarter now showed that his confidence was misplaced.

The timing for this equity raise was challenging and getting worse
by the day. Since the Lehman weekend, the capital markets had become
more turbulent. Goldman Sachs and JPMorgan Chase had tapped the
capital markets for fresh funds, but General Electric had run into trouble with its capital raise. The prices of bank stocks were dropping and
it wasn't clear how much investor interest was still out there for Bank
of America. Because of the tanking economy, it was almost certain that
other banks would try to raise fresh capital. If BofA waited any longer,
there might not be any money left for a sale of stock. The market in
general appeared to be going into a free fall, with the S&P 500, a broad
index of stocks, suffering a double-digit collapse, one of the worst swoons
since the great crash of 1929.

The Charlotte bank faced yet another problem in going to the markets to raise capital. For years it had been telling the investing public what a well-run institution it was, what a safe investment it was. Unlike the New York banks, which had played fast and loose with investor funds, Bank of America managed its loans and investments conservatively and paid a fat dividend every quarter. Its stock traded well above the level of JPMorgan Chase because of the perception that the bank, headquartered down in Charlotte, was removed from the ills that infected Wall Street.

The revelation that BofA was mired just as deeply in the financial mess that engulfed Wall Street would expose it to charges of gross mismanagement, especially in the wake of the agreement to buy Merrill Lynch for $29 a share.

For more than a year, since the $21 billion cash purchase of the LaSalle bank system in Chicago in 2007, Lewis's corporate treasury department had recommended that the bank raise capital. Then came the $4 billion Countrywide acquisition earlier in 2008, followed by the agreement to buy Merrill in a generous, all-stock deal.

All along, the message from Lewis had been the same: BofA didn't need to raise more capital, and didn't need to cut its dividend, which sent precious cash out the door to shareholders every quarter. Now, faced with a recession much harsher than he had foreseen and a mammoth acquisition of a business he didn't fully understand, Lewis needed to take drastic steps, putting an equity raise in motion.

Along with a small team, O'Kelly and Doug Baird, head of equity capital markets at BofA, starting putting together a plan—dubbed "Project Panther," after Charlotte's pro football team—to raise $10 billion in fresh capital to replenish BofA's depleted coffers.

Thain got wind of the capital-raising efforts and on Saturday dispatched Lisa Carnoy and Dan Cummings, Merrill's co-heads of equity capital markets, to BofA's Manhattan offices to pitch in. Together, the group identified the top twenty institutional investors to whom BofA would market its securities, as well as the universe of top BofA shareholders. Several pages of the plan were given over to the sales pitch, highlighting the arguments as to why investors should buy more BofA stock, while another page presented some of the opposing arguments that would likely surface during the sales campaign. The team would script a presentation for Lewis to read to a small number of investors on Sunday, then polish it for the rest of the sales team to use Monday evening, when the earnings announcement would take place.

On Monday, having learned there would be a 6 p.m. conference call headed by Lewis to get the institutional sales teams on board, Thain himself showed up on the third floor of One Bryant Park, where equity sales and trading was based, and said he wanted to participate in Lewis's conference call. O'Kelly, caught in an awkward position, suggested that Thain take up the matter directly with Lewis, especially since the Merrill acquisition was one of the primary drivers behind BofA's need for fresh capital. Thain called Lewis, and secured permission to join the call. In addition to Merrill's institutional sales force, Thain would also reach out to his firm's thundering herd of brokers across the U.S., enlisting the 16,000 financial advisors in the effort to move BofA's new stock.

The call began right after the earnings announcement. Instead of addressing the obvious issue—BofA's lagging earnings—the pitch that the two CEOs wanted their salespeople to use was simple and uninspired, a litany of the usual bromides associated with any merger, asking investors to buy on faith, without providing any concrete rationale to spur purchases. "We're the best" was a recurring theme, along with "We're going to dominate our industry." Another slogan maintained that "One plus one will equal four!" At the end, when questions were allowed, none of the thousands of brokers on the line, members of Merrill's thundering herd, had any queries. As for Merrill's institutional sales force, many of the rank and file tuned in, but several of the unit's top managers had simply gone home rather than wait around and participate in the phone call. Thain was undeterred by their absence.

"Okay," said Thain to his troops on the joint conference call. "Let's show our new parent company what we're capable of doing. Let's impress our new boss!"

That evening and the next morning, BofA and Merrill went to market to sell new shares in its company. The market had turned ferociously hostile and BofA's admission that it needed capital, just three weeks after insisting that it would not have any problems financing the acquisition of Merrill Lynch, lent an air of desperation to the entire affair.

If there was ever a moment for Thain to prove to Lewis the value of the Merrill Lynch franchise, this was it. The bank that had just agreed to buy Merrill was in desperate need of cash, and who was better positioned to raise that cash in the stock market than Merrill Lynch and its thundering herd of brokers?

The sales forces of BofA Securities and Merrill Lynch hit the phones, talking up the prospects of an investment, but the evidence of the Charlotte bank's problems were now on full display for investors, even before the Merrill Lynch deal was consummated.

Based on feedback from the sales teams on Tuesday, the equity raise would not go smoothly. The price of BofA stock had been above $30 a share, but there was no way investors would pay that for new shares in the bank. Around 2:00 p.m., Lewis convened another call, with Thain, Carnoy, O'Kelly, and other members of the sales effort, to find out if the capital raise would be possible after all. The goal was to raise $10 billion, but the "indications of interest" that the sales force had received at that point only amounted to a couple of billion dollars. Since investors were not willing to pay anything close to $30 a share, some members of Lewis's management team wondered whether the whole effort should be postponed until the stock price bounced back up and the economy improved.

More than a dozen people crammed into an office on the trading floor at One Bryant Park as Lewis, piped in on a speakerphone, asked for an update. O'Kelly was candid about what he was hearing in the marketplace. Investors saw no reason to pay a premium for BofA stock. Given the bank's own increasingly cloudy outlook for the economy, the market didn't think its loan loss allowance, at 2.2 percent, was realistic. JPMorgan Chase was setting aside funds for losses in the 2.6 percent range. Worse, BofA's "tangible common equity" ratio—a measure of the bank's financial strength—was far below the industry average. Lewis and his management team had clung to the notion that Bank of America was well capitalized because its "Tier 1 capital ratio" was close to the industry norm, but in the harsh financial environment in which banks were now operating, the Tier 1 ratio—which regulators relied upon—was viewed as less pertinent than the real-world metrics of the tangible common equity ratio. And in the real-world metrics of a negative market, O'Kelly explained, BofA was viewed as a bank with severe weaknesses.

After Lewis heard him out, the CEO paused, then asked the group what the offering price of BofA's stock should be. Neither Thain nor anyone else in the room appeared eager to offer an answer, and then O'Kelly approached the speakerphone and said, "Twenty-two dollars a share." There was a long silence on the Charlotte end of the phone line as Lewis digested the information. That price was a big comedown from where BofA's shares were trading. It was as though the real world had finally come crashing down on headquarters in Charlotte.

Lewis finally spoke, asking the group if they should go ahead with the plan. O'Kelly turned around and looked at everyone in the room, opening up the floor for anyone who wanted to speak. Thain, who was standing in the back, almost out of sight near the door, remained quiet, observing but not participating.

Finally, O'Kelly answered, "Yes, we should do it. We have to do it." The markets were as bad as anything he'd seen in his eighteen years, he said, and this might be the bank's last opportunity to raise capital for some time. Also, having disclosed a severe shortage of capital to the markets already, O'Kelly said, it would be even more dangerous to abandon the effort midstream.

Lewis agreed, and the joint sales teams spent the rest of the day selling as aggressively as they could. At a price of $22 a share, more buyers emerged. At one point, Thain himself offered to pitch in with the effort, assuring the BofA sales team that he would "make a few calls" to bring in some large investors. During the long slog of selling on Tuesday, Thain moved around BofA's trading floor, wandering through various offices offering to help out, or musing over the difficulties everyone was facing.

At one point, he came up with a rationale to explain why it was so hard to sell all the new stock. "I think we should go with 'Nobody has any money,' when we talk to Ken," Thain said, first to one BofA man-ager, then another. "That should be our position."

It took the full day, but by nightfall, the Charlotte bank had raised the $10 billion it needed. Although Merrill's institutional sales force had contributed to the capital raise, Lewis began to have doubts about Thain, whose contributions to the effort did not impress his new masters.

Through the course of the day, BofA's own share price slumped, dropping from the $30 range to $23, nearly matching the price of the offer. When it was all over, Lewis held another call in which he thanked the sales teams from both companies. He didn't know it at the time, but Lewis had successfully extracted the last slug of affordable capital the markets had to offer that year. Future capital raises, courtesy of the fed-eral government, would be far more painful to Lewis and his sharehold-ers than any of the funds raised on October 7.

ON THE FIRST WEEKEND in October, Greg Fleming attended a reunion of Yale Law School graduates, class of 1988, in New Haven, Connecticut. After the exhaustion of the previous twenty-four months, he found it strangely relaxing to mix with a collection of people who had nothing to do with Wall Street, Merrill Lynch, or Bank of America, and to be protected from his professional troubles by the wall of academia that fortified his alma mater.

On Friday evening, before the opening dinner, Fleming and his wife, Melissa, visited the dean of the law school, Harold Koh, in his office. At previous meetings, Koh had encouraged Fleming to think about taking some time off from Wall Street and come to the school's Center for the Study of Corporate Law, where he could enjoy a hiatus from the grind of the capital markets, teach a course, and recharge his batteries. Koh repeated his offer, and this time it sounded more attractive than it ever had before. As he had on previous occasions, Fleming thanked the dean for his offer and said he'd "think about it," but in this instance, he actu-ally meant those words.

. . .

IN EARLY OCTOBER, three Merrill Lynch executives—general counsel Rosemary Berkery and two HR executives, Michael Ross and Peter Stingi—drove from Manhattan to the Warren, New Jersey, headquarters of the Chubb Group of Insurance Companies. Ross and Stingi took a car from Merrill Lynch, while Berkery drove herself from a different meeting.

When they arrived they went up to the office of John Finnegan, Chubb's CEO, who, as a member of the Merrill Lynch board of directors, chaired the firm's compensation committee. A board meeting was scheduled for October 27, and every year, prior to the late October board meeting, it was customary for Berkery to review some of the issues that the compensation committee would be considering at that board meeting, especially bonus payments for the bank's top performers, as well as its most senior executives. What was unusual about this year was that Berkery was conducting the preparatory meeting in person, rather than by telephone, which had been the norm in previous years.

Up through 2006, the process had become routine. Stan O'Neal sent the recommendations for himself and his team, via Berkery, to Alberto Cribiore, who had been head of the committee prior to Finnegan. In October 2007, Finnegan's first year as head of the compensation committee, the normal bonus process for the top five executives hit a roadblock with the sudden revelation of subprime-related losses at Merrill Lynch and O'Neal's ouster.

Because of the losses, O'Neal received no bonus or severance at his departure, but his accumulated stock and vested options allowed him to walk away from Merrill Lynch, which was mortally wounded by bad bets made on his watch, with $161 million in cash and stock. Because of Merrill's huge losses, Fleming and McCann received stock options, but no cash bonus for 2007.

In March 2008, the House Committee on Oversight and Government Reform, chaired by California congressman Henry Waxman, held a hearing to look at the outsized pay packages on Wall Street. Among the witnesses called to justify their payouts were Chuck Prince, former CEO of Citigroup, Angelo Mozilo, former CEO of Countrywide Financial, and O'Neal. Finnegan was also called as a witness before the congressional panel, where he was forced to justify the sums paid to O'Neal. The experience sensitized him to the public relations ramifications of multimillion-dollar bonanzas on Wall Street.

Berkery reviewed several of the topics that were on the agenda for the October 27 meeting, including the $5.8 billion bonus pool that had been specifically set aside for Merrill's employees as part of the September 15 merger agreement. Peter Stingi had put together a proposal to accelerate the decision making process concerning the year-end bonuses. Normally, the compensation committee would render final decisions on bonus allotments in January, after the end of the year. That way, bonus amounts could be allocated according to the actual performance turned in by employees over the course of the entire year.

This year, things would be different. Bank of America would be in charge come January, so Stingi proposed that the compensation committee move up the decision making process into early December, so that the cash portion of the bonuses—money that Merrill Lynch had been setting aside all year for incentive-based compensation—could be paid out in December, at a time when Merrill Lynch was still independent.

Finnegan listened sympathetically to the proposal about the revised bonus schedule and seemed to be in agreement on the timing. He asked about the amount that had been set aside—the $5.8 billion—and was told that the sum represented the upper limit of what BofA agreed to allow, since it was consistent with 2007 aggregate bonus levels. Finnegan said he thought the total seemed a bit high, given than 2008 had turned out to be a much worse year than 2007.

The next topic on the agenda, Berkery said, concerned bonus payments for the top five executives at Merrill. Because her own bonus was on that sheet, she recused herself from any discussion of the matter. Instead, she handed Finnegan a sheet of paper with the proposed payouts.

"This is the current thinking about what we might want to do," she said.

When Finnegan saw the bonus numbers for Thain and his top deputies, his eyes were agog. According to the sheet, Thain, as CEO, would receive a cash bonus of $40 million, and Fleming was to get $25 million.

Bob McCann would receive a similarly sized bonus, while Nelson Chai and Rosemary Berkery would receive something in the area of $15 million each.

Finnegan recoiled at the numbers handed to him.

Berkery pointed out they should not be considered "bonuses" in the literal sense, since Merrill Lynch had no earnings for the year. It would be better to think of them, she said, as "strategic transaction payments," which were intended to reward the executive team for making the BofA deal happen.

"Are you guys completely out of your minds?" the director asked. The bonus requests were "crazy," he said. There was no way Finnegan could give his approval to anything in the same time zone as what Thain was requesting.

Berkery left the room. Stingi let it be known that the bonus numbers were not something that he had been asked for guidance on. He was merely a courier on this request. Stingi warned Finnegan that Thain had an "emotional interest" in the matter and that there would likely be a collision down the road over the issue.

Berkery returned. The three Merrill Lynch executives left Finnegan's office shortly thereafter. Outside, before she even got into her car, Berkery called Thain to report in on Finnegan's opinion about the bonus request.

Shortly thereafter, Thain called Finnegan and said the figures weren't his doing. He blamed Berkery and Stingi for "getting out in front" of him on the topic, and promised to revisit the matter with Finnegan before the board meeting later that month.

DURING HIS VISITS TO Merrill Lynch in New York, Steele Alphin spent most of his time with his top deputy, Andrea Smith, and John Thain.

Alphin also spent some time getting to know Greg Fleming, and visited him at his office one afternoon to talk about the way things worked in Charlotte. Like Thain, Fleming was trying to get a better sense of how things worked at BofA headquarters, particularly with regard to personnel decisions.

With his crisp white shirt and erect posture, Alphin seemed a throwback to a different era, an "organization man" devoted to his employer. He talked about the value system that had been inculcated at Bank of America under Hugh McColl, Lewis's predecessor, and how important that value system was to the bank. "Trust" and "teamwork" were the two most important elements of the bank's culture, of its value system.

Fleming had sat down on a couch in his office, and Alphin was in a chair between him and the window, which was facing southwest. The sun had now gotten low enough that it was shining directly into Fleming's eyes as Alphin spoke. When he noticed Fleming blinking, Alphin offered to change his seat, but Fleming insisted that it was not a problem and that he keep speaking.

The value system was very important at Bank of America, Alphin continued, and what the people in his department wanted to create was an "inclusive meritocracy." In order to accomplish that, BofA had put a tremendous focus on creating an HR department unlike any other in the country. Most big companies rely on their human resources departments as an ancillary service, for screening job applicants and such, and companies tend to staff HR departments accordingly. At Bank of America, HR is a central part of the company's decision making processes, Alphin said. The department is stocked with people who have succeeded at various businesses inside the organization, who have deep operating experience, and a respect for the culture of teamwork and trust that permeates the entire operation. It's that culture that separates the bank from its competitors, Alphin continued, and when the company buys another bank, such as Merrill Lynch, it is essential that Bank of America's culture, its DNA, be spread through the new entity. The most crucial part of any acquisition, any combination of an outside entity into Bank of America, is the preservation of the Charlotte culture.

Fleming had trouble seeing Alphin clearly but listened closely, as he could tell that the chief administrative officer was on a roll about something that mattered to him.

That's where his department comes in, Alphin said. Every time there's an acquisition, some of the new people get it immediately and blend in with Bank of America. Others take more time. They're smart in their own narrow way, or they have an expertise in one part of one business, but they don't understand how the entire bank operates. Some of those people can be taught, Alphin said, if they're willing to learn. That's good. They are welcomed into the bank with open arms and they fight side by side on the same team as Charlotte.

What the bank cannot do, and will never do, Alphin said, is allow a different culture, a subculture of any kind, to take root in the organization. That would never be tolerated on his watch. And so, going forward, he continued, it was absolutely critical that the people selected from Merrill Lynch to be part of Bank of America understand that culture and adhere to it.

With tens of thousands of employees, how could you tell who understood the culture and who didn't? Fleming asked.

Through observation of behavior, productivity measurements, and evaluations from peers and superiors, Alphin said. It actually wasn't difficult to determine early on who would fit into the Bank of America culture and who wouldn't. The important thing was to lie back and watch, and it would become clear with time whether or not someone was fitting in.

"We're like the wolf," Alphin said, leaning over on his chair, a playful smile on his face. "The wolf doesn't hunt for packs of animals. It stays behind the pack and looks for the weak ones that can't keep up, or the ones who wander from the pack."

Fleming was transfixed.

"My advice to you is for you to stay up front with the herd," Alphin said, warming to his topic. "Stay at the front of the pack. If not, the wolf will get you. And remember, the wolf is usually hungry and rarely fails."

Fleming started to say something but didn't know what to say. Alphin continued.

"It's your decision, but the view is better from the front of the pack. Do know there is a wolf and he will get you. And the wolf is hungry." Alphin made a playful biting motion with his teeth as he smiled, accompanied by a clawlike gesture with his hand, in case Fleming didn't grasp the meaning of his words. "He'll git you."

· · ·

DESPITE THE DECISIONS BY the Federal Reserve chairman Ben
Bernanke and treasury secretary Hank Paulson to bail out AIG and allow
Morgan Stanley and Goldman Sachs to become bank holding companies, with full access to the Federal Reserve, the U.S. banking industry
continued to suffer in late September and early October.

Paulson championed the passage of a $700 billion bailout fund to buy
the toxic assets on the balance sheets of the nation's banks. After a surprise
defeat in the House of Representatives, a version of the program was approved by the Senate, then ultimately approved by the House and signed
into law on October 3 as the Emergency Economic Stabilization Act.

But even the new bailout fund failed to restore confidence in the
banking system. The Federal Deposit Insurance Corporation had just
seized Washington Mutual, one of the largest mortgage providers in the
country. Wachovia, the nation's fourth-largest bank—and a once formidable rival to NationsBank in Charlotte—was also on the verge of collapse, a victim of its decision to pay $25 billion to acquire Golden West,
a subprime mortgage provider, at the height of the real estate bubble in
2006. A tentative deal for Citigroup to acquire Wachovia with government aid was trumped by a bid from Wells Fargo in San Francisco, which
saw an opportunity to extend its retail banking reach to the East Coast.
Citi's failure to close the Wachovia deal impaired its image in the eyes
of investors.

Paulson and Bernanke were still concerned about a loss of public
confidence in financial institutions, which, if it became widespread,
could lead to a depression. Goldman Sachs had raised $5 billion in new
funds from Warren Buffett, and Morgan Stanley agreed on a similar
arrangement with Mitsubishi UFJ, a Japanese bank, but the future of
these investment banks as well as Citigroup and other major lenders still
seemed in doubt. Goldman stock, which had been a high-flyer since the
firm went public in 1999, continued its monthlong slide, dropping below
the $100 per share mark on October 10.

On Monday, October 13, Paulson and Bernanke summoned the

heads of nine major banks to Washington, D.C., to invite them to participate in a new government idea, the capital purchase program. In addition to Ken Lewis and John Thain, the regulators brought in the top executives of Goldman Sachs, Morgan Stanley, Citigroup, JPMorgan Chase, Wells Fargo, Bank of New York Mellon. and State Street.

Once the nine men gathered in a conference room at the treasury department that afternoon, Paulson made what was, in effect, an offer they couldn't refuse. In an effort to restore confidence in the financial system, the U.S. government would invest tens of billions of dollars in individual banks, in the form of preferred stock. The new capital would shore up the banks' balance sheets at a time of heightened public concern. In order for the program to work, Paulson said, it was important for every bank to participate. That way there would not be any stigma attached to participation in the program.

The big retail banks—JPMorgan Chase, Citigroup, and Wells Fargo—would get $25 billion in government funds, while Bank of America was slated to receive $15 billion. The investment banks—Merrill Lynch, Goldman Sachs, and Morgan Stanley—would each receive $10 billion. Bank of New York Mellon would get $3 billion and State Street would receive $2 billion.

The program would allow each of these banks access to capital at relatively low rates, since the banks would only have to pay a 5 percent annual dividend to the government for several years, at which point a rising dividend would encourage the banks to buy back the preferred shares. But there was one catch to the program: Executive compensation at the banks receiving the funds would be restricted.

The economic devastation wreaked by the bursting of the real estate bubble and the collapse of Lehman Brothers had exacerbated public outrage at the multimillion-dollar pay packages common on Wall Street. To address that contentious topic, the $700 billion bailout fund—known as the "troubled asset relief program" or TARP—placed restrictions on the types of golden parachute payments that could be made to top executives. The same limits would apply to banks that participated in the new capital purchase program.

When Paulson and Bernanke opened the matter up for discussion, Dick Kovacevich, chairman of Wells Fargo, expressed reservations about any government ownership of his bank. Jamie Dimon of JPMorgan Chase and Citigroup CEO Vikram Pandit agreed to seek board approval for the program that afternoon.

Thain and his former Goldman Sachs colleague, Lloyd Blankfein, inquired about the technical aspects of the investment, such as how the warrants would be priced. Thain then bored in on the topic of executive compensation, asking a series of questions about how participation in the program would affect a bank's ability to attract and keep top executives, and whether pay restrictions might be continued under a new administration in 2009.

Ken Lewis didn't like what he was hearing from his future colleague. Thain's line of questioning suggested to him that the Merrill Lynch CEO viewed access to $10 billion in federal funds as a possible escape hatch from the merger agreement with BofA. And Thain's focus on executive compensation was a reminder to Lewis of how much he hated Wall Street's mania for multimillion-dollar bonuses. "If we spend another second talking about executive compensation, we are out of our minds," the Bank of America CEO finally said, before urging everyone to stop wasting time and sign on to the program.

Despite the protests from Kovacevich, the nine bankers eventually got approval from their boards of directors to participate in the program, which was announced formally the following day.

Lewis still felt uneasy about Thain and the possibility that he might try to tap in to the government funds to extricate himself and Merrill Lynch from the proposed deal. Picking up on Thain's interest in executive compensation, Lewis struck an agreement with him that Merrill Lynch would not access its $10 billion in TARP funds until the new year, by which time the deal would have closed. By not drawing down the funds sooner, Thain ensured that Merrill Lynch would be free to pay out year-end bonuses as the bank saw fit, and not according to the dictates of a government program.

. . .

SEVERAL DAYS AFTER THE meeting in Washington, and after he and Lewis had reached an agreement over how Merrill Lynch would access the $10 billion that had been set aside for it, John Thain hosted a conference call to discuss Merrill Lynch's third-quarter performance, which had resulted in a loss of $5.1 billion.

During the call, Thain was asked about how Merrill would use its $10 billion. As was the case with his public pronouncements regarding the need to raise more capital, or the sale of BlackRock shares a few months earlier, Thain responded without thinking through the political ramifications of what he was saying, telling the analysts that the money was "just going to be a cushion." The statement sparked angry complaints to Hank Paulson by lawmakers who took Thain's comment to mean that the bailout funds—which Paulson had sold as being absolutely necessary to save the system—were nothing more than a mere cushion to help Wall Street banks keep operating the same old way. Paulson called Thain and chided him for the politically insensitive remark.

HAVING ACCEPTED LEWIS'S OFFER to become president of global banking, securities, and wealth management, Thain quickly assembled his own management team to run the three businesses under his supervision. He put Greg Fleming in charge of investment banking, and named Tom Montag to run sales and trading. As for the wealth management business, the core of which was Merrill's thundering herd of financial advisors, Thain still wanted Peter Kraus to get the job, not Bob McCann, whom he considered to be more of a salesman.

In the first month following the agreement to sell to Bank of America, Thain kept looking for ways to reverse Alphin's early declaration that Kraus would not be a member of the team going forward.

During Alphin's subsequent visits, Thain insinuated Kraus into situations involving BofA's chief administrative officer, or arranged for some pretext that would result in Kraus dropping by his office "unexpectedly" while Alphin was there. Following one such encounter, in which Kraus was particularly solicitous, the former Goldman Sachs banker invited

Alphin to stop by his own office down the hall after his session with Thain was over.

"You should come down and see my art," said Kraus, as he left the office.

Steele Alphin glared at Thain.

"You haven't told him yet, have you?"

Thain shook his head sheepishly, like a teenager admitting to his parents that he hadn't done his homework.

"You've got to talk to him," said Alphin. "We don't want him as part of the company."

Thain nodded and said he'd handle it.

"If you don't deal with this," Alphin continued, "it will have an impact on how you're viewed at the bank. It will *erode* your standing at the company."

Thain said he understood.

"My view is that there's two ways to do things," Alphin said. "There's the easy way, and then there's the hard way. Now, personally, speaking for myself, I prefer the easy way, but I'm willing to do things the hard way, if it's for my company. Do you understand?"

Thain understood.

ON FRIDAY, OCTOBER 17, Ken Lewis announced who would be on his management team following the acquisition of Merrill Lynch. Of the ten-person group, eight executives were already on the team, including Steele Alphin, Amy Brinkley, Greg Curl, Brian Moynihan, and Joe Price, the chief financial officer. John Thain would join the roster of direct reports, as would Anne Finucane, BofA's head of marketing and communications, who had worked closely with Brian Moynihan and Chad Gifford at Fleet Financial.

When Greg Fleming learned the news, he called up Alphin to complain.

"I haven't not been on a management team in fifteen years," said Fleming.

"Sorry, Greg, but down here, the management team consists of Ken's direct reports only."

"I think I should be on the management committee. I'm in charge of corporate, commercial, and investment banking. That's responsibility for $20 billion in revenues."

"I hear you," said Alphin. "But that's the way it is."

"I'm not happy with it. Should I talk to Ken directly?"

"No," said Alphin. "That's not a good idea."

"Okay," said Fleming in resignation. "I can live with it. I'll move on. But I just want to make you aware that that's something that's important to me."

"Duly noted," said Alphin, more amused than put off by the display of petulance.

ON SATURDAY, OCTOBER 18, Bob McCann was driving to his daughter's field hockey game in suburban New Jersey when the phone rang. He could tell from the caller ID number that it was John Thain on the line, so he pulled off the road into a parking lot to take the call.

Earlier in the month, Thain had spoken to McCann about staying on through 2009 in his position as head of the thundering herd, adding that he could count on a payout of anywhere from $9 million to $12 million in Bank of America stock if he committed to the organization for at least a year. McCann agreed to stay on, but reiterated his long-standing request for a larger role at the bank.

By way of making up, Thain tried to explain that what had happened at the "town hall" on September 15 was a misunderstanding—a joke—not an attempt to embarrass McCann in front of everyone. McCann figured this was about as close to an apology that he would get from the boss, and the discussion ended.

Now, sitting in a New Jersey parking lot on a Saturday morning, McCann knew that whatever Thain had to say to him could not be good.

Thain explained that Peter Kraus, the executive he wanted to put in charge of global wealth and investment management—i.e., McCann's boss—would be leaving Merrill Lynch and Bank of America.

"It's a shame that Peter won't be staying," Thain said.

McCann listened, saying nothing.

"Bob, are you there?"

"Yes, John, I'm here. You'll have to tell me why that's such a shame about Peter."

"It wouldn't have been that bad, Bob. Peter's really good at this stuff."

"You'll forgive me if I don't agree with you," said McCann.

Thain said an announcement would go out from Bank of America sometime the following week, with the names of his management team. The slot that had been designated for Peter Kraus would be left vacant until they found the right person for the job.

"Thanks for sharing that with me," said McCann.

ON OCTOBER 20, Tom Montag paid a visit to One Bryant Park to check out his future offices and speak to some of BofA's top sales and trading executives. Once the merger was complete, Montag was planning to keep most of his Merrill team in place and fire the majority of BofA's traders. Knowing that their jobs were at risk, the BofA people gave Montag the red-carpet treatment, extending every courtesy and trying to make him feel comfortable. But Montag, always blunt and to the point, dispensed with the courtesies and probed for information that could help him figure out what kind of a company he was going to be working for. Montag was familiar with the big leagues of capital markets trading and he had always thought of BofA Securities as a second-tier operation. The events of the previous months, including the firing and rehiring of respected research analysts, had only reinforced that notion.

Among others, he met with Bruce Thompson and Alastair Borthwick in capital markets, Gerhard Seebacher and Mike Meyer in fixed income, Paula Dominick in research, and Brian Brille in investment banking. Montag, who had already received $27 million in cash from his Goldman stock, and was guaranteed a payday of $40 million, asked almost everyone a similar series of questions: "Do you think these guys are serious about the investment banking business? What idiot made the decision to sell the prime brokerage business? Do you think they're going to sell Merrill Lynch's prime brokerage business? Do you get paid here? Do you get your people paid? Why are you still here? Why haven't you blown out of here?"

THROUGHOUT OCTOBER, SCORES OF "transition team" associates from Charlotte migrated to New York every week from Monday through Thursday, to work on the integration of the two operations.

Brian Moynihan, who had been in charge of BofA's own investment bank, was put in charge of the transition team, which held meetings twice a week with "leadership team" representatives of more than twenty different business units from Merrill and BofA. May Lee, who had essentially been supplanted as Thain's chief of staff by Andrea Smith, served as Moynihan's counterpart on the transition team, helping to chair the meetings, which took place in the "town hall" room on the third floor of Four World Financial Center.

Nelson Chai retained the title of CFO of Merrill Lynch, but by early October, Neil Cotty, a member of BofA's finance team, was on the premises as acting CFO. Merrill's top internal accounting people—Chris Hayward and Dave Moser—routed every important document, including their daily updates, to Cotty.

Meanwhile, BofA's HR people spread out through Merrill Lynch's headquarters to take the measure of the exotic creatures who would be joining their organization. At the executive level, BofA committed itself to various management trends popularized on business school campuses across the country. In recent years, the Charlotte bank had devoted its internal education programs to the "six-sigma" management program embraced by Jack Welch, the former CEO of General Electric who embarked on a new career as a management guru following his retirement.

BofA executives put a lot of stock in psychological profiles and Myers-Briggs personality tests, which, among other things, purport to determine whether an individual is an introvert or an extrovert. Using the language of Myers-Briggs, Alphin judged Thain early on to be an introvert. In October and November, Alphin's subordinates tried to determine what kinds of personalities would be joining the team.

Paul Wetzel had been left without any specific duties. The Merrill Lynch strategy function would be eradicated by BofA's strategic planning department and Wetzel's boss, Peter Kraus, had no future with the Charlotte bank.

May Lee promised Wetzel he'd be part of the transition team representing Merrill Lynch, but when that program was formally launched, he was left off the roster. With nothing to do, Wetzel had conversations with Greg Fleming about the possibility of returning to investment banking, maybe on an international level. He also spoke with Joe Price about whether there might be room for him in treasury, but the options he heard about didn't sound attractive.

One day Wetzel received a visit in his office from a woman in BofA's HR department. She asked him a series of questions that had little to do with banking, but instead focused on his personality and how he felt about certain hypothetical situations, about his moods and whether or not he considered himself happy.

On another occasion, Wetzel and several of his colleagues were shepherded into a small conference room where two women from BofA's marketing team were waiting. The women said they wanted to get a better sense of how BofA and Merrill Lynch were perceived in the marketplace.

"When you think about Bank of America," one of the marketing women asked Wetzel, "what kind of car do you think about?"

"Uh, I don't know," said Wetzel, puzzled. "I'm not really much of a car guy."

"When you think about Merrill Lynch, what kind of a car do you think about?"

"You should ask my wife. She knows a lot more about cars than I do."

DURING THE SEPTEMBER WEEKEND that the merger agreement between Merrill Lynch and Bank of America was struck, the deal carried risks on both sides. Thain had to weigh the risks of staying independent versus the possibility that he was selling a historic franchise for far too little. Lewis had been willing to pay a premium for Merrill Lynch in the hope that the acquisition would turn into a long-term bargain.

After the events of late September and early October, when investors fled Wall Street in droves, and Treasury Secretary Paulson decided to invest $125 billion directly into nine of the nation's top banks, the transaction began to look like a lopsided deal in favor of Merrill Lynch. It was clear that the company would not have survived on its own, and every week during October its losses mounted.

Merrill Lynch treasurer Eric Heaton became so alarmed at his firm's deteriorating finances that he was convinced Bank of America would try to renegotiate the deal. Starting in October, he put together weekly reports for Greg Fleming to use when he received the inevitable call from BofA's Greg Curl seeking to renegotiate the terms of the transaction. Each of the reports was devised to help Fleming frame the best possible argument as to why the Merrill deal, as it was structured, still made sense for BofA. But throughout October, even as Merrill Lynch recorded more losses in one month than it had ever sustained in its history—losses that were shared with BofA executives on a daily basis—the inevitable call from Curl never came. Instead, there was radio silence from BofA's top executives in Charlotte on the matter of Merrill's financial health, as if they didn't know or didn't care what the investment bank's financial condition was.

DURING THE WEEK OF October 20, Thain embarked on a multination tour of the Middle East. Fares Noujaim, the ex–Bear Stearns banker who had been hired in June to run the region, arranged most of Thain's appointments, which, at the CEO's request, were with government officials as well as investors and clients.

The trip occasioned wonderment at Merrill Lynch since almost no one, including Margaret Tutwiler, Thain's head of communications, knew why the boss was doing it. Thain's sudden disappearance not only puzzled subordinates at Merrill but engendered suspicion among his peers in Charlotte.

Some of the men and women who reported directly to Ken Lewis had extended Thain a warm welcome after his decision to stay on board and encouraged him to visit Charlotte so they could get to know him better. Politely but consistently, Thain rebuffed those invitations, responding that he'd be happy to meet with whoever was extending the invite on their next visit to New York.

It was Fleming who traveled to Charlotte regularly, introducing himself to his new team and befriending some of Lewis's direct reports. His trips were so frequent that they drew needling remarks from Thain about how much time Fleming was spending ingratiating himself at Bank of America headquarters.

Now Thain was in the Middle East, conferring with government officials and some of Merrill's largest investors, including the Kuwait Investment Authority.

On the last night of the trip abroad, Thain and Noujaim stopped in Beirut, Noujaim's overseas base of operations, for a long dinner and a bottle of wine before embarking on the flight back to New York. Once they were airborne, Noujaim departed from the subject of the previous few days' conversations—the economic state of nations in the Middle East and their common concern about the U.S. capital markets—to ask Thain if he was worried about what was going to happen at Merrill Lynch once Charlotte took over.

"We're going to be fine," Thain said confidently. "I'm going to be the next CEO of Bank of America."

"Really?" asked Noujaim, who had worked on enough deals to know that chief executives who acquire other companies usually don't turn the reins of power over to the executives from the companies they acquire.

"I know what you're trying to say," replied Thain. "But this is different. Ken Lewis told me the job was all but mine."

THAIN RETURNED FROM THE Middle East just a few days before the October 27 board meeting. Earlier in the month, after learning of Finnegan's discomfort with the original proposal for executive bonuses, he promised the compensation committee chief that they'd talk again in the days leading up to the full board meeting about a more realistic target for special payments to himself, Fleming, and the other members of his team.

But the Middle East junket had taken him away from that plan, so at the board meeting, the topic was not discussed. Instead, given Finnegan's inclination to adjust the size of the total bonus payments downward from the upper limit of $5.8 billion, management recommended a bonus pool of $4.7 billion for the year, with a caveat that the number could be further adjusted depending on how the fourth quarter progressed.

Thain also told directors that he had designated Peter Kraus, who would be leaving Merrill Lynch at the end of the year, to be in charge of the bonus-setting process at the bank.

After the board meeting, Finnegan paid a visit to Thain's office, so the two men could resume their discussion of executive bonuses.

Thain conceded that in the post-TARP environment, where the government had provided emergency funds to prop up ailing banks, the world had moved away from the first set of bonus numbers presented by Rosemary Berkery. Instead of $40 million for him, a cash bonus in the range of $20 million would probably be more realistic.

Finnegan balked again, saying the compensation committee had held a preliminary discussion on the matter and didn't feel comfortable with a big payout, given what had happened on Wall Street in the last two months. There was also a question about how to structure any kind of bonus payment, given that Merrill lost money throughout the year and had to be sold.

Thain suggested that the compensation committee think about any year-end payments as "success fees" triggered by the sale of Merrill Lynch to Bank of America.

CHAPTER 17

MOUNTING LOSSES

ON NOVEMBER 3, BANK of America and Merrill Lynch filed a joint proxy statement with the Securities and Exchange Commission, a 243-page tome that described the proposed acquisition of Merrill Lynch by BofA. Investors in both banks were advised to read the merger proposal closely, so they could make an informed decision when it was time to vote on the deal five weeks later, December 5.

The proxy statement was crammed with financial results and ratios from both banks, and contained a copy of the original agreement reached between Merrill Lynch and BofA on Sunday, September 14. In discussing the acquisition, BofA told its shareholders that Merrill Lynch would not be allowed to pay outsized compensation packages to its executives without the express approval of Charlotte. But left out of the 243-page disclosure was the agreement specifying that Merrill Lynch could pay out as much as $5.8 billion in bonuses to its employees for 2008.

On Tuesday, November 4, Illinois senator Barack Obama defeated Arizona senator John McCain in the presidential election. Obama's victory meant the White House would return to Democratic Party control for the first time in eight years. McCain's defeat also foreclosed any chance that existed for John Thain to succeed Hank Paulson as U.S. treasury secretary.

Thain had emerged a year earlier as McCain's primary fundraiser and leading supporter on Wall Street. The Arizona senator's short-lived lead in the polls, in early September, evaporated with the collapse of Lehman Brothers and the subsequent government bailout of AIG. The creation of the $700 billion TARP fund, by a Republican administration, fueled populist anger at the banking industry to the point where McCain and his running mate, Alaska governor Sarah Palin, blamed "greed on Wall Street" as the driving force behind the financial crisis and the nation's economic woes. Even if McCain had won the election, his anti–Wall Street rhetoric in the final weeks of the campaign suggested that John Thain, an ex–Goldman Sachs banker who presided over the sale of Merrill Lynch, would probably not emerge as a popular candidate for treasury secretary.

NEIL COTTY, THE BOFA EXECUTIVE who had been dispatched from Charlotte to serve as acting CFO of Merrill Lynch in the last quarter of 2008, spent the entire month of October monitoring the bank's performance.

Merrill's internal accounting people sent him a preliminary report indicating a pretax loss of $6.1 billion for the month, a staggering sum. In a November 5 e-mail to his boss in Charlotte, CFO Joe Price, Cotty passed along the revised figures with a terse note: "Read and weep."

By November 9, when the final marks for October came in, the total loss had climbed to $7.5 billion, a one-month record, almost as much as Merrill Lynch had lost in the entire fourth quarter of 2007, its worst quarter ever.

ON NOVEMBER 11, MERRILL LYNCH hosted its annual banking and financial services conference in New York City. The conference provides a forum for the heads of Wall Street banks and large consumer banks to talk to analysts and institutional investors. Given what had happened in the capital markets throughout 2008, this conference generated more intense interest than any similar gathering in recent years.

The key speakers included Lloyd Blankfein, CEO of Goldman Sachs, and top executives from other Wall Street firms. At a conference sponsored by his own company, John Thain, fresh off his agreement to sell Merrill Lynch to Bank of America, would get the privilege of delivering the opening address.

For most of the year, at least until the weekend of September 13–14, Thain had been more optimistic about the state of the economy than many of his Wall Street peers. At the January Davos meetings, he said he did not believe the economic problems in the U.S. would necessarily translate into a global recession. Throughout the first quarter of 2008, after raising almost $13 billion in fresh capital, he had assured investors that Merrill Lynch had enough capital for its future needs. In the spring, he had blown off a preliminary inquiry from Lone Star about the sale of Merrill's toxic CDOs, at a time when the price being suggested would have forced Merrill Lynch to book a loss of several billion dollars, triggering the need for yet more capital to be raised.

Even after the frantic month of July, when Merrill Lynch had been forced to sell its stake in Bloomberg to fill one capital hole, manufacture an agreement to sell FDS to plug another hole, and pull the trigger on the Lone Star CDO sale, generating another loss that had to be filled with an equity raise of common stock, Thain had remained generally optimistic, as evidenced by his interest in acquiring Fortress Investments in August.

Then came the weekend of Lehman's bankruptcy and Thain's difficult but necessary decision to sell Merrill Lynch, followed a month later by Hank Paulson's insistence that every big bank accept a huge slug of taxpayer funds. Now, at long last, Thain embraced the severity of the moment, declaring at the conference that the current markets were the worst since the Great Depression.

"Right now, the U.S. economy is contracting very rapidly. We are looking at a period of global slowdown," Thain said. "This is not like 1987 or 1998 or 2001. The contraction going on is bigger than that.

We will in fact look back to the 1929 period to see the kind of slowdown we are seeing now."

Later that day, Thain presided over a conference call with the management development and compensation committee of Merrill Lynch's board, which consisted of Finnegan, the chairman, Armando Codina, Virgis Colbert, and Aulana Peters.

The special meeting had been scheduled to discuss two government requests, or warnings, about plans to pay out year-end bonuses following the decision by Treasury to prop up Wall Street banks with taxpayer funds. In the House of Representatives, congressman Henry Waxman of California had asked representatives of all the banks that received TARP funds to provide details about what kind of bonus payments they had made in the past two years, and whether the access to TARP funds would affect bonuses for 2008. On the state level, New York attorney general Andrew Cuomo had also written to Wall Street's biggest banks, requesting similar details about plans to pay out bonuses.

Once the meeting was scheduled, Thain decided to add an item or two to the agenda, concerning the payment of bonuses at Merrill Lynch.

Peter Stingi, the head of HR at Merrill, formally presented a schedule by which the committee would approve bonus payments for top employees on December 8, a full month ahead of the usual timetable. The downside of the plan was that bonuses—which are intended to reward performance across an entire year—would be allocated according to eleven months of work, leaving open the prospect that once people had been guaranteed a bonus, they would have less incentive to apply themselves in December. The alternative would be to wait until January before deciding on bonus levels. That approach had its own drawback: The Merrill Lynch board would no longer exist in January, and final decisions on incentive compensation would be made by Bank of America's board, which would be less inclined to go along with the eye-popping bonus payments that were normally handed out on Wall Street each February.

After some debate, the compensation committee took the position that it was their responsibility to allocate the bonuses, not the responsibility of BofA's board, so they adopted the accelerated schedule and agreed to meet again on December 8 to give their final approval to bonus payments. Finnegan, who had recommended that the bonus pool come in lower than the $5.8 billion that had been stipulated in the merger agreement, once again suggested that the pool be reduced, in light of the difficult markets and the government's decision to plow $125 billion into the nation's top banks.

Thain updated Alphin on Merrill's plan to pay out bonuses early, but mentioned nothing of the compensation committee meeting.

THE NEXT DAY, NOVEMBER 12, Treasury Secretary Paulson delivered a speech in Washington outlining a change in plan for the $700 billion TARP fund that had been approved by Congress in early October. Instead of using the funds to buy the weakest assets housed at domestic banks, Treasury would stay out of the business of buying toxic financial waste. The TARP funds would be available for banks that needed a capital investment, but the government would not relieve the banks of responsibility for bad purchases over the previous few years.

Paulson's announcement raised concerns about investment banks such as Merrill Lynch, Morgan Stanley, and Goldman Sachs, which would have benefited the most from an organized program to purchase troubled assets. It was now apparent that all three institutions were on a pace to set records for poor performances in the quarter.

Some large investors in Bank of America, who had expressed concerns about the risks in acquiring Merrill, now became even more concerned about the possibility that the deal could turn into a black hole for the Charlotte bank.

The news didn't get any better at Merrill Lynch. Nelson Chai, who still held the title of CFO of Merrill Lynch, sat down with Joe Price, who had flown up from Charlotte, and Neil Cotty, who had been monitoring Merrill's performance practically since the day the merger agreement was signed, to present a forecast of Merrill's fourth-quarter performance.

The losses from October totaled $7.5 billion, and Merrill had already lost more than $1 billion on top of that. On an after-tax basis, that meant a loss of $5.4 billion for the quarter, even if everything stayed flat for the next seven weeks. But Cotty knew that some other problematic positions weren't even part of Chai's forecast, suggesting that the loss for Merrill's final three months would probably be even bigger.

PRICE WAS FOCUSED ON the magnitude of Merrill's losses. Along with Greg Curl, who negotiated the Merrill deal, he met with Tim Mayopoulos, BofA's general counsel, and Teresa Brenner, another BofA lawyer, to talk about whether Merrill's losses through October, as well as its projected losses for the quarter, would have to be disclosed to investors prior to the December 5 shareholder vote on the acquisition.

"Five billion dollars is a lot of money," Mayopoulos said, adding that disclosure might be necessary. He promised Price that he would do some further research into the matter.

After that meeting, Mayopoulos and Curl called Ed Herlihy, the mergers-and-acquisition lawyer at Wachtell, Lipton who had helped midwife the Merrill Lynch deal, and asked that Wachtell lawyers find out whether Merrill's losses through October warranted any kind of special disclosure to shareholders.

BACK IN CHARLOTTE, ANDREA SMITH learned from Steele Alphin that Merrill Lynch had negotiated the ability to pay out as much as $5.8 billion in bonuses as part of its agreement, despite the mounting losses. What's more, Alphin told her that Thain was planning to pay those bonuses out in December, before the year had actually ended.

Smith had been working closely with Thain, so she was surprised that she hadn't been alerted to the plan and was concerned about whether Merrill Lynch could compress a three-month process into six weeks. She called Fleming to find out more.

"How are you all going to pay at the end of December when you haven't even started the process?" she asked.

"Did you not know that we had a meeting with the board's comp committee?" Fleming said, surprised that Smith had not been kept informed.

"I did not know."

"Have you seen the minutes?"

"I haven't seen anything."

Smith relayed this information to her boss. Alphin was surprised that Thain had discussed the early payment of bonuses with him just one day earlier without ever mentioning that a board committee had already approved the plan.

Alphin called Thain to discuss the matter further. Bank of America never paid out year-end bonuses before the year had actually ended. Thain explained that a clause negotiated in the September 15 merger agreement specifically allowed Merrill Lynch to pay out its own bonuses for 2008. That clause was not part of the 243-page proxy statement sent to investors, but it was nevertheless part of the deal, and it allowed Merrill to pay as much as $5.8 billion—the equivalent of its 2007 bonus pool—to its employees. Since the Merrill Lynch board would be dissolved after the acquisition was completed, on or about December 31, it made sense to move the process forward by a few weeks, he explained.

Alphin said he was not pleased with the decision but acknowledged that it was within the power of Merrill Lynch's board to pay the bonus money as it saw fit. He insisted that Andrea Smith be allowed some input into the decision-making process and Thain agreed.

ON THURSDAY, NOVEMBER 13, Mayopoulos and Brenner followed up with the lawyers at Wachtell, Lipton.

In a long conference call with Herlihy and two other Wachtell lawyers—Eric Roth and Nick Demmo—the group discussed the looming losses at Merrill Lynch. One of the Wachtell lawyers recalled what had happened a decade earlier in the merger between NationsBank and San Francisco–based Bank of America. The deal was agreed to in April 1998, with a scheduled closing date in late September. But by the time September arrived, the collapse of the Russian ruble and the meltdown at Long Term Capital Management had changed the economic scene drastically. Bank of America's investment in the D.E. Shaw hedge fund was losing massive amounts of money in the weeks leading up to the transaction's close, creating hundreds of millions of dollars in losses for

BofA and its CEO, David Coulter. Those losses hadn't been disclosed to shareholders, and the lack of disclosure led to litigation after the merger was completed, not to mention the ouster of Coulter from the new management team in Charlotte, and his replacement as Hugh McColl's heir apparent by Ken Lewis.

Eventually, the group agreed that some kind of disclosure to investors would make sense in the current situation.

"Given Merrill Lynch's numbers, both companies could make a disclosure about a week before the vote," said Mayopoulos. "Our results are not fabulous, either."

"What about writing a trend disclosure?" asked Herlihy, suggesting that the banks focus less on the actual losses that had piled up and more on the general market trends through the quarter.

"How much detail should go in there?" asked Mayopoulos.

"Not much," said Herlihy, recommending that the trend disclosure be modeled on a standard "management discussion and analysis" statement found in every quarterly report.

"If Merrill Lynch breaks even in November, that's a $7 billion loss for two months in the quarter," said Mayopoulos.

"Maybe we should just refer to the past trend of losses and say that has not abated," said Nick Demmo, Herlihy's deputy. "We expect it to be no better than this, or it might be worse than the $7 billion."

The conversation about what the shareholders should be told kept on in this vein until Mayopoulos asked for some clarity.

"But do we all agree that there must be some disclosure?"

"If we do," said Herlihy, "let's just make sure it's balanced."

"Right. This is not the end of the world," said Mayopoulos.

Then the lawyers discussed how BofA should approach Merrill about the disclosure. That might be a tough sell, since the disclosure of greater losses could spook antsy BofA shareholders to vote against the deal. Mayopoulos said he would ask Joe Price to talk to Thain or Fleming about it. The lawyers decided not to let Merrill's law firm, Shearman & Sterling, handle the disclosure, at least in the initial stages.

As to when the disclosure should be made, the lawyers talked about

December 1, the Monday before the Friday shareholder vote, but decided that was too close. One of the Wachtell lawyers came up with a better idea: Friday, November 28, a full week before the shareholder vote and, best of all, the day after Thanksgiving, when it would receive the minimum attention. Everyone agreed. The date was perfect. The lawyers said the disclosure, if there was to be one, should be written by November 25 or 26, before the holiday. The meeting ended with Mayopoulos saying he'd have Joe Price reach out to Merrill Lynch early the following week.

PRICE MET WITH THAIN and Chai in Thain's office the next day to discuss Merrill's latest projections and ask whether they were planning to make any special disclosures to their shareholders about the magnitude of the losses. Thain said he had no plans to, that Merrill didn't offer mid-quarter guidance or updates as a matter of practice and that he saw no reason to depart from that practice.

DESPITE THE PROGRESS THAT Merrill Lynch had been making on the accelerated payment of bonuses to its people, the issue of Thain's own bonus continued to be a sticking point with Finnegan on the compensation committee. Rather than engage on a particular number, Finnegan—who seemed afraid to confront Thain directly—kept saying that it would be difficult to pay out large cash bonuses in the current environment, where populist anger at Wall Street had reached epidemic levels.

Peter Kraus, whom Thain had designated as Merrill's lead man on the bonus pool, joined his friend's cause in lobbying for a sizeable payout for the CEO. The two men held a joint conference call with Finnegan to urge the Chubb CEO to award a cash bonus of at least $10 million to Thain.

In previous discussions, Thain had reminded Finnegan that at Goldman Sachs, the company always rewarded executives for delivering. Now, with Kraus at his side, the Goldman argument gained force. Kraus said that he and Thain had been talking to Lloyd Blankfein, Goldman's CEO, and Blankfein insisted he was not going to buckle to the public pressure against getting paid.

"But Goldman Sachs is different from Merrill Lynch," said Finnegan. "They have earnings."

ON SUNDAY, NOVEMBER 16, Goldman Sachs announced that its top seven executives, including CEO Lloyd Blankfein and chief financial officer David Viniar, would not accept any bonus for 2008.

From that point on, when Thain spoke with Finnegan he no longer argued that he and his team should get a bonus because that's the way they did things at Goldman Sachs. Instead, he told Finnegan, "You have to do it because it's the right thing."

By this time, Thain had come to an understanding with Alphin that his bonus would be less than whatever Ken Lewis got paid for 2008. In his discussions with Merrill's board, Thain scaled back his request from $40 million to $20 million and eventually to $10 million. Because Merrill had no earnings, and he didn't qualify for a straight-out bonus, Thain described the payouts as "success fees," to be given because he and his team had succeeded in finding a buyer, and therefore protecting shareholder interests. Finnegan suggested that the terrible economic conditions in the capital markets, and Merrill's ballooning losses, made it difficult to justify any kind of bonus payments for the top executives. Thain objected strenuously, insisting over and over again that the board had to pay bonuses to him and his direct reports. "You *have* to do it," Thain repeated in his conversations with Finnegan.

Eventually Finnegan called Charlotte for guidance. He knew that Alphin, BofA's chief administrative officer, was not happy with the decision to pay bonuses to Merrill Lynch employees on an accelerated basis, but Alphin conceded that it was up to Merrill Lynch, as an independent company, to make the ultimate decision. Tim Mayopoulos, the general counsel in Charlotte, had also made that point clear to Alphin.

Finnegan had another incentive to stay in touch with Alphin. He, along with Virgis Colbert and Charles Rossotti, were the three Merrill Lynch directors who had been invited to join BofA's board following the acquisition. Finnegan wanted to make sure that whatever decisions he made as chairman of the compensation committee on bonus payments to Thain and his top executives would be in sync with the thinking of BofA's board in Charlotte.

Alphin told him that the worsening economic climate, and BofA's struggles in the fourth quarter, meant that whatever bonus Lewis received for the year would be minimal.

ON THURSDAY, NOVEMBER 20, just two weeks before Bank of America shareholders were scheduled to vote on the Merrill Lynch acquisition, Tim Mayopoulos convened a conference call with the Wachtell, Lipton lawyers and Joe Price to discuss whether it would be necessary to disclose Merrill's October losses prior to the vote.

Ken Lewis remained supportive of the deal, but if a legal determination had been reached to disclose Merrill's October losses to shareholders, it could cause shareholders to vote against it, depriving Lewis of the prize that would define his legacy. The lawyers at Wachtell didn't think any additional disclosures were necessary, since every Wall Street bank had been losing money in the tumult of the current financial crisis. It wasn't as though Merrill Lynch was stumbling at a time when other banks were earning record profits. Further, Mayopoulos learned that Merrill's October losses, and its fourth-quarter projections, fell within the range of the bank's previous quarterly losses, so the group agreed, as of November 20, that there was no need to impose additional information on shareholders.

Meanwhile, doubts had begun to spread through the capital markets about Citigroup's ability to continue functioning, given that its balance sheet was weighed down by hundreds of billions of dollars' worth of questionable real estate–backed assets. The bank's share price—which had sunk from the mid-teens in October to the $10 range in early November—sank after Paulson's announcement that the government would not purchase risky assets from banks. Starting on Monday, November 17, Citi shares plunged in Lehman-like fashion, from a high of $9.81 at the beginning of the week to a low of $3.05 by Friday. It was clear that there was a run on Citi stock, and it was equally clear that Citi—unlike Lehman—could not be allowed to fail without causing catastrophic damage to the global economy.

Over the weekend of November 22 and 23, the team of Paulson and Bernanke, in consultation with Tim Geithner, who was about to be named the next treasury secretary in the incoming Obama administration, fashioned a new bailout for Citi, investing another $20 billion into the bank, and providing a guarantee of support for $270 billion in questionable assets.

The Citigroup bailout, announced Monday, November 24, buoyed the bank's share price, driving it back up above $7 by the Thanksgiving holiday. It also planted an idea among some of the BofA people in Charlotte, who were suffering from a case of buyer's remorse about the losses at Merrill Lynch. Merrill's woes were clearly impacting BofA's share price, which had dropped from $34 at the time the deal was announced in September to a low of $10 on the Friday before the pre-Thanksgiving Citigroup rescue.

That morning, in Charlotte, Lee McEntire of BofA's investor relations team sent a memo to Joe Price and treasurer Jeff Brown asking what effect a "Citi like plan," involving an extra infusion of government capital, would have on Bank of America's balance sheet.

DAYS BEFORE THANKSGIVING, John Thain's communications chief, Margaret Tutwiler, spoke with her boss about an interview request from the *Financial Times*—the salmon-colored business newspaper. According to the written request for an interview, two *FT* journalists were planning to write an article about how John Thain had proven to be the one Wall Street executive in 2008 who was smart enough to zig while everyone else was zagging. Thain had been the first one to sell his entire portfolio of toxic CDOs, and on that momentous weekend in September, he had proven to be astute enough to sell Merrill Lynch at a good price rather than watch it disintegrate into bankruptcy the way Lehman Brothers had. Thain and Tutwiler agreed that the article would be positive for him, so an interview was scheduled for Monday, December 1, four days before the shareholder vote.

. . .

FLEMING'S FREQUENT TRIPS TO Bank of America headquarters were part of his personal mission to become a prominent member of the BofA team. During his long acquisition spree, Hugh McColl used to tell employees and executives of the banks he had acquired that there's a seat on the NationsBank train for you, but the train is leaving the station and if you want to be part of this bank, you'd better get on board.

Fleming wanted a seat on that train. He worked assiduously to ingratiate himself with Lewis's crowd, and bonded with Curl, with whom he'd negotiated the Merrill Lynch sale, Liam McGee, the head of retail banking, and David Darnell of commericial banking, who would become one of Fleming's direct reports.

Fleming also developed a good rapport with Lewis himself, and had several lengthy one-on-one conversations with the CEO in his office on the fifty-eighth floor. Although he never directly claimed credit for the sale of Merrill Lynch to BofA, Fleming made it clear to the people he dealt with in Charlotte that he'd been a longtime proponent of the strategic pairing of Bank of America with Merrill Lynch.

Curl enjoyed Fleming's company, and the men usually spent time together after Fleming's business with the commercial banking team had concluded. Curl talked about his background in naval intelligence, and regaled Fleming with tales about some of his secret missions in Vietnam. Late one afternoon, Curl invited Fleming to join him and a few of his colleagues downstairs at Sonoma, the unofficial watering hole of the bank's top executives. Lewis was there, and the chemistry between Fleming and his new "teammates" began to click.

Early on, Fleming figured out that Alphin was a guy he needed to work with in order to maximize his influence in Charlotte. In their first conversations, Fleming talked passionately about the potential of the combined companies. The chief administrative officer—whose job it was to separate the wheat from the chaff among executives at banks acquired by BofA—was initially put off by Fleming's ardor, but eventually came to see the young Merrill Lynch executive as a man with a future in the organization.

Alphin picked up on something else: a veiled hostility between

Thain and Fleming. When he was visiting Merrill headquarters in New York, it was not uncommon for Thain to ask Alphin to relay a message to Fleming and vice versa. Not only did the two men avoid direct contact with each other, they telegraphed their mutual discomfort to outsiders.

Prior to the weekend of September 13 and 14, it was clear to Fleming that he had no future at Merrill Lynch under John Thain. But the merger agreement had changed the equation. Peter Kraus, the most immediate threat to Fleming, was out of the picture. And Fleming now saw an opportunity to use his superior people skills to build his own power base in Charlotte, out from under Thain's shadow.

CHAPTER 18

WELCOME TO THE ASYLUM

THE THANKSGIVING HOLIDAY WAS less festive than usual for most Merrill Lynch employees. Rank and file staffers, particularly those who worked outside the capital markets business, faced the inevitable takeover by BofA with considerable dread. In general, people who produced revenues for Merrill Lynch—including the financial advisors, the investment bankers, and the traders—would be safe. In a month, they'd be under new management, but most would still have their jobs and their Merrill Lynch stock would be worth something.

People in staff jobs, such as the lawyers in the general counsel's office, the marketing and communications staffers, and everyone in HR, feared for their jobs and salaries, but also dreaded the prospect of being kept on, since working for BofA—described by its own CEO as the "Walmart of banking"—would mean absorption into a parallel universe where the ability to perform a job well was less important than the ability to conform to a top-down system of command.

Twice a week, clusters of staffers from various support functions gathered in the third-floor conference room—the place where Merrill Lynch town hall meetings were held. The clusters sat along the sides of a giant U-shaped table. At the head of the table, heading up the transition teams, were Brian Moynihan—who had lost his position as head of BofA's investment banking operations as a result of the Merrill deal—and May Lee, John Thain's chief of staff.

Within the clusters were the Merrill Lynch employees, many of whom were still traumatized at what had happened to their company. Just two years earlier, they were working for one of the biggest and best-performing banks on Wall Street, and now here they were, scrambling on the floor of their own building, hoping to land a job with a Charlotte bank.

The sense of dread felt by the Merrill Lynch employees was only magnified by what they saw in the eyes of their counterparts at Bank of America: abject fear. The BofA people seemed to consider it a great privilege to be part of the transition process—an honor bestowed on them by their masters in Charlotte. All the same, the "honor" of being part of the team did not confer any confidence that they would emerge from the process with their jobs. Behind the façade they put on about the privilege of working on the transition, the BofA people had enough experience to know that every Merrill Lynch employee in the room—every Merrill Lynch employee in their department—was a mortal threat to their livelihood.

Merrill Lynch employees understood that since they worked for the failing bank that had to be acquired, it was now their lot to grovel for positions in the new organization. What did not make sense, or inspire much confidence in the future, was that BofA's own employees had also assumed the same groveling posture, exuding a sense of desperation that they might not make the cut.

IN THE EXECUTIVE SUITE at Bank of America headquarters in Charlotte, the Thanksgiving holiday had been anything but restful. Merrill Lynch's losses continued to swell through November, and Ken Lewis was concerned that going through with the purchase of Merrill Lynch, the crown jewel he had been pursuing for years, could end up causing irreparable damage to his own bank and his legacy. The strategic rationale behind the combination of Merrill Lynch and Bank of America still made sense, but not at the price that had been negotiated in September.

On December 1, Joe Price held a meeting in his office on the fifty-eighth floor with Greg Curl—who had negotiated the Merrill Lynch deal—and Tim Mayopoulos, the general counsel. Price asked Mayopoulos's opinion about a section in the merger agreement having to do with a "material adverse change," or, as the lawyers referred to it, the "MAC clause." A standard component of any contract to buy or sell a company, the MAC clause provides an escape hatch in case one of the companies involved in a takeover sustains a catastrophic impairment.

Anyone who enters into a contract to buy a house knows that if that house burns down between the time of the agreement and the closing date, there's no obligation to complete the purchase of the house. Likewise, any company that enters into an agreement to buy another company wants an assurance that if the target company breaks down irreparably between the time of the original agreement and the closing date, the acquiring company can back out of the deal.

Lawyers for Merrill Lynch had spent what seemed to be a disproportionate amount of time on Sunday, September 14, defining a "material adverse change" as narrowly as possible. They inserted language saying that even if Merrill's losses were disproportionately worse than other banks' losses in the quarter, it would not be grounds for terminating the agreement. The specificity insisted on by the Merrill lawyers was now holding up under the pressure of the cratering capital markets.

Price asked Mayopoulos if the losses at Merrill Lynch in October and November constituted a "material adverse change" in the merger agreement. Mayopoulos, who had already reviewed Merrill Lynch's losses for the previous five quarters and determined that there was no need to disclose the October losses as anything out of the ordinary, didn't think that Bank of America had just cause to invoke the MAC clause. Merrill's stock price had dropped 60 percent over the previous three months, but BofA's own share price had dropped by a comparable amount, down 57 percent. As for Merrill's losses, they were bad, but still within the range of what the company had done over the past year. And even BofA, which had been earning money every quarter throughout the credit crisis, was now on track to post a loss for the quarter, its first quarterly loss in seventeen years. No, Mayopoulos concluded, the current situation did not constitute a MAC, and Bank of America would be risking a long, expensive, and losing court battle if it tried to invoke the clause.

Price thanked him and the meeting was over. Later, Price visited Lewis in the CEO's office to update him on all the latest developments with regard to the merger.

WITH THE SCHEDULED CLOSING date less than a month away, Bank of America's human resources department was consumed with making decisions about which people would get which jobs in the combined organization. Merrill Lynch executives assumed they would be able to make most of the final personnel decisions about those working in the capital markets. For all other areas, though, the vast majority of positions would go to BofA employees.

Meanwhile, Lewis and Alphin saw the upcoming acquisition of Merrill Lynch as an opportunity to realign their organization. In order to show that they were serious about cutting expenses at all levels, they planned to ask Bruce Hammonds, head of the credit card division in Delaware, to step down on January 1. They also decided to realign the sixteen-member board of directors. As was their custom following a major acquisition, BofA would add several directors from the acquired company. Back in October, Lewis had planned to use the Merrill acquisition as an opportunity to prune the current board. Meredith Spangler, whose family had been with the bank dating back to the NCNB days, had reached the retirement age of seventy-one and would not stand for reelection. Ken Lewis and Temple Sloan, the lead director, decided it was appropriate for Chad Gifford, who had voiced concerns about the Merrill Lynch deal, to step down as well. It would not do to allow Gifford's questioning of Lewis's judgment—expressed openly, in front of other board members—to pass without consequence. Going back to the McColl era, directors at the Charlotte bank had learned to trust the wisdom of the chief executive and refrain from asking any questions that forced the CEO to justify his actions.

ON DECEMBER 3, TWO days before the shareholder vote, a conference call was arranged between Lewis and Thain to discuss Merrill Lynch's fourth-quarter performance. Also dialing in were BofA's top finance people—Joe Price and Neil Cotty—as well as Nelson Chai, who still held the title, though not the duties, of Merrill Lynch's CFO position.

Even though November was over, Merrill's internal accounting people were still trying to put a price on its hard-to-value assets, a process made more difficult by the lack of trading across all markets in October and November. But at a minimum, Merrill Lynch was on track to record a $7 billion loss for the fourth quarter, even if nothing went worse in December. The actual operating loss for the quarter was close to $11 billion, but corporate losses generate tax benefits and in Merrill's case, the tax benefit would reduce the losses by approximately $4 billion.

Cotty, who by now was developing a feel for the way things were going at Merrill, wanted a meaningful forecast for what the quarter's totals would be. He suggested that everyone assume an additional $3 billion in losses for the remainder of the month, which would bring the total operational losses for the fourth quarter to $14 billion, or $8.9 billion after the tax benefit generated by the losses. Thain thought the projection was a bit severe, but ultimately agreed to work with Cotty's numbers.

One source of Merrill's worsening losses was a series of positions known as "basis trades" in its fixed-income book. In these trades, some of which had been entered into by Osman Semerci's team in 2006 and early 2007, Merrill Lynch bought long-term bonds and matched these bonds with credit default swaps that guaranteed their value. The tiny difference between what Merrill paid to hedge its position and the income that the underlying assets generated added incrementally to the firm's revenues but clogged its balance sheet. In most circumstances, the trades reliably generated a risk-free return, but under certain severe economic conditions—like what the market was going through in the fourth quarter of 2008—the correlations became uncorrelated and Merrill's positions began bleeding losses. Other Wall Street firms were also suffering from the blowup in "correlation trades" or "basis trades." The losses were yet another by-product of Semerci's strategy of expanding Merrill's balance sheet to maximize near-term revenues in the FICC department.

In a separate meeting with Joe Price, BofA treasurer Jeff Brown expressed his concern over the magnitude of Merrill's losses and urged him to make a special disclosure to shareholders prior to the December 5 vote. Using language that sounded like it had been scripted by lawyers, Price assured Brown that no disclosure was necessary. But Brown persisted, saying Merrill's losses had gone beyond what the marketplace could have been expecting. Price repeated the legal verbiage he used earlier. Finally, Brown could take it no more and insisted that the magnitude of Merrill's losses was something that, by law, shareholders needed to know about.

"Listen, Joe," said Brown, "I don't want to be having this conversation with you next time through a glass wall over a telephone."

THAIN'S CASH BONUS FOR 2008 was getting smaller by the day. A few weeks earlier, the Merrill Lynch CEO agreed that his bonus for the year would be smaller than Ken Lewis's by about $2–3 million. Now, about a week before Merrill's board would meet to approve bonuses for all employees and sign off on the biggest bonuses for the top executives, Alphin was telling Thain that Lewis wouldn't even be getting $10 million.

"We're more at $8 million right now," said Alphin, referring to projections for Lewis.

"So that means $5 million or $6 million for me," said Thain.

"It's probably going to be five."

"Hmmmm. Can't you get me to six?"

Alphin laughed.

"Well, if that changes, let me know," said Thain.

"If it does change, I don't anticipate it getting bigger."

After the exchange with Alphin, Thain called Finnegan, the head of Merrill's compensation committee, to relay the latest news from

Charlotte. Thain said he was willing to accept a bonus of as little as $5 million, which would keep him subordinate to Lewis in the bonus pool.

Once again, Finnegan questioned whether any payment to Thain or his other top executives could even be termed a "bonus," given Merrill's woeful performance for the quarter and the year. By now, Thain had become completely frustrated with Finnegan's intransigence on the subject. He told Finnegan he didn't care what the board wanted to call the payments—success fees, transition payments, whatever—he had a team of people to take care of, including Nelson Chai, who'd given up his New York Stock Exchange bonus the year before to join Merrill, and the board had to take care of those people.

"You have to do this," he told Finnegan forcefully.

ON THURSDAY, DECEMBER 4, Thain received a call from Win Smith, son of Winthrop H. Smith, one of the founders and first CEOs of the modern-day Merrill Lynch. Smith planned to attend the shareholder meeting the next day and wanted to make a statement, not only in favor of the deal, but about what had happened at Merrill Lynch over the previous decade. According to standard procedure at such meetings, shareholders are allowed a maximum of three minutes to speak, and they speak from their seats or from a microphone in the seating section. Smith said his statement would last a little more than ten minutes. It contained some pointed criticism of Merrill's board of directors. Smith asked if he might be allowed to speak from the front of the conference room. Thain said he would be happy to oblige.

Through an intermediary, Thain let Finnegan know that if the compensation committee didn't come through on the executive bonuses, it would mean war, and Thain had the media on his side.

KEN LEWIS SPENT THE evening of December 4 in the ballroom of the Plaza Hotel in Manhattan at a black-tie dinner hosted by *American Banker,* the trade publication, where he was being honored as Banker of the Year.

In his acceptance speech, Lewis thanked his "teammates" at Bank of America, but warned the audience that the financial services industry, which had metastasized from 8 percent of the S&P 500 in terms of market capitalization to 22 percent, had gotten ahead of itself. Bankers needed to be reminded that they were in the business of helping other companies grow, Lewis said, and not in the business of enriching themselves, which had become common practice on Wall Street.

ON FRIDAY, DECEMBER 5, a small group of Merrill Lynch shareholders gathered in the third-floor conference room to vote on the proposed sale of the company, founded by Charlie Merrill in 1914, to Bank of America. John Thain had assured board members that their presence was not required, and that the vote would merely be a formality. Indeed, most shareholders had cast their ballots by mail or electronically, so there was no drama as to the outcome.

Rather, there was an almost funereal sense that the end of an era had arrived. After the formal announcements regarding the purpose of the meeting were made, the floor was opened to shareholders to speak their piece. Win Smith waited his turn, and then walked to the front of the room, where he would be visible to the cameras sending the proceedings to every internal TV monitor at Merrill's offices around the globe. There were reporters from wire services in the room to capture the event. John Thain stood just a few feet away from the guest speaker, visible to all.

Smith first read a letter from Merrill Lynch Magowan, grandson of Charlie Merrill. Magowan described the experience of voting for the sale of Merrill Lynch as comparable to "attending a funeral" and criticized the reign of Stan O'Neal, during which the company took on massive amounts of leverage without adequate risk controls.

Then Smith began his own speech. "Like Merrill Magowan I have been privileged to know every CEO of Merrill Lynch from Charlie Merrill to John Thain," he said. "Most of them, including John, were principled leaders who never placed their interests ahead of those of the firm. Most of them valued and promoted the principles that Charlie Merrill created and most of them cared deeply for the welfare of their fellow colleagues."

Smith spoke for several minutes about what Merrill Lynch had always stood for, about how Charlie Merrill had built the firm around the policy of putting the interests of the customer first, and how the organization had always treated its own people with respect, leading to its nickname, Mother Merrill. His years at Merrill Lynch, said Smith, echoing those of a former colleague, "were like catching lightning in a bottle."

After voicing support for the Bank of America deal, Smith said that at a time when the company was about to move forward, some things needed to be said. The time had come to set the record straight with regard to the board of directors and its decision to install Stan O'Neal as CEO a few years earlier. (Like Magowan, he refused to dignify O'Neal by even uttering his name, referring to him instead as a "former CEO.")

"Today did not have to come," Smith said. "Today is not the result of the subprime mess or synthetic CDOs. They are the symptoms. This is the story of failed leadership and the failure of a board of directors to understand what was happening to this great company, and its failure to take action soon enough. I stand here today to say *shame* to both the current as well as the former directors who allowed this former CEO to wreak havoc on this great company. Shame on them for allowing this former CEO to consciously and openly disparage Mother Merrill, throw our founding principles down a flight of stairs and tear out the soul of the firm."

Smith enumerated the depredations done to the Merrill Lynch culture under the O'Neal regime, before turning once again to the board of directors.

"Shame, shame, *shame* for allowing one man to consciously unwind a culture and rip out the soul of this great firm. Shame on them for allowing this former CEO to retire with a $160 million retirement package, and shame on them for not resigning themselves."

For just about everyone in the room, Smith's stemwinding tirade against O'Neal and the company's board provided a cathartic release to all the frustration, sadness, and financial loss spawned by the epic mismanagement of the recent past, which doomed a once mighty franchise.

COMPARED TO THE MERRILL Lynch vote, the shareholder meeting in Charlotte went smoothly, with almost no debate and no dissent and no criticism of directors for abandoning their fiduciary duties to shareholders. When the votes were counted, Bank of America investors approved the acquisition of Merrill Lynch, with 82 percent of the votes coming in favor of the deal.

AFTER THE SHAREHOLDER MEETING, Thain went uptown to join Fleming at the last gathering of Merrill Lynch's international advisory committee, a group of CEOs that met once a year to share their views on what was going on in the global economy.

When Fleming noticed Thain's arrival, he thought the CEO seemed as exuberant and upbeat as he had been in his entire year at Merrill Lynch.

OVER THE WEEKEND OF December 6 and 7, Thain's public relations team at Merrill Lynch fielded several phone calls from Susanne Craig of *The Wall Street Journal*. Craig had somehow learned that Thain was planning on asking for a bonus—possibly as high as $10 million—at Monday's board meeting. Did Thain or Merrill Lynch have any comment?

Margaret Tutwiler, Thain's communications director, immediately recognized that any story about her boss's request for a bonus would be a public relations disaster. She counseled Thain to take Sue Craig's call and inform her that he was planning to ask for a bonus of zero at the Monday meeting. Thain refused.

He was outraged that someone—Finnegan, he presumed—had leaked the story to the press. He believed firmly that he was right, that he deserved something, even if it was only a couple of million dollars, for preserving the value of Merrill Lynch shares. If he forfeited his bonus because of a leak to the media, he'd be stooping to the level of whoever it was that planted the story and he steadfastly refused to do that, despite Tutwiler's advice.

ON MONDAY, DECEMBER 8, the compensation committee of Merrill Lynch's board of directors met to consider what kind of bonuses should be paid out to Thain and his top four executives. *The Wall Street Journal* had published its story that morning about Thain's plan to ask for a bonus. As Tutwiler predicted, the story went off like a bomb at Merrill Lynch, and even though the compensation committee would consider Thain's request, it was apparent from this embarrassing disclosure that Thain had no chance now of getting a cent in bonus money for 2008.

When Thain arrived to make his argument before the committee, he was visibly agitated by the newspaper story. He lashed out at the directors and demanded to know who leaked the story to *The Wall Street Journal*. His harangue went on for several minutes before he asked Finnegan, point-blank, if he had spoken to Sue Craig.

"She called me at home," said Finnegan. "I picked up the phone."

Thain knew that any further argument on his own behalf would be fruitless. Exasperated, he left the room.

FLEMING, WHO HAD BEEN advising Thain against asking for cash bonuses for the top executives, felt humiliated by the story because it portrayed Merrill Lynch management as being obsessed with its own pay at a time when the entire U.S. economy was heading into recession and enraged citizens were calling for jail time for Wall Street CEOs.

As Kraus consulted with Thain in his office, Fleming came by and asked if he had told the board that he, Fleming, would be fine with stock options. Fleming had made this argument to Thain and Kraus several times in recent weeks, asking for a year-end reward that was aligned with shareholder interests. In spite of his overt dislike of Fleming, Kraus embraced the younger man's suggestion of stock options, especially after Goldman Sachs announced that its top executives would do without bonuses for the year. But Thain still wasn't persuaded.

Fleming went upstairs and sent word in to Finnegan and another member of the compensation committee, Virgis Colbert. One at a time, he told them that he had no interest in a cash bonus for the year and that if stock options were available, that would be fine for him. The two men thanked Fleming before returning to their deliberations.

THAT MORNING, IN RESPONSE to the bonus story, New York attorney general Andrew Cuomo sent an open letter to the Merrill Lynch board describing Thain's attempt to secure a bonus as "nothing less than shocking." Through the first three quarters of 2008, Cuomo noted, Merrill Lynch had lost $11 billion and was saved only by Bank of America's agreement to buy the franchise. "Clearly, the performance of Merrill's top executives throughout Merrill's abysmal year in no way justifies significant bonuses for its top executives, including the CEO," he wrote.

OWING TO HIS RELUCTANCE to pay any cash bonuses, Finnegan had brokered an agreement with Kraus in November that Thain's arguments on behalf of bonuses for his top reports should be made to the whole board, rather than to the compensation committee.

Usually, a CEO will make an argument in front of the compensation committee justifying bonuses for himself and his top team, and then the committee takes the case before the entire board for approval. But Finnegan had decided well ahead of the final showdown that Thain would be a better advocate for the bonuses. Thain considered it cowardly on the part of Finnegan to wash his hands of the matter, but Finnegan, who couldn't bring himself to approve bonuses for a leadership team that presided over more than $11 billion in losses, wouldn't budge. Finnegan also knew that forcing Thain to make his case directly to the full board put the CEO in a weakened position. It would be clear to every director that the compensation committee did not approve of Thain's bonus arguments.

To make matters worse, Thain would be throwing himself at the mercy of the board just three days after Win Smith had vented his pent-up fury against the current and former directors who oversaw Merrill's demise. Thain had not only allowed Smith a public forum for his broadside, but stood directly beside him in a show of support as the founder's son berated the board and accused it of abdicating its responsibility to shareholders. The image of Thain standing behind Smith had been beamed to every office of Merrill Lynch around the world, and some of the directors watched it, too. None of the board members attended the meeting, especially after Thain had told them it would be a non-event. And so even if they wanted to, the directors had no chance to defend themselves.

When Thain returned to the boardroom at midday to make his pitch for all his top executives, he carried a copy of the Cuomo letter, as well as another letter from former Merrill Lynch CEO Dan Tully, which had been sent to the board that morning.

"As a partner of this great firm and shareholder of fifty years, I unhesitantly recommend that a bonus of at least $10 million be paid to John Thain," Tully wrote. "He inherited this mess and did a 'far exceed' job of cleaning it up and saved the franchise by initiating the sale to Bank of America. I hesitate to interfere in your decision but feel this is fair and well deserved."

Despite Tully's support it was now clear that Thain would have to forgo his own bonus. Nevertheless, he gamely argued in favor of bonuses for his team.

Thain urged the board to consider a multimillion-dollar bonus for Bob McCann, head of Merrill's thundering herd, because McCann's business functioned well throughout the financial crisis and had been a reliable source of revenues for the firm. Thain also asked the directors to take care of Nelson Chai, his CFO, who had given up a secure position at the NYSE to follow him to Merrill Lynch, without any guarantees. As for Rosemary Berkery, the general counsel, Thain said it would be unfair to deprive her of a bonus. Morgan Stanley had announced earlier that day that its top three executives—John Mack, James Gorman, and Walid Chammah—would not accept a bonus for the year. Thain argued that Morgan Stanley's general counsel was getting a bonus, and that Berkery should, too. Finally, Thain argued in favor of Fleming, his president, who had been fully involved in every major initiative that year, from the capital raises to the sale of Bloomberg and, ultimately, in negotiating the Bank of America deal. Like McCann, Fleming had received no bonus in 2007 and it wasn't fair for him to have to miss out on a bonus for the second straight year, the CEO argued.

His argument over, the board prepared to go into executive session without Thain to discuss the matter further. But Thain wouldn't budge. He refused to let the directors bring their lawyers and compensation consultants into the room, and he was adamant about not leaving.

Instead, he wanted to hear from the directors themselves what they felt about bonuses, not receive a message that had been filtered through paid advocates.

Finnegan implored Thain to step outside, so that the board could deliberate on its own, but the CEO stubbornly resisted. Finally, Finnegan himself got up and left the boardroom to meet with the board's attorney, who was waiting outside. The attorney explained to Finnegan that if the board wanted to go into executive session, it was within its power to order Thain out of the boardroom. Finnegan went back inside to relay that message, but Thain refused to leave. Nearly an hour later, Finnegan emerged once again to consult with the board's lawyer.

"I told him everything you told me to say, and he still won't leave," Finnegan said to the attorney. He then returned to the boardroom, accompanied this time by the attorney.

Finally, at Thain's insistence, the board agreed to discuss the CEO's request for bonuses for his top team. As head of the compensation committee, Finnegan would go last, so it was up to someone else to be the first to speak. Charles Rossotti, former commissioner of the IRS who had joined the Carlyle Group, a buyout fund, spoke first. He made a well-reasoned, cogently argued case against bonuses for anyone, building his arguments one layer upon another. Finnegan was pleasantly surprised that someone not on the compensation committee had grasped the issues so clearly and articulated them so well. Even Thain, seething about what had happened in the media, had no argument he could use to rebut Rossotti's reasoning.

It was clear that Merrill's board of directors was not going to pay a bonus to anyone. One of the board members put the matter directly to Thain, telling him it would probably be best if the four members of his top management team followed his example and asked for nothing, because if Thain persisted in his quest to secure bonuses for them, and the board voted against it, that story wouldn't look very good in the newspapers either.

Thain stormed out of the boardroom and down the hallway to the stairs in the chairmen's gallery. A moment later, Kraus, who'd been waiting in a conference room nearby, emerged, asking, "Did John leave?" as he bustled down the hallway in pursuit of his boss.

Thain returned to his office and had his assistant arrange a meeting of his four most senior colleagues. Thain, Rosemary Berkery, Nelson Chai, and Peter Kraus went to a conference room, and Greg Fleming and Bob McCann were patched in on the speakerphone.

"Hello, everybody," said Thain, telling Fleming and McCann that he was sitting with Berkery and Chai. "And Peter Kraus is here, just for laughs.

"I have a wonderful opportunity for you," he continued, his tone distorted by a combination of exasperation and sarcasm. "We met with the board all day, and our wonderful board is giving us the opportunity to not accept a bonus for this year."

Fleming jumped in. "John, did you tell the board that I had specifically asked for stock options instead of a bonus?"

No response.

McCann spoke in favor of Berkery, asking why she had to be punished for losses generated on the business side, which had nothing to do with the general counsel's office. But he had recognized that morning how damaging the *Wall Street Journal* story had been to Thain, and how damaging it would be for everyone.

"John, you're not really asking us if we want to give up the bonus. You're telling us that the board doesn't want us to get a bonus. And if we don't agree, we will be told we are not going to get a bonus, and that could end up in the press."

"I didn't want to put it that way, but yes," Thain admitted.

"Okay, so I guess I volunteer, John. And by the way, can I go back to work now?"

The others followed suit. When Thain returned to the boardroom that afternoon, he lodged his one official compensation request, the one that would be recorded in the minutes of the board meeting for posterity: that neither he nor his top four direct reports receive a bonus for 2008. The board unanimously agreed with his suggestion.

Aulana Peters, a member of the compensation committee, expressed her relief at not having to vote against Thain's wishes. "Thank God!" she said.

If McCann realized the damage that the *Wall Street Journal* story had done to Thain, Fleming felt that the CEO had unnecessarily dragged the entire group into the mud alongside him. He had been in frequent touch with Finnegan over the previous two months, especially since Finnegan would be one of the Merrill directors joining the BofA board. He knew that the compensation committee was going to be hypercautious about any cash bonus payments or "success fees" that Thain requested. Fleming had urged Thain to ask for stock options instead of cash, but time and again the CEO ignored him. Instead, Thain had pushed Finnegan over and over for a cash bonus, to the point of shouting at him.

One level down in the organization, people who had worked closely for Thain over the previous year recognized the behavior pattern. An engineer by training, Thain focused on problems in isolation, and when he reached a conclusion on an issue, he dug in and stood his ground. Thain had concluded that he and his management team deserved a cash reward for saving Merrill Lynch and protecting the company's shareholders from bankruptcy, and he fought obstinately for it, to the point of avoiding a compromise solution—a request for stock options in the new company.

Thain never saw his campaign for a cash bonus in the larger context of a public backlash that had swelled up against Wall Street. His former colleagues at Goldman Sachs recognized the public relations ramifications associated with huge multimillion-dollar bonuses on Wall Street, but he didn't. Finnegan had been dragged before Congress in March of that year and forced to defend the indefensible compensation paid out to Stan O'Neal. There was no way Finnegan was going to let himself be dragged down there again. Thain didn't see the bigger picture, only the individual pixels.

THE NEXT DAY, THAIN flew down to Charlotte to attend Bank of America's post–shareholder vote board meeting. Lewis and Alphin had been outraged at the article in *The Wall Street Journal*, but to Thain's relief, that outrage was directed at Merrill's board for what the Charlotte executives perceived as a violation of trust. Thain told them Finnegan had leaked the story to the *Journal*. Lewis growled about Finnegan's behavior and said there was no way he would tolerate such a character on his board.

THE BOFA BOARDROOM, on the sixtieth floor of the Bank of America Corporate Center—known in Charlotte as the "Taj McColl"—is the highest room in the tallest structure not just in the Carolinas but between Philadelphia and Atlanta as well, a monument to McColl's overweening ambition. To access the boardroom, directors have to enter through a hall in which hang the portraits of the bank's previous three CEOs: Addison Reese, Tom Storrs, and McColl.

When Thain entered the majestic boardroom on December 9, at the peak of the "tiara" that served as the crown of the BofA headquarters, he marveled at the high ceiling, the huge board table—suitable for a U.S. president planning a war—and the military precision, the formality of the proceedings. Everything about the room, including the beige carpet underfoot, which was patterned with the bank's flagscape logo, added to the sense of power and authority invested in the chamber.

Ken Lewis sat midway along one side of a large, football-shaped table almost thirty feet long. Only board members were allowed a seat at that table. Subordinates, including all of Lewis's direct reports, sat to the rear of the room, with their backs against the wall, to respond when spoken to, not to initiate any discussion. The distance between the business unit heads and the board was far greater than the few feet separating the straight-back chairs from the sprawling table.

Thain took his place in the room, among the executives who populated BofA's management team. For the first time in more than a decade, he literally did not have a seat at the table. He sat near Amy Brinkley—the former head of marketing whom Lewis had put in charge of risk management at the nation's largest bank—and Tim Mayopoulos, the general counsel, who didn't even report to the CEO. There was Joe Price, the youthful CFO, who seemed to be in a constant state of fear in Lewis's presence. Even Steele Alphin, Lewis's closest confidant at the bank, adopted a different demeanor in the boardroom, saying "yes, sir," when Lewis spoke to him, like a sergeant responding to a general.

At Goldman Sachs, Thain had worked with the most brilliant minds on Wall Street, and proven himself to be among the best of that group. At the New York Stock Exchange, he took a team of well-meaning but middle-of-the-road talents and propelled them to a better place. At Merrill Lynch, where Stan O'Neal had decimated an entire generation of seasoned executives, Thain had found smart people in unexpected places. But BofA was different. The management here didn't seem to be interested in high IQs. Just the opposite. Greg Curl, Lewis's dealmaker, was the only player on this roster who could make it on Wall Street, Thain thought. And there was Alphin. He was smart in a different way. He didn't know much about the capital markets, but he had a certain animal cunning that made him very effective at what he did.

As the board meeting proceeded, Lewis called for a financial update on what was going on with Bank of America and Merrill Lynch. Joe Price stood, went to the podium and walked the board through BofA's fourth-quarter numbers, which showed the bank headed toward its first quarterly loss in seventeen years. Then Price started to describe Merrill Lynch's financial performance so far in the quarter, using numbers that had been packaged by Neil Cotty, along with his $3 billion estimate for future losses over the rest of December. Thain wondered why they hadn't asked him to participate. Only later in the meeting was Thain called upon directly, and asked to describe the current condition of the capital markets. He stood up.

"Things are terrible right now," he said.

And that was it. There was no follow-up question, no request for more information, or for insight into where things were going. Thain sat down silently, acclimating himself to BofA's "don't speak until you're spoken to" culture. Perhaps he should have volunteered more color to the board, explaining that many of the paper losses now being sustained were likely to be reversed with the inevitable pickup of capital-markets activity in January. But there would be time enough to show this board his talents at future meetings. Steele Alphin had assured Temple Sloan, the lead director, that he, John Thain, had strong leadership skills.

The formal board meeting was followed by an executive session unlike any Lewis had ever held during his tenure as CEO. Lewis, who seemed tightly wound, listened as several of the board members questioned him about the magnitude of the losses that were appearing on BofA's books, as well as on Merrill Lynch's books. None of the directors were panicking, but the pushback Lewis was getting from his mostly handpicked board was as straightforward and challenging as he'd ever heard in his seven years as CEO. Some of the board members were taking their responsibilities toward shareholders seriously.

Toward the end of the session, Lewis surprised everyone with the announcement that Brian Moynihan, who had been in charge of BofA's own investment bank until the deal to acquire Merrill Lynch, was leaving the organization. With the forced retirement of Bruce Hammonds on January 1, Moynihan had been offered Hammonds's job as head of the bank's credit card operations, based in Wilmington, Delaware. But Moynihan, who was raising a family outside of Boston, didn't want to uproot his wife and kids for something that was at best a lateral move.

In the four years since Bank of America had acquired Fleet, Moynihan had been Lewis's loyal and unflinching supporter. He had taken over broken businesses and fixed them at Lewis's request, followed orders from headquarters without question, and slashed costs mercilessly when Alphin told him it was necessary. He even tore up his contract in his first year, a contract that guaranteed him a big payout following the change in control from Fleet to BofA, to demonstrate his loyalty to the cause. And now he'd come to the end of the line. At BofA, when a Marine is ordered to jump on a grenade, he jumps first and asks questions later. But after watching the arrival of Thain eclipse him in the organization, Moynihan decided that a one-way ticket to Wilmington, Delaware, was too much to ask, even of him.

After Moynihan turned down the credit card assignment, Lewis reached the inevitable conclusion: "Then I guess you're going to leave the bank," he said. Moynihan didn't want to leave, and begged Lewis to find some other role for him, but the CEO was clear. There were no second chances. Either you accepted every assignment or you were out.

Throughout the day of the board meeting in Charlotte, Moynihan urged Lewis to reconsider and allow him to commute from Boston for the job, but Lewis was adamant.

And thus the Bank of America career of Brian Moynihan had come to an end, effective at the end of the week. Thain's arrival at Bank of America had resulted not only in the loss of a high-profile job on Wall Street for Moynihan—who had never really been accepted as part of the "in" crowd by Lewis and Alphin—but in an offer so unpalatable that Moynihan would have to leave the bank rather than accept it.

In the executive session that followed the full board meeting, Chad Gifford and Thomas May—two of the directors who had come on board following the acquisition of Fleet in 2004—complained bitterly about Moynihan's departure, displaying a hostility that Lewis had rarely seen among his directors. They had known Moynihan for some time, and he was the last senior executive from Fleet still at BofA. Other top executives from that deal had long since left, once they figured out that they would never crack the "Charlotte Mafia." With the Moynihan announcement, the session ended, and the out-of-town directors made their way to the airport for the flight home.

AFTERWARD, TIM MAYOPOULOS, WHO was surprised by the magnitude of the Merrill Lynch losses described by Joe Price at the board meeting, went to Price's office seeking an explanation. He had been counseling Price that no special disclosures were necessary as long as Merrill's losses stayed within a particular range, but the newly revised figures suggested that Merrill had busted through the outer limit of what Mayopoulos had been using as his guideline. On the fifty-eighth floor, Price's administrative assistant informed him that the CFO would be busy for the rest of the afternoon.

Mayopoulos returned to his office on the fifty-seventh floor. There was a lot to do. Among other things, Mayopoulos reviewed a draft press release that had been prepared announcing Moynihan's departure from the company. The headline read, "Bank of America Planning to Reduce Work Force," followed by a sub-headline that said, "Brian Moynihan Leaving the Company." Mayopoulos scanned the announcement for any statements that might cause legal problems. He looked closely at the boilerplate quotes contained on the second page of the release:

"I have enjoyed my time at Bank of America, but it is time to pursue new challenges," Moynihan said.

"Brian has been an outstanding executive who has taken on and done well with every challenge we have thrown at him," said Ken Lewis, chairman and chief executive officer. "We know he will do well at whatever he chooses to do."

THE BOARD MEETING OVER, Lewis held a 2:00 p.m. meeting of his management committee on the fifty-eighth floor to review compensation and bonuses for BofA's executives and employees. But the question about the credit card business remained unresolved. Bruce Hammonds, the head of the credit card business, hadn't planned on retiring. It was just that he had been told by Lewis and Alphin that, given the mounting losses, it was important for at least one top-level executive to leave the bank, as a sign that BofA was paring back. To ease the pain, Lewis gave him a generous retirement package. Now, with Moynihan's refusal to take the credit card job, they asked Hammonds to stay on. But Hammonds, once he had gotten his head around the idea of retiring, decided that he liked the idea, so he said no, he wasn't coming back.

During the compensation discussions, Barbara Desoer, who had been put in charge of BofA's mortgage business, including the Countrywide operations, asked Amy Brinkley about David Onorato, one of the top lawyers who worked for Mayopoulos, the general counsel. Mayopoulos and his legal team reported to Brinkley, the chief risk officer, and Onorato, a highly regarded lawyer, had recently quit.

"He tried to hold us hostage," Brinkley said, referring to an ultimatum that Onorato had given her about his compensation, saying that if BofA didn't pay him what he was worth in the marketplace, he'd leave.

Several attendees nodded. It was widely known at the management committee level that the legal team, starting with Mayopoulos, was always whining about pay. The issue of pay for BofA's lawyers had become so contentious that Alphin had shut Mayopoulos down earlier in the year, practically yelling at him that he didn't want to keep hearing the incessant complaints from the legal team about money.

As the management meeting drew to a close, Alphin suddenly perked up and snapped his fingers.

"I have an idea," he said, getting up and asking Lewis if he had time for a private meeting.

AT 3:29 P.M., LEWIS sent an e-mail to his board members, marked confidential. "We have come up with a solution for Brian Moynihan. He will become General Counsel and report to me directly. He can stay in Boston for some time and eventually will move to Charlotte. With this move, we have upgraded the General Counsel position and keep a very talented individual. Please keep this confidential since we have not talked to all of the affected individuals. Ken."

Late that afternoon, after the corporate jet they were riding in landed in Boston, Gifford and May sent effusive notes of gratitude to Lewis.

"Ken—that's great news for our company . . . good for you and good for Brian and it's good for our shareholders. best Chad."

"I think that's a great move. With what's ahead you need a strong bench. Hope Santa brings you a quick economic recovery. All the best, Tom."

THERE WAS ANOTHER PIECE of unfinished business to be handled. Lewis called John Finnegan and informed him that he would not be invited to sit on Bank of America's board. The call lasted about forty-five seconds. Compared to Chad Gifford's open questioning of Lewis's judgment the previous September, Finnegan's actions were inexcusable. In Lewis's view, directors were supposed to support the CEO, not undercut him.

Thain dialed Fleming in New York.

"I have some news for you!" he said in a gleeful tone. "Your friend John Finnegan's not going to be on the board."

"What happened?"

"I told Ken that he leaked the bonus story."

"Do you know that for a fact?" asked Fleming, with an edge in his voice.

"He's off the board!"

PETE KELLY ARRIVED IN Charlotte from New York early the next morning. He reported to his new boss, Tim Mayopoulos, to learn more about what was expected of him.

The meeting took place in a conference room on the fifty-seventh floor of the Bank of America building, just down the hall from Mayopoulos's office. Kelly was going to become general counsel to the investment banking unit of Bank of America–Merrill Lynch. Bill Caccamise, a BofA veteran who had been tapped for that job, would become chief counsel of the Merrill Lynch private client business. Kelly was among the few Merrill Lynch lawyers who had been offered a position in the new organization, but it was only because Thain and Fleming had fought hard on his behalf that his appointment had been approved by Alphin and HR. The Kelly decision embarrassed Mayopoulos, since he had to move Caccamise out of a position that had already been promised to him.

In recent weeks, Kelly had sensed some reluctance on the part of Mayopoulos to have him on his team. Now, alone with his new boss, Kelly watched that reluctance burst forth in a spasm of contempt.

"I picked you for this position," Mayopoulos said with an edge in his voice. "You're going to do the job the way I tell you to, and don't forget it."

"We'll see about that," replied Kelly, who knew he had been forced on Mayopoulos by Thain and Fleming.

"No. We won't see about that. That's the way it's going to be. I know more about investment banking than you do. I'm better at this than you are!"

"If saying it makes it so," snapped Kelly. "Otherwise, it's up to the client to decide."

"You need to manage your ambition. I'm going to be micromanaging everything you do, so don't get cute with me. You're going to do exactly what I tell you to. You're going to hire the people I tell you to hire, and you're not going to send a letter to any client, at any time, until I've approved it."

"It's not going to work that way," said Kelly, whose Irish was now up.

"Yes, it is," Mayopoulos hissed. "That's the way we do things here. I don't care who your friends are."

Kelly could tell that Mayopoulos, even as a lawyer, wasn't accustomed to pushback from subordinates. The general counsel was becoming enraged by Kelly's responses. But Kelly had decided, before flying down that morning, that if he couldn't operate the way he wanted to in his new job, then he didn't want the position. He would dare Mayopoulos to fire him rather than conform to whatever management system they tried to cram down his throat.

After about an hour, Mayopoulos took Kelly to a different conference room, where they were joined by Caccamise and David Grimes, the chief operating officer of BofA's legal department.

Now it was three against one, but the tone of the meeting turned more professional. Mayopoulos recommended which lawyers would be the best fit to work in Kelly's unit, and Caccamise seconded those choices, having known the candidates from BofA Securities.

Kelly, who didn't want to be forced into making rash personnel decisions about his unit, stood his ground.

"I don't think I need you three guys in a room telling me how to run this unit," he said. "I'll figure it out on my own."

"You just don't get it, do you?" said Mayopoulos. "I decide how this is supposed to work, not you!"

"I'm responsible for this area," Kelly insisted. "I'll make the calls."

They had come to an impasse, and Kelly felt Mayopoulos may have reached the breaking point with him.

The door opened, and Mayopoulos's secretary entered the room. "Tim, Amy Brinkley needs you for a moment in your office. It's important," she said discreetly.

Mayopoulos was adamant as he left the conference room. "We're going to finish this," he snapped at Kelly. "Don't you go *anywhere*."

He strode down the hall toward his office and entered. When he saw Brinkley, his boss, he greeted her.

"Tim, Ken is replacing you as general counsel," she said coldly. "He just decided this. Brian Moynihan is going to become the new general counsel."

Mayopoulos was stunned and couldn't even get a word out.

"You are terminated from Bank of America as of this moment, and you are to leave the premises immediately. You can't take anything with you. There's someone from HR outside the office who has your severance papers."

And with that, Brinkley left, and in walked a man from Steele Alphin's department holding a sheaf of papers. He took Mayopoulos's corporate ID card, company credit card, BlackBerry, and office keys, and put them down on the desk. Then, having done everything but read him his Miranda rights, he escorted Mayopoulos to the elevator and down to the executive garage in the basement of the building, and got into Mayopoulos's car so that he could physically escort him off the premises.

Kelly and Caccamise were still waiting in the conference room about thirty minutes later when Mayopoulos's secretary returned. "Mr. Mayopoulos won't be back today," she informed them, and then closed the door.

Grimes left.

Kelly looked at Caccamise. "I don't know what my next move here is," he said. But Caccamise said nothing. After about fifteen minutes, the same woman returned. "Could you please follow me?" she said, leading the two lawyers up to a smaller conference room on the fifty-eighth floor, the executive suite.

On the way up the stairs, Kelly figured out how it would go down: They'd bring him to the executive floor, shoot him, and give the job to Caccamise.

The two men arrived at a small conference room to find Brian

Moynihan sitting there, immersed in paperwork. Kelly had met Moynihan several times through the transition process.

"Tim's no longer with the company. I'm the general counsel now,"
said Moynihan, as Kelly just stared. "I'm really busy right now, so I don't
have much time to talk."

"Well, uh, you're the third general counsel I've been reporting to
today," said Kelly. "I was just told what my job was by Mayopoulos, but
I'm not sure he even wanted me working for him."

"Don't worry about it," said Moynihan, who appeared to be distracted with a number of issues. "I've heard good things about you. Forget what Tim said. I'm busy, so we'll talk another time, but I'm glad
you're on the team."

Kelly and Caccamise left the office. Kelly went straight to the airport, where he called Fleming.

"Greg, this place is a lunatic asylum. We *have* to get out of here. I
met with Mayopoulos this morning and in the middle of the meeting,
they *took him out*. It's insane!"

CHAPTER 19

AN OFFER THEY COULDN'T REFUSE

BY LATE AFTERNOON, Pete Kelly had returned to Merrill Lynch's offices. Kraus, Fleming, and others were having a meeting with John Thain on the thirty-second floor when Kelly walked in.

"I thought you were in Charlotte," said Thain.

Kelly then recounted the entire episode with Mayopoulos, blow by blow, culminating in his being summoned to the fifty-eighth floor for a brief audience with Moynihan.

"You've got to be exaggerating," said Thain.

"No. It's the God's honest truth."

Thain laughed and shook his head. Just another episode of *The Beverly Hillbillies*.

ONCE THE MERRILL LYNCH board of directors gave its approval to the employee bonus pool on December 8, the department heads went into high gear to determine who would get how much. Andrea Smith also worked nonstop to reduce many of the discrepancies that arose between the size of bonus payments at Merrill Lynch and the bonuses for BofA employees with similar jobs.

At the top end, Smith's hands were tied. Thain had guaranteed payouts of $40 million for Montag and $30 million for Kraus. Several of Merrill's top international investment bankers—Andrea Orcel and Fares Noujaim—were also on track for eight-figure payouts. Smith could whittle down their numbers somewhat, but Bank of America had no comparable bankers to whom she could make a line-by-line comparison.

As she looked deeper into the organization, Smith found opportunities to ratchet the Merrill Lynch bonus payments downward. Where she saw a Merrill Lynch employee on track for a $3 million bonus, while a comparable BofA employee was getting $1 million, she cut the Merrill bonus number down to $2 million.

In Charlotte, Ken Lewis was worried about Merrill's losses. He knew that the federal government had just promised an extra $20 billion to Citigroup to shore up its capital base and agreed to insure Citi against damage from more than $270 billion of its weakest assets. In his mind, BofA was a much healthier bank, and was performing an important service for the U.S. economy and the capital markets by acquiring Merrill Lynch. There had to be some way to get the federal government to give BofA a little support, along the lines of Citigroup, even if it was just protection against some of Merrill's worst assets.

ON FRIDAY, DECEMBER 12, Joe Price received yet another update from Neil Cotty in New York. At Cotty's request, the Merrill financial group had made some quick estimates of what its losses would be for the month, and new sum, a guesstimate of $18 billion pretax, was forwarded to Charlotte. Price shared the information with Curl.

There was also disturbing information about Bank of America's own earnings. In just two weeks, its projected losses for the quarter had quadrupled, to $1.4 billion. The figure was small compared with Merrill Lynch's numbers, but the losses reflected badly on BofA's own management and would cut into the bank's precious capital reserves at a time of maximum external pressure.

. . .

BY MID-DECEMBER, BUSINESS began winding down for the year at Merrill Lynch headquarters. Tom Montag, who had assembled his capital markets trading teams for January, headed to his home in Hawaii for the last three weeks of the month. All things considered, 2008 had been a good year for Montag, one of the top trading floor managers on Wall Street. He would be paid $40 million for joining Merrill Lynch on August 4, and his new employer had kicked in more than $80 million to reimburse him for the loss of his unvested Goldman Sachs stock. Of that $80 million, about a third—or $27.7 million—had been paid to him as a cash bonus on August 20. The remainder had been paid to him in the form of restricted stock priced at the level where Merrill shares were trading in early August, $26.39. Given what had happened to Merrill shares since, the restricted stock was worth less than half its original value, but unlike Lehman shares, Merrill stock was still worth something.

It was Peter Kraus's good fortune that he didn't fit into Bank of America's "culture." On December 22, he was named CEO of Alliance-Bernstein, an investment management firm with almost $500 billion under management, from institutional investors as well as wealthy private clients. In addition to the $30 million he had coming due since joining Merrill Lynch in September, Kraus received an additional $50 million to make him whole on the Goldman Sachs holdings that he forfeited. About a third of that that sum—or $16,872,995—was paid out as a cash bonus on September 10, days before Merrill Lynch agreed to sell to Bank of America, and the rest was awarded in restricted units of Merrill stock.

Thain finally found a position for Nelson Chai, his CFO. On December 18, he announced that Chai would become president of the Asia Pacific region for BofA's global banking business, reporting directly to him. Margaret Tutwiler would stay on as Thain's head of corporate communications, and Noel Donohoe, another one of Thain's early hires at Merrill, would remain in his risk-management position.

. . .

ON SUNDAY, DECEMBER 14, while spending a weekend in New York, Ken Lewis got on a call that had been scheduled with Price and Curl to discuss BofA's investment in the China Construction Bank. During this call, Lewis asked for the latest figures from Merrill Lynch. After hearing about the $18 billion projected pretax loss, he declared that the numbers justified an attempt to invoke the "material adverse change" clause, and urged his subordinates to get working on plans for a MAC.

Spooked by the prospect of recording the first quarterly loss in seventeen years, Alphin's HR department fired a group of "band one" managers—executives who worked one rung below the c-suite—without warning on December 15.

Like other purges of senior executives which had occurred over the years, this one was not a surgical incision designed to tweak the perfor-mance of a department, but a peremptory, across-the-board wipeout of several million dollars' worth of salaries and benefits executed to create the impression that Charlotte was keeping costs under tight control. But the suddenness of the firings suggested some level of panic on the fifty-eighth floor at BofA's own mounting losses.

Over the next several days, Price, Curl, and Brian Moynihan, the new general counsel, worked with lawyers at Wachtell, Lipton to mar-shal arguments in favor of invoking the MAC clause. The BofA team made sure not to ask Wachtell's lawyers for their opinion as to whether a MAC claim had any legitimate basis in fact. They simply informed the Wachtell lawyers of their intent to call the MAC and asked for support-ing materials. The Wachtell attorneys complied.

Weeks earlier, lawyers from Wachtell had prepared a memo present-ing arguments as to how difficult it would be for BofA to invoke the MAC clause. But it was part of the Charlotte bank's DNA not to take the advice of lawyers too seriously. After all, NCNB would never have been able to take over First Republic in Texas in the late 1980s if it had played by all the rules, rules that were stacked in favor of the establishment banks in New York. Lewis and the BofA team felt the same way about the MAC clause. The hell with what the lawyers said, they were going to do it.

In conversations with BofA executives, including Price and

Moynihan, the Wachtell lawyers discussed two previous cases where the government had supported a major bank in 2008. In the first case, the Federal Reserve helped limit any exposure for JPMorgan Chase when it acquired Bear Stearns the previous March. In the other case, just weeks earlier, Treasury provided $20 billion in fresh capital to Citigroup and guaranteed support for some of that bank's toxic assets.

On the afternoon of Wednesday, December 17, Lewis made his move, calling treasury secretary Hank Paulson and telling him that Merrill's rising losses had caused his board to reconsider the acquisition. (He was careful to say "the board" was reconsidering, and not that he, the CEO, was reconsidering the deal he'd struck back in September.) Bank of America's directors were thinking of invoking the MAC clause to unwind the deal, Lewis added. Paulson said this was an extremely serious matter and the men arranged to meet at 6:00 that evening at the Federal Reserve in Washington to discuss the issue.

Lewis, Price, and Moynihan flew to the nation's capital to talk about Merrill Lynch's losses and the Charlotte bank's plans to scuttle the deal. Paulson and Ben Bernanke, the Federal Reserve chairman, advised against that, with Bernanke adding that any such move would undermine confidence in Bank of America, not just Merrill Lynch.

Lewis then suggested an alternative: How about a relief package modeled on the one that Citigroup received a month earlier? The regulators said they'd think about it, and cautioned Lewis not to do anything rash, but to keep them apprised of the situation.

Two days later, Lewis called Bernanke to say that Merrill's pretax losses had swelled to $22 billion and the situation was urgent. Worse, Lewis himself didn't seem to know where the losses were coming from. Paulson convened a conference call for BofA executives to discuss the problem with a gaggle of Fed bankers from Virginia to New York. Lawyers from Wachtell, Lipton, who had privately and candidly advised their client of the difficulties in winning a MAC court case, were now making the opposite argument to officials from the Federal Reserve: BofA had a compelling case with the MAC and had every reason to believe they could pursue it.

But the BofA executives and their Wachtell lawyers did not know that the number crunchers working for the Federal Reserve had figured out that the Charlotte bank was mired in its own financial problems even without Merrill Lynch. These subordinates saw Lewis's threat of a MAC clause as nothing more than a crude bargaining tool to get the federal government to kick in some financial support for a poorly negotiated deal. After this second presentation, Bernanke and Paulson had come to the same conclusion: Lewis was using the threat of a MAC as leverage to get the type of taxpayer support that Citi had received a month earlier.

On Sunday, December 21, Lewis called Paulson at his vacation home in Keystone, Colorado, to say yet again that he wanted to invoke the MAC clause. The Merrill Lynch acquisition was supposed to close in ten days and Lewis wanted to know if the Feds were going to do anything about it.

Paulson warned Lewis that such a move would demonstrate a lack of judgment so severe that he would use it as grounds to fire Lewis and remove his entire board of directors. The government had already invested $15 billion in Bank of America and, given what was going on in the markets, had become the most powerful stakeholder in the enterprise. Lewis took the threat seriously and backed off, suggesting to Paulson that they "de-escalate."

UNAWARE OF THE PROBLEMS Merrill Lynch's losses were causing Lewis and his team, John Thain was preparing to leave New York on December 20 for his annual Christmas holiday in Vail, Colorado.

He mentioned it to Steele Alphin a day or two before his departure.

"Are you sure it's a good idea to go, John?"

"Steele, we always go skiing this time of year. My family will be there, it's all arranged."

"All right, it's your call."

"It's not like we're leaving civilization. You can reach me by phone and fax and e-mail. Things usually slow down around Christmas anyway."

On his last day at the office, Thain had to sit through a long meeting, the final gathering of senior executives of Bank of America and Merrill Lynch, to review everything that needed to be done prior to the deal's closing, scheduled for December 31. Thain seemed disengaged during the meeting and almost impatient, as if he couldn't wait for it to be over so he could go on holiday.

DESPITE HIS FREQUENT TRIPS to Charlotte, his incessant court-ing of his new colleagues, and his belief that the combination of Bank of America and Merrill Lynch would create a financial powerhouse, Greg Fleming had trouble acclimating himself to the BofA way. He had been put in charge of investment banking and corporate banking at the new organization. With Thain's help, he had been able to get Pete Kelly a position as the top lawyer for his group, but inexplicably he was not able to get Charlotte to approve his request to bring Eric Heaton to his invest-ment banking team. He pleaded his case with Andrea Smith in her office on the thirty-second floor.

"I want him to run our financial institutions group, it's incredibly important," said Fleming.

"Eric's very good at what he does," said Smith. "We've decided that he should stay in treasury, at least for now," she replied.

"Andrea, he's done treasury. He did a great job for us during a very trying time. Now he wants to get back to investment banking. We should let him do that."

"Eventually, we can make that happen. But for now, finance needs him in treasury."

"But it's not what *he* wants to do. Besides, it pays about a third of what he'd make as an investment banker. Why would he go along with that?"

"When bank management asks you to do something, they expect you to do it. That's the way it is here," Smith said.

"He's a very smart guy. Why should he stay here when he can get a better job elsewhere?"

"He's close to you," said Smith. "He's not going to go anywhere."

"But I'm not going to take advantage of that. Listen, your company agreed to pay $50 billion for us. This is what you're spending the $50 bil-lion on, the expertise we have in this stuff."

Fleming had several versions of this same conversation with Smith, and it always frustrated him because it always ended the same way. It was like an out-of-body experience trying to convince the Charlotte executives why it made more sense to put people in the jobs *they* wanted, as opposed to the jobs where management most needed them.

LEWIS ARRANGED A CONFERENCE call with his board on December 22 so he could apprise them of the latest developments with Merrill Lynch and federal regulators. He reported to the group that Paulson and Bernanke had assured him of financial support if he completed the acquisition of Merrill Lynch, as scheduled, on January 1. He added that if the bank continued with its plan to invoke the MAC clause, Paulson indicated that the removal of Bank of America's board and top management would be necessary.

It was not uncommon, particularly before the agreement to buy Merrill Lynch, for one or two of the older BofA directors to doze off during board meetings. But as Lewis described Paulson's threat to remove the bank's management and board, all of the directors tuned in with laser-like focus.

The financial support for the deal, which was still being worked out, would not be available before the closing, Lewis continued, but Paulson had assured the CEO that the money would come shortly afterward, by the time earnings were scheduled to be announced on January 20.

Lewis said that both regulators—Paulson and Bernanke—were willing to support his position that the extraordinary help being provided by the government would come out of a concern for Merrill Lynch's unexpected losses, not because of Bank of America's own problems managing its business. It was important that this rescue be seen as "a Merrill issue."

Lewis recommended that the board proceed with the acquisition along the terms set forth by the federal government.

No longer the compliant bunch that rubber-stamped every one of Lewis's initiatives, BofA's directors discussed the situation at length, trying to figure out the best way forward. Lewis and their own lack of oversight had brought them to a difficult place, where the future of their own bank was in jeopardy. They were faced with a difficult choice. If

BofA tried to bail out of the Merrill deal, the Charlotte bank could trigger a financial panic worse than the bank runs of the previous September, and expose BofA to a massive legal judgment brought by the estate of Merrill Lynch. If the directors accepted the government's offer of assistance, they would be saddling their shareholders with Merrill Lynch's black hole of losses.

It fell to Meredith Spangler, the oldest member of the board, to ask Lewis the one hardheaded question that needed to be asked: Can you get this in writing? Her question was met with widespread support by the other directors, and Lewis said he'd ask.

Ever loyal, the board remained firm in its support of Lewis, and accepted his recommendation to proceed with the deal, insisting only that he ask for some kind of written guarantee. But when the meeting had ended, Lewis knew that he'd lost the uncritical and unconditional board support he had enjoyed during his seven years as CEO. The directors would see him through this one emergency, but he'd brought them too far out on a limb. If he made one more mistake in the wake of this deal, he could face a vote of no confidence. He would have to make sure that didn't happen.

LEWIS ASKED PAULSON IF the treasury department could provide BofA with a letter, so that the board could approve the government's rescue package with a written commitment of some kind. Paulson said that wouldn't make sense, since any kind of letter would require a public disclosure of what was going on.

Lewis said he was concerned about Thain. Even though he was on a ski vacation in Vail, if the Merrill CEO found out what was going on, he'd go ballistic. Thain hadn't called in yet, Lewis continued, but he might check in any day now. Paulson agreed with Lewis that Thain should be kept out of the information flow, at least for the time being.

IN THE WEEK BEFORE Christmas, Merrill Lynch employees began learning what their 2008 bonuses would be. It was generally understood that since 2008 was a horrible year, culminating in the sale of the organization, that bonus payments would be off from previous years. But most of the employees who received incentive compensation for 2008— from an extra $100,000 to $1 million—sensed that BofA's overseers, particularly Andrea Smith, had exercised some prerogatives in cutting the bonuses back.

Smith continued to oversee the transition of Merrill Lynch into the newest division of Bank of America. She spoke to Alphin every day in order to keep him apprised of what was going on in New York. He periodically asked her about Thain and whether he had been checking in from Vail. Smith reported one phone conversation she had with Thain in the midafternoon. The Merrill Lynch chief was in good cheer. He was having lunch at the moment Smith called in a nice restaurant with the minister of finance of Mexico, and the men were enjoying a glass of wine.

"Sounds like a good old party," Alphin said to his protégé.

"Yes, it does," Smith replied.

FLEMING WORKED ON THE days leading up to Christmas. Professionally, it was the most depressing week of his life.

Just a year earlier, after Thain had arrived, he and his group worked furiously on a two-part capital raise. Thain was a terrific closer, and they completed the first round of the capital raise on Christmas Eve. Christmas Day, Fleming interrupted the festivities at his home to place a call to a bank in Tokyo, in an effort to bring Mizuho into the next round of capital-raising.

Fleming hadn't liked the Christmas interruption at the time, but he would have traded anything to be back in that situation now, fighting for his firm. In late 2007, Merrill Lynch, the bank where he had worked since 1992, had been in the middle of a comeback. It had been exciting to be part of that, to be part of making it happen.

And then came 2008. The whole world, it seemed, was headed toward the cliff. And Thain—the great John Thain who had helped run Goldman Sachs and saved the New York Stock Exchange—arrived amid expectations that everything could be turned around.

Rationally, Fleming knew the sale to BofA was for the best for the employees and shareholders. Emotionally, it was another story. He couldn't be there for the last few days of Merrill Lynch's existence. He couldn't bear to be around—to be *there*—when they pulled the plug on it. His wife, Melissa, had things to do between Christmas and New Year's, but he didn't, so on Saturday, December 27, he took his three children out west to Deer Valley, Utah, for a few days of skiing.

The physical activity of skiing was good, since it distracted him, and the company of his children, when he engaged directly with them, took his mind off Merrill Lynch. But in the confines of the hotel room at night, when the kids were asleep or watching TV, he could think of only one thing: *It was over.*

Somewhere out there—in the world of Bank of America–Merrill Lynch—a bright future lay ahead for Greg Fleming. He'd been telling himself that for several months now, and he'd believed it, particularly in October and November. But he no longer saw that bright future and, deep down, could no longer will himself to believe it was there.

It had taken three full months, but it was all hitting him now. That night in September, after the deal was signed, he walked back to his hotel in the wee hours and he was so exhausted, so numb, that he didn't really feel what was happening. He knew that an emotional day of reckoning would eventually arrive, and now it had. Totally. Greg Fleming was feeling it all. It was coming down on him in buckets. He was *drowning* in it, and he couldn't escape, not even by flying two thousand miles away from New York to go skiing with his kids.

For the past sixteen years Fleming had devoted himself to Merrill Lynch. He'd had a fantastic career, met wonderful people, worked like a dog and lived like a king, made more money than he ever dreamed possible, and risen almost to the very top. How lucky could a guy be?

Merrill Lynch wasn't a job, or a series of jobs. It was an institution that changed America, that restored the faith of the average citizen in the stock market in the 1940s and 1950s. Merrill Lynch was an integral part of the economic miracle of the United States in the second half of the twentieth century, channeling capital from everywhere in the country—from Des Moines, Duluth, Dothan, Decatur, and every other town across the U.S.—to thousands of small businesses, helping them grow into larger businesses. All that stuff about bringing Wall Street to Main Street—Fleming actually *believed* that.

And as of Thursday, January 1, that Merrill Lynch, the one he'd worked for since 1992, would be gone, forever.

FROM DECEMBER 28 through December 30, representatives from the Federal Reserve worked closely with BofA's Joe Price and Brian Moynihan on the general outline of the government's rescue package for the Merrill Lynch acquisition.

In Charlotte, as BofA executives focused primarily on Merrill, the realization was dawning on people that Bank of America itself had been poorly managed over the past year and that its exposure to consumer credit problems would make for a difficult 2009. While no one said it out loud, it was clear at the executive level that BofA's looming financial problems were the result of a massive failure in its risk-management division, headed by Amy Brinkley.

Until 2007, Brinkley, who had begun her career at NCNB in 1978, seemed like a lock to be Lewis's eventual successor. She had held important positions in different parts of BofA over the course of her career. She had the right pedigree, not just having started with the old NCNB but having graduated from UNC Chapel Hill, McColl's alma mater. But those deep Charlotte roots, and her friendship with Lewis (she and her husband were regular dinner companions of Ken and Donna Lewis), could not protect her from the fallout of the bank's financial problems.

At 4:00 p.m. on December 30, Lewis held another conference call with his board of directors. He reported that the government had been unable to provide him with a written guarantee of financial support for closing the Merrill acquisition, but that he and Joe Price had received numerous verbal promises of support from Paulson, Bernanke, and Kevin Warsh, the Fed governor who had taken over the point position for the government on the transaction.

For the better part of an hour, Lewis recited all the reasons why it made sense to proceed with the Merrill purchase, and the hazards of trying to break it off. Lewis concluded with his judgment that the deal should go forward, for the good of the country and Bank of America, and opened the call to the directors. The discussion which ensued was the most frank, contentious, and freewheeling debate at the board level since the old NCNB took over First Republic Bank of Texas two decades earlier.

Directors hit Lewis with a barrage of questions about Merrill's books and the due diligence that went into the review of Merrill's assets. Several wanted to know whether Merrill's traders had doubled down in the fourth quarter, making risky bets and swinging for the fences, confident that even if the bets didn't work out, BofA would be there to save them.

Lewis said he didn't know, but he did not believe that to be the case.

What about Thain? one of the directors asked. Did he have any explanation for this explosion in losses, other than what he said a few weeks earlier, that the "markets were terrible"?

Lewis said he hadn't heard from Thain in two weeks.

Temple Sloan, who had never been fond of Thain in the first place, seethed with anger at Thain's absence during such a pivotal moment in the bank's history.

CHAPTER 20

ONE TEAM, SHARED VALUES, SHARED FUTURE

"LEGAL DAY ONE." That's what it's called at Bank of America when a deal formally closes and a new bank is acquired. "Customer day one," which was when the combined organizations started serving customers under a new name, usually followed a few months later. January 1, 2009, was legal day one for the absorption of Merrill Lynch into Bank of America. After all the sturm und drang of December, the deal had finally closed. In September, when BofA stock was at $34 a share, the all-stock transaction placed a value of $29 per share for Merrill shares, which amounted to a $50 billion purchase price. In the intervening months, BofA shares had dropped to $13 a share, reducing the value of the transaction to about $19 billion.

Ken Lewis issued a statement to all 300,000 employees of his new company on "flagscape," the bank's internal website and news forum.

"With our merger with Merrill Lynch closed, today is our first day of business as one company. Today is a day to focus on new teammates and new opportunities. . . . From this day on, we are one team, with shared values, shared goals and a shared future."

With New Year's on a Thursday, the winter holiday was unusually long. John Thain stayed in Vail through the following weekend. At the Eagle Bahn Gondola, he ran into Neil Cotty, who was replacing Chai as his CFO. Thain and Tom Montag both returned refreshed from their vacations and ready to work on Monday, January 5.

For Thain, "legal day one" had another meaning: reentry into life working for someone else. It had been five years since he had had a boss of any kind, and even during the final four years at Goldman Sachs, when he reported to Paulson, Thain had enjoyed an unusual amount of autonomy.

On his first day back, Thain received a call from Lewis, telling him in capsule form what had transpired over the previous two weeks—about the threat of the MAC clause, the government's strong recommendation that the deal go through as planned, and the pledge of financial support that would be sorted out by January 20, the date of the fourth-quarter earnings call.

Thain was caught flatfooted. He had been away for more than two weeks and had missed everything. While he was relaxing with the family at Vail, the deal had almost fallen apart, and BofA's own financial condition had entered the red zone. He wondered why Lewis hadn't asked for his help. Given his own long relationship with Paulson, surely he could have helped work everything out.

Thain was also exposed. For the past thirteen months, his title as CEO of Merrill Lynch ensured that bad news would get to him quickly, whether it was Eric Heaton coming up to his office a year earlier to tell him the fourth quarter 2007 losses were worse than expected, or Greg Fleming calling him at his vacation retreat in the Adirondacks in late June to deliver similar news about the second quarter's earnings.

Heaton and Fleming had been shut out of the late-December events in Charlotte, so neither man was in a position to warn Thain about what was going down. As for Steele Alphin, he advised Thain against going to

Vail—at a time when Lewis was already trying to change the terms of the Merrill deal—but Thain hadn't heeded him.

Thain and Lewis were scheduled to host a joint town hall appearance in New York that week, but Lewis canceled.

BOB McCANN RETURNED FROM vacation that day with one purpose, to leave the company where he had spent twenty-six years. McCann had been humiliated at the September 15 town hall meeting, and a month later, he had been humiliated again when Thain announced his management team and specifically noted that McCann wouldn't report directly to him, but to a player to be named later, who would serve as a buffer. McCann had spent far too much of his life on the road, away from his family. Now that he had turned fifty, he asked himself if he really wanted to keep doing this, for a man who didn't respect him and in a company that didn't seem to respect its people. The answer was clear.

McCann went up to the thirty-second floor to speak to Thain face-to-face. When he announced his resignation, Thain acted sympathetic, as if he too knew how difficult it would be to work in the new, Charlotte-driven environment. Thain made no effort to dissuade McCann from leaving. He issued an internal statement that day lauding him for his years of service, wishing him well, and announcing that Dan Sontag, McCann's deputy, would take over as day-to-day head of the private client business.

ON WEDNESDAY MORNING, JANUARY 7, Fleming flew to Charlotte on the corporate jet. Lewis greeted him in his fifty-eighth-floor office and bade him sit down. After a minimum of small talk, Fleming got to it.

"Ken, I've been spending a lot of time thinking about this and decided that it's best if I leave." Fleming explained that the dean of his alma mater, Yale Law School, had invited him to spend a sabbatical lecturing students, and he felt this was the right moment in his career for something different.

Lewis, not an emotive man, studied Fleming for a moment. "You can't do that," he said pleasantly. "Steele and I were just talking this morning, and we want you to take on the wealth management position, in addition to what you're doing. That would be an expansion of your responsibilities and you would report directly to me."

Fleming paused as Lewis's offer sank in. The CEO was willing to let him run almost everything that used to be Merrill Lynch, except for sales and trading. This could cause a problem with Thain. "Wealth management reports to Thain now," Fleming said. "He wouldn't like that if it suddenly started reporting to me."

Lewis looked at Fleming and spoke without a trace of emotion in his voice. "He'll have to make his own decision on that."

Lewis reminded the younger man of all the opportunities that lay ahead of him at Bank of America and urged him to reconsider. "I want you to sleep on it."

FLEMING RETURNED TO NEW YORK and spent the balance of the day weighing the offer. With wealth management reporting to him, along with corporate and commercial banking, he'd be responsible for about 70 percent of the revenues generated by the division formerly known as Merrill Lynch. That was $35 billion. Thain's responsibilities would be whittled down to capital markets, about half that amount. And the promotion for Fleming would be an absolute humiliation for the former boss.

After all the acrimony that had built up between him and Thain, particularly since September, Fleming was surprised by how little appeal the prospect of hurting Thain held for him. Here was a chance to *crush* the guy, and Fleming had no appetite for it.

That evening, he and Melissa had dinner with Eric Heaton. Fleming reviewed the reasons that had caused him to tender his resignation in the first place. He had been battling with John Thain for six months. Kraus was now gone, but the tensions with Thain were as bad as ever and would only get worse. Dealing with Bank of America's HR department was another impediment. He couldn't even name his own team without Charlotte giving approval. Finally, there was the burnout factor. He had barely survived the regime of Stan O'Neal before John Thain was installed as his boss. The result was two years of almost nonstop, emergency room triage.

Lewis's offer changed the equation. Thain would either be out or to the side. As for burnout, it was easier to handle the grinding schedule of a big job if you were in charge. Fleming would be reporting directly to Lewis. The Bank of America CEO had his issues, but as a boss, he would be far better to work for than Thain or O'Neal.

And yet. He'd still be working for Bank of America. He'd still have to seek approval from Alphin or Andrea Smith when he wanted to make a key hire or tap someone from elsewhere in the bank. On how many other issues would he be constrained from doing what he thought best, in as quick a manner as possible?

Then again, this was the opportunity of a lifetime. To have one of the top jobs at one of the most powerful financial institutions in the world. And he was still young. If Lewis retired in a few years, he would have an opportunity to succeed him. He could not pass this up. This is why he put in all those hours over all those years. This was why he had sacrificed so much of his personal life: for the chance to get a shot at the top job. He couldn't walk away from it all right now. He had come too far and done too much. He had invested too much of his life in the game. This was how the whole system worked.

After several hours of back-and-forth with his wife and Heaton, they broke up for the evening. Fleming chatted some more with Melissa on the ride home, and it became clear to him what he had to do.

"I'm going to take it," he told Melissa. "This is the job I've worked sixteen years for."

They went to bed at midnight, but Fleming and his wife woke at 4:00 the next morning and talked about the job and about what lay ahead. After almost two hours, Fleming realized something: He didn't want it. The time had come to get off the train. Once he came to that conclusion, Fleming felt a strange sense of liberation.

Later that morning, he called Lewis.

"Ken, I've got a long life ahead. I really appreciate the offer, but I have to say no."

Lewis paused, taken aback. "I'm disappointed," he said. "I wish you'd made a different decision. Now that you're leaving, I can't lose Thain."

Fleming thanked Lewis for all his help and support, and the decisiveness he showed in September when Merrill Lynch was in trouble.

"This will be one of my biggest regrets about this," said Lewis, who asked Fleming not to mention the previous day's offer to anyone.

THE DIE CAST, FLEMING went to Thain's office to inform him of his decision to accept a post at Yale Law School. His former CEO was incredulous.

"Why are you doing this?" Thain demanded. "You're blowing up your career. You'll be running this place in a few years." Thain cited other former Wall Street executives who'd quit and gone to academia as examples of wasted careers.

"I've made up my mind," Fleming said. "Melissa's with me on this."

"McCann's not a loss, but you are. This will look bad to Lewis."

"I saw Lewis yesterday. He knows all about this."

Thain was apoplectic. "How could you not have told me first?!"

That's all Fleming needed to hear. Thain really didn't care what he was doing to Greg Fleming's career, he thought. Thain only cared about what Greg Fleming was doing to John Thain's career by dealing directly with Lewis.

FLEMING CAME IN THE next day, Friday, January 9, to assist with whatever transition matters he might be able to help out on. Normally, when a banker leaves his place of employment, he's gone that day and not allowed back because of competitive concerns. Since Fleming was leaving Merrill Lynch for a job in academia, not at a competing bank, the same kind of "garden leave" rules didn't apply.

Still, there wasn't much for him to do that last day, because the merger had just closed. Fleming said good-bye to a few people that afternoon, although his close friends knew they'd remain in touch.

What a strange way to leave the place where he'd spent the previous sixteen years, he thought, as he approached the elevator bank on the thirty-second floor for that final ride down. Throughout his career at Merrill Lynch, he had always hoped this day would never come, or if it did come, his departure would be marked with a celebration of some kind, preferably a retirement party, since he never wanted to work anywhere else.

He had come *that close* to becoming CEO of Merrill Lynch before Stan O'Neal allowed the place to blow up. Then John Thain arrived, but the man touted as Mr. Fixit couldn't protect Merrill Lynch from the financial crisis of 2008. Finally, Ken Lewis offered him the job he'd worked for over the past sixteen years, but Fleming had woke up the previous morning and realized he didn't want it. What Lewis offered sounded a lot like the job he'd been working toward, but it wasn't Merrill Lynch, and never could be again.

The elevator arrived down on the second floor, he passed through the turnstile, down the escalator, and Greg Fleming left the building.

ON MONDAY, JANUARY 12, Lewis was in New York to get to know members of Thain's team. At lunchtime, Thain escorted Lewis up the stairs connecting the thirty-second floor to the thirty-third-floor executive dining room. As he came to the top of the stairs, Thain pointed out all the pictures of his predecessors hanging on the wall.

"This is our chairmen's gallery," said Thain, pointing out the paintings of Charlie Merrill, Winthrop Smith senior, and Don Regan. Lewis paid no attention whatsoever.

BY THE MIDDLE OF that week, it was apparent that a huge shift was under way in the capital markets, which had nearly seized up during the fourth quarter of 2008. Money was flowing again, investors were buying and selling securities—mostly of the plain vanilla kind—but the flow activity was a welcome relief from the near shutdown of the previous quarter.

On January 14, as Thain was leaving the office to meet his wife for dinner, he called Alphin to continue an ongoing discussion they had been having about a retention package for him and his top people for 2009. Fleming's departure had increased Thain's importance to the organization, because now there was no one who could step in if he left for a different job on Wall Street.

Time and again, the former Merrill CEO had discussed with Alphin the inequity of what had happened to him through the sale of his company. Because he had no change in control clause, he was exposed, and now he made it clear that he wanted some kind of general promise for himself and his key people to make it worth their while to stay on through 2009. The fact that BofA was about to receive another slug of taxpayer money seemed irrelevant to him.

"It's not going to happen, John."

"You can get this done, Steele."

"I know I can. I'm not sure I want to."

"Don't you understand how Wall Street works?"

Thain had already told Alphin he was meeting Carmen for dinner.

"John, you've got a lovely wife. Go have a nice dinner, have a good bottle of wine, and let's stop talking about this."

Alphin couldn't understand it. He had met with and spoken to Thain dozens of times since the deal was struck in September. In so many ways, John Thain was a brilliant man. His understanding of the business was unparalleled. But he had some blind spots. Alphin knew Thain well enough to understand that the incessant conversations they had about money, about compensation, had nothing to do with greed. John Thain was not a greedy person. He was a dedicated family man who put his wife and kids before everything else. Alphin came to view Thain's focus on money as symptomatic of Wall Street's out-of-control bonus culture.

Taken in narrow terms, Thain was right to ask for a certain level of compensation. But nobody in New York seemed to understand the bigger picture. Alphin didn't go to an Ivy League school, and he wasn't even the top student at the school he did attend, but he understood a few things about Wall Street. The whole reason everything almost came crashing down in 2008 was twenty-five years of nonstop focus on bonus checks, on compensation. Why did Lehman Brothers go out of business? Because their people kept doing real estate deals long after the market had turned. It produced bigger bonuses for them. Why did AIG keep selling those foolhardy insurance policies on CDOs? Because it was easy money and led to bigger bonuses. Why did Merrill Lynch need to be saved in the first place? Because O'Neal let his guys run wild in the CDO market so they all could get bigger bonuses. Bank of America could *never* have bought Merrill Lynch if the people up there hadn't been so obsessed with their own bonuses that they were blind to the dangers of what they were doing. The people at Merrill Lynch came crawling to Charlotte because of their own self-inflicted wounds. The whole reason John Thain worked for Ken Lewis, and not the other way around, was that bonus culture they had up there in New York. And even Thain, with all his degrees from Harvard and MIT, couldn't see it. That's what twenty-five years on Wall Street would do to a man.

FROM JANUARY 12 TO 14, Bank of America's share price slipped, in heavy trading, from just under $13 a share to just over $10, amid general uncertainty over the economy and the impending shift of power in the White House from President Bush to President-elect Obama. But on January 15, word started leaking out of Washington that Bank of America was going to receive a special package of taxpayer funds, presumably to help it cover losses associated with the acquisition of Merrill Lynch.

The news, the first public disclosure that BofA had been in any kind of trouble, led to a binge of trading in the stock—552 million shares traded that day—and drove the price down to a low of $7.35. The bank announced that it would move its earnings announcement up from inauguration day, January 20, to the next day, Friday, January 16. That evening, Ken Lewis held a conference call with his board of directors. The meeting was surreal. A few hours earlier, a Charlotte-bound U.S. Airways flight experienced engine trouble after taking off from LaGuardia Airport in New York. The captain, Chesley "Sully" Sullenberger, made a split-second decision to ditch the airplane, an Airbus A320, in the Hudson River rather than take a chance on being able to get back to an airport. More than a dozen BofA employees were on the flight, heading back to Charlotte after a four-day workweek in New

York. Miraculously, the plane landed intact on the Hudson and stayed afloat for hours, allowing rescue teams to get everyone out alive.

Lewis assured the board that everyone was safe and out of harm's way, and then began describing the final details of the government rescue package, which had been firmed up that week. It was an important piece of unfinished business that Hank Paulson had to wrap up before leaving office.

The final numbers for Merrill Lynch were staggering: operating losses of $21 billion for the quarter, which generated a tax benefit of $6 billion, for a net loss of $15 billion. BofA sustained a $1.7 billion loss of its own, its first quarterly loss in seventeen years. The government had agreed to supply $20 billion in taxpayer funds to fill the hole caused by Merrill Lynch—essentially providing a loan to subsidize a $19 billion transaction—and protect up to $118 billion in bad assets held on the books of both institutions. Between the $15 billion in TARP funds that had been given to BofA in October, and the $10 billion that had been set aside for Merrill Lynch, the extra $20 billion brought the government investment in Bank of America to $45 billion, exactly the same level as Citigroup. Lewis said the bank's dividend would be cut to a penny per share.

Most of the directors, including Gifford, were shocked by the magnitude of it all, and the damage that the Merrill Lynch acquisition had done to their beloved bank. "Unfortunately, it's screw the shareholders," he wrote in an e-mail to Tom May, another BofA director from Fleet.

Temple Sloan, who had never warmed up to Thain in the first place, was nearly beside himself with anger about what had happened, and how the Merrill CEO had disappeared during the two most important weeks in the bank's history. The Boston directors believed that Moynihan would do a better job as head of the investment bank, and none of the other directors felt any particular loyalty to Thain. In the boardroom, the sentiment was almost universal that Thain should have known how bad things were going to be.

The next morning, Bank of America released its earnings results to the public. After a compressed one-hour call, most of which was spent reviewing the results and describing the government's $20 billion investments, only a few questions were allowed. But Lewis reiterated his belief in Merrill Lynch's ability to help BofA grow, and expressed his support for Merrill's former CEO, saying, "We are happy that John Thain has assumed a major role at Bank of America."

Another 495 million BofA shares traded that day with the closing price sinking to $7.18. The public disclosure of the extra government aid, on top of Merrill Lynch's massive losses, sparked several lawsuits accusing Lewis of withholding important information from shareholders prior to the December 5 vote at which the acquisition was approved.

The Bank of America board also came under fire for its role in the matter, with critics castigating directors for abdicating their fiduciary responsibilities to shareholders. Over the next several days, through the inauguration of President Obama, Lewis spent almost all of his time dealing with board members and his inner circle of advisors in Charlotte.

Lewis and Alphin were in nonstop contact throughout the weekend and into the following week, trying to figure out the best way to keep the board—particularly the Boston directors, who were up in arms—from turning on the CEO. There was also the matter of John Thain. Starting with Thain's performance in BofA's October capital raise, Lewis had begun to question whether Thain was the right person to lead Bank of America. When Lewis struck the deal to buy Merrill Lynch in September, he assumed that Thain had a large and loyal following at his company. But the departures of McCann and Fleming showed that his support did not run deep. Then there was Thain's remoteness. Not only had he gone off to Vail in late December, but he never checked in with Lewis, and now Lewis was fielding complaints from some of Thain's direct reports, such as David Darnell, that they couldn't get him to return phone calls or reply to e-mails.

In New York, Thain focused on his job overseeing the Merrill Lynch legacy businesses. Sales and trading operations continued to generate stronger revenue than anything he'd seen since joining Merrill thirteen months earlier. January was on track to be an extremely strong month, with $5 billion in revenues already on the books. The values assigned to Merrill's assets, which had slumped in the fourth quarter, leading to most of the losses, were already on the rebound.

On Monday, January 19, Lewis got a call from Badr Al-Saad, managing director of the Kuwait Investment Authority, who had invested more than $1 billion in John Thain's vision for Merrill Lynch a year earlier. After the reset in July, Al-Saad had lost patience with Thain. At the end of the year, he sent a letter to Lewis urging him not to give Thain any kind of bonus. In this phone call, after the announcement of losses for the fourth quarter, Al-Saad was more blunt, telling Lewis he should fire Thain.

Thain, meanwhile, was looking forward. As a sign of confidence in the future of Bank of America, Thain bought 84,600 shares in the bank at about $6 per share. He had finally succeeded in getting his restricted shares of Merrill Lynch converted into BofA stock, so his total stake in the Charlotte bank was 764,546 shares. Only two other insiders, Lewis (with 2.3 million shares) and Meredith Spangler (with 6.3 million), held more. Thain also continued planning his annual trip to Davos for the following week. He had lined up interviews with the BBC and other media outlets, even though some of his own people asked him if he really thought it was a good idea to assume such a visible role at the World Economic Forum following everything that had been going on at Bank of America.

On Monday, January 19, the *Financial Times*—which had been planning to publish a long feature about how John Thain was the one Wall Street executive smart enough to avoid disaster in 2008—started preparing a different story, one that focused on the December bonus payments at Merrill Lynch. The paper asked BofA how Merrill Lynch, which had posted operating losses of $28 billion for the entire year, could pay out more than $3 billion in bonuses just days before the U.S. government agreed to supply Bank of America with an additional $20 billion in taxpayer funds to help finalize the acquisition.

A spokesman for the bank in Charlotte was not able to get a statement to the paper, and the story did not run. The same thing happened on Tuesday. On Wednesday afternoon, after being informed that the story about early payment of bonuses at Merrill Lynch would be published the next day, a BofA spokesman supplied the following statement to the *Financial Times*: "Merrill Lynch was an independent company until January 1 2009. John Thain decided to pay year-end incentives in December as opposed to their normal date in January. BofA was informed of his decision."

In New York, Thain had no idea that a story about the accelerated bonuses was in the works, and was not informed on Wednesday afternoon of the statement BofA had issued concerning his role in the matter. Instead, he received word that Ken Lewis would be coming up to New York the following day, and would like to speak with him late in the morning, around 11:30.

Thain didn't understand the reason for the visit, so he approached Andrea Smith.

"Do you know why Ken's coming up tomorrow?"

"He's coming to see clients, I think."

ON THURSDAY, JANUARY 22, Thain did what he did every morning on his drive into the office. He started reading the five newspapers that were delivered to his home each day in Rye: the *Financial Times, The Wall Street Journal, The New York Times, USA Today,* and the *New York Post.* On this morning, he got no further than the *Financial Times,* which had splashed the Merrill Lynch bonus article on the front page. Thain was outraged about the story, which implied that there was something surreptitious or underhanded about the December bonus payments, and he was angry at the statement from BofA, which laid the blame on him. He and Tutwiler couldn't understand why Bank of America would pin the payment of Merrill Lynch bonuses on him, especially since the bonuses had been negotiated in the September agreement. Not only had Thain kept Alphin informed of the process, but Andrea Smith had played a role in determining the amounts paid out.

Andrew Cuomo, the New York attorney general, issued a statement condemning the bonuses. And then, shortly after 10:00 a.m., there was a report on CNBC about the furniture Thain had ordered for his office a year earlier. Charles Gasparino, an on-air editor, had gotten hold of a list of the expensive furniture that had been installed in Thain's office that detailed the price of each article, as well as the fee for Michael Smith, the celebrity home decorator. The total bill for the office makeover was $1.2 million, he announced.

On top of the news about Merrill's fourth-quarter losses, the $3 billion in bonus payments that had been reported in the paper that morning, and the controversy surrounding the additional $20 billion in taxpayer funds that had been loaned to BofA in order to help it close the Merrill Lynch deal, the story about Thain's $1.2 million office seemed like one outrage too many.

And then Gasparino reported that Lewis was on his way to New York at that moment to discuss Thain's future with the bank. By 11:00 a.m., the story of Thain's office and the bonuses had become the buzz in the Financial District, and the real-time report that Lewis was en route to New York, possibly to fire Thain, had turned the spectacle into the Wall Street version of O.J. Simpson in the Ford Bronco, with thousands of bankers and traders glued to their TV sets.

While Thain's possible ouster was being reported on TV, employees on BofA's equity trading floor were transfixed by the developments. Hundreds were scheduled to be fired that day as part of the Merrill Lynch takeover in capital markets. Many hoped that Thain's departure, if it was indeed taking place, might lead to a rethinking of the bloodbath that was about to ensue.

Thain sat alone in his office, watching the TV reports with horror. He couldn't believe what was happening to him, or that his prospective dismissal was being turned into a media circus. The quote from BofA in the morning's newspaper article about the bonuses was misleading. Furthermore, somebody had leaked the fact that Lewis was coming up to visit him, possibly to fire him. As for the stuff about the office, Thain had no idea how that had gotten out. He was now trapped in that office and there was nowhere to go while the soap opera of his future at BofA was being played out on television.

Lewis arrived on the thirty-second floor at 11:30 and entered Thain's office. The two men sat down.

"I have bad news," Lewis said. "This is not going to work out."

"I don't understand, Ken."

"The board blames you for the fourth quarter."

"The losses in the fourth quarter are going to come back this quarter. They're already coming back."

"You can never succeed me. We want you to resign. We want Brian Moynihan to replace you."

"This doesn't make any sense."

"This is what we decided. There's not much more to say."

Lewis got up, shook Thain's hand and wished him the best.

"I guess I know where the leak came from," said Thain as Lewis was leaving.

"We didn't leak this."

"Well, I didn't know why you were coming here."

As Lewis was leaving the office, he almost collided with May Lee, who had seen the report on TV and bolted out of a meeting and run toward Thain's office. Lewis slipped by her and left the area. Thain's assistant, Susan, stood up and asked what had happened.

"Let's just wait," said Lee, and the two women stood there for a moment, frozen.

Thain remained in his office, alone and stunned. Nothing like this had happened to him before. Ever. What kind of an organization would act this way? At Goldman Sachs, when the going got tough, people hunkered down and pulled together as a team. They didn't throw bodies overboard.

Thain recalled Mayopoulos. This is exactly what they did to Tim Mayopoulos. They were treating Thain the way they treated the general counsel a month earlier.

Thain went to his door, opened it, and looked out at Lee.

"Well, I guess that's it," he said to his chief of staff. "We're going home."

Lee came into Thain's office and sat down in front of his desk.

"Okay, let's make a list of people you need to call," she said.

Thain sat down at his desk, the same desk he had at Goldman Sachs, and which he had brought with him to the New York Stock Exchange. He called his direct reports, starting with Montag, who was in Asia. He wasn't even clear on what this meant for Montag, who, after the conversation, thought he was going to be fired as well.

He called other people in the organization to make sure they heard it officially from him, and then started packing his things.

By noontime, the calls starting coming in for him, from his friends, longtime colleagues, and others who had come to know and respect John Thain over the years.

Jamie Dimon, the CEO of JPMorgan Chase, called to express his sympathy and support. Several senior executives from Goldman Sachs—a place that you never truly leave—also reached out to him.

Finally, Hank Paulson called. After all they'd been through at Goldman, especially the removal of Corzine, and the NYSE, where Paulson had been helpful and supportive, and the September weekend at the Fed, where Hank had pushed him toward BofA, here was Paulson, now without a job for the first time in his adult life, calling to offer some encouraging words to Thain.

Around 3:00 p.m., after saying good-bye to the people closest to him, Thain left the office and was driven home.

OVER THE NEXT FEW DAYS, the *Financial Times* and other newspapers began to report Bank of America's involvement in the early payment of bonuses. Day by day, the true story of BofA's role in the bonus payments dribbled out. Still, Thain had to endure a torrent of news coverage about his failure at Merrill Lynch, and the $1.2 million office, culminating in a statement by President Obama condemning Wall Street executives for using taxpayer money to fund their luxurious lifestyles. It was crazy, Thain thought. The money for the office had been spent a year earlier, before any taxpayer funds were sent to Wall Street.

Thain's wife, Carmen, was appalled at the way her husband was being treated.

Less than a week after his firing, Thain gave an interview to Maria Bartiromo on CNBC, in which he apologized for the office and explained that no taxpayer money was involved. He did the interview from a studio in New York, wearing a suit and tie. Bartiromo was in Davos, where he should have been. Thain promised to reimburse Bank of America for the full cost of the office. But he also said that the office had been built at a time when the economic outlook was different, reflecting his own view a year earlier that the worst was over.

John Reed, the former Citibank chief who had recruited Thain to the NYSE, called to console him, and suggested that they get together, with their wives, for dinner. Other calls continued to pour in over the weeks following the firing.

Then one day Thain got an e-mail from someone he'd never met, an executive at Warburg Pincus.

Dear John,

I tried to call, but figured you were busy.
I have no real insight into this, but I do know your past accomplishments, and I know you just didn't become a raving asshole overnight. If you ever want to talk about it, let me know . . .

David Coulter

CHAPTER 21

THE BOSTON MAFIA

THE GOVERNMENT'S $20 BILLION arrangement to get Bank of America to complete its acquisition of Merrill Lynch sparked a storm of controversy. Several large shareholders filed lawsuits immediately, claiming that BofA's executives, starting with CEO Ken Lewis, had kept them in the dark about the massive losses building up at Merrill Lynch prior to the December 5 vote on the deal. In response to the public outcry—and to explain why it never informed its own shareholders of the depth of Merrill's problems—BofA issued a carefully worded statement to the media saying the bank asked for government help only after the forecast for Merrill's losses increased dramatically in the second week of December (that is, after the December 5 shareholder vote).

At the summit meeting in Washington, D.C., the previous October, treasury secretary Hank Paulson, along with Federal Reserve chair Ben Bernanke and New York Fed chief Tim Geithner, had committed to invest $15 billion in BofA and $10 billion in Merrill Lynch. The additional $20 billion brought the sum total of taxpayer funds propping up

Bank of America to $45 billion, the same level as Citigroup, which was widely viewed as the basket case of the industry.

On the day that Merrill Lynch's accelerated bonus payments were disclosed in the *Financial Times,* New York State attorney general Andrew Cuomo launched his own investigation. After the "Wall Street bailout" announced the previous October, Cuomo had sent letters to the heads of the New York banks receiving the funds, warning them against using taxpayer money to pay outsized bonuses to their top executives. Now, after learning that executives at Merrill Lynch had doled out $3.6 billion in bonuses even while racking up losses of $21 billion for the year—losses that forced BofA to beg for the additional infusion of $20 billion in taxpayer money—Cuomo was outraged.

His immediate focus was on Merrill Lynch and its former CEO John Thain. According to the statement given by BofA to the *Financial Times,* decisions about bonus payments were made by Thain and his board, acting independently, and only after those decisions were made was the Charlotte bank informed.

Within days of the disclosure of the bonus payments, however, the facts surrounding BofA's involvement in the process emerged. Not only was Charlotte fully aware of Merrill's plans, but the issue of bonus payments had been negotiated in the September merger agreement hammered out between Greg Fleming and Greg Curl, yet never disclosed to shareholders prior to the December 5 vote. And not only was BofA aware of the bonus payments, but it inserted itself into the process, recommending that Merrill pay out 70 percent of the bonuses in cash, with the rest in stock, as opposed to Merrill's usual practice of paying out 60 percent in cash. Finally, Andrea Smith, the bank's top HR executive in New York, was actively involved in decisions about bonuses, slashing payments for a wide variety of Merrill Lynch officers to bring them more in line with the lower levels of pay doled out by Charlotte each year.

Cuomo's prosecutors in the case, Benjamin Lawsky, Eric Corngold, and David Markowitz, issued subpoenas to senior executives from Merrill Lynch and their counterparts at Bank of America, starting with Thain and Lewis. Thain was the first to show up for a deposition, arriving at the

AG's office in lower Manhattan on February 19, raising his right hand and explaining his actions with regard to the bonuses

The question-and-answer process went smoothly until Lawsky began to zero in on specific payments Thain made to some of his top people. Thain's lawyer, Andrew Levander, cut off the line of questioning, explaining that any discussions of specific payments to individuals would violate BofA's confidentiality policies. Lawsky was puzzled and asked Thain if he had not, in fact, been fired. He had, Thain replied, adding that there was no severance agreement between him and BofA. Lawsky couldn't understand why the former CEO would adhere to the policies of an organization that had cut him loose and with which he no longer had a financial relationship.

Over several weeks, Cuomo's team took depositions from Lewis and his top people, including chief administrative officer Steele Alphin, CFO Joe Price, strategy chief Greg Curl, general counsel Brian Moynihan, and Andrea Smith. The prosecutors soon dug into the topic of Lewis's approach to Hank Paulson in December and his threat to invoke a material adverse change clause to break up the Merrill deal. They also fought with BofA's lawyers, who refused to turn over any information about how much money was paid to individual Merrill Lynch executives. Eventually, backed by a state judge, Cuomo's team got BofA to turn over a list of who received what at Merrill Lynch. In return, the AG's office promised not to disclose any of the name-specific payments to the public.

On February 11, Cuomo revealed that Merrill Lynch had paid out bonuses of $1 million or more to over seven hundred employees for 2008. The four top recipients of bonuses received $121 million, while twenty people received bonuses of at least $8 million and fifty-three got bonuses of at least $5 million.

The aggregate disclosures surrounding bonus payment increased the public anger toward Wall Street, especially in the wake of the $700 billion TARP fund that Paulson had secured from Congress the previous fall. At the same time Cuomo disclosed the Merrill payouts, executives at AIG—the insurance company that had been bailed out with taxpayer funds the previous September—were planning to pay bonuses to their own people, the ones responsible for unwinding the mess that AIG's financial products group had created at the company. The prospect of bonuses at AIG led to more public anger, and the House of Representatives, in an emotional spasm of outrage, endorsed a proposal to tax bonuses by up to 90 percent. Cooler heads in the Senate let the matter drop and the bill died.

In addition to the battle with Cuomo, BofA was being investigated by the House Committee on Oversight and Government Affairs, which wanted to know why and how Paulson decided to pay out an additional $20 billion to the Charlotte bank. The Securities and Exchange Commission also launched a probe into whether BofA had provided adequate disclosures to its shareholders about bonus payments at Merrill, and the mounting losses at the Wall Street bank.

On top of the regulatory reviews, Lewis came under increasing fire from his own shareholders for pushing forward with an acquisition that nearly destroyed Bank of America. An investor in Houston, Jerry Finger, succeeded in adding a proposal to BofA's annual proxy statement urging shareholders to strip Lewis, the CEO, of his additional title as chairman at the bank's annual meeting in late April.

Finger had been an investor in BofA for more than twenty years, since the days when NCNB invested in his small Houston bank. In the late 1980s, he served as Hugh McColl's eyes and ears on the ground in Texas and recommended that McColl take a look at First Republic Bank, a failing Dallas-based lender that the Federal Deposit Insurance Corporation had planned to auction off. Republic had been the largest bank in Texas, and McColl's success at winning the FDIC's support for his takeover of the bank marked a pivotal moment in the transformation of NCNB into what became Bank of America. Jerry Finger had remained a loyal shareholder of the bank for almost twenty years, but he objected to Lewis's proposed takeover of Merrill Lynch when it was announced the previous September and voted against it on December 5, without even knowing the depth of Merrill's financial problems.

Thus, Lewis spent a good portion of February, March, and April preparing for depositions from Cuomo's prosecutors, preparing for his own testimony to Congress, and reaching out to prominent shareholders and investors at large to assure them that the Merrill Lynch acquisition would pay off for the bank eventually.

Bank of America's share price, which had been above $50 a share in 2007, before the credit crisis began, and sunk to $34 the previous September, when the Merrill deal was announced, was now below $5 a share. A substantial portion of the bank's shareholders were angry at Lewis for weakening BofA's balance sheet and diluting the value of their holdings. Lewis's own employees were angry with him for the damage he had inflicted on the share price. Making matters worse was a draconian policy regarding bonuses awarded by BofA to its own employees in February 2009. Because of its weak financial position, the bank reduced the size of its already meager bonus payments and spread them out over several years, a consequence of its dire financial position.

Thain's firing ended up having an effect quite different from the one achieved through the dismissal of David Coulter a decade earlier. Instead of uniting everyone at the bank, Thain emerged as a polarizing figure. Legacy Merrill employees lost any trust they had in the management in Charlotte. BofA employees, meanwhile, felt a grudging respect for the fact that Thain had gotten his people paid and snookered Lewis into overpaying for the franchise. But whatever envy BofA people felt didn't carry over to warm regards for their new colleagues. Time and again, as BofA's share price floundered in the $3 to $5 range, an employee in Charlotte would meet a new colleague from New York. Once the Charlotte employee learned that his new colleague had been at Merrill Lynch, he'd say, "Great. That means I don't have to shake your hand," and walk away.

BANK OF AMERICA'S ANNUAL shareholder meeting was scheduled for April 29 in Charlotte. In the weeks leading up to the meeting, not only had Lewis been consulting with the bank's largest investors, but Temple Sloan, the board's lead independent director, also met with major shareholders, encouraging them to support Lewis. Sloan himself was facing a battle to retain his own position on the board. As the lead director, he became a lightning rod for much of the anger over Lewis's misadventures with Merrill Lynch and the federal government. Many shareholders criticized Sloan for not providing any adult supervision over Lewis and his team. In his haste the previous September to acquire Merrill Lynch at seemingly any price, and in his inability to see the magnitude of Merrill's financial problems, Lewis had nearly destroyed the bank that had been painstakingly built by his predecessors over five decades, and Temple Sloan had allowed that to happen.

A separate proposal was also added to the proxy statement urging shareholders to boot Lewis out as CEO, but few of BofA's major investors, including Jerry Finger, thought that proposal had a chance. The chairman proposal, however, was a different matter. BofA's own canvassing of investors showed that the proposal to strip Lewis of his title as chairman had a chance at succeeding.

On April 23, Cuomo issued a preliminary summary of his investigation to members of Congress involved with the TARP program. For the first time, Cuomo's investigation disclosed to the public the various back-and-forth negotiations between Lewis and Paulson surrounding Lewis's threat to pull out of the Merrill deal the previous December. Until Cuomo's report, only a small group of people close to Lewis and at the highest levels of government were aware of the strong-arm tactics used by Paulson to coerce Lewis into completing the Merrill deal. Most embarrassing to Lewis, just a week before the shareholder meeting, was the disclosure that Paulson had issued a threat: If Lewis tried to stop the Merrill deal by invoking the MAC clause, Paulson said he'd remove Lewis and his entire board at BofA. Lewis's top people saw the timing of the Cuomo report as anything but an accident, a political stunt designed to inflict maximum damage on the Bank of America CEO prior to his annual meeting.

On April 29, hundreds of BofA shareholders descended on Charlotte to participate in the most contentious annual meeting ever held by the bank. The meeting took place in the Belk Theater, connected to the base of BofA's tower. Not coincidentally, hundreds of the bank's own employees (who are referred to as "associates" or "teammates") packed the auditorium, filling up most of the main floor and pushing some of the protesting shareholders up into the balcony, where they would be less likely to draw attention.

Almost in unison, the BofA employees, identifiable by their flag-scape pins, stood to applaud when Lewis took the podium to review the events of the past year. In his speech, Lewis defended himself from the accusations of shortsightedness that had been piling up.

"As CEO of your company, it is my job to make decisions that will build earnings power and financial stability over the long term," he said. "I understand that shareholders and associates are going through a lot of short-term pain. But I believe that we have built the best and most diversified financial services company in the industry, and that when economic conditions return to normal, no one will be better positioned than Bank of America to thrive and win."

The associates also clapped at various pauses following Lewis's recitation of particular accomplishments in 2008 and his description of the mighty engine of earnings he had constructed with the acquisitions of Merrill Lynch and Countrywide.

"This year I will celebrate my fortieth anniversary with this company, and I do mean celebrate," he said in conclusion. "The best evidence that I made a good career decision when I graduated from college is that I have gotten up every morning throughout my career looking forward to coming in to work, collaborating with my teammates, competing in the marketplace, and winning with friends. I appreciate every opportunity you have given me. I am proud of our shared accomplishments. And I have been honored to serve our customers and clients, and all of you. This has been an incredibly difficult and painful year for all of us. But we are building this company for the long term. I continue to believe we have built the best financial company in the industry, and that our results over time will bear that out."

Following his presentation, the BofA employees gave Lewis another rousing round of applause.

The question-and-answer session that followed the chairman's report was much livelier than it was in other years, with a motley assortment of people—from Florida retirees who made the trip because they had nothing better to do, to concerned investors who owned millions of dollars' worth of BofA stock—approaching the microphones to express their views. One investor complained about Lewis's pay—even though Lewis received no bonus for 2008—and another criticized the special perk given to Chad Gifford, one of the Boston directors: 120 hours of use of the corporate jet each year. But most of the questioners pushed Lewis on the topic of the Merrill acquisition. In the early afternoon, the bank's corporate secretary read the results of the shareholder vote, which showed a strong majority in favor of Lewis retaining his position as CEO. The vote on whether Lewis could keep his title as chairman, however, remained too close to call, and the meeting was adjourned.

It wasn't until a few hours later that the bank announced that the proposal to strip Lewis of his title as chairman had actually passed. The vote was a stunning rebuke to a sitting CEO who, until the previous year, had been lauded as one of the best bankers of his generation.

HIGH UP ABOVE THE AUDITORIUM, in the boardroom on the sixtieth floor of the Bank of America tower, when the final results of the shareholder vote had been tabulated, Lewis accepted the verdict with equanimity. Leading up to the shareholder meeting, he had pushed the idea that Temple Sloan could replace him as chairman.

The idea never gained traction, since Sloan had come to be perceived as a yes-man for Lewis and as the anchor of the informal Charlotte Mafia that controlled the board. The consensus among directors was that the subject should be discussed in further detail, especially since Sloan was reelected to the board by only 63 percent of the shareholders who cast ballots, the lowest total among all directors. Most of the investors who cast votes at annual meetings represent large, institutional shareholders and control big blocs of votes. In general these shareholders tend to support existing management. As a result, most CEOs and directors, even controversial ones, usually receive north of 90 percent of the shareholder votes at their annual meetings. The fact that Lewis mustered only 67 percent of the yea votes and Sloan got even less showed a significant level of dissatisfaction toward the existing power structure at BofA.

For the first time since the 1960s, when Addison Reese kept the peace between the directors brought together in the merger of American Commercial in Charlotte with Security National in Greensboro—the merger that created NCNB—control of the bank was in play. By now there was a newfound wariness among the Carolina directors toward the small but relatively tight faction of the board from Boston. In the discussion that ensued, the various groups sought out a compromise candidate to become the next chairman. Given BofA's new status as a ward of the state, the directors agreed that the next chair should be someone well-connected in Washington, in contrast to Lewis, who hated dealing with government officials.

A consensus formed around Walter Massey, retired president of Morehouse College in Atlanta, who had been on the board of the old Bank of America in San Francisco before the merger with NationsBank, and therefore belonged neither to the Carolina camp nor the Boston group. Massey was not regarded as a particularly strong director, but he was well connected. He knew Valerie Jarrett, a longtime friend of President Obama. As an added benefit, he was a year away from retirement age, so his tour of duty would only be twelve months.

The board announced that Massey would replace Lewis as chairman. Right after the annual meeting, the Office of the Comptroller of the Currency surprised the bank by issuing it a "memorandum of understanding," or MOU in banking terminology. The memorandum was a regulatory directive ordering the bank to consider changes in the composition of its board of directors, changes in its top management ranks, and a plan to improve its capital base, which had been severely weakened by the acquisitions of Countrywide and then Merrill Lynch.

Massey and Gifford traveled to Washington. The two board members interpreted their conversations with regulators in Washington and the memorandum of understanding from the OCC as a mandate to replace those directors who lacked financial expertise with a new crop of directors steeped in the banking industry. They also urged Lewis to replace the weakest members of his management team, which had been unprepared for and overwhelmed by the events of 2008.

With Gifford's support, Massey contacted Charles Tribett, an old friend from the executive recruitment firm Russell Reynolds, and asked him to begin a search for new board members. Over the next few months, BofA added six new directors to replace the ten directors who were encouraged to leave or stepped down of their own accord. Several of the departees, including Temple Sloan, were Carolina stalwarts who had always rallied around Lewis. In their place were directors with more experience in banking but no regional ties to the Carolinas.

On June 4, under increasing pressure from the board to identify a successor, Lewis replaced his longtime friend Amy Brinkley with Greg Curl as chief risk officer. For Brinkley, it was an unfortunate conclusion to a career which, until 2008, had been marked by one success after another.

Brinkley's departure also meant that the next CEO of Bank of America would not be a product of the old NCNB culture. At the upper-management level, she was the last culture carrier from the old days, a graduate of UNC Chapel Hill—Hugh McColl's alma mater—who started her career at NCNB in 1978, when Tom Storrs was CEO and the bank was still fighting with Wachovia for bragging rights to North Carolina.

IN THE LATE WINTER, Lewis had endured several hours of questioning, under oath, at the hands of prosecutors from the New York Attorney General's office. On June 11, he testified before the House Committee on Oversight and Government Reform about the unusual deal he had struck with Paulson and Bernanke the previous December for $20 billion. Some of the committee members, mostly Republicans, expressed sympathy with Lewis's plight and blamed Paulson and Bernanke for forcing BofA to accept the taxpayer money in return for completing a deal that Lewis wanted to break off. Others, mostly Democrats, expressed deep skepticism about Lewis's motives and insinuated that his threat to invoke the MAC clause was a ploy designed to shake down the federal government for the extra infusion of taxpayer funds. In subsequent weeks, the committee questioned Paulson and Bernanke on the same topic.

Over the summer, the board continued to press Lewis to put some kind of succession plan in place. In response, Lewis announced the hiring of Sallie Krawcheck on August 4 as head of the bank's wealth management operations, overseeing what had been the Merrill Lynch thundering herd. Krawcheck had run Smith Barney, Citigroup's investment advisor group, before being pushed out by Vikram Pandit, the CEO who was chosen to replace Chuck Prince.

Lewis and Alphin used Krawcheck's arrival as an opportunity to move other pieces on the management chessboard. Moynihan, who had been struggling in his attempt to rebuild Merrill Lynch's investment banking operations, was put in charge of retail banking, the most visible division of the company. He replaced Liam McGee, who was told he would not get an opportunity to be CEO.

To replace Moynihan as head of investment banking, Lewis promoted Tom Montag—John Thain's $40 million man—who had emerged as one of the most valuable executives at the bank through the billions of dollars in profits that his division was generating. Without the contributions of Montag's unit, BofA would have posted losses in the first two quarters of 2009.

In announcing Krawcheck's hiring and the reconfiguration of his management team, Lewis declared publicly that the race to identify his successor had formally begun. He had also created the expectation among investors that he would continue in his job as CEO for at least two more years.

On the same day that the management reorganization was announced, the SEC struck a deal with BofA calling for the bank to pay $33 million to settle allegations that it did not properly disclose the agreement to allow Merrill Lynch to pay billions in bonuses for the year.

Later that month, Lewis went to his vacation home in Aspen for a few weeks, to recover from the most trying year he had ever endured in his professional life. He stopped shaving and he brooded about what had happened to him, his bank, and his job. Lewis thrived on order and consensus, especially when he was the one giving the orders and declaring what the consensus should be. Ever since becoming CEO, he had reported to the board of directors, technically speaking. But, in fact, he had always been the master of his board. As for Gifford, he had also been supportive, especially since he had received such a generous package of perquisites upon selling Fleet to BofA, including an office and secretary, and 120 hours of flying time on the corporate jet each year. Until the 2009 shareholder meeting, when a power vacuum suddenly occurred in BofA's boardroom, Gifford had never tried to bite the hand that fed him.

But now things were different. The new chairman, Massey, often sided with Gifford, who had come to wield considerable influence over him. The new directors understood that their reason for being on the BofA board was to act responsibly and serve the best interests of shareholders, so they pushed back on many of Lewis's suggestions, forcing him into the unusual position of defending himself in front of his directors.

When Lewis returned from vacation after Labor Day, he was a changed man. The fact that he was sporting a beard for the first time in his professional life sent shockwaves through an organization where the preferred shirt color was white and men kept their hair short. It was as if he had wandered into the building clad in sandals, Bermuda shorts, and a tie-dyed T-shirt. People gossiped about the beard all day.

Shortly after 9:00 a.m., Steele Alphin came into Lewis's office.

"I don't think I want to do this anymore," Lewis said. Even Alphin, Lewis's closest confidant at the bank, who had worked with him for twenty-seven years, was stunned. Lewis tried to explain his feelings. A few hours later, the two men had lunch together in the executive dining room on the fifty-ninth floor, and later took a walk. Alphin urged his friend to think about the ramifications of what he was doing, about all the people who depended on him. That evening, Lewis's wife, Donna, reiterated the same message, and the CEO, feeling a sense of obligation to the 300,000 people who reported to him, changed his mind and decided to stay.

About two weeks later, Steele and Debbie Alphin went out to dinner with Ken and Donna Lewis in Charlotte, something the couples did on a regular basis. But this time, something about Lewis's demeanor was different. The four friends engaged in the usual small talk throughout the meal, but afterward, when they split up, Debbie Alphin turned to her husband and said, "He's going to retire, isn't he?"

"You're right," Alphin replied. "He is going to retire."

On Monday, September 28, Lewis and Alphin flew to Boston to tell Gifford and the other Fleet directors that he was planning to step down at the end of the year. Two days later, after a client meeting in New York, Lewis spoke to his entire board on a conference call from One Bryant Park to tell them of his plans.

The news shocked the bank's employees and investors, and caught the board by surprise. Several senior executives, including Montag and Krawcheck—who had been lured to the bank by the prospect of being a candidate for the top job when Lewis was scheduled to step down, either at the end of 2010 or 2011—were caught short, since neither had been with the bank long enough to be a serious candidate for the corner office.

A special search committee, headed by Massey but dominated by Fleet directors including Gifford, began the process of finding the next CEO. In a meeting the following Monday, October 5, Lewis recommended giving the job to his deputy, Greg Curl, but Massey and other directors demurred, insisting that the board conduct a wide-ranging search which would include outside candidates. All of Lewis's power, the dominance which he exerted over the board during his eight years as CEO, had evaporated. Now, he was just one of fifteen directors at the company, and tarred with the reputation of being the man who put Bank of America in hock to the U.S. taxpayer. The last thing the board would do was blindly take his advice on the matter of selecting the next CEO.

The $45 billion in TARP money given to Bank of America was a cloud that hovered over the bank. It was a huge debt that would have to be paid back, with interest, to the government, so it would be a drag on earnings at a time when BofA was struggling with the economics of a recession. The money also carried a stigma, since it lumped BofA in with Citigroup as the industry's biggest wards of the state. The healthiest banks to receive government funds the previous year, such as State Street and Goldman Sachs, had already paid their TARP money back. TARP money also put BofA at a disadvantage in terms of hiring and retaining its top people, because TARP recipients were limited in what they could pay their top executives. The financial restrictions would affect the selection of the next CEO, because any executive who had the talent and track record to take on the job would command a financial package of at least $10 million on the open market. But BofA's obligations to the federal government would not allow for such extravagance.

Lewis learned firsthand the power of the government in setting pay. Kenneth Feinberg, the special "pay czar" appointed by treasury secretary Tim Geithner to review compensation packages at TARP banks, recommended that Lewis—who had earned $1.2 million in salary for 2008 but received no bonus—get zero for 2009. Lewis fought with him for several weeks but in October, after announcing his departure, decided to give in and put the matter behind him. He wrote a check for approximately $900,000 to his own bank to cover the salary he had received through the first nine months of the year.

For most of 2009, BofA had been fighting with various regulators. The bank's lawyers tried to resist New York attorney general Andrew Cuomo's attempts to find out who was paid what at Merrill Lynch in 2008 and, when Cuomo's prosecutors tried to find out why the bank didn't inform its shareholders of the pre-arrangement on Merrill's bonuses, BofA executives invoked the attorney-client privilege, which protected sensitive conversations and documents from having to be disclosed.

In September, a federal judge rebuked the SEC for reaching a $33 million settlement with the bank over the issue of disclosure of the Merrill Lynch bonuses, because the commission didn't identify who at the bank was responsible for the lack of disclosure. In an embarrassing setback, the judge, Jed Rakoff, ordered the SEC to drop its charges if it couldn't identify an individual at fault in the matter, or go to trial to prove its case in court.

Cuomo's prosecutors issued their own threat to BofA's board in September, announcing that they were at the stage of deciding whether to bring charges against some of the bank's executives, but that they were being hindered by lack of access to important evidence protected by the attorney-client privilege. In an attempt to put all these matters behind it, the bank waived that privilege in October, allowing Cuomo's prosecutors, as well as the SEC and investigators from the House Committee on Oversight and Government Affairs, to search through a trove of fresh documents in the case, and re-interview key witnesses to ask about the advice they were given by counsel.

THE SEARCH COMMITTEE OF the board received a roster of outside candidates from Russell Reynolds, the recruiting firm selected by Massey. Of the top managers at the bank, the only two executives being given serious consideration for the top job were Curl, who was well liked by the BofA board, and Brian Moynihan, who was the favored candidate of Gifford and the Fleet directors.

On November 17, Gifford and Moynihan testified before the House Committee on Oversight and Government Affairs, along with Tom May, another Fleet director who was still on the BofA board, and Tim Mayopoulos, the general counsel who had been summarily fired a year earlier. Democrats on the committee—particularly Dennis Kucinich of Ohio—were convinced that Mayopoulos's firing was evidence of a sinister plot at the bank to deceive shareholders and government officials alike. Mayopoulos testified about his firing, and said that even a year later he had no idea why he had been let go. Moynihan testified that he didn't know why Mayopoulos was fired, either, except that the bank was going to have to lay off thousands of people as a consequence of its acquisition of Merrill Lynch. On two occasions, members of the committee asked Moynihan whether he was a candidate to be the next CEO of Bank of America, and both times Gifford interrupted to say it would be unfair to force Moynihan to discuss the matter in public.

IN EARLY DECEMBER, Bank of America announced the government would allow it to pay back the $45 billion in TARP funds, thus restoring it to the realm of healthy banks and allowing the company's board and management to operate with a free hand. For a once proud organization that had been humiliated by the events of 2009, the agreement to pay back TARP funds provided a huge morale boost. It also raised the possibility that the bank could name one of its own executives—either Moynihan or Curl—to be CEO. Both men had played large roles in convincing regulators that BofA was healthy enough to repay its obligation to the state, and the board was determined that the next CEO should be someone who worked well with regulators and enjoyed credibility in Washington, D.C.

Of the two men, Curl became the favored candidate of most of the board members, because he had been the lead negotiator in Washington on the TARP repayment. Just as important, Curl's age, sixty-one, meant that he would only be in the job for two to three years, which would allow the board to take a closer look at all the top management candidates for the job, including Montag and Krawcheck.

The board's selection committee also invited Robert Kelly, the well-regarded CEO of Bank of New York Mellon, to interview for the job. Kelly had been CFO of Wachovia, and therefore had ties to Charlotte, an important consideration for the board. But information started leaking to the media about compensation discussions between BofA and Kelly, which served to embarrass the executive and make it more difficult for him to be seen openly campaigning for the job. Kelly surmised that someone on the board did not want him to get the job.

In early December, most of the directors were leaning toward Curl. One director even sent an e-mail to a friend of Curl's, advising him of the news. But as the board's opinion solidified around Curl, there was another leak to the media, this one regarding testimony given in the Cuomo investigation. *The New York Times* reported an embarrassing inconsistency in Curl's statements to Cuomo's prosecutors. In April, during the first round of the Cuomo investigation, Curl was asked whether he ever sought legal advice as to whether Merrill's fourth-quarter losses should be disclosed to shareholders. Curl said he had done so, and mentioned a specific conference call he had with attorneys from Wachtell, Lipton. Because of the attorney-client privilege, Cuomo's prosecutors were not able to ask for any more details about that meeting. But after BofA waived its attorney-client privilege in the matter, prosecutors Ben Lawsky and David Markowitz reinterviewed Curl and asked him about the conference call. There was no documentation of the call, either with e-mails or diary entries, and none of the Wachtell lawyers involved recalled discussing the subject with Curl. Curl said he no longer had any recollection of the call.

With the Cuomo investigation still proceeding, Curl ceased being a viable candidate. At a meeting in Charlotte on December 16, most of the bank's directors, with the exception of William Boardman, who wanted an outside candidate, were ready to award the job to Moynihan. Over the course of the afternoon, Boardman consulted with other directors, and ultimately decided to make the choice of Moynihan unanimous.

At a time when the board's search committee was dominated by legacy Fleet directors from Boston, and the bank's communications apparatus was controlled by legacy Fleet executives still based in Boston, the candidacies of Kelly and Curl had been hurt by embarrassing leaks to the media. Moynihan's candidacy, by contrast, hadn't been the subject of any such leaks.

In interviews following his selection, Moynihan insisted that Charlotte would remain the headquarters for the bank, and that he would be spending a lot of time at his office in the Queen City. But it was clear that an era had come to an end. There had been a transfer of power at Bank of America, not just from one CEO to another, but from a regional clique of directors and executives committed to Charlotte and the Carolinas to a smaller, more politically nimble group committed to New England.

The next morning, after the Belk auditorium filled up with hundreds of BofA employees, Lewis took the stage to introduce Moynihan as the next CEO, and received an ovation that was long and loud.

"You're always humbling with your expressions," Lewis began. "This is not about me, this is about Brian." Lewis explained how he had met Moynihan six years earlier in New York, during the negotiations to acquire Fleet.

"I was impressed by Brian at that point," Lewis continued, before striking a lighter note. "Many of you know him because he's been in so many different jobs. And so hopefully he'll be in this job much longer than the last three or four."

The crowd laughed, as did Moynihan, who was sitting on a chair nearby as Lewis continued to ad lib.

"A CEO's legacy is the next CEO, so you know I want him to do well. If you do know him, you know he is very smart, and that he shares our values. He doesn't have a huge ego. He's not going to be some pompous CEO which you can get sometimes in banking."

BofA's directors had been criticized for the length of time it took to name a new CEO, and the relative lack of enthusiasm among top bankers for the Charlotte job.

"Another unique characteristic about him is that he wanted the job," said Lewis, to general laughter. "That may end up being in the category of 'be careful what you wish for.'" Lewis had often cited his mother in public speeches, most recently quoting her as saying he ought to pay the TARP money back. He wrapped up his introduction of Moynihan on a homey note, saying, "You're happy, I'm happy, *my mother's* happy," and giving the microphone to his successor.

And then, before Moynihan could speak, Lewis returned to the center of the stage and said one more thing into the microphone: "One final point. And thank God he's one of us!"

Unlike his last big appearance in the auditorium, during the annual meeting when he was on the defensive, fighting for his job, on this day he was lighter. Lewis looked exhausted, drained from the experience of the previous fifteen months, but relieved and even a little sad that it was all over.

Lewis came into the office for another week, working almost until Christmas. Befitting the events of the previous year, he did not want any kind of farewell party or celebration to mark his departure. Instead, after his last day, he and Alphin dropped by Sonoma for one last drink on the way home. Given the cold weather, Alphin ordered a Buffalo Trace bourbon with a splash of water. Lewis, as always, had a Johnnie Walker Black. The two men downed their spirits slowly, spoke sparingly, and went their separate ways, an atomic unit no more.

. . .

ON FEBRUARY 4, 2010, New York attorney general Andrew Cuomo filed civil fraud charges against Lewis and Joe Price, accusing the men of deceiving their own shareholders by not disclosing the extent of the losses at Merrill Lynch prior to the shareholder vote, and of turning around and using the threat of a MAC clause to get the federal government to pump an additional $20 billion into BofA in order to complete the deal.

Cuomo built his case around the firing of Tim Mayopoulos, claiming in the complaint that accompanied the charges that Price and Lewis hid the extent of Merrill's losses from the general counsel. Once Mayopoulos learned of the magnitude of Merrill's losses, in the December 9 board meeting attended by Thain in Charlotte, he tried to meet with Price to learn more. The following day, Cuomo said, Mayopoulos was fired because "he was the man who knew too much." A few days prior to the December 5 shareholder vote on whether BofA should acquire Merrill Lynch, Price and Curl had asked Mayopoulos whether Merrill's growing losses would give BofA justification for invoking the MAC clause. Mayopoulos had said no. Two weeks later, his successor, Brian Moynihan, would say yes, allowing BofA to invoke the MAC clause, which was the result that Lewis and his top management wanted. Attorneys for Lewis and Price proclaimed their innocence and vowed to fight the charges in court.

On February 8, just days after Lewis was charged with fraud and a little over a year after he'd been unceremoniously fired, John Thain returned to the workforce as chief executive of CIT, a company which made loans to small businesses, but which had nearly crashed during the financial crisis of 2008. Thain, whose annual salary was pegged at almost $6 million, mostly in restricted stock, would be responsible for cleaning up some of the problems encountered by Jeffrey Peek, the former CEO. Peek had come to CIT in 2003, after losing out to Stan O'Neal in the race to succeed David Komansky as CEO of Merrill Lynch.

AFTER LEAVING BANK OF AMERICA in late December, Lewis seemed to disappear from Charlotte for a while, but his portrait, installed in the gallery outside the sixtieth-floor boardroom in 2009, assures his continued presence.

The painting of Lewis is unusually colorful, given the subject's blunt, monochromatic personality, and shows him reclining, uneasily, on the corner of a sofa. The expression on Lewis's face, one of slight puzzlement, shows that the artist captured an essential aspect of the man, his profound discomfort with outside scrutiny and his lack of interest in managing his own image.

Next to Lewis's portrait is the painting of McColl, the man who spent almost as much time constructing his own legend as he did building his bank. McColl had served a stint in the Marine Corps as a first lieutenant before joining American Commercial Bank in 1959. But his exploits and conquests in the banking industry allowed him to don the trappings of a general in the world of finance. His portrait accurately reflects this enlarged status. Unlike Lewis, who sat uncomfortably while the artist captured him, McColl dominated his portraitist, projecting the mien of authority he wanted to see reflected on canvas.

Next to McColl's portrait, on the other side of the passageway that leads to the elevator bank, is a painting of Tom Storrs. Colorful in a style similar to Lewis's portrait, the painting of Storrs shows a benign figure reclining easily in a chair, wearing his glasses, instead of holding them, as McColl and Lewis are. The disarming smile suggests a man comfortable as he is, and betrays no hint of the keen intelligence that lay within.

Finally, beside Storrs is the portrait of the founder of NCNB, Addison Hardcastle Reese, seated at an angle almost perpendicular to the artist, casting a penetrating stare directly at those who look upon him. The backdrop behind Reese, which dominates the painting, is completely black, leaving the impression of a deep and impenetrable void, out of which Reese created something of enduring value.

Back in 1755, to get to the area now known as Charlotte, the first known European settlers traveled down the Great Wagon Road that ran southeast from Pennsylvania and parallel to the Appalachians. What is now Charlotte's uptown business district is framed on a grid built around the intersection between that original wagon road, now known as Tryon

Street, and a crosspath, now known as Trade Street. Just as the original streets were formed on a bias away from the north-south meridian, modern-day Charlotte is configured along similar lines. The Bank of America tower, situated at the heart of old Charlotte, at the corner of Tryon and Trade, conforms to this bias. And so the portraits of the only four men to have run what was the North Carolina National Bank, which became NationsBank, which became Bank of America and which now owns Merrill Lynch, hang on a wall high up above the old city, forever facing northeast, in the direction of New York and Boston.

EPILOGUE

THE DECLINE AND FALL of Merrill Lynch is a sad tale, even within the survival-of-the-fittest ethos of Wall Street and the larger context of the free enterprise system, where no company is immune from the pressures of competition.

No one died as a result of the sale of Merrill Lynch to Bank of America. Unlike the bankruptcy of Lehman Brothers, where shareholders and thousands of employees saw their holdings wiped out, Merrill Lynch shareholders ended up with something, not nothing.

And yet, the failure of Merrill Lynch—the collapse of a mighty financial institution that embodied the concept that all investors could partake in the magic of the capital markets—is different from what happened at Lehman, as well as Bear Stearns, the other Wall Street banks that succumbed to the financial crisis of 2008.

The modern incarnation of Merrill Lynch dates from 1940—in the aftermath of the stock market crash of 1929 and the Great Depression—and was predicated on the notion that average Americans could realize handsome returns in the stock market, as long as a trustworthy advisor helped show them the way. In order to instill confidence in the firm's earliest customers, Charlie Merrill abolished the commission system, by which salesmen were rewarded on the volume of products they could push on their investors. By paying his salesmen straight salaries, Merrill proved to his earliest customers that his firm was there to serve as a guide to prudent investing. (For competitive reasons, Merrill's successors eventually put the sales force back on commission, but by then, the firm had already established itself as the leader in the field.)

With the benefit of hindsight, it's easy to see the strategic brilliance of Charlie Merrill's vision: He built a company that distributed stocks to average U.S. investors at the cusp of the second half of the twentieth century, an era of unparalleled growth in the world's largest economy.

But innovative businesses can't maintain their dominance forever. Their very success breeds competition and by the 1970s, Merrill Lynch needed to expand into other areas of the capital markets—such as investment banking—in order to keep growing. Not only did the firm's management feel the need to expand, but after the firm went public, Merrill's own investors demanded ever higher returns from the company, more than could be generated simply through its army of financial advisors.

Thus, by July 2001, when Stan O'Neal was designated by the board of Merrill Lynch as heir apparent to the sitting chief executive, David Komansky, the firm was struggling with overexpansion into areas far afield from its bread-and-butter financial advisory business. The dot-com bubble had just burst, puncturing the outsized profits Merrill was earning as an investment bank that arranged initial public offerings for technology firms, and cutting into the revenues that its thundering herd of financial advisors was generating through the distribution of those stocks.

The events of September 11, 2001, only exacerbated the economic difficulties facing Merrill Lynch, Wall Street, and corporate America.

Following the terrorist attacks, and a full year before he was officially named CEO, O'Neal took charge of the company. Critics including this author have noted that he used the massive downsizing initiated after September 11 as cover for the elimination of any executives with the seniority and wisdom to question his judgment. But to some degree, such management purges are a common practice in the business world. There is a natural tendency among chief executives to surround themselves with like-minded people, subordinates who share their vision.

There is also a significant body of evidence to support the notion that under Stan O'Neal, Merrill Lynch became more of a meritocracy than it had been at any time since the Don Regan era. For that, O'Neal deserves some credit.

In order to tell the story of how Merrill Lynch ultimately ran aground, I have spent the past two years trying to learn, in as much detail as possible, how a firm that not long ago was perceived as invincible suddenly found itself at the mercy of a severe economic downturn. Merrill Lynch had always survived downturns, protected from the convulsions of the capital markets by its reliance on the steady, if modest, returns of its financial advisory business.

The failure of Merrill Lynch resulted, in part, from the same drive toward meritocracy that O'Neal used to improve the firm's profits from 2003 through the first half of 2007. O'Neal correctly perceived the flaws of the old "Mother Merrill" culture, a sales culture which glossed over the weaknesses of many of its own people in the spirit of "taking care of our own." That culture had to change, or at least be modified, in order for the firm to remain competitive on Wall Street.

What O'Neal did not realize was the danger of eviscerating one corporate culture without establishing another one in its place. Until he came to power, the financial advisory business had always been the core of Merrill Lynch. Under O'Neal, the emphasis shifted to more profitable activities in the capital markets. Like every other Wall Street bank, Merrill Lynch under Stan O'Neal chased profits wherever they were to be found from 2004 to 2007. And like every other Wall Street bank—including Bear Stearns and Lehman Brothers—Merrill Lynch rode the boom in financial services of those years to unprecedented profits.

By 2006, Merrill's financial advisory business had become a stepchild while the area which generated the biggest revenues—sales and trading—took center stage. It was at this point that the fateful decision to put Osman Semerci in charge of Merrill's fixed income, commodities, and currencies business was made.

Success, as the saying goes, has a thousand fathers, while failure is an orphan. In that spirit, neither O'Neal nor his top lieutenant, Ahmass Fakahany, is eager to take credit for Semerci's promotion. Semerci was promoted to his job by Dow Kim, the executive in charge of all sales and trading activities at Merrill Lynch. But it is beyond dispute that Kim promoted Semerci only after his first choice for the job—Jeff Kronthal—was overruled and after his second choice—Jack DiMaio—was vetoed by Fakahany and O'Neal. Short of quitting the firm, it would have taken an act of signal defiance on Dow Kim's part to ignore his bosses' wishes and pass over Semerci for the promotion.

Semerci makes a convenient scapegoat for the fall of Merrill Lynch. The record of his tenure as head of FICC is clear: According to a presentation made to Merrill's board of directors following his firing, on Semerci's watch, the FICC department put more than $30 billion worth of CDOs on Merrill's balance sheet.

And yet, efforts to portray Semerci as some kind of rogue trader don't ring true. He was put in charge of the firm's FICC division because of his success as a salesman in London and Tokyo. Given his lack of experience in risk management, and the strong support he enjoyed in the executive suite, it stands to reason that Semerci felt his mandate was to grow revenues as quickly as possible.

In fact, not only was Semerci *not* a rogue trader, he was far closer to being the model employee of the recent boom era. He was a product of Wall Street's bonus culture, which rewards employees according to how much revenue they produce for their firm. He rose quickly at Merrill Lynch because he demonstrated an uncanny ability to sell complex financial products to institutional investors and banks around the world. Up until his promotion, Semerci had been rewarded for his ability to produce, to deliver results in the near term, without regard for the long-term consequences of his actions. O'Neal was so smitten with the hard-charging young salesman that he advertised him to the board as someone with the potential to succeed him as CEO.

To the extent that Semerci was able to run the FICC department without the normal oversight he should have had, the fault, ultimately, lies with O'Neal. Because Semerci was perceived as being O'Neal's guy, his decisions and trading activities did not receive the pushback or scrutiny they should have. This is where O'Neal's battle to rid the firm of its vestigial culture ultimately damaged the entire enterprise. The collegiality of the old Mother Merrill culture would never have allowed Semerci to run the FICC department in such an unfettered fashion. Once the old culture disappeared, it was, by default, replaced with a new culture, the dysfunctional, dog-eat-dog value system favored by O'Neal. The perception that Semerci had the CEO's full support gave the young salesman the license to act as he saw fit.

On multiple occasions, Stan O'Neal has accepted general responsibility for what happened at Merrill Lynch, but the former CEO's statements of contrition only address the issues from an altitude of 30,000 feet. They are based on the premise that as chief executive, O'Neal was responsible for anything that happened at Merrill Lynch. Therefore, the company's collapse was his fault. While the logic behind this position is unassailable, it is also unsatisfying, since it seems to absolve any individuals at Merrill Lynch—from traders in the fixed-income division to members of the company's board of directors—of responsibility.

In retrospect, it is difficult to believe that Merrill's board of directors never ordered an investigation into what happened at the company. Up through the second quarter of 2007, Merrill's performance was spectacular, and the profits generated by the fixed-income department—led by Semerci, who was presented to the board as a rising star—were nothing short of breathtaking. Then, in a span of three months, Merrill's miraculous profits evaporated, the rising star was quietly dismissed, and the CEO claimed the sky was falling and Merrill Lynch had to be sold to Wachovia immediately.

It is understandable that the board would lose confidence in O'Neal and dismiss him. It is incomprehensible that the directors would accept the explanation put forth by O'Neal and his management team about what happened, and then turn the fate of the firm over to Alberto Cribiore, a director who had sought employment at Merrill. The situation cried out for a full independent investigation on behalf of shareholders.

COULD JOHN THAIN HAVE saved Merrill Lynch? As with most hypothetical questions, the answer to this will never be certain. Thain's supporters uniformly feel that Merrill Lynch, by the time he arrived in the fourth quarter of 2007, was a lost cause and that any attempt at financial triage was doomed to failure. This view provides convenient sanctuary to those who want to avert their eyes from their former leader's missteps.

In retrospect, Thain's greatest shortcoming during his year at Merrill Lynch was his belief, grounded in decades of experience on Wall Street, that the economic downturn of 2007 would be short-lived. This was a reasonable position, based on the way markets had rebounded from previous downturns. This outlook also appealed to the directors of Merrill Lynch, who, after more than four years of continuous growth, were suddenly being told by O'Neal that the sky was falling and the firm needed to be sold.

With the benefit of hindsight, Thain should have raised twice the amount of capital he brought in to Merrill Lynch in his first six weeks on the job. Understandably, he wanted to keep the dilution of existing shareholders to an absolute minimum, but Thain's optimism about how much capital Merrill Lynch needed cost him.

There should be no confusion as to whether Thain bears any responsibility for the fall of Merrill Lynch. He does not. He was unable to repair the damage wrought under O'Neal, but he did not inflict any of that damage himself.

AS FOR KEN LEWIS, his legacy as Bank of America CEO will be defined by whether the acquisition of Merrill Lynch benefits shareholders in the long term. In the near term, the acquisition of Merrill Lynch seems to have paid off. During 2009, when years of poor credit oversight and mediocre management at BofA resulted in an ocean of red ink related to bad loans, Merrill's performance in the capital markets carried the bank to profitability.

Yet the acquisition of Merrill Lynch came at a steep price to BofA shareholders. In early September 2008, BofA's share price was $34 and the number of outstanding shares was 4.4 billion. BofA's market capitalization was almost $150 billion. As of this writing, BofA's share price is just under $14 and the number of shares outstanding is 10 billion. Its market capitalization is $140 billion, less than what it was two years earlier. Because of the Merrill Lynch deal, and the subsequent capital raises necessitated by Bank of America's weakened capital position, the value of the bank's shares has been diluted: A stake in the bank in September 2008 is worth less than half of what it used to be in terms of share price, and it accounts for a much smaller slice of the entire enterprise. On top of that dilution, the bank's annual dividend to shareholders, once generous, is now a pittance.

Shareholders clearly suffered. And by the last days of December 2008, as Lewis searched for a way to abort the Merrill Lynch deal, he had exposed Bank of America to dangers that were unthinkable just a few months earlier. In less than two years, Lewis had taken one of the strongest banks ever created, an institution that was impregnable in terms of its size, scope, and capital position, and turned it into a ward of the state.

Bank of America's dependence on the federal government in 2009 led to another change at the bank, one which has altered its character permanently: BofA's board of directors is no longer closely tethered to the business communities of North and South Carolina. This shift in governance, prompted by regulators, was a sign of how much Bank of America had outgrown its roots as the old North Carolina National Bank. The expansion of BofA's board is a positive step from a corporate governance point of view, since it increases the board's independence from the bank's top management.

But the change in the bank's character marks a peculiar kind of loss. In an era of huge, multinational corporate behemoths that employ hundreds of thousands of people, the idea that Bank of America—one of those behemoths—could still be run by the leading citizens of Charlotte and environs carried a sentimental appeal. Beyond the bank's deep commitment to its North Carolina roots, its executives' simplistic view that

Wall Street represented the Sodom and Gomorrah of finance also made sense. After all, Bear Stearns, Lehman Brothers, and Merrill Lynch ran into trouble by engaging in reckless financing activities that had no ostensible purpose other than to generate fees that increased their bonus pools.

BofA has now lost the remaining vestiges of provincial innocence that protected it from the worst excesses of Wall Street. More than at any time in its fifty-year history, the institution once known as NCNB is now just like many other big banks.

IN THE WAKE OF the 2008 financial crisis, investors and the general public have expressed outrage at the government's bailout of the banking system and the enormous pay packages doled out on Wall Street. Many believe that the failures of the biggest investment banks could only have been the result of some kind of criminal activity or fraud.

According to this view, top executives at Bear, Lehman, and Merrill should be held accountable for the failures that occurred on their watch. But the desire for retribution against the leaders of these firms should be weighed against the fact that there is no law against making bad business decisions. Following the collapse of Enron almost a decade ago, the Justice Deparment swept into Houston and put a number of executives on trial. In the fevered aftermath of Enron's collapse, prosecutors won a string of convictions. But one by one, starting with the conviction of Arthur Andersen, the auditing firm, many of these convictions were overturned on appeal, usually because the district court was too liberal in what it determined to be criminal conduct.

The same dynamic holds for the financial crisis of 2008. Just because the top managers at failed investment banks took foolish risks and made profoundly bad business decisions does not mean they broke any laws.

After Merrill's surprise announcement of a $4.9 billion write-down in its fixed-income division in October 2007, the Securities and Exchange Commission opened an investigation into the matter, as is routine whenever a public company surprises its investors with a sudden, unforeseen loss. SEC attorneys interviewed a number of Merrill Lynch employees who worked in fixed income, finance, and risk during the months leading up to the disclosure and combed through thousands of documents but found no immediate cause for action.

Most of the laws regarding adequate disclosure of earnings were codified in the Securities and Exchange Acts of 1933 and 1934. The laws are civil, meaning that people who break them pay fines, but don't have to go to jail. And in most cases, acts that constitute securities fraud have a five-year statute of limitations, after which no charges can be filed.

As for the actions of those who brought about the demise of Merrill Lynch, there is no statute of limitations, at least in the court of public opinion. The sinking of this great American institution, one that restored the nation's faith in the capital markets following the Great Depression, demands notoriety.

To the individuals responsible for this travesty, the infamy of their deeds will attach forever.

NOTES

THE RAW MATERIAL FOR this book grew out of a variety of sources. The vast majority of the information on which I based this story came from interviews. In all, I interviewed more than 120 people, a process which consumed somewhere between 250 and 300 hours. Of those 120-plus interviewees, there were 15 individuals who gave me, in aggregate, some 150 hours of their time.

In addition to these interviews, I had access to a variety of e-mails, confidential workpapers, and transcripts from internal presentations at Merrill Lynch and Bank of America, as well as court documents filed by New York attorney general Andrew Cuomo, the Securities and Exchange Commission, and plaintiffs lawyers. A yearlong investigation by the House Committee on Oversight and Government Reform also yielded a trove of useful documents from federal regulators, including minutes of board meetings, and pertinent testimony.

Finally, I tapped in to an ocean of basic factual information, available through corporate websites and standard news accounts of events that took place years ago. In those cases where I relied on an important piece of information uncovered and published in a book, a news story, or a magazine profile, as opposed to a widely circulated fact or announcement, I am providing a citation of the source material below. In this effort, I have tried to be complete, but am certain that I must have made some mistakes of omission.

Historical stock prices throughout are from Bloomberg.

PROLOGUE

1 **Waccabuc:** golf scores from Metropolitan Golf Association website.
2 **Roanoke, grew up in Wedowee:** "Shaking Up Merrill," by Emily Thornton, with Anne Tergesen and David Welch, *BusinessWeek,* Nov. 12, 2001.
2 **"The modest sums of the thrifty":** from an unpublished history of Merrill Lynch, by William Ecenbarger, obtained by the author.
3 **"bullish on America":** Ibid.
3 **"In 2001":** "Merrill Picks Heir Apparent to Top Job," by Joseph Kahn, *The New York Times,* July 25, 2001; "Merrill Lynch Names O'Neal President," by Charles Gasparino, *The Wall Street Journal,* July 25, 2001.
3 **"O'Neal was about to meet with Ken Lewis":** *Too Big to Fail,* by Andrew Ross Sorkin, Viking, 2009, p. 314.
6 **played golf almost every day:** Metropolitan Golf Association website.
7 **"Through a series of mergers":** *The Story of NationsBank,* by Howard E. Covington, Jr., and Marion A. Ellis.
9 **"Curl and Lewis . . . exchanged glances as the moments ticked by":** *Too Big to Fail,* p. 315.

CHAPTER 1. THE YOUNG TURK

11 **"My name's Tom Spinelli":** transcript of Stan O'Neal's presentation at Merrill Lynch annual meeting in Princeton, New Jersey, April 27, 2007.
16 **caused investors such as Merrill Lynch to seize some of the CDOs as collateral:** *The Sellout,* by Charles Gasparino, Harper Business, 2009, p. 265.
37 **Stan O'Neal was one of the best paid executives on Wall Street:** O'Neal's compensation figures taken from documents prepared on behalf of Rep. Henry Waxman, then chairman of the House Committee on Oversight and Government Reform, for a hearing on executive compensation, March 7, 2008.
38 **O'Neal's wife, Nancy Garvey, got her own car and driver:** Merrill Lynch proxy statements filed with the SEC.

CHAPTER 2. A QUESTION OF CHARACTER

40 **After being the top deal guy in the 1980s:** "The Man Who Cost Merrill Shareholders $50 Billion," by William D. Cohan, *Fortune,* April 15, 2010.
40 **pitching the young Merrill Lynch executive on deals:** "Deals & Dealmakers: How Merrill CEO Warms to Risk—Chief O'Neal Gives Green Light to Private Equity Deals, an Area Wall Street Firm Exited in the 1990s," by Randall Smith, *The Wall Street Journal,* Dec. 8, 2005.
40 **he raised $650 million to start his own fund:** "The Man Who Cost Merrill Shareholders $50 Billion," by William D. Cohan, *Fortune,* April 15, 2010.
41 **Cribiore sent him an expensive case of French white wine:** Ibid.

41 **Finally, Cribiore approached O'Neal:** Ibid.
42 **Cribiore was almost nonchalant in his response:** Ibid., and author interviews. Cribiore maintains that the Bank of America discussion with O'Neal never took place.
46 **"It was a wild ride":** Gasparino, *The Sellout,* p. 302.
46 **in April 2008, Semerci was hired by Duet:** "Semerci, Former Merrill Executive, to Run Duet Group," by Yalman Onaran, Bloomberg News, April 7, 2008.

CHAPTER 3. BEAT THE WACHOVIA

47 **Torrence Hemby, the bank's president, had been looking for a leader:** *The Story of NationsBank: Changing the Face of American Banking,* by Harold E. Covington, Jr., and Marion A. Ellis, University of North Carolina Press, 1993, p. 27.
47 Subsequent pages, describing the growth of NCNC, are also based on *The Story of NationsBank.*
49 **Ken Lewis was born in Meridian, Mississippi:** Interview with Jeff Richardson, Aug. 29, 1996; transcript located in the Southern Historical Collection's NationsBank archives, Wilson Library, University of North Carolina, Chapel Hill.
50 **His starting salary was $8,000:** "Ken Lewis: The Pure Prototype of the NCNB Cause," by John Taylor, *Florida Trend,* Feb. 1, 1987.
50 **Lewis's father, Vernon, had grown up dirt poor:** Jeff Richardson interview, Wilson Library.
51 **"In 1989, McColl pulled off one of the signal achievements":** *The Story of NationsBank,* pp. 212–42.
53 **Lewis overheard a remark from a neighboring table about NCNB:** Jeff Richardson interview, Wilson Library.
54 **McColl had once described Kemp as the better leader and Lewis as the better manager:** Ibid.

CHAPTER 4. BETRAYAL

64 **"Barry, I don't need your advice":** "Bull by the Horns: As Merrill Digs Out, No. 2 O'Neal Moves Fast to Reshape Firm," by Charles Gasparino, *The Wall Street Journal,* Nov. 2, 2001.
78 **O'Neal was grateful for the dinner invitation and met with Fink at Sistina:** Gasparino, *The Sellout,* p. 312.
78 **O'Neal checked his messages and saw one from a reporter at *New York Times*:** Ibid.
81 **The most successful CEO of Merrill Lynch in the modern era:** From the unpublished history, by Ecenbarger; also, *Still Bullish on America,* William A. Schreyer, self-published.
85 **O'Neal fired some 22,000 people in the next year . . . :** "Putting the Muscle

Back in the Bull: Stan O'Neal May Be the Toughest—Some Say Most Ruthless—CEO in America," by David Rynecki, *Fortune,* April 5, 2004; also, "Have Merrill Lynch's Bulls Been Led Out to Pasture?" by Landon Thomas, Jr., *The New York Times,* Jan. 5, 2003.

CHAPTER 5. THE LISTING SHIP

90 **Fleming and Fink had a strong relationship:** "Merrill Lynch's Keystone—With BlackRock Pact, Fleming Seals His Deal-Making Status," by Randall Smith, *The Wall Street Journal,* February 17, 2006.

92 **Merrill Lynch had been hiding losses from its subprime mortgage–related assets:** "Deals with Hedge Funds May Be Helping Merrill Delay Mortgage Losses," by Susan Pulliam, *The Wall Street Journal,* Nov. 2, 2007.

92 **O'Neal cut off Dan Bayly:** "Deals and Consequences," by Landon Thomas, Jr., *The New York Times,* Nov. 20, 2005.

110 **Fleming insisted that Cribiore call Fink:** Gasparino, *The Sellout,* p. 341.

113 **"Charlie Merrill would turn over in his grave":** "Merrill Lynch Hires NYSE Chief as CEO," by the author, *USA Today,* Nov. 14, 2007.

114 **"He is a seasoned and decisive leader":** Reuters, "Fleming Expresses Confidence in Merrill's Future," by Tim McLaughlin, Nov. 26, 2007.

CHAPTER 6. THE ADVENTURES OF SUPER-THAIN

116 **He was a star on his high school wrestling team . . .** (and other details from Thain's background in Illinois): "The Adventures of Super-Thain," by Justin Schack, *Institutional Investor,* June 14, 2006.

117 **That summer, he shipped off to Cincinnati:** Ibid.

123 **Thain's move to the Exchange:** "NYSE's Steady Pilot," by Joe Weber, *BusinessWeek,* Feb. 28, 2006.

125 **When Thain called his first management committee meeting to order** (and other details about Thain's arrival at the Exchange): "The Exchange Faces Change," by Julie Creswell, *Fortune,* Aug. 9, 2004.

129 **Thain fires the barber at the NYSE:** "The Taming of Merrill Lynch," by Gary Weiss, *Portfolio,* April 14, 2008.

134 **Then there was the special elevator:** Sorkin, *Too Big to Fail,* p. 139.

137 **Details about Thain's office and the bill for individual items:** "John Thain's $87,000 Rug," by Charlie Gasparino, the *Daily Beast*/CNBC, Jan. 22, 2009.

139 **John Thain reached out to Stan O'Neal:** Sorkin, *Too Big to Fail,* pp. 141–42.

CHAPTER 7. THE SMARTEST GUY IN THE ROOM

148 **Thain arrived the evening before his speech:** "The Taming of Merrill Lynch," by Gary Weiss, *Portfolio.*

154 **"When you're the smartest guy in the room":** "Merrill's Repairman," by Lisa Kassenaar and Yalman Onaran, *Bloomberg Markets,* February 2008.

154 **In an interview with a French newspaper:** *Le Figaro,* March 8, 2008.

154 **That same month, he told a Spanish newspaper:** *El Pais,* March 16, 2008.

157 **"He is a very popular guy":** "Merrill's Risk Manager—New Chief John Thain on What Led to the Losses and Why He's Hiring Goldman Sachs Executives," by Susanne Craig and Randall Smith, *The Wall Street Journal,* Jan. 18, 2008.

CHAPTER 8. PROFIT INTO LOSS

163 **Alan Schwartz, Bear's newly installed CEO, went on TV:** Interview with David Faber, CNBC, March 12, 2008.

166 **In early April, Thain traveled to Japan:** *Nikkei Report,* April 3, 2008.

166 **Within hours, CNBC reported Chai's quote on its website:** "Merrill May Need to Raise More Capital," by Charles Gasparino, cnbc.com, April 16, 2008.

171 **Kraus . . . would also receive a salary of $600,000 . . . :** "Merrill's $10 Million Men," by Susanne Craig, *The Wall Street Journal,* March 4, 2009.

174 **On May 21, an investor named David Einhorn gave a speech:** Sorkin, *Too Big to Fail,* pp. 106–108.

177 **"And if we were to raise more capital . . .":** Ibid., p. 136; Fair Disclosure Wire, June 11, 2008.

178 **To that end, Thain met the mayor for breakfast:** Sorkin, *Too Big to Fail,* pp. 147–48.

CHAPTER 9. TERMINATED WITH PREJUDICE

180 **At the time of that acquisition:** "Bank of America Reaffirms Promises, CEO Lewis Meets State, City Officials, Offers Few Specifics," by Sasha Talcott, *Boston Globe,* Sept. 1, 2004.

183 **In January 2008, following the strategic review:** "Bank of America Cuts 25% of Its Analysts, People Say," by Jeff Kearns and Eric Martin, Bloomberg News, Jan. 24, 2008.

184 **In spite of his position at the top of the nation's largest bank:** "Crisis Changes Rules of Game for Prime Brokers," by Renee Schultes, *Financial News,* April 7, 2008.

CHAPTER 10. FIRESALE

197 **Michael Bloomberg started his career as a trader:** *Bloomberg by Bloomberg,* by Michael Bloomberg, John Wiley & Sons, 1997, p. 32.

CHAPTER 11. THE CHAIRMEN'S GALLERY

207 **This most unusual character:** unpublished manuscript by Bill Ecenbarger.

207 **He helped bring Kroger, Kresge, and First National public:** *For the Record, From Wall Street to Washington,* by Donald T. Regan, Harcourt, 1988, p. 130.

208 **He was rewarded for his service in 1958:** unpublished history by Bill Ecenbarger.

211 **A genial Pennsylvania native, Schreyer grew up:** *Still Bullish on America,* by William A. Schreyer.

211 **Never again would the firm aspire to be the market leader:** Ibid.

214 **In the fall of 1998, after the meltdown at Long Term Capital:** "The Merrill Steamroller Encounters Potholes," by Joseph Kahn, *The New York Times,* March 20, 1999.

214 **In early 1999, Komansky started talking:** "Merrill Plays Down Speculation of Step Toward Chase," by Charles Gasparino, *The Wall Street Journal,* March 22, 1999.

231 **Fleming had been quoted in a news story:** "No Thain, No Gain," by Daniel Fisher, *Forbes,* March 13, 2008.

CHAPTER 12. A CALL TO ARMS

241 **Paulson was late arriving . . . from the airport:** *On the Brink: Inside the Race to Stop the Collapse of the Global Financial System,* by Henry M. Paulson, Jr., Business Plus, Hachette Book Group, 2010, p. 189.

242 **Geithner opened the meeting:** Ibid., p. 191.

243 **After working in the Pentagon in the early 1970s:** Ibid., p. 27.

243 **Exactly ten years earlier, in September 1998:** *The Partnership: The Making of Goldman Sachs,* by Charles D. Ellis, Penguin, 2008, 2009, p. 597.

244 **But Corzine and Paulson did not get along:** Ibid., p. 609.

245 **Thornton, a colorful investment banker:** Ibid., pp. 530–32.

246 **The postponement of Goldman's IPO:** Ibid., p. 606.

246 **The men were so close that in his will:** Ibid., p. 614.

246 **Paulson declared that Lehman was in deep trouble:** *On the Brink,* p. 192.

247 **Thain's driver took him to a restaurant:** *Too Big to Fail,* pp. 305–306.

CHAPTER 13. THE LONGEST DAY

250 **Geithner reiterated his stance:** *Too Big to Fail,* p. 311.

251 **Before hanging up, Herlihy:** Ibid., p. 314.

252 **Sometime after 10:30, the group comprised:** Ibid., p. 321.

253 **"We have to figure out how to organize ourselves":** *On the Brink,* pp. 197–98.

263 **The treasury secretary warned his former subordinate:** Ibid., pp. 203–204.

265 **After brief opening remarks from Thain:** *Too Big to Fail,* p. 331.
270 **Fleming said he was going to ask for a "three-handle,":** Ibid., p. 339.

CHAPTER 14. SUNDAY BLOODY SUNDAY

284 **In an emergency situation such as the one:** *On the Brink,* p. 207.
287 **"Have you done what I recommended and found a buyer?":** Ibid., p. 211.

CHAPTER 15. THE CHARLOTTE MAFIA

326 **It was Ken Lewis who finally carried the day:** *McColl, the Man with America's Money,* by Ross Yockey, Longstreet, 1999, p. 527.
327 **Prior to McColl's negotiations with Coulter:** Ibid., pp. 548–49.
329 **After earnings were reported:** "Hootie's Blow: Ousting of Coulter Isn't the Only Fracture at the new Bank of America," by Rick Brooks, Greg Jaffe, and Martha Brannigan, *The Wall Street Journal,* Oct. 23, 1998.
330 **The enormous payout to Coulter vilified him:** "BofA Chief Is Shown the Door," by Arthur M. Louis, *San Francisco Chronicle,* Oct. 21, 1998.

CHAPTER 16. PROJECT PANTHER

345 **When Paulson and Bernanke opened the matter up for discussion:** *On the Brink,* pp. 364–65.
346 **Paulson called Thain and chided him for the politically insensitive remark:** Ibid., p. 371.

CHAPTER 17. MOUNTING LOSSES

361 Details concerning the meetings involving lawyers for Bank of America and Wachtell, as well as internal discussions at BofA, come from court documents filed by the New York Attorney General's office and the Securities and Exchange Commission, as well as documents made public by the House Committee on Oversight and Government Reform.

CHAPTER 18. WELCOME TO THE ASYLUM

370 Details concerning internal BofA discussions about Merrill's losses come from court documents filed by the New York Attorney General's office and the Securities and Exchange Commission, as well as documents made public by the House Committee on Oversight and Government Reform.
378 ***The Wall Street Journal* had published its story:** "Thain Spars with Board Over Bonus," by Susanne Craig, *The Wall Street Journal,* Dec. 8, 2008.

CHAPTER 19. AN OFFER THEY COULDN'T REFUSE

398 **Spooked by the prospect of recording the first quarterly loss:** "Bank of America Said to Fire Executives Before Merrill Closing," by David Mildenberg, Bloomberg News, Dec. 15, 2008.

399 **On the afternoon of Wednesday, December 17:** *On the Brink,* pp. 425–27.

400 **On Sunday, December 21, Lewis called Paulson:** Ibid.

CHAPTER 20. ONE TEAM, SHARED VALUES, SHARED FUTURE

416 **But on January 15, word started leaking out:** "Bank of America to Get Billions in U.S. Aid; Sides Finalizing Terms for Fresh Bailout Cash," by Dan Fitzpatrick, Damian Paletta, and Susanne Craig, *The Wall Street Journal,* Jan. 15, 2009.

420 **On this morning, he got no further than the *Financial Times*:** "Merrill Delivered Bonuses Before BofA Deal," by the author and Julie MacIntosh, *Financial Times,* Jan. 22, 2009.

CHAPTER 21. THE BOSTON MAFIA

429 **not only had Lewis been consulting with the bank's largest investors:** "BofA Faces Pressure to Split Top Roles," by Dan Fitzpatrick and Joann S. Lublin, *The Wall Street Journal,* April 17, 2009.

436 **When Lewis returned from vacation after Labor Day:** "In U.S. Regulators, Lewis Met His Match," by Carrick Mollenkamp and Dan Fitzpatrick, *The Wall Street Journal,* Nov. 10, 2009.

440 **But information started leaking to the media:** "Bank of America Can't Sign New CEO," by Dan Fitzpatrick and Joanne S. Lublin, *The Wall Street Journal,* Dec. 16, 2009.

440 ***The New York Times* reported an embarrassing inconsistency:** "Bank of America Executive Under Scrutiny," by Louise Story, *The New York Times,* Dec. 7, 2009.

441 **At a meeting in Charlotte on December 16:** "How BofA CEO Survived Board Split," by Dan Fitzpatrick, *The Wall Street Journal,* July 6, 2010.

441 **Moynihan insisted that Charlotte would remain the headquarters:** "City Leaders Cheer Welcome News," by Stella M. Hopkins, *Charlotte Observer,* Dec. 17, 2009.

ACKNOWLEDGMENTS

THIS BOOK COULD NOT have been written without support from the *Financial Times*. The newspaper provided me with an incomparable platform and calling card. In November 2008, an editor at the *FT*'s Weekend Magazine asked me and one of my colleagues, Henny Sender, to write a feature-length piece on John Thain, the Merrill Lynch CEO. At the time, the theme of the article was to highlight Thain's perspicacity and show how, compared to other Wall Street CEOs, he seemed to have made all the right moves during the financial crisis. As events unfolded, the story went in a different direction. "The Shaming of John Thain" was published in the *FT*'s Weekend Magazine on March 14, 2009.

Rose Jacobs, the *FT* Weekend editor who assigned the article and worked closely with me for four months on it, is near the top of the list of *FT* colleagues who deserve a hearty thank-you. Gary Silverman, the paper's U.S. news editor, helped me in my day-to-day coverage of Merrill Lynch and Bank of America through his voluminous knowledge of the industry and his superb editing skills. Francesco Guerrera, the paper's finance and business editor, supported me tirelessly through the financial crisis and encouraged me to write this book. Members of the capital markets team, including Michael MacKenzie, Aline van Duyn, and Nicole Bullock, all tried to help me understand Bank of America's unusual statement that Merrill's losses didn't seem to be a problem until the second week of December 2008, when the bearish and volatile credit markets actually turned benign. Anuj Gangahar provided me with excellent color on John Thain and his tenure at the New York Stock Exchange, and Brooke Masters, a fellow refugee from the federal courtroom circuit, generously gave me time and advice whenever I asked.

Thanks also to Lionel Barber, the *FT*'s editor in chief, and Gillian Tett, the paper's U.S. managing editor, for supporting this project and giving me the time and space to see it through. Gillian, who in 2009 published her own book on the financial crisis, *Fool's Gold,* was particularly empathetic, given her first-hand knowledge of the process.

Then there's Chrystia Freeland, who hired me at the *FT* in 2008 and, up through her departure, was an enthusiastic supporter of this book. In bringing me to the *FT,* she afforded me the opportunity of a lifetime, and for that I will be forever grateful.

Thanks to my former Harvard classmate Norb Vonnegut, who traded in his Wall Street career for a new life writing fiction, starting with his debut novel, *Top Producer.* Norb introduced me to his agent, Scott Hoffman, who spruced up my book proposal and found a home for this project at Crown Business. Thanks to the entire team at Crown, in particular to my editor, John Mahaney, and Tina Constable, the group publisher.

Finally, to everyone who has expressed amazement at my ability to hold down a full-time job and write a book, I can only say: You should meet my wife. Without Cathy Taylor—who, in addition to her own work as a blogger, freelance editor, social media guru, and conference organizer, took care of our two children practically every night and weekend for more than nine months—this couldn't have happened. She made this book, and so much more, possible. Nor could I have done this without my cousin Mike Farrell, a versatile handyman who provided me with something every aspiring author has to have: a room of one's own.

INDEX